Psychiatric Rehabilitation

Psychiatric Rehabilitation

Carlos W. Pratt

Kenneth J. Gill

Nora M. Barrett

Melissa M. Roberts

SCHOOL OF HEALTH RELATED PROFESSIONS
UNIVERSITY OF MEDICINE AND DENTISTRY OF NEW JERSEY
SCOTCH PLAINS, NEW JERSEY

ACADEMIC PRESS

San Diego   London   Boston   New York   Sydney   Tokyo   Toronto

This book is printed on acid-free paper.

Copyright © 1999 by ACADEMIC PRESS

All Rights Reserved.
No part of this publication may be reproduced or transmitted in any form or by any means, electronic or mechanical, including photocopy, recording, or any information storage and retrieval system, without permission in writing from the publisher.

Requests for permission to make copies of any part of the work should be mailed to: Permissions Department, Harcourt Brace & Company, 6277 Sea Harbor Drive, Orlando, Florida, 32887-6777.

Academic Press
a division of Harcourt Brace & Company
525 B Street, Suite 1900, San Diego, California 92101-4495, USA
http://www.apnet.com

Academic Press
24-28 Oval Road, London NW1 7DX, UK
http://www.hbuk.co.uk/ap/

Library of Congress Catalog Card Number: 98-89453

International Standard Book Number: 0-12-564245-8

PRINTED IN THE UNITED STATES OF AMERICA
99   00   01   02   03   04   EB   9   8   7   6   5   4   3   2   1

This book is dedicated to people with psychiatric disabilities and to the psychiatric rehabilitation professionals who strive to improve the quality of their lives and promote their recovery.

Contents

Part II   *Psychiatric Rehabilitation Principles and Methodology*

Part III   *Applications of Psychiatric Rehabilitation Principle and Methodology*

Chapter 6 *Psychiatric Rehabilitation Day Programming*

Chapter 7 *Vocational and Educational Rehabilitation*

Chapter 8 *Case Management Strategies*

Chapter 9 Residential Services and Independent Living

Chapter 10 Consumers as Advocates and Providers of Supports and Services

Chapter 11 The Role of the Family in Psychiatric Rehabilitation

Acknowledgments

Writing this textbook was a mammoth project that, at each step, seemed to grow larger rather than smaller. At this juncture it is tempting to consider whether we would have approached this work with as much enthusiasm had we realized the scope of the task. Writing the first textbook dedicated to the emerging field of psychiatric rehabilitation, we had the sense that we were breaking new ground. Despite our best efforts, some readers may find the text lacking in some areas. We would like to hear about these. This book is one more step in the ongoing project to define and refine psychiatric rehabilitation. As such, we welcome and encourage suggestions, criticism, and reactions from our readers.

One of the most gratifying things about this work was the generous and very helpful support we received from members of the psychiatric rehabilitation community, as well as from our friends and colleagues. Input from the following people greatly improved the book: Sylvia Axelrod, Irwin Badin, Gary Bond, Bill Butler, Judi Chamberlin, Linda Chalakani, Laurie Curtis, John Farmer, Ruth Hughes, Ed Manos, Lisa Schmidt, Fran Ulrich, and Sandra Wulach.

The University of Medicine and Dentistry of New Jersey and Montclair State University provided important logistical support for this project from its early stages to its completion.

Brian Hartman corrected early drafts, and Ron Siiter provided sound technical advice and moral support to the project. Norma Crosier, Jim Schmidt, Mohammad Shafiq, and others helped us gather information for the book.

Introduction

This text is organized into three parts, covering (1) major mental illness, (2) psychiatric rehabilitation, and (3) community-based services. Part I, Understanding the Nature of Severe and Persistent Mental Illness, contains three chapters that provide the reader with basic information about severe and persistent mental illness and explain why psychiatric rehabilitation is needed. Chapter 1 outlines a case study that conveys the impact of mental illness on the life of one young man. Chapter 2 provides an overview of what we know about the causes of these illnesses and an introduction to psychiatric diagnosis. Chapter 3 describes the treatment, course, and probable outcomes of these disorders—in short, what happens to people with severe mental illness. Part I is not intended to take the place of an abnormal psychology text, but rather focuses on specific issues about some of the mental disorders commonly experienced by users of psychiatric rehabilitation services.

The two chapters in Part II describe the psychiatric rehabilitation enterprise. In Part I the reader gains some understanding of what people with serious mental illness are up against. Part II explains the overall thinking behind psychiatric rehabilitation and what principles can guide the interventions that will improve the life of a person with severe and persistent mental illness. Chapter 4 is devoted to the goals, values, and guiding principles of psychiatric rehabilitation. Chapter 5 covers the basic methodology or approach used in psychiatric rehabilitation regardless of settings or specific application.

Part III is composed of six chapters describing the application of psychiatric rehabilitation principles to community services. These chapters examine the services that are actually performed and provide some case examples of consumers receiving these services. Some of the applications mentioned may not be traditionally thought of as psychiatric rehabilitation. Nonetheless, they are based on many of the same principles that guide effective psychiatric rehabilitation services. Although Part III describes many of the psychiatric rehabilitation services currently in use, it is by no means exhaustive. For example, psychiatric rehabilitation in inpatient settings is not addressed. Considering how new this field is and what we still have to learn, new strategies of psychiatric rehabilitation are certain to emerge in the future.

Some Comments on Language

Language is a powerful tool. The way we speak about people reflects our beliefs about them on many levels. When we refer to someone with a disability by the label of that disability—for example, calling someone a schizophrenic or someone else a quadriplegic—we imply that the disability is the most important feature about that person. People sensitive to this kind of labeling have promoted the use of "people-first language." Putting the person first in our language—such as saying "a person with schizophrenia" or "a person who has quadriplegia"—acknowledges the person first and then, if necessary, the presence of a disability.

Client and *consumer* are also terms that can be used to refer to someone with a disability. Some activists among people with disabilities have expressed a preference for the term consumer over the term client, asserting that a consumer or customer is someone with options and choices whose satisfaction with purchased goods and services is important to the provider of those goods and services. Others have expressed a preference for client, seeing that too as a valued role in which one seeks the input of professionals without relinquishing the decision-making function. Over time, as we become more sensitive to these issues as a society, these terms may move in and out of favor.

The authors of this textbook believe that whatever the word used to refer to someone with a disability, it must be respectful and reflect the inherent value of that individual. Throughout this textbook, we use the terms *person with a disability*, *consumer*, and *client*. In all cases, our intent is as stated—to be respectful and to acknowledge the value of all individuals.

Part I

Understanding the Nature of Severe and Persistent Mental Illness

The Experience of Mental Illness
An Introduction to Psychiatric Rehabilitation

Chapter 1 begins with the case of Paul, a young man diagnosed with a major mental illness, schizophrenia. After reading Paul's case you will cover basic definitions of major mental illness, disability, and stigma. Most importantly, this chapter introduces you to the field of psychiatric rehabilitation, a newly emerging set of methods, strategies, and concepts for the community treatment of persons with major mental illness. The final section of the chapter discusses how psychiatric rehabilitation knowledge is developed and the sources of that knowledge for professionals and students. After reading this chapter you should have a basic understanding of the goals of psychiatric rehabilitation.

This chapter will answer the following questions:

1. What are some of the symptoms and problems that might afflict a young person stricken with a major mental illness?

2. What is major mental illness and how is it defined?

3. What is psychiatric rehabilitation?

4. How and when did the practice of psychiatric rehabilitation begin?

5. What is the state of psychiatric rehabilitation today?

Introduction

Psychiatric rehabilitation, also known as psychosocial rehabilitation, is a comprehensive strategy for meeting the needs of persons with severe and persistent mental illness. A true understanding of psychiatric rehabilitation (PsyR) starts with an awareness and sensitivity to the personal experience of severe and debilitating mental illnesses.

Unlike many common diseases that have very predictable symptoms and outcomes, the consequences of mental illness vary considerably from person to person. This is true even of individuals diagnosed with exactly the same condition. Take, for example, two persons both diagnosed with chronic undifferentiated schizophrenia. One may have auditory hallucinations (hearing voices), whereas the other person is plagued by paranoid ideas but experiences no auditory hallucinations. The history or course of mental illness may also differ from person to person. Some people will have many relapses, others will get sick again very infrequently. In addition, each person will adjust and respond to their illness differently. One person will be severely disabled throughout the course of his or her life, another will cope well and overcome this disability.

The Case of Paul

Like any person's story, Paul's is unique. But Paul's story also resembles millions of similar case histories that unfold every year throughout the United States and around the world. Each of us has ideas and attitudes about mental illness that we get from personal experience, from the media, or from speaking with others. Some of these ideas are accurate. Others are half-truths and myths. Some are just plain wrong. As you read the following case study of Paul, try to be aware of the attitudes and ideas you have about mental illness. Also, consider the following questions.

1. Why did Paul become ill when he did? Were there any events or situations that might have led to Paul's illness?
2. What kinds of things did Paul experience as he became ill? Were these things all caused by the disease itself?
3. Could Paul's illness have been predicted?
4. How did Paul's family handle the situation? Should they have done something different?
5. Are there any clues to how Paul will respond to treatment?

Paul began to realize something was wrong when he couldn't follow the lectures in his classes. Almost any stimulus—a crack in the chalkboard, the inflection of a particular word—would become as important as what the professor was saying. Even in his favorite class, Introduction to Anthropology, taught by a professor he really liked, Paul could not keep his attention on the material. Nineteen years old, a college freshman, living away from home for the first time in his life, Paul found school was becoming a nightmare. An A—/B+ student in high school, now halfway through his first college semester, Paul was

The Case of Paul Continued

losing his ability to concentrate. He strained to listen and take good notes but his thoughts were confused. He could not seem to maintain his focus on the subject of the lecture. Instead, he would hear a particular word, go off on a tangent, and lose the focus of the lecture. After class, he would struggle to summarize the main points of the lecture, but nothing seemed to stand out. Everything was of equal importance. At first, Paul felt mainly frustration, but as his inability to focus continued, his anxiety increased and he began to feel frightened.

In high school Paul hung around with a group of college-bound, but not particularly motivated students. Blessed with a moderately high IQ, Paul could usually get above-average grades by paying attention in class and cramming for his finals. His one love was anthropology. He could spend hours reading about the customs, rites, and religious beliefs of small tribes in the Amazon Basin or the South Pacific. Margaret Mead was one of his heros, and he dreamed of going to live among a primitive people and studying their culture. For Paul, the most interesting thing about these cultures was how their aboriginal belief systems differed from his own, which stressed scientific explanations for things.

Paul's neighbor Nancy was his love interest during high school. Like Paul, Nancy was on the quiet side and shy, and they got along well together. Paul and Nancy would ride bikes, go to the movies, play computer games, and study together. They were best friends and talked about getting serious, although their relationship had not developed that far as yet. It was a real tragedy for Paul when she moved out of state with her family the summer after their sophomore year. At first they wrote to each other weekly, but the connection grew weak and after about 6 months they hardly corresponded at all.

Paul played right field on the junior varsity baseball team during his sophomore year in high school. The coach saw him as a mediocre player, and Paul only played when the team was ahead. He did not go out for baseball again as a junior. Instead, he joined the computer club and began spending most of his time playing Dungeons and Dragons and other computer games. Likable but shy, Paul spent a lot of his free time with his computer during his junior and senior years.

Paul's friend Kevin was also a member of the computer club and spent many hours hacking and playing Dungeons and Dragons with Paul. As they became friendlier, Paul felt safe confiding in Kevin. They often talked about their hopes and dreams for the future and their pet likes and dislikes. Although they were not considered popular, Paul and Kevin were liked by most of their high school peers. Kevin was really serious about computers. He planned to be a math and computer science major in college, and his motivation to get the grades he needed to pursue his goal rubbed off on Paul.

Childhood had been a happy time for Paul. As the firstborn he got plenty of attention and love from his parents, as well as a lot of encouragement. The feelings he had when he thought of his family were friendship, love, fun, and support. His father worked as a personnel manager for a large manufacturing company. Paul's father liked his job, loved his family, and usually had a kind word for everyone. Paul's mom worked as a medical technician at the local laboratory. She was proud of this job because it required technical

The Case of Paul Continued

skill. She also liked it because she could schedule her own hours to make time when she was needed by her family. It was no secret that her family came first. Paul's sister, Alice, was a junior in high school and his younger brother, Ted, was in the eighth grade.

Going away to college had seemed like a great adventure to Paul. During orientation he met his future roommate Ira, who came from out of state. A psychology major, Ira shared Paul's interest in computers, fantasy games, and hacking. But best of all, he had assured Paul that they could both use the new, latest model computer Ira's parents had bought him for college. An instant friendship emerged. At first, as classes started Ira had the same positive effect on Paul's study habits as his friend Kevin. Like his mother, whom he looked up to, Ira wanted to pursue his Ph.D. in psychology. Being very organized, he made sure that he and Paul set aside a block of time each evening to be used only for studying. Ira and Paul joked about becoming nerds, but Paul was secretly glad for the discipline.

Several weeks after he noticed he was having trouble focusing on lectures, Paul found himself feeling both suspicious and angry with Ira. Whenever Ira said something to him, Paul would become suspicious of what he meant or what he might be up to. He felt that Ira was letting him use his computer to lure him in and take control of their relationship. He began to refuse to use the computer so that he would not feel like he was being manipulated. But not using the computer made him angry, and he blamed that on Ira as well. He found that no matter how much he wanted to mend their relationship, he was not really able to be friendly with Ira. When he tried to communicate, he felt manipulated and controlled. When he withdrew, he felt angry and rejected.

At the same time he noticed that he was having trouble relating to his professors. He felt they were manipulating him as well. Studying every night had given Paul a real edge in his classes, and early on his professors had pegged him as one of the brighter students. Now, after an excellent start his apparent total reversal was a real shock to his professors. Several of them asked to speak with Paul after class, asking if everything was alright. Paul denied any problems yet wondered why they were singling him out, as he still had a good average. Paul decided that he was being held to a stricter standard than the other students and that he was being closely observed by the school. After several of these inquiries, Paul found it harder and harder to get to class. His inability to concentrate made it seem pointless anyway. Instead, he spent his time alone in the computer lab playing computer games. Failing every class, Paul left for home before finals.

His parents were worried and confused by Paul's behavior. Telephone conversations with Paul had alerted them that something was wrong but left them puzzled. Paul talked about isolation, people manipulating and controlling him, and being "observed" by the school. Their first thought was that Paul was using drugs but he denied it and showed none of the telltale signs. When he got home it was obvious to his parents that something was wrong. Both were very upset. After long discussion they decided to ask Paul to see Dr. Williams, the family doctor. Paul had always liked Doc Williams, and the doctor was clearly fond of Paul. Ashamed of his poor performance at school and confused by his own thoughts and feelings, Paul agreed to see Dr. Williams the following week.

The Case of Paul Continued

Home in a safe place and feeling less suspicious, Paul was able to tell Dr. Williams everything that had been happening to him. As he conveyed his story he felt that much of what he told the doctor made no sense. Why had he mistrusted his new friend? Why was he unable to concentrate in class? Why had he started cutting classes? All the behaviors, thoughts, and feelings he reported seemed strange, as if they had happened to someone else. Dr. Williams listened to Paul's story and reassured him that it was not uncommon for students going away to college for the first time to have an anxiety reaction. He suggested that Paul see a colleague of his with special training to work with these types of problems, a psychiatrist named Dr. Kline.

During the week he had to wait before his appointment with Dr. Kline, Paul started to become withdrawn and suspicious of his family. During evening meals he heard a voice telling him that he was not his mother's child. His parents tried to hide their own anxiety by accepting Paul's odd behavior. When he saw Dr. Kline, Paul was so suspicious that he had trouble relating his story. Dr. Kline suggested that Paul consider signing himself into a hospital for a period of observation and treatment. He assured Paul that this was the best course of action and that he would be able to leave if he ever changed his mind. Feeling very distrustful, Paul refused the hospital as well as the medication Dr. Kline prescribed. Paul stayed home throughout that winter and into the spring. He became progressively withdrawn and uncommunicative. Most of the time he stayed in his room listening to music. During June, Paul told his mother that Dr. Kline was giving him orders by broadcasting thoughts to him telepathically. As these symptoms increased, Paul became agitated and threatening. Finally, at Dr. Williams suggestion, Paul's parents took him to the county hospital where he stayed for 60 days.

After 60 days in the hospital, Paul felt like he was not ready to be discharged. He was still hearing voices, feeling withdrawn, and on a high dose of injectable medication, but the nurses assured him that living at home and attending the community mental health center would be much better for him. Paul had visited the mental health center before he was discharged. His intake worker had given him a tour of a special program for people with problems like his. People there seemed friendly and the program looked interesting, but he still was not sure. His parents were both hopeful and concerned about Paul's return. At the suggestion of the hospital social worker, they told Paul that if he was going to live at home he would have to attend the program at the center.

Paul's first week at the program was difficult. He still was not sure what was wrong with him. His doctors at the hospital had been vague about his condition. When he thought about being mentally ill he became really scared, tried to think about something else, or decided he was just suffering from stress. While he and the intake worker at the program were filling out his initial treatment plan, the worker told him that he should expect to be at the program for a long period of time and that his diagnosis was schizophrenia.

Paul was not exactly sure what that meant. But at the same time he knew it was what he had dreaded all along. He felt fear growing in the pit of his stomach. His old life was over, the worker was telling him that he was insane.

Discussion of Paul's Case

Paul's story raises a number of important questions about mental illness that you will learn about as you read this book. Many of these issues are very controversial. Throughout this text you will see that depending on training and orientation, theorists, researchers, and mental health professionals often have very different answers to these questions.

One important issue involves questions of **etiology,** or the cause(s) of such illnesses. What caused Paul's illness? Could someone have predicted that Paul would become ill by observing his development, and could the illness have been prevented? Partly because there is still a great deal we do not know about the etiology of the major mental illnesses, this is an area of great controversy and heated debate. Some professionals believe that aspects of Paul's personal history, environment, and family life may help us to understand the cause of his illness. Others feel that these issues have no bearing on the disease because it is essentially biological not environmental. Most important, the etiological beliefs held by professionals, family members, and people like Paul lead to choices of specific treatment strategies.

Another important issue that is raised is the question of **prognosis** or the probable course or outcome of the disease. What is the probable course of Paul's disease? Will he recover with medication and treatment? Or will he become progressively more confused, alienated, and withdrawn over time? Can the prognosis of such a disease even be established? Although there is increasing agreement among professionals on the prognosis of these diseases, there is such great variability between people with the same illness that predicting or determining prognosis remains as much an art as a science.

The final and most important issue remains: What is the best way to help Paul and other people like him? As you will see, there are many aspects to the care of mental illness. Specific beliefs about the etiology of these diseases lead to specific treatment strategies. **Treatment** is usually considered to be any action designed to cure a disease or reduce its symptoms. **Rehabilitation**, on the other hand, is usually defined as any action intended to reduce the negative effects of the disease on the persons everyday life.

To help explain this difference, let's consider a stroke victim who has lost her ability to walk. A doctor might prescribe anticoagulants, blood pressure medication, a change in diet, and regular exercise to help reduce the probability of future strokes. These prescriptions would be considered treatment. The doctor might also prescribe physical therapy to help return the patient to the highest level of physical mobility after the deficits caused by the stroke. This therapy, aimed at returning the patient to normal or near normal functioning, would be considered rehabilitation. Finally, a rehabilitation worker making a home visit might recommend that a ramp be built to the front door, that doorknobs be changed to levers, and that the bathroom be fitted with hand bars. These modifications to the patient's environment would also be considered part of the rehabilitation process.

The differences between treatment and rehabilitation seem clear for the stroke patient. For the person experiencing severe mental illness, the difference between treatment and rehabilitation is not so clear. Some professionals believe that it is a mistake to make a distinction between the treatment of mental illness and a process of rehabilitation. Many practitioners and researchers believe that the rehabilitation process itself has a direct and positive effect on the disease (Anthony & Liberman, 1986). Almost all PsyR professionals believe that treatment and rehabilitation are complementary processes.

The importance of the differences and similarities between treatment and rehabilitation will become evident as you progress through this text. This issue is vital when considering questions such as "Who provides treatment or rehabilitation? What is the role of the psychiatric rehabilitation practitioner? What kinds of services should be provided?"

This textbook provides answers to many of these questions. Real people, like Paul and his loved ones, are dependent on the answers. You will also learn about new, challenging, and complicated questions about the best ways to help persons with severe mental illness.

The Major Mental Illnesses

Serious and persistent mental illnesses, like the one that struck Paul, afflict many people in our society and around the world. In the United States approximately 2.1 to 2.6% of the population suffer from a mental illness, which reduces one's ability to perform living and working tasks effectively (IAPSRS, 1994). This translates to 5,250,000 to 6,500,000 people. In 1990 Irv Rutman, president of Matrix Research Institute, estimated that in the United States the *minimum* number of persons who where **chronically mentally ill** was 2 million.

Within the population of people with mental illness, more than 2,500,000 people are diagnosed with schizophrenia. For society as a whole, schizophrenia, which strikes an estimated 1% of the population, is by far the most devastating and the most feared mental illness. In addition, there are several other mental illnesses that cause untold suffering and disability. The *Diagnostic and Statistical Manual of Mental Disorders*, Fourth Edition, (*DSM-IV*), of the American Psychiatric Association recognizes recurring depressive disorders, bipolar and unipolar disorders (commonly known as manic depressive disorders), schizoaffective disorder, and organic brain syndromes among others as major mental illnesses that can become chronic, cause psychosis, and lead to psychiatric disability.

Today there is increasing awareness that people who experience severe mental illness often suffer from other serious maladies as well. These dually diagnosed individuals may be coping with substance abuse problems, developmental disorders, severe learning disorders, and chronic physical illnesses at the same time they are struggling with their mental illnesses. As you might imagine, the problems raised when someone is suffering from more than one disorder at the same time can be very difficult. Which disorder should be treated first? Does the treatment of one disorder negatively affect the treatment of another disorder? Which disorder is causing the symptoms that are present? Special programs for people who are dually diagnosed, staffed by professionals who are cross trained to address multiple problems, are increasing around the country.

The Symptoms of Mental Illness

Mental illnesses may present a wide variety of symptoms. Most professionals classify the symptoms of the major mental illnesses into two categories: positive symptoms and negative symptoms. **Positive symptoms** refer to what is added to the individual because of the disease. **Psychosis**, the faulty interpretation of reality due to incorrect sensory perceptions (**hallucinations**) or thoughts (**delusions**) are good examples of positive symptoms.

Negative symptoms refer to things that the individual has lost because of the disease. Social withdrawal and an inability to experience pleasure (anhedonia) are typical examples of the kinds of negative symptoms someone with severe mental illness experiences. The great majority of persons experiencing these conditions are diagnosed with schizophrenia or a bipolar disorder (manic depression). Chapters 2 and 3 will cover the cause, symptoms, and treatment of mental illness in depth.

The Causes of the Major Mental Illnesses

The pathological process that causes these conditions is still poorly understood (Anthony & Liberman, 1986). Nevertheless, there is consensus within the psychiatric rehabilitation profession that these conditions have a strong biological component (Dincin, 1990; Taylor, 1987). With the development of increasingly sophisticated soft tissue and metabolic imaging techniques such as CAT, PET, and MRI scans, researchers have been able to demonstrate actual changes in brain tissue and brain functioning corresponding with psychotic episodes (Taylor, 1987; Torrey, 1995; also see Nancy Andreasen, *The Broken Brain*, 1984). At the same time, researchers have looked at the contribution of genetics by tracking the lifespans of individuals with schizophrenic and nonschizophrenic parents (Marcus et al., 1987) and studying identical and fraternal twins (Torrey, 1995, and others). These studies provide strong evidence that genetics play an important role when someone is stricken with a major mental illness. Despite these advances, the cause of major mental illness is not known. Chapters 2 and 3 will cover the symptoms, diagnosis, probable causes, probable courses, and outcomes of these illnesses.

BOX 1.1
Biographical Sketches—Early Theorists

Emil Kraepelin (1856–1926)

An eminent German psychiatrist, Kraepelin is credited with establishing the first classification system for the major mental illnesses. He was also the first clinician to recognize the difference between dementia praecox (schizophrenia) and manic-depressive illness. After receiving his M.D. from the University of Wurzburg in 1878, Kraepelin continued his neurological studies and studied with the father of the new field of psychology, Wilhelm Wundt. This work led to the publication of Kraepelin's *Compendium der Psychiatrie* (Concise Summary of Psychiatry) in 1883. Kraepelin divided mental illness into exogenous conditions, which were caused by external factors and

were therefore treatable, and endogenous conditions, which he believed were caused by biological or hereditary factors and which he considered incurable. Using this classification strategy, Kraepelin saw manic-depressive illness as exogenous and therefore treatable and dementia praecox as endogenous and essentially incurable. Kraepelin believed dementia praecox stemmed from organic pathological changes in the brain. He is also credited with classifying three important subtypes of dementia praecox: catatonia (halted motor activity), hebephrenia (regression to a vegetative state), and paranoia (delusions of persecution or grandeur).

Eugene Bleuler (1857–1939)

One of the most influential psychiatrists of his time, Bleuler is credited with introducing the term *schizophrenia* by combining two Greek words meaning "split" and "mind." Rather than the split personality of popular fiction, Bleuler believed that the "split" was usually between the person's cognitive (thinking) and affective (emotional) processes. A Swiss psychiatrist, Bleuler studied medicine at the University of Bern, was appointed professor of psychiatry at the University of Zurich, and became director of the Burgholzli Asylum in Zurich. It was at Burgholzli, where he worked from 1898 to 1927, that he conducted his ground-breaking studies of schizophrenia. In 1911 he published *Dementia Praecox oder Gruppe der Schizophrenien* (Dementia Praecox: Or the Group of Schizophrenias). Contrary to the professional wisdom of his day, Bleuler believed that the schizophrenias were actually several different diseases, that they were not necessarily incurable, and that the course of the disease was not always negative. During Bleuler's later career he was assisted by Freud's disciple Carl Gustav Jung. Under the influence of Freud's theories, Bleuler became convinced that schizophrenia could have psychological rather than biological causes and that it could be treated using psychoanalytic techniques.

CONTROVERSIAL ISSUE
Schizophrenia (or Neurotransmitter/ Stress Syndrome)

Since Bleuler coined the term *schizophrenia* and distinguished it from dementia praecox, the term has been widely used in psychiatry. The *DSM-IV* and its predecessors, *DSM-I*, *DSM-II*, *DSM-III*, and *DSM-III-R*, have consistently used the term *schizophrenia*, modifying it with disease categories such as paranoid, catatonic, and undifferentiated. Today literally hundreds of thousands of persons in the United States carry a diagnostic label of schizophrenia.

The term *schizophrenia* is widely used by the media and entertainment industries, where it has become the very essence of major mental illness. The paranoid schizophrenic label used by the media conjures up images of wild-eyed assassins who kill and maim for no apparent reason.

The term *schizophrenia* is also used to denote seeming contradictions in people, organizations, or polices. The Iran-Contra scandal was often labeled the product of a schizophrenic policy of selling arms to our enemies in order to raise money to support our allies. This misuse of the term also reinforces the common misconception that schizophrenia is a form of multiple personality disorder, which it is not.

The clear abuse of the term and increased understanding of these illnesses has prompted debate about the continued use of *schizophrenia* as a diagnostic label. Jerry Dincin, the executive director of Thresholds, a large psychiatric rehabilitation agency in Chicago, Illinois, believes that the diagnostic label *schizophrenia* should be changed to **neurotransmitter/***stress syndrome* (Dincin, 1990). This new diagnostic label captures both the biological basis (neurotransmitter) and the environmental vulnerability (stress) aspects of the major mental illnesses. But more important, *neurotransmitter/stress syndrome*, or a similar term, does not carry the stigma and negative connotation of a label like schizophrenia. Dincin used an analogy from the developmental disabilities field to make his point: The *morons*, *idiots*, and *imbeciles* (which were the professional diagnostic labels used) of 30 years ago have been replaced by a term with much less negative impact—Down's syndrome (Dincin, 1990). The probable relationship of neurotransmitters to major mental illness will be discussed in more depth in chapter 2.

The actual costs of changing such a label might be enormous. Besides the obvious changes in charts, records, and diagnostic manuals, a great deal of retraining would need to take place within the mental health delivery system and the systems that pay for treatment.

One might also consider the media's response to such a change. Popular culture would still need a label for "mad men," because individuals with these labels supply the motivating force for many real and fictional stories of crime and violence. Could *neurotransmitter/stress syndrome* become the stigmatized label of the future?

Psychiatric Disability

Without effective rehabilitation, a major mental illness can disable a person for life. Often striking during the late teens and early twenties, life disruptions like the one Paul experienced are very common with these illnesses. When school, work, and family are disrupted, the individual cannot acquire the skills needed to function and cope with the demands of modern life. Without these skills, which many take for granted, the individual cannot function successfully.

These conditions tend to be long lasting as well as severe. Thus, they often stunt or retard normal intellectual, social, and vocational development or lead to conditions where acquired skills are lost due to disuse. This lack of ability, whether because skills were lost or never acquired, is the hallmark of psychiatric disability. Although psychiatric symptoms can often be controlled by medication and therapies, the disability caused by the condition often persists. The analogy of a physical trauma may help to clarify this issue. A person who loses the use of his legs because of an automobile accident becomes disabled because he lost skills such as walking and running. The damage from the accident persists or is permanent even after the physical danger has passed.

Many PsyR theorists and researchers such as William Anthony and Robert Liberman believe that the degree of psychiatric disability is related to the individual's **premorbid** skill level. In addition, they believe that higher skill levels can reduce the intensity of psychiatric illness. The contributions of these skill theorists are covered in chapter 5.

Disability is an important medical and social concept. The Americans with Disabilities Act of 1990, which is discussed in chapter 7, defines disability as a substantial limitation in a major life activity (Lawn & Meyerson, from Liberman 1993). Another important medical body, The World Health Organization, defines disability as an inability to participate or perform at a socially desirable level in such activities as self-care, social relationships, work, and situationally appropriate behavior.

Most important for Americans, the Social Security Administration has outlined four key areas of psychiatric disability: (a) activities of daily living (ADL) (e.g., grooming, hygiene, maintaining a household, managing finances); (b) social functioning (with family, friends, community, and in the workplace); (c) concentration, pace, and task persistence (ability to function for 6 to 8 hours without supervision); and (d) the ability to tolerate competitive work (Lawn & Meyerson, from Liberman, 1993). Duration of disability is also an important factor. To meet the Social Security Administration's definition, the disability has to be continuously present for at least 12 months.

The Stigma of Major Mental Illness

When someone has a major mental illness, the diagnosis itself can cause serious problems. As Hall, Andrews, and Goldstein (1985) pointed out "Schizophrenia is . . . a sentence as well as a diagnosis" (p. 3). The person labeled schizophrenic carries a powerful stigma to which other people react with fear and rejection. Because the symptoms of these diseases can affect how a person thinks, feels, behaves, and communicates, the effects of the disease are often apparent to other people. Unlike common symptoms like coughing, sneezing, or running a fever, these effects or symptoms are often not attributed to a disease. More often, because they are so little understood, psychiatric symptoms are sometimes attributed to supernatural, spiritual, or demonic causes.

Mental illness is so frightening that healthy persons often refer to people with mental illness using the name of their mental illness. Someone with schizophrenia becomes known as a schizophrenic by most people they come in regular contact with. Someone with paranoid schizophrenia may be called a paranoid. By contrast, the individual suffering from diabetes is only rarely identified as a diabetic by friends and acquaintances and then only when it is pertinent, such as when meals are being planned. E. Fuller Torrey, M.D., a psychiatrist who treats, researches, and writes on schizophrenia, believes that persons experiencing schizophrenia are treated like the lepers of the 20th century (Torrey, 1995). The term *stigma* originally referred to the ancient practice of marking villains so that others would know that they were criminals and be on their guard. Many persons today react in the same way when they meet a person they think is mentally ill.

People's reaction to stigma refers to what Coleman (1986) called "the dilemma of difference." We are all aware and generally accept that everyone is different in many ways. When some differences are deemed unacceptable, people with undesirable characteristics or differences may be stigmatized. What a given society chooses to stigmatize is relative. In the past, some societies considered persons who today might be diagnosed with schizophrenia as higher beings who were specially gifted and able to commune with God. Saint Francis of Assisi was known to speak with the animals, which was considered proof of his saintly nature. Today, our first reaction might be to consider such behavior evidence of a psychotic process.

Much of the stigma around mental illness has its roots in ignorance and fear. This is not surprising because until very recently there was little evidence to support any theory explaining mental illness. Some scholars even questioned the existence of mental illness. Thomas Szasz, M.D., believes that mental illness is simply a learned behavior which, for some people, is a realistic reaction to modern society. Today, as we are beginning to get a clearer understanding of mental illness, we can begin to combat the stigma left by centuries of ignorance and fear.

The stigma surrounding mental illness can be eliminated. Stigma is relative so it can be changed. Knowledge about the disease can eradicate the stigma it carries. The ignorance that has surrounded mental illness since the beginning of history is being lifted by modern psychiatry with the advent of imaging techniques like CAT, PET, and MRI, genetic research, the development of new drugs, and other breakthroughs. Although we fear cancer and have compassion for those who are stricken, medical science has increased our understanding of the disease and reduced the stigma cancer patients once experienced. In the same way, future citizens educated about mental illness will fear the disease, not the person.

The community treatment of mental illness also has the potential of reducing stigma. Treating persons experiencing severe and persistent mental illness in the community means that at one time or another everyone will come in contact with them. This exposure to persons with mental illness is a powerful tool for reducing the stigma that surrounds the disease. As most psychiatric rehabilitation workers will tell you, persons with mental illness are no different from you and me, except for their disease. Keeping these persons in institutions added to the stigma surrounding the disease. Accepting them into the community will help eliminate the stigma because working and living with them day by day will highlight their basic humanity, not their disability.

Psychiatric Rehabilitation

In the helping professions, the term *rehabilitate* means to restore to an optimal state of constructive activity. Of course, what is optimal is relative to the individual. An individual's optimal level of constructive activity depends on several factors. How well a person functions depends on how severe his or her illness is at the time, the severity of the person's disability, the abilities they still possess, the outside supports that are available, and what some theorists call the patient's *stage of recovery*. Stage of recovery refers to the individual's ability to cope with the disease and disability and the individual's self-image as a functioning person. The concept of recovery will be dealt with in some depth in chapter 4. Psychiatric rehabilitation (PsyR) refers to efforts to restore persons with psychiatric disabilities to optimal states of constructive activity. Many persons with severe and persistent mental illness may be disabled in many if not most aspects of their life.

There are a number of definitions of PsyR reflecting a range of philosophical and technical differences among practitioners (Anthony, 1979; Anthony & Liberman, 1986; Hughes, 1994; Rutman, 1994). Ruth Hughes, the executive director of the International Association of Psychosocial Rehabilitation Services (IAPSRS), provides an excellent general definition with which most PsyR practitioners can agree:

> The goal of psychiatric rehabilitation is to enable individuals to compensate for, or elim-inate the functional deficits, interpersonal barriers and environmental barriers created by the disability, and to restore ability for independent living, socialization and effective life management. (*Introduction to PsyR*, p. 11)

In 1992 *The Psychosocial Rehabilitation Journal* asked its readers to submit defini-tions of PsyR. The following definition of PsyR, which received an honorable mention in the contest, captures both the humanity and the hope inherent in the rehabilitation process:

> Psychosocial rehabilitation means that a person who before was afraid to go into a store to order an ice cream soda can now be an ice cream store manager. (Martha Green in Rutman, 1994, p. 8)

The Emergence of Psychiatric Rehabilitation

Practitioners of PsyR are united in believing that persons with severe and persistent mental illness can achieve greater independence and a better quality of life through psychiatric rehabilitation services. This assumption, that persons with psychiatric disabilities can be successfully rehabilitated, is in marked contrast to the beliefs of mental health workers of only a few generations ago. Until the late 1970s and early 1980s the conventional wisdom about severe mental illness was that it took an insidious downward course with little or no hope of recovery. Prior to 1987, the *DSM-III* (*Diagnostic and Statistical Manual of Mental Disorders*, Third Edition) published by the American Psychiatric Association stated that the most common course of schizophrenia consisted of acute episodes followed by "increasing residual impairments" (p. 185). In contrast to this pessimistic view, recent research has demonstrated that, even for those with severe psychiatric disability often labeled as "backward" patients, the long-term prognosis is positive (DeSisto, Harding, McCormack, Ashikaga, & Brooks, 1995; Harding, Brooks, Ashikaga, Strauss, & Breier, 1987; Torrey, 1995).

Another positive development is the work PsyR researchers, practitioners, and consumers of psychiatric rehabilitation services are doing to develop the concept of recovery from psychiatric disability. Even though some of the disabilities caused by major mental illness may be lifelong, the field of PsyR is rapidly learning and defining what it means to "recover" from the disabilities caused by major mental illness (Anthony, 1993; Deegan, 1988). The concept of recovery is discussed in greater detail in chapter 4.

Deinstitutionalization

The emergence of PsyR as a unique enterprise can be directly traced to the **deinstitutionalization** movement of the late 1960s and early 1970s. Between 1960 and today, approximately 90% of the persons in long-term state psychiatric institutions have been discharged into the community. Based on current population estimates, to date approximately 900,000 persons experiencing severe and persistent mental illness have either been discharged from psychiatric hospitals or not institutionalized (Torrey, 1995). When the policy of deinstitutionalization began, literally thousands of patients who had been institutionalized for much of their adult lives were moved into the community for treatment. Many, if not most, of the community mental health workers with traditional mental health training were unprepared for this challenge (Farkas et al., 1988; Stern & Minkoff, 1979). In many areas of the country, the deinstitutionalized patients were deemed inappropriate for the community services in place at the time. This was despite the fact that the major impetus for the nationwide federal funding of community mental health centers was specifically to care for this population. Workers trained to provide individual psychotherapy for persons with psychodynamic problems tended to classify these people as not being good treatment cases. Marianne Farkas, of the Center for Psychiatric Rehabilitation, Boston University, believes that this newly deinstitutionalized population had low patient status because they were not highly verbal and did not demonstrate high rates of treatment success (Farkas et al., 1988). As a result, many persons with chronic mental illness were relegated to programs staffed by less educated persons with nontraditional academic degrees and paraprofessionals.

Torrey (1995) asserted that only about 5% of the 789 federally funded community mental health centers (CMHCs) accepted the challenge of providing appropriate services to the deinstitutionalized population. The majority of the centers focused their efforts on providing counseling, psychotherapy, and consultation and education in the broader area of mental illness. Mostly because the CMHC staff members were ill equipped to deal with persons with major mental illnesses, these patients became increasingly isolated and remained underserved in the community.

The academic preparation of mental health professionals did not adjust to the needs of the deinstitutionalization movement. This poor academic response was caused by both a lack of recognition of the plight of this population and a lack of awareness of the treatment strategies necessary to aid them. A review of introductory undergraduate psychology textbooks carried out as late as 1992 revealed that lobotomy was written about more than psychiatric rehabilitation (Halter, Bond, & De Graaf-Kaser, 1992). None of the 28 introductory textbooks mentioned common PsyR approaches, such as the Clubhouse model (Fountain House, Horizon House, etc.), the National Institute of Mental Health's Community Support System, or social skills training. In addition, hospital treatment was given much more coverage than community treatment at a time when hospital stays were being reduced and hospitals were being closed.

In addition to the textbooks, the clinical focus of most undergraduate curricula has remained on the more traditional psychodynamic, cognitive, and behavioral models of treatment and etiology. Graduate education has often side stepped the issue of treating persons with major mental illnesses by stating that this population is not appropriate for the treatment strategies that graduate-level institutions are training students to use.

Despite growing scientific evidence that the major mental illnesses have a strong biological component if not cause, some schools of social work granting the masters of social work (M.S.W) degree have maintained their traditional focus on psychodynamic approaches, emphasizing individual therapy aimed at uncovering past trauma. There is some evidence that this type of intense, interpersonal treatment can be harmful for persons with major mental illness (Linn, Caffey, Klett, Hogarty, & Lamb, 1979). The neglect of the proper care for persons with these illnesses is especially troubling given the traditional emphasis social work has placed on social welfare and championing the needy and downtrodden. Persons diagnosed with major mental illness constitute one of the most rejected, stigmatized, disadvantaged, and needy groups in our nation.

Community workers providing services to this newly deinstitutionalized population faced another problem. Not surprisingly, spending years in an institutional setting like a large psychiatric hospital caused many of the patients to become **institutionalized**. This institutionalization syndrome caused functional deficits, atypical or inappropriate behavior, and extreme dependency in long-term patients (Lehrman, 1961; Ridgeway & Zipple, 1990; Schmieding, 1968). This syndrome often mixed with their mental illness increasing their level of psychiatric disability. Awareness of the debilitating effects of long-term institutionalization provided increased emphasis to the community mental health principle of least restrictive treatment environment. This principle holds that every individual should be provided treatment in the least restrictive environment possible. For example, consider a patient who might equally benefit from hospitalization or a community treatment program. The patient should be treated in the community program because it is a less restrictive treatment environment and less likely to promote institutional behavior.

Psychiatric Rehabilitation Terminology and Language

Each profession has its own peculiar jargon of words, names, and sayings. Psychiatric rehabilitation is no different. The language we use can reflect our attitudes and prejudices. The words we use to describe others may also designate whether we consider them to be either like us or different from us. When we label people we relegate them to a particular category. Some categories can be innocuous ("She's an Oilers fan"), some negative ("He's an ex-con"), and some may frighten ("He has AIDS"). As the labels help determine how we feel about someone they tend to determine how we will react to that person in the future. This issue is particularly important for persons with mental illness.

Since the deinstitutionalization movement and the advent of community treatment, the labels given people who experience severe and persistent mental illness have begun to take on some very specific meanings. When these persons are hospitalized they are known as patients because they are in a medical environment. After discharge if they attend a Clubhouse type day program, they are often known as members. The member label conveys the philosophy of egalitarianism, sharing, and inclusion espoused by Clubhouse programs. Conversely, if they attend a more traditional community mental health center, they are probably known as clients. This labels them as recipients of the center's services. Persons living in residential facilities, whether operated for profit or by a publicly funded community mental health facility, are usually known as residents. (See Table 1.1.)

Recently, some persons unhappy with current labels have begun calling themselves consumers (meaning consumers of mental health services). Other persons have labeled themselves survivors. For some, the survivor label represents the fact that they have been able to exist with a terrifying illness. For others, the label denotes their displeasure with the services they have been provided. As increasing numbers of persons with mental illness become employed in psychiatric rehabilitation some of these persons have labeled themselves prosumers, indicating their joint professional-consumer status. As you can see, how a person with mental illness labels him- or herself or how a professional labels that person can carry a great deal of meaning about an individual's status and the kinds of services he or she is receiving and expects to receive.

TABLE 1.1
Labels: What People with Mental Illness Are Called

Setting	Traditional Label	Nontraditional Label
Hospital	Patient	
Clubhouse	Member	Consumer
		Survivor
Community mental health center	Client	Consumer
Residential facility	Resident	
PsyR worker	Peer Worker	Prosumer
Other labels		Participant
		Recipient

One survey of 300 persons receiving mental health services found that *client* was the most popular term (48%), followed by *patient* (20%), and *consumer* (8%). The remainder of those surveyed (24%) responded *other* or *don't care* (Mueser, Glynn, Corrigan, & Baber, 1996).

Consumer groups and PsyR professionals concerned with combating the negative effects of stigma have emphasized the need for people-first language. For example, rather than calling someone a schizophrenic, which is calling them their disease, using people-first language the individual would be called a person who has schizophrenia. This may seem a subtle difference, but it is very important for the person being so labeled.

The statement in Box 1.2 was put out by the Center for Community Change through Housing and Support at the University of Vermont.

BOX 1.2

Choosing Words with Dignity

The words we choose to use to portray people with mental illness reflect our attitudes and beliefs about the value, dignity and worth of people with disabilities. Our words influence the public perception and acceptance of people with disabilities. People with disabilities are people first and foremost, who also happen to have a disability, or a different set of abilities.

Progressive mental health systems use, at all times, descriptive words that emphasize the person's worth and abilities, not the disabling condition. They understand that people may have a disorder or disability but the people are not the disability. They also recognize that people are diminished when they are described by diagnosis (e.g., "schizophrenic," "paranoid," "borderline"), by slang (e.g., "psychos," "schizos"), and by phrases that negatively categorize them (e.g.

"the mentally ill," "the chronically mentally ill," "young chronics," "retarded," "dually diagnosed"). Medical terms such as "patient" are not used in these systems to refer to people who are not in medical settings, because they are inconsistent with rehabilitation and community support philosophy.

It should be the written and public policy of all systems and agencies working with people with disabilities not to use the labels like "the seriously mentally ill" or use terms like "he is a bi-polar disorder." It should be the policy of all programs to consult with consumers and ex-patients in their states to identify a phrase or phrases that are respectful of individual dignity and reflect the preferences of the majority of individuals. Some phrases with general growing acceptance are "people with psychiatric disabilities," "persons with severe and persistent mental illness," "ex-patients," or "consumers." All current and future documents should reflect this policy.

Developing Psychiatric Rehabilitation Knowledge

Early practitioners of psychiatric rehabilitation learned their trade by experience through a trial-and-error process. The typical community-based mental health center was designed for persons who did not require long-term institutionalization. When the national policy of deinstitutionalization began, community workers and services were confronted with a large, recently released population that did not respond well to the existing treatment modalities and services. It soon became apparent that neither the existing community services nor the types of services previously offered in the psychiatric hospitals were effective for helping this new group adapt to the community environment. Many of the community mental health workers assigned to this population began devising new strategies and services to meet their needs. These pioneer workers struggled to develop treatment philosophies consistent with the goals of community treatment. They often had to design programs for this new population where none had existed. Without recourse to references or handbooks, using emerging concepts like least-restrictive treatment environment, client involvement, and **normalization** as guidelines, innovative programs and services were created. These new services were evaluated by their success or failure. Of course, many of these solutions failed or were later discarded as better solutions were developed.

Some successful models already existed in places like Fountain House in New York City and Horizon House in Philadelphia. These successful programs, which we will deal with in greater depth in chapter 6, served as models for the services that were being developed in communities around the country.

Because no formal education about psychiatric rehabilitation existed at the time, programs tended to hire bright, young, motivated individuals and teach them psychiatric rehabilitation on the job as it was practiced at that setting. Much of what was known was handed down from supervisor to supervisee, and the staff from individual programs tended to share the same ideas and philosophy. Knowledge was also picked up at the yearly conferences of emerging PsyR professional associations or from journal articles on PsyR that appeared infrequently in publications dedicated to other disciplines.

The process of developing new programs and services based on emerging philosophical concepts made psychiatric rehabilitation a very creative profession in the 1970s and 1980s. Without models or reference points, program staff were free to create programs in many forms, and they did. Psychiatric rehabilitation services today cover a wide range of styles, types, and philosophies. This wealth of program types and designs has provided excellent opportunities for testing and refining PsyR theories and practices. Today the PsyR field periodically experiences a shaking out of some of these ideas as new knowledge is acquired and agreement is reached on what are the most effective (able to produce results) and efficient (able to produce results economically) forms of PsyR services.

Psychiatric Rehabilitation: A Science or an Art?

Is PsyR a science, an art, or some combination of both? The three goals of any scientific inquiry are (a) description (what is the process or thing?), (b) explanation (how does it work?), and (c) prediction (what will happen in the future?). These principles can be applied to severe mental illness. We would like to (a) describe the effects of severe mental illness, (b) explain why mental illness has these effects, and (c) predict the course and outcome of these illnesses. The same set of principles can be applied to PsyR interventions. We need to (a) describe a PsyR intervention or strategy, (b) explain how the intervention or strategy works, and (c) predict what the outcome of the intervention or strategy will be. Many dedicated PsyR practitioners believe that approaching the task from this technical-scientific perspective will produce the best results for their clients.

Research produces knowledge. Scientific PsyR knowledge is developed through rigorous systematic research based on the scientific method of observation, description, control, and replication. In the sense of PsyR this means that, in general, if we apply the same treatment to the same population under the same conditions we expect to get the same results. To foster this type of scientific knowledge, several research centers focusing specifically on PsyR and the community treatment of persons with severe mental illness have received public funding. Notable among these research centers are The Center for Psychiatric Rehabilitation at Boston University; The Mental Health Research Center in Madison, Wisconsin; and Thresholds in Chicago, Illinois.

For research to be effective, procedures have to be carried out in as systematic a fashion as possible. This helps to ensure that the treatment under study can be replicated. This holds true for the population being studied, the treatment or rehabilitation environment, the amount of treatment provided, the way the treatment is provided, and the measurements taken. The hallmark of science is not truth, it is replication. In the field settings where PsyR takes place, replication is a formidable task that usually leaves much to be desired.

Brainstorming sessions, sometimes with staff and consumers combined, to develop creative strategies for achieving PsyR goals and objectives are a far cry from the systematic precision required to conduct valid research. Creating new programs and strategies can be an art and some of the creations are ingenious—for example, using consumers as job coaches to help other consumers learn and keep regular jobs in the community, or helping consumers learn about their illnesses by participating in discussion groups where they read and discuss research literature from PsyR journals. The development of strategies like these are often serendipitous. New strategies and techniques are also developed by improving on the ideas of others. The executive director of a very large rehabilitation center in the Midwest who is known for developing innovative programming often states that he really isn't that intelligent, he mainly steals other people's ideas and then improves on them. Of course, we can judge the intelligence of this strategy by observing the effectiveness of the programs he develops.

Many of these creative solutions work, as the staff and consumers who utilize them will attest. But what is it about them that works and what should another PsyR program do to ensure that they will work for them? Many of the solutions that appear to be effective, to staff and consumers alike, in fact are not. A common mistake, for example, is crediting a new strategy with rehabilitation gains when the improvement is actually caused by a Hawthorne effect. You may have heard about the experiments at the Hawthorne plant of the Western Electric Company in Cicero, Illinois, during the 1930s. Researchers found that no matter how they manipulated the lighting intensity in the workrooms, (higher, lower, or no change), production went up. They concluded that the workers were responding to being studied, not to the changes in lighting intensity. In the case of PsyR, a Hawthorne effect implies that the consumers' improvements or gains are caused by the attention they are getting because they are using the new strategy, not because of the strategy itself.

Scientific Literature and Meetings

Starting from a small group of psychiatrists, psychologists, social workers, and other professionals working and publishing in related areas, PsyR research has come into its own during the past decade. The first regular issue of *Schizophrenia Bulletin*, a quarterly journal of the National Institute of Mental Health, was published in 1974. This journal is dedicated to facilitating "the dissemination and exchange of information about schizophrenia." In 1977 the International Association of Psychosocial Rehabilitation Services (IAPSRS) and the Boston University Center for Psychiatric Rehabilitation launched the *Psychosocial Rehabilitation Journal*, today called the *Psychiatric Rehabilitation Journal*. This quarterly journal has been the primary source for PsyR research, evaluation, and ideas. Several other journals regularly carry PsyR research and evaluation reports: *Psychiatric Services*, an American Psychiatric Association journal; *Community Mental Health Journal*, the journal of the National Council of Community Mental Health Centers; and *The Journal of Mental Health Administration*, sponsored by the Association of Mental Health Administrators. Articles about PsyR also appear in journals from the fields of psychology, psychiatry, social work, and other disciplines.

International, national, and local PsyR conferences are excellent places for discussing PsyR research, evaluation, and ideas. Initially, these conferences provided the only opportunity for PsyR professionals to get together with others doing the same work to share ideas. Today's conferences include consumers and family members and take in a broad spectrum of issues and interests. IAPSRS, which holds a yearly conference at a major city in the United States or Canada, has chapter organizations in more than 40 states and provinces. These state organizations also sponsor conferences, meetings, and institutes on special topics. The World Association for Psychosocial Rehabilitation (WAPR) sponsors a congress of PsyR professionals every 2 years at a major world city. WAPR congresses are genuine multilingual, multicultural events with presentations by PsyR professionals representing countries from the Americas, Europe, Asia, and Africa.

These worldwide conferences help to emphasize the global nature and impact of severe mental illness. With slight variations, the incidence of diseases like schizophrenia are constant both around the world and over time. The plight of persons experiencing severe and persistent mental illness in third-world countries is especially troubling. At the 1989 Congress of the World Association for Psychosocial Rehabilitation, Dr. Vijay Nagaswami of the Schizophrenia Research Foundation, Madras, India, stated that "In developing countries . . . the mentally ill continue to languish and can be considered lucky if they receive even medication" (Nagaswami, 1989, p. 20). The international PsyR movement is actively promoting the sharing of knowledge and ideas to meet this challenge.

Creating Psychiatric Rehabilitation Professionals

IAPSRS, the largest organization of psychiatric rehabilitation professionals in the United States, has taken the initiative in establishing PsyR as a profession. Like other professionals, such as doctors, lawyers, and public school teachers, this requires that the person providing PsyR services be licensed by the state where the professional provides services. To be licensable by states a profession needs to have clear guidelines spelling out who practitioners are, what special knowledge they have, what services they provide, and their standards and ethics. In short, how are these professionals unique. In the case of psychiatric rehabilitation professionals the question is, what do PsyR professionals do that is different from social workers, psychologists, and other human service professionals?

As a first step toward professionalization, IAPSRS has outlined a set of practice guidelines and a code of ethics for PsyR professionals. In addition, it has established a national registry for PsyR professionals. Based on their level of education and amount of experience, this allows individuals to be designated as either a registered psychiatric rehabilitation practitioner (RPRP) or as an associate psychiatric rehabilitation practitioner (APRP). The IAPSRS publishes an annual book listing all the individuals who are registered PsyR professionals.

Although the registry is a first step in identifying PsyR professionals, the next major step toward licensure is the establishment of a test-based certification system. The development of a written test that can be used on a national basis to evaluate PsyR knowledge is a complicated and time-consuming task. IAPSRS is committed to and has begun this task, which will provide states with the objective criteria they need to begin licensing PsyR professionals.

Summary

Being struck with a major mental illness can be a devastating experience that may affect a person's entire life. Particularly because they tend to strike during the late teen/early adult years, these diseases can create, severe disability. Despite the disruption these diseases create, we are still unclear as to their cause. Contrary to psychodynamic theories, it has recently become clear that these conditions are biologically based. One of the major sources of disability is the stigma that is attached to these diseases. Increased knowledge and education are helping to reduce stigma, but there is still a long way to go.

Psychiatric rehabilitation encompasses the community treatment and rehabilitation of persons with severe mental illness. In its present form, psychiatric rehabilitation began in response to the deinstitutionalization movement in the late 1960s. Psychiatric rehabilitation is emerging as a unique discipline with its own body of research, journals and publications, and professional organizations and conferences. The major U.S. organization, IAPSRS, is actively working toward the professionalization of PsyR personnel and services.

Class Exercise
Knowledge and Attitudes about Severe Mental Illness

This exercise is designed to establish a baseline for the classes knowledge and attitudes about severe mental illness. Students can complete this exercise individually or in small groups. Students should respond to the following scenario.

Imagine that you are a case worker in a psychiatric rehabilitation program. A new client, diagnosed with schizophrenia and recently assigned to your case load, asks you the following questions. How do you respond?

1. Why did I become ill? What causes this disease?
2. I feel okay right now. Will I get sick again?
3. How long will I have this condition? Will I ever get better?
4. Will I be able to have a "normal" life?

Discuss students' answers to these questions. This textbook will thorughly deal with the issues raised by these questions.

References

American Psychiatric Association. (1974). *Diagnostic and statistical manual of mental disorders* (3rd ed.). Washington, DC: Author.

American Psychiatric Association. (1994). *Diagnostic and statistical manual of mental disorders* (4th ed.). Washington, DC: Author.

Andreasen, N. C. (1984). *The broken brain: The biological revolution in psychiatry*. New York: Harper and Row.

Anthony, W. A. (1979). *The principles of psychiatric rehabilitation*. Baltimore: University Park Press.

Anthony, W. A., & Liberman, R. P. (1986). The practice of psychiatric rehabilitation: Historical, conceptual and research base. *Schizophrenia Bulletin*, *12*(4), 542–559.

Center for Community Change through Housing and Support, University of Vermont. "Choosing words with dignity." (Date unknown)

Coleman, L. M. (1986). Stigma: An enigma demystified. In S. C. Ainlay, G. Becker, & L. M. Coleman (Eds.), *The dilemma of difference* (pp. 211–232). New York: Plenum Press.

Deegan, P. E. (1988). Recovery: The lived experience of rehabilitation. *Psychosocial Rehabilitation Journal*, *11*(4), 11–19.

DeSisto, M. J., Harding, C. M., McCormack, R. V., Ashikaga, T., & Brooks, G. W. (1995). The Maine and Vermont three-decade studies of serious mental illness. *British Journal of Psychiatry*, *167*, 331–342.

Dincin, J. (1990). Speaking out. *Psychosocial Rehabilitation Journal, 14*(2), 83–85.

Farkas, M. D., O'Brien, W. F., & Nemec, P. B. (1988). A graduate level curriculum in psychiatric rehabilitation: Filling a need. *Psychosocial Rehabilitation Journal, 12*(2), 53–66.

Hall, W., Andrews, G., & Goldstein, G. (1985). The cost of schizophrenia. *Australian and New Zealand Journal of Psychiatry*, *19*, 3–5.

Halter, C. A., Bond, G. R., & De Graaf-Kaser, R. (1992). How treatment of persons with serious mental illness is portrayed in undergraduate psychology textbooks. *Community Mental Health Journal*, *28*, 1, 29–42.

Harding, C. M., Brooks, G. W., Ashikaga, T., Strauss, J. S., & Breier, A. (1987). The Vermont longitudinal study of persons with severe mental illness I: Methodology, study sample and overall status 32 years later. *American Journal of Psychiatry*, *144*, 718–726.

Hughes, R. (1994). Psychiatric rehabilitation: An essential health service for people with serious and persistent mental illness. In IAPSRS, *An Introduction to Psychiatric Rehabilitation*. Columbia, MD: Author.

International Association of Psychosocial Rehabilitation Services (IAPSRS). (1994). *An Introduction to Psychiatric Rehabilitation*. Columbia, MD: Author.

Lehrman, N. S. (1961). Do our hospitals help make acute schizophrenia chronic? *Diseases of the Nervous System*, *22*(9), 489–493.

Liberman, R. P. (Ed.). (1993). *Handbook of psychiatric rehabilitation*, Boston: Allyn & Bacon.

Linn, M. W., Caffey, E. M., Klett, C. J., Hogarty, C. E., & Lamb, H. R. (1979). Day treatment and psychotropic drugs in the aftercare of schizophrenic patients. *Archives of General Psychiatry*, *36*, 1055–1066.

Marcus, J., Hans, S. L., Nagler, S., Auerbach, J. G., Mirsky, A. F., & Aubrey, A. (1987). Review of the NIMH Israeli kibbutz-city study and the Jerusalem infant development study. *Schizophrenia Bulletin, 13*(3), 425–437.

Mueser, K. T., Glynn, S. M., Corrigan, P. W., & Baber, W. (1996). A survey of preferred terms for users of mental health services. *Psychiatric Services, 47*,7, 760–761.

Nagaswami, V. (1989). Community based rehabilitation of persons suffering from chronic psychoses in developing countries. *Proceedings of the II Congress of the World Association for Psychosocial Rehabilitation* (p. 20). Barcelona, Spain.

Ridgway, P., & Zipple, A. M. (1990). The paradigm shift in residential services: From the linear continuum to supported housing approaches. *Psychosocial Rehabilitation Journal, 13*(4), 11–31.

Rutman, I. D. (1994). What is psychiatric rehabilitation. In IAPSRS, *An Introduction to Psychiatric Rehabilitation.* Columbia, MD: Author.

Schmieding, N. J. (1968). Institutionalization: A conceptual approach. *Perspectives in Psychiatric Care, 6*(5), 205–211.

Stern, R., & Minkoff, K. (1979). Paradoxes in programming for chronic patients in a community clinic. *Hospital & Community Psychiatry, 30*(9), 613–617.

Szasz, T. (1976). *Schizophrenia: The sacred symbol of psychiatry.* New York: Basic Books.

Taylor, E. (1987). The biological basis of schizophrenia. *Social Work,* March–April, 115–121.

Torrey, E. F. (1995). *Surviving schizophrenia.* New York: Harper Perennial.

Chapter 2

Symptoms and Etiology of Severe and Persistent Mental Illness

People with a variety of severe and persistent mental illnesses can benefit from psychiatric rehabilitation services. The most common diagnoses of the people in these programs are from the schizophrenic and mood disorder categories. The symptoms of these major mental illnesses are often catastrophic in their impact, threatening the integrity of the person's thoughts, feelings, and sense of self. Today we understand that these illnesses are brain disorders that have severe physiological, psychological, and social consequences. Their causes seem to be related to an interaction of heredity and environment. The vulnerability to these disorders appears to be genetic—that is, inherited. This genetic vulnerability apparently interacts with environmental and developmental factors that provoke the onset of these disorders.

This chapter will answer the following questions:

1. *What are the most common symptoms of the major mental illnesses?*
2. *What are the current scientific theories about the etiology (cause) of these conditions?*
3. *How does stress affect people who have severe mental illnesses?*

Introduction

The goal of psychiatric rehabilitation is to help individuals recover from the catastrophe of serious mental illness. The disabling nature of these disorders is due to both their severity and their persistence. Psychiatric rehabilitation programs serve people with a variety of disorders, primarily individuals recovering from psychoses, as discussed in chapter 1. In a recent nationwide study of 13 psychiatric rehabilitation (PsyR) programs, 65% of the individuals served had schizophrenic disorders, 25% had mood disorders (bipolar disorder, unipolar disorder, major depression, etc.), and 10% had a variety of other conditions (Arns, 1998). Therefore, this chapter focuses primarily on schizophrenia, giving some attention to the major mood disorders.

Symptoms

Symptoms are literally signs or indicators of an illness or disease. They are also a cause of suffering for the individual with the disease. According to the traditional medical model, the observance of symptoms, or their simultaneous occurrence in specific patterns, leads to the diagnosis of the underlying disorder. As an example, a young child may have the sniffles, be cranky, tug at his or her ear, and have a fever. The doctor examines the middle and inner ear and sees that it is red. All of these are symptoms or indicators of the illness commonly known as an ear infection. The earache, although a symptom of an infection, is also causing suffering for the child. Of course, the treatment is usually to provide antibiotics to stop the infection, which also relieves the child's pain.

The symptoms of mental illness, as discussed in chapter 1, involve the senses, emotions, and cognition (thinking). Literally, these symptoms shape how the person perceives, thinks about, and reacts to the world around her or him. Besides being indicators of a serious illness, the experience of these symptoms by the individual (like the child's earache) can become a preoccupying and consuming experience of the person's life. In the case of the earache, the situation is temporary and specific. In the case of the most serious mental illnesses, both the severity and persistence of symptoms is often all encompassing and disruptive to the person's functioning at home, school, work, and in the community in general.

Persistence of Symptoms over Time

One of the most devastating features of these conditions is that psychiatric symptoms often recur and persist, in one form or another, for the entire life of the individual. Indeed, these illnesses used to be referred to as *chronic* mental illnesses. The individuals who experienced these disorders were often insensitively referred to as *chronics*. Fortunately, this terminology has fallen out of favor for a couple of reasons. The first reason is the emergence of person-first language. The second is the fact that *chronic*, which simply means "lengthy," has gradually become equated with low functioning and hopelessness. The overall negative associations of this label turned out to be not only inaccurate and but also very harmful (Harding et al., 1992). Chapter 3 discusses the new evidence about the inaccuracy of the chronic label.

Nevertheless, the fact that psychiatric symptoms may persist, despite treatment, creates one of the most important challenges of PsyR. In short, how can we help people live meaningful, productive lives despite the severe difficulties their symptoms present?

The Symptoms of Schizophrenia

Schizophrenia is the most common disorder of persons who utilize psychiatric rehabilitation services (Arns, 1998). Partly because the symptoms of schizophrenia are so varied and numerous, diagnosing the disorder is difficult and takes time. Other serious disorders must be ruled out. For example, many drug reactions look strikingly like schizophrenia during the acute phases of the illness, hence the term *psychedelic* drug, referring to a class of drugs which causes psychotic-like symptoms. But these drug-induced conditions are short-lived and thus are very different in their impact on the life of the individual.

The symptoms of severe and persistent mental illness are ongoing rather than transient experiences. In the case of schizophrenia, an individual's most serious symptoms may last several days to many years, waxing and waning in intensity. As of yet, there are no laboratory tests and no direct outward physical signs of mental illness. Although there are some subtle physiological signs, they are not diagnostic in themselves. For example, as we will discuss later in this chapter, some people with schizophrenia and other mental illnesses have a smaller head size, perhaps due to difficulties in their prenatal development.

Positive and Negative Symptoms

According to the official manual of the American Psychiatric Association, *DSM-IV* (APA, 1994), the characteristic symptoms of schizophrenia can be categorized into two broad groups: positive symptoms and negative symptoms. Specifically, the positive symptoms appear to reflect an excess or distortion of normal functions, whereas the negative symptoms appear to reflect a diminution or loss of normal functions (p. 274). It is important to note that negative symptoms are considered much more difficult to treat and are often times much more disabling than positive symptoms. Positive and negative symptoms are described and illustrated below, they are also summarized in Box 2.1.

BOX 2.1
Positive and Negative Symptoms of Schizophrenia

The positive symptoms of schizophrenia include distortions or exaggerations of

1. thinking and ideas (delusions)
2. perception and sensations (hallucinations and illusions)
3. language and communication (disorganized or bizarre speech)

4. behavioral self-control (grossly disorganized or catatonic behavior)

Negative symptoms include losses or deficits in

1. the range and intensity of emotional expression (flat affect)
2. the fluency and productivity of thought and speech (alogia)
3. the initiation of goal-directed behavior (avolition)

We will consider negative symptoms first. Clearly, all the symptoms of schizophrenia are negative in the sense that they are harmful. However, this class of symptoms is referred to as *negative* because it is characterized by the absence of something that is normally present. For example, avolition and anhedonia are common negative symptoms. In these terms, the prefix *a* is similar to *anti* and literally means not. Thus, avolition is the lack of will power or motivation. Anhedonia means *not* in pursuit of pleasure and the term refers to an inability to experience pleasure. Both are common negative symptoms of people recovering from psychotic disorders. Many mental health professionals mistake these symptoms, which are common among people with severe and persistent mental illness, as simply a choice not to be motivated. Consider the experience of Pete, a newly hired psychosocial rehabilitation staff person:

> "I went to the rooms throughout the program and then to the work units, but it was all the same. Most of the time, it seemed members of the program were sitting around, doing nothing, staring into space. Some staff were really good at engaging the members, but the members had a hard time sustaining it. People seemed to move slowly, they were slow to smile." Pete thought to himself, "why are these people so negative and down, so unwilling to do anything?"

In contrast, positive symptoms such as hallucinations, delusions, and most thought disorders are, in a sense, more blatant signs of a disorder. They are known as positive symptoms because they are added to the individual's experience as a result of the disease. For example, when someone with schizophrenia or another mental illness hears voices, it is defined as a positive symptom because these auditory hallucinations are something added by the disease.

Sometimes people who have serious mental illnesses appear distracted, mumble or talk to themselves, and seem to be bewildered or in their own world. These behaviors are secondary to positive symptoms such as auditory hallucinations or other internal stimuli, which are described in detail later in this chapter.

Delusions

Among the most common positive symptoms of psychosis (defined in chapter 1) are **delusions**—bizarre beliefs or ideas that the person cannot be talked out of. A common type of delusion is the feeling that one's actions are under the control of others. Consider Sal's experience:

> Sal was a bright man who formerly worked as a teacher. Since developing schizophrenia, he thought that two individuals were controlling his actions: Marlboro Man and Frank. These were not their real names, he said, but code names, aliases. They were real people, cousins of Sal's, but Sal thought they were controlling his life, intervening to make him fail, talking to his students (when he still had them), talking to his employers, who would then fire him. Sal thought they caused his other symptoms, polluted his water, and contaminated his bathroom. Once, Sal started teaching at a day program, helping his fellow consumers to learn Spanish. When the students had the normal difficulties—making mistakes, confusing pronunciation, and so on—Sal gave up. In explanation he said, "It's no use, it's Marlboro Man and Frank, interfering again." In the early phases of Sal's illness he talked about the two men, but in the active phase he was totally preoccupied with them. Even when he was relatively well, they were always in his thoughts.

Another category of delusions, grandiose delusions, involve believing one has great worth, power, knowledge, a special identity, or a special relationship to God or a famous person. Typical grandiose delusions include believing one is God or Jesus Christ. Other typical delusions are believing oneself to be especially famous, beautiful, or influential.

> Louise, a plain-looking person, average in many ways, arrived at her day program one day saying and believing that she was a famous designer of clothes and that a new perfume had been named after her.

Other types of delusions might include believing there are evil or negative forces targeting one's self or a loved one. Examples include believing the Mafia is harassing you or the CIA or FBI has you under surveillance. These delusions can also take the form of ideas of reference, in which an individual believes special messages are being sent to him or her by the radio, television, computer, or even in an everyday remark.

> Carol, a middle-aged woman with schizophrenia, had not been hospitalized for many years. She was concerned because she thought television programs were sending special messages just for her and she knew this was a bad sign. She wished to reassure her caseworker (and herself) that she was not getting ill. She called up her caseworker on the phone and said she had something to tell her. Carol's comment was, "Oh, no, I won't let the TV bother me."

The impact of delusions on an individual's behavior can be extreme, with the individual taking specific actions in response to a belief. Uncontrolled emotional responses such as inappropriate laughter and crying occasionally occur. Delusions may occur by themselves or simultaneously with the next major symptom we will discuss: hallucinations.

Hallucinations

Other psychotic symptoms include hallucinations or incorrect sensory information that the individual experiences as real. The individual must deal with heightened internal stimulation (often in the form of a hallucination) or exaggerated experiences of external stimuli (illusions). The most common hallucinations, usually worst in the active phases of illness, are auditory in nature. Poor concentration and attention span seems to be a natural outgrowth, in part, of these sensory experiences, although as discussed later there may be other reasons for distractibility, including various types of thought disorder.

Auditory hallucinations may include any variety of experiences, such as a voice keeping up a running commentary on one's actions or thoughts or multiple voices conversing with each other. These hallucinations can take various forms:

- Voices speaking one's thoughts aloud. As one man said, "I have very loud thoughts."
- Two or more voices arguing. As one woman said to her case worker, "I heard the voices of the staff here at the program yelling at each other. It started as two voices, later more voices were added, including yours. Later, it was like 18 voices or something like that. It was so overwhelming I stayed in bed and never got out."
- Voices commenting on one's actions are another form of hallucination. One patient reported that he did not like walking around his neighborhood. It was pleasant and safe enough, except he could not stand the chatter of his neighbors commenting on his behavior. He could hear their voices as he passed their homes.
- A voice or voices telling or ordering the individual to do a specific thing. These *command hallucinations* can have dangerous consequences. A woman who had jumped from a bridge into the river reported that voices had been telling her to jump for several days before she complied.

Thought Disorders

In addition to delusions and hallucinations, individuals may experience thought disorders, which are symptoms associated with cognition or thinking (i.e., the processing of information). In schizophrenia, the cognitive symptoms are quite prominent and include thought disorders, thought broadcasting, thought insertion, and racing thoughts. Consider the story of Betty, who experienced thought broadcasting:

> "For years, I could never understand why people acted certain ways, especially why they never responded to me when I sent them messages. Then I went to a psychoeducation group. For the first time, I realized that not everybody thought as I did. For a long time, I believed people could hear my thoughts. I could hear theirs. At first, I didn't believe that people could not hear my thoughts, because as far as I'm concerned I still hear others' thoughts."

Other individuals complain of very intrusive thoughts being put into their heads or not under their control.

> Elise believed that her parents and doctors conspired against her by arranging to have a surgical procedure performed on her while she was asleep. She thought the procedure involved the insertion of "metal patterns" in her brain, which controlled many of her thoughts and actions. This delusion system provided an explanation for Elise who experienced some of her thoughts as being intrusive and inconsistent with her thinking prior to the onset of her illness.

Other people experience racing thoughts, such as Tommy who stated:

> "My thinking is all messed up, it moves really fast and makes me nervous because I can't keep up with it."

The Experience of Symptoms

Sometimes it is difficult to tell specifically which symptoms someone is suffering from. At the same time it is apparent that he or she is currently experiencing one type of psychotic symptom or another.

> Andrea was meeting with her doctor and told her that she was no longer taking her medicine. When her doctor asked why, Andrea responded, "Because God told me not to take it." The doctor tried to persuade Andrea several different ways including saying to her "God helps those who help themselves," but Andrea just kept repeating, "God told me not to take it." Almost exasperated, the doctor said, "Andrea, God told me to tell you to take the medicine." The doctor was very startled when Andrea said, "OK".

Was this evidence of a grandiose or religious delusion, that God was sending direct messages, or was it an auditory hallucination? After all, if you were hearing a disembodied voice, where would you think it was coming from?

The impact of symptoms on the person can vary markedly, and younger individuals are a at higher risk for acting in response to both hallucinations and delusions.

> Rachel, a meek, mild, middle-aged woman who has suffered from schizophrenia for most of her life, recalled how she lost the custody of her children more than 10 years ago because she responded to a delusion. She thought her crying infant son had been sent by the devil, so she threw him out the window. Fortunately, he survived, but she lost custody of all three of her children. Since then she has committed no violent acts. Over the years she has developed a good, but generally long-distance relationship with her children. She has held several jobs and has some close friends. In retrospect, she can not believe what she did, particularly since she rarely acts in response to her symptoms now. Today, occasionally she feels hostile, angry, or a bit suspicious, but she knows that this is often a sign that she needs some assistance.

Sometimes bizarre acts are committed when individuals act on hallucinations and delusions. Although these events are quite dramatic, they are also rather rare in that most individuals who experience these symptoms do not act in such a manner.

Some individuals are quite accommodated to their symptoms and although they certainly would prefer not to have them, they experience a relatively peaceful coexistence with them.

> When it came Catherine's turn to speak about the experience of auditory hallucinations at a psychoeducation group, this generally cantankerous 70-year old said with a grin, "Yeah, sure, I hear voices, but what the hell? I argue with them, put them in their place, and that's the end of it. I don't let them bother me."

While, experiencing severe symptoms, the self-regulation of one's behavior becomes more difficult, as was evident with Rachel's experience. Often, however, along with the psychotic symptoms the individual has some self-awareness, as Catherine's comments indicate. Consider this vignette:

> Andrew had not been doing well lately. He hid from the outreach workers when they came to his home. One day, he became convinced that his voices would abate if he jumped in the river—that is, they would be "washed away." Andrew went down to the polluted river in his city and jumped in. In the water, he felt his nostrils fill with water and realized he was drowning. He swam to safety. Sopping wet, he walked to the local mental health center where he was a client and asked for help.

Although his behavior seemed very bizarre and dangerous, Andrew was not totally out of touch and had some awareness of his actions. Perhaps, like Catherine, he might be able to develop a proactive stance toward his symptoms and self-regulate his behavioral responses in the future accordingly.

Were Andrew's actions in response to a delusional belief? Did voices tell him to do it? Or was it a thought disorder, an example of concrete thinking, the "washing away" idea taken too literally? Andrew's own description of his experience was not clear enough to ascertain what symptoms prompted his behavior. In a sense, the answers to all those questions are not what was really important at the time. Behavior is often the result of an array of symptoms rather than a response to one symptom. What was very important is that both he and his helpers recognized that he was in the acute or active phase of the illness and that his behavior had become unpredictable.

Most remarkable of all is that many individuals who experience these symptoms still manage to care for themselves and others. Many maintain their own homes, hold jobs, or attend school despite their symptomatology.

Phases of Schizophrenia

The duration (see Box 2.2, Criterion C) of an episode of schizophrenia must persist for at least 6 months for an accurate diagnosis to be made (APA, 1994). The symptoms a person experiences during an episode may vary considerably depending on which phase of the illness is present.

The **prodromal** phase (before the full syndrome) is a period of deterioration in functioning and increasing symptoms, both positive and negative. In "The Case of Paul," from chapter 1, Paul's inability to focus on college lectures, his suspicious feelings about his roommate and professors, and his increasingly withdrawn behavior were all indicative of the prodromal phase of schizophrenia.

The **acute** or **active phase** is the time period of the most severe and extreme stages of full-blown symptoms. It is when positive symptoms are most prominent. In "The Case of

---

BOX 2.2

Diagnostic Criteria for Schizophrenia Excerpted from DSM IV (APA, 1994, p. 285)

A. Characteristic symptoms: Two (or more) of the following, each present for a significant portion of time during a one month period (or less if successfully treated):

(1) delusions [i.e., bizarre beliefs or ideas]
(2) hallucinations [usually auditory, i.e., "hearing voices"]
(3) disorganized speech (e.g., frequent derailment or incoherence)
(4) grossly disorganized or catatonic behavior
(5) negative symptoms, i.e., flat affect, alogia, or avolition

B. Social/occupational dysfunction: For a significant portion of the time since the onset of the disturbance, one or more major areas of functioning such as work, interpersonal relations, or self-care are markedly below the level achieved prior to the onset (or when onset is in childhood or adolescence, failure to achieve expected level of interpersonal, academic, or occupational achievement).

C. Duration: Continuous signs of the disturbance persist for at least 6 months. This 6-month period must include at least 1 month of symptoms (or less if successfully treated) that meet Criterion A (i.e., active phase symptoms) and may include periods of prodromal or residual symptoms. During these prodromal or residual periods, the signs of the disturbance may be manifested by only negative symptoms or two or more symptoms listed in Criterion A present in an attenuated form (e.g., odd beliefs, unusual perceptual experiences).

[Additional criteria caution the diagnostic clinician to rule out other physical and psychiatric disorders as well as considering the presence of preexisting developmental disorders of childhood.]

Paul," hearing voices, increased suspicion and withdrawal, and the belief that his doctor was giving him orders by broadcasting thoughts to him telepathically all occurred during the active phase of Paul's illness.

The **residual phase** is when symptoms become milder. Both positive and negative symptoms decrease, but negative symptoms are more likely to persist. Pauls's story left off when he was most likely nearing the end of the active phase of the schizophrenic episode. In a few months Paul's symptoms would probably have decreased, and although he still might have been withdrawn and felt mistrustful, his auditory hallucinations would probably have decreased in frequency and intensity as he entered the residual phase of the illness.

How the Phases of Schizophrenia Affect Consumers' Lives

To experience the course of the phases of schizophrenia only once would be disruptive enough. Unfortunately, many individuals experience this dreaded sequence of phases repeatedly, resulting in numerous and unpredictable disruptions to their life. Persistent negative symptoms during long residual phases with occasional bursts of positive symptoms may dominate the person's existence, making it difficult for the individual to concentrate or focus, even on simple day-to-day tasks. Functional deficits associated with the disorder interfere with goal-directed behavior involving one's career and lifestyle. Thus, a disproportionately large number of people with schizophrenia are chronically unemployed, have not finished their education, do not reside in their own homes, are unmarried, and are estranged from their relatives. Later in this book we will address how the interventions of psychiatric rehabilitation can help these individuals to cope more effectively, regain control over their lives, and pursue these life goals.

Mood Disorders

More common than schizophrenia, mood disorders are estimated to affect from 5% to 20% of the general population. Compared to schizophrenia, mood disorders affect a smaller proportion (about 25%) of persons served in psychiatric rehabilitation programs (Arns, 1997). This is probably because mood disorders cover a wide spectrum of symptoms and functional deficits. Some individuals have relatively mild or moderate symptoms that do not have a significant negative effect on the person's day-to-day functioning requiring PsyR services. Others have occasional bouts of mood swings intermixed with long periods of good mental health. It is also common for people with other serious disorders to experience mood disorders as well.

The most serious mood disorders are episodic, recurrent, and cause significant functional deficits. There are three types of episodes associated with mood disorders (APA, 1994). Keep in mind that every individual with a mood disorder does not necessarily experience each type of episode.

Depressive episodes are characterized by extreme sadness or emptiness lasting most of the day, every day, for 2 weeks or longer. **Manic episodes** are marked by an elevated mood, in which the person feels excessively "up" or "high," and occasionally is excessively irritable, for a week or more. In a **mixed episode**, a person meets the criteria for both types of episodes, cycling through depressive and manic phases of the illness. When an individual experiences one or more recurrent episodes of depression, they may be diagnosed with major depression, recurrent (APA, 1994). Individuals who experience more than one instance of two of the three types of episodes may have what is known as bipolar disorder, formerly called manic-depression. Both major depression and bipolar disorder may or may not have some of the psychotic features previously described, such as hallucinations and delusions.

Most people know what it is like to be "down in the dumps" for a day or two. Some have had longer bouts of feeling sad, perhaps accompanied by insomnia or a change in appetite. By contrast, consider the following:

> Marian has a middle-management position in a large company. She generally enjoys her work, but she has not made it in to the office for almost 3 weeks. She cannot rouse herself in the mornings. When she finally does get up, close to noon, she has trouble getting anything done, even a load of laundry. It seems to take an eternity to get herself up, walk to the kitchen, and make herself a cup of coffee. She feels sadder than she can remember, except perhaps when her father died 4 years ago. But this seems worse now, because at least after her father's death she could be distracted by friends and forget her sorrow for brief periods. Her current sadness has a different quality, like she is at the bottom of a pit with no hope of getting out or ever feeling happy again. She finds herself crying for hours at a time, but she cannot figure out why she is weeping. Marian knows she needs help, but cannot motivate herself to even make a phone call.

Marian is experiencing a major depressive episode. Although some of her symptoms may have been experienced by many people not diagnosed with a major mental illness, Marian's symptoms are more severe and of longer duration. In fact, she is experiencing a severe, persistent, and extremely disabling mental illness. The criteria for making this diagnosis are outlined in Box 2.3.

BOX 2.3
Criteria for Major Depressive Episode (APA, 1994, p. 327)

A. Five or more of the following symptoms have been present during the same 2-week period and represent a change from previous functioning; at least one of the symptoms is either (1) depressed mood or (2) loss of interest or pleasure. (Note: Do not include symptoms that are clearly due to a general medical condition, or mood-incongruent delusions or hallucinations.)

(1) depressed mood most of the day, nearly every day, as indicated by either subjective report (e.g., feels sad or empty) or observation made by others (e.g., appears tearful). Note: In children or adolescents, can be irritable mood.

(2) markedly diminished interest or pleasure in all, or almost all, activities most of the day, nearly every day (as indicated by either subjective account or observation made by others).

(3) significant weight loss when not dieting or weight gain (e.g., a change of more than 5% of body weight in a month) or decrease in appetite nearly every day. Note: In children considerable failure to make expected weight gains.

(4) insomnia or hypersomnia [excessive sleep] nearly every day.

(5) psychomotor agitation [excessive movement] or retardation [slowed movement] nearly every day (observable by others, not merely subjective feelings of restlessness or being slowed down).

(6) fatigue or loss of energy nearly every day

(7) feelings of worthlessness or excessive or inappropriate guilt (which may be delusional) nearly every day (not merely self-reproach or guilt about being sick).

(8) diminished ability to think or concentrate, or indecisiveness nearly every day (either by subjective account or observed by others).

(9) recurrent thoughts of death (not just fear of dying), recurrent suicidal ideation without a specific plan, or a suicide attempt, or a specific plan for committing suicide.

B. The symptoms do not meet the criteria for a mixed episode.

C. The symptoms cause clinically significant distress or impairment of social, occupational, or other important areas of functioning.

[Criteria D and E caution clinicians to rule out substance use, other medical conditions, and simple bereavement.]

Reprinted with permission from the *Diagnostic and Statistical Manual of Mental Disorders, Fourth Edition.* ©1994 American Psychiatric Association.

The symptoms of a manic episode are almost literally the opposite of those of a depressive episode. They are outlined in Box 2.4. Consider the case of Mark, a fairly average, married, middle-aged fellow who recalls his earlier manic episodes with a mixture of amusement, embarrassment, and regret.

"It is pretty wild being in that state. There is even some fun, if you don't get into too much trouble. You have a great feeling of self-confidence. You don't so much as feel

---

BOX 2.4
Criteria for Manic Episode (APA, 1994, p. 332)

A. A distinct period of abnormally and persistently elevated mood lasting at least 1 week (or any duration if hospitalization is necessary).

B. During the period of mood disturbance, 3 (or more) of the following symptoms have persisted (4 if the mood is only irritable) and have been present to a significant degree:

1. inflated self-esteem or grandiosity
2. decreased need for sleep (e.g., feels rested after only 3 hours of sleep)
3. more talkative than usual or pressure to keep talking
4. flight of ideas or subjective experience that thoughts are racing
5. distractibility (i.e., attention too easily drawn to unimportant or irrelevant external stimuli)
6. increase in goal-directed activity (either socially, at work, or school, or sexually) or psychomotor agitation [extreme restlessness]
7. excessive involvement in pleasurable activities that have a high potential for painful consequences (e.g., engaging in unrestrained buying sprees, sexual indiscretions, or foolish business investments)

C. The symptoms do no meet criteria for a mixed episode

D. The mood disturbance is sufficiently severe to cause marked impairment in occupational functioning or in usual social activities or relationships with others, or to necessitate hospitalization to prevent harm to self or others, or there are psychotic features.

E. The symptoms are not due to the direct physiological effects of substance (e.g., a drug of abuse , a medication, or other treatment) or a general medical condition (e.g., hyperthyroidism).

Reprinted with permission from the *Diagnostic and Statistical Manual of Mental Disorders, Fourth Edition.* ©1994 American Psychiatric Association.

---

that you are the president, but feel you have pull with him. I'd always get my hands on a really big, fancy car, which I would rent or even buy. I would head for another state, spending wildly until my credit got cut off. Somehow, I would have a pretty girl on my arm, at least some of the time. The stuff I did! I can't believe my wife didn't divorce me. She almost did, more than once, even though she was coming to realize that, bizarrely enough, all this was due to an illness."

Another individual, Robert, with a history of manic phases, put it this way:

"I would set out, say to hitchhike to Hawaii. Yeah, hitch rides, leave the East Coast, ignore the fact that the Pacific Ocean was in the way, even if I got across the country. Of course, I had to hitchhike, I had already cracked up my car, left my job, stopped paying my mortgage, lost my condo. But I would have big plans for myself."

Both men also described very dark periods. Robert said:

"I'd get so I would lose my confidence, not get out of bed, not shower for weeks or change my clothes. The mornings were the worse. Night, was not so good either. I'd be in bed, not asleep, not wanting to get up."

Mark noticed a cycle or pattern that was seasonal.

"It got so I dreaded the fall, the short days before winter set in. Even on medication, I still feel the changes in myself according to the time of year."

Of course, what is so remarkable is the extremes in symptoms within the same individuals—two opposite poles, thus the term *bipolar disorder*.

There are many individuals who only experience depressive episodes, such as Marian, described earlier, or Ann:

> "In a way, everything stopped. I didn't take care of anything, anybody—my husband, my kids, no one, not even myself. I mostly did nothing. I thought a lot about death, even suicide, but I did not even have the energy to do anything about it."

Whereas individuals in manic phases are at risk for harming themselves or others through their impulsive and sometimes dangerous behavior, people in depressive phases are at greater risk for suicide.

> Una had made many attempts on her life, so many it was not taken very seriously and these were called gestures. But she knew for certain she wanted to die. During her last depressive episode, as she was getting better, she started to make plans. She was tired of it all and of all the medications that never really gave her relief. This time she succeeded in slitting both her arms and bleeding to death before she could be found.

Are Schizophrenia and Mood Disorders Different?

Although schizophrenia is characterized by its psychotic symptoms and a mood disorder is characterized by its emotional or affective symptoms, the distinction between the two diagnostic categories is not always so clear. For example, both Robert and Mark who were diagnosed with bipolar disorders experienced grandiose delusions. They said their thoughts raced quickly, and Mark said that at times he heard voices. Consider what happened to Dave:

> Dave had racing thoughts. Sometimes he imagined he was a mafiosio and at other times, a saint. He talked fast and incoherently. At times he would suddenly become sullen and withdrawn. He was treated with antipsychotic medication for many years, without much improvement and many side effects. He died in the state hospital. Later on, when his daughter was diagnosed with bipolar disorder, manic, it occurred to the other members of the family that Dave may have been incorrectly diagnosed as having schizophrenia and, therefore, improperly treated all those years.

Many individuals exhibit the symptoms of both schizophrenic and mood disorders. Their diagnoses do not fit neatly into either category. Consider the story of Tara.

> Tara's mental health workers considered her to have schizophrenia because when she became ill she heard voices, had mixed-up thoughts, paced constantly, and believed she was controlled by aliens. When not sick, she was often cheerful and vivacious. Recently, she sounded sort of hopeless and said "I can't do anything." Her caseworker was so used to hearing so many of her clients say that, she barely noticed. Then Tara began to stop her usual social and volunteer activities. Her personal hygiene became very poor. She stared off into space and basically stopped talking.

Does Tara really have schizophrenia? Does she have another type of psychosis? Is she someone who has schizophrenia but now is also experiencing a depressive episode? Are these the signs of a catatonic episode, perhaps the most bizarre form of schizophrenia in which movement stops altogether?

Tara's flat affect (the lack of expression of emotions), her withdrawal, and her poor concentration are indicative of any variety of illnesses (see *DSM-IV*). Too often mental health professionals, including psychiatrists, jump to conclusions about a person's diagnosis. The risks associated with an incorrect diagnoses are great, because the choice of psychotropic medication is, in large part, based on the diagnosis. The wrong medications are not only unhelpful, they can be directly harmful due to both side effects and the aggravation of other symptoms. For example, antidepressant medication can increase symptoms of psychosis. Also, antipsychotic medication can bring on depressive symptoms. Issues about medications will be discussed further in chapter 3.

The symptoms of mood disorders and schizophrenia resemble each other and in some cases may even be identical. Indeed, many individuals meet the criteria for both schizophrenic and mood disorders at different times throughout their lives or occasionally even at the same time. Individuals who have schizophrenic symptoms and also meet the criteria for one of these mood disorders are classified as having schizoaffective disorder, which has two subtypes: bipolar and depressed (APA, 1994).

Relevance to Psychiatric Rehabilitation

This brief overview of psychiatric symptomatology among persons with severe and persistent mental illness is intended to help the reader grasp the highly disruptive nature of these disorders. The symptoms of these disorders are far more serious than the ups and downs of everyday life. Nor are they like the transient effects of experimenting with drugs or alcohol. Their impact is all encompassing, causing extreme distress and disrupting the living, working, and learning of the individuals who experience these illnesses. It is important for PsyR professionals to have a clear understanding of what their clients are up against and what they are literally dealing with every day. It is hoped that some understanding of the nature of symptoms allows us to feel empathy for someone struggling with a severe mood or thought disorder.

Professionals who have knowledge of symptoms can also help consumers learn about, monitor, and cope with the phases of their illnesses. In addition, this knowledge is sometimes useful in helping clients to communicate with their psychiatrists. However, it is important to understand that most psychiatric rehabilitation interventions do not directly address the symptoms of these illnesses; rather, they address the impairments caused by the disruptiveness, severity, and persistence of the symptoms. PsyR professionals emphasize and build on the healthier features of the person: his or her strengths and interests.

Unfortunately, many professionals tend to overemphasize symptoms, sometimes even missing alternative, simpler explanations. For example, social withdrawal is a common behavioral symptom of persons with severe and persistent mental illness. The extreme, of course, is the individual like Eva who does not speak at all or seek the company of others. But is Eva withdrawn because of her illness?

> Eva spoke rarely, if at all, uttering occasional words in a thick Italian accent. Her psychiatrists and caseworkers must have written a thousand times in her chart "socially

withdrawn." One day, a thought occurred to one of Eva's caseworkers. The caseworker went to another member of the program who spoke Italian and asked him to talk to Eva. When he did, Eva's face brightened immediately. She then produced long, coherent sentences in Italian. The consumer-translator said, "She speaks Italian, definitely, a southern dialect, but I understand her, although she murders a beautiful language."

Clearly, Eva's social withdrawal was not a symptom of what the staff had assumed it to be.

Similarly, mental health professionals tend to not only overemphasize symptoms but to dwell on crises and bizarre behavior, perhaps because they make for juicy war stories. The strengths and personal interests of mental health consumers are sometimes overlooked due to this bias on the part of professionals.

Leonard was a young, lanky fellow who wore a leather jacket and talked to himself in a combination of tough street language and apparent gibberish, which was referred to as a thought disorder and even described as "word salad." It was difficult communicating with him and engaging him in any activities. Sometimes he would try to speak to people and one day all one could hear was "LBJ, Sam Rayburn, U.S. Senate" and the like. Because of his incoherent speech, Leonard's staff person attributed all of this to delusions of grandeur mixed with a good dose of thought disorder. She assumed that Leonard believed he spoke to or knew great U.S. political leaders. However, one day, this staff person asked Leonard to talk more slowly, repeat himself, and so on. The staff person soon found out that Leonard was quite a history and politics buff. His facts were accurate, and he did not believe he was talking with great historical figures. His trouble expressing himself, directly related to the symptoms of his illness, obscured a great interest of his.

Now Leonard's psychiatric rehabilitation professional had found an interest around which to engage Leonard and perhaps also a strength on which to build. Subsequent chapters will explore how psychiatric rehabilitation helps consumers to utilize their strengths, overcome functional deficits, and ultimately achieve their goals.

The description of dire symptoms in this chapter might lead one to conclude that the outlook is hopeless, but this is far from the case. Indeed, many of the individuals described in this chapter who experienced serious problems have continued to struggle with their disorders and achieved successful lives. Chapter 3 will address the long-term outcomes of these conditions.

Dual Diagnosis

The term *dual diagnosis* refers to the presence of two coexisting conditions. The two dual diagnoses most often encountered in PsyR services are mental illness and substance abuse (i.e., drug or alcohol) and mental illness and developmental disability. In both cases, the presence of a dual diagnosis has historically been a complicating factor for providing adequate and appropriate services. Mental health providers often knew little about drug abuse or developmental disability and may have either declined to provide services to someone with a dual diagnosis or provided mental health services without addressing the coexisting disability. Similarly, substance abuse service providers and developmental disability service providers often either addressed only the issues with which they were familiar or declined to provide services altogether. Recently the presence of coexisting conditions and the ways that those conditions affect each other have received greater attention.

Mental Illness and Developmental Disability

The term *developmental disability* encompasses a number of conditions, including cognitive disabilities (i.e., mental retardation), autism, cerebral palsy, epilepsy, brain injury, and spina bifida.

> A Developmental Disability is a severe, disabling condition that arises in infancy or childhood, persists indefinitely and causes serious problems in language, learning, mobility and the capacity for independent living. (New Jersey Developmental Disabilities Council, 1997/1998, p. 1)

Since the mid-1800s when the first segregated schools were developed for children with mental retardation, most people with severe developmental disabilities have been institutionalized for most of their lives. The first segregated schools were designed to be small, personal, individualized, and temporary with services designed to develop skills necessary for success in the community. Instead, they quickly became large institutions "designed to protect society from children with retardation who might grow up to be depraved and dangerous adults" (Mauch, 1991, p. 3). A target of the **eugenics** movement at the turn of the century, people with developmental disabilities were often sterilized.

During the 1950s, parents of people with developmental disabilities began to demand a greater focus on educational and developmental approaches to services. The idea of institutions as the only service option was rejected and some parents began to keep their children with developmental disabilities at home. Parental organizations such as the Association for Retarded Children (ARC) emerged. ARC, which later changed its name to Association for Retarded Citizens and more recently became simply The Arc (Roberts, 1996), became a strong advocate for family members. During the 1960s and 1970s, litigation and advocacy led to the establishment of rights such as public education and services in the least-restricted environment for people with developmental disabilities (Mauch, 1991). The work of many people such as Wolfensberger, who articulated the principle of normalization that is discussed in chapter 4, and Marc Gold, who demonstrated that people with the most severe cognitive disabilities could learn complex skills, fueled the fire of dissatisfaction with institutional care. These new ideas about the rights and abilities of people with disabilities ultimately led to the development of supported employment (discussed in chapter 7) and other community-based supports for people with developmental disabilities. During the 1980s and 1990s, many state institutions were downsized or closed as more and more people with developmental disabilities are being supported to live, learn, work, and socialize in the regular community (Mauch, 1991, Schwartz, 1992, Torrey, 1993).

Incidence of Mental Illness and Developmental Disability

Studies of people with developmental disability living in the community suggest that among these individuals 20% to 35% experience a coexisting mental illness (Parsons, May & Menolascino, 1984; Torrey, 1993). However, Parsons and colleagues cautioned that these studies include many children under the age of 12 and therefore should not be considered a true reflection of incidence among adults (Parsons et al., 1984). More recently, Szymanski, King, Goldberg, Reid, Tonge, and Cain (1998) reported an incidence rate for schizophrenia and other psychotic disorders and mood disorders among people with developmental disability to be similar to that found in the general public. They further reported that the incidence of personality disorders appears to be higher than usual but suggest that this may be "related to maladaptive personality traits resulting from negative social experiences" (p. 14). Furthermore, the full gamut of mental illnesses has been found among people with developmental disabilities (Torrey, 1993).

Diagnosing mental illness in a person with developmental disability is sometimes a difficult task. The diagnostic process includes self-report of thoughts, feelings, and symptoms. For individuals with significant impairments in communication this may be difficult if not impossible. Often diagnosis then is based on reported behavior, such as an increase in aggression, self-injury, tearfullness, withdrawal, and so on. These same behaviors can also be indications of physical illness, psychological stress, or dissatisfaction (Stark, McGee, Menolascino, Baker, & Menousek, 1984; Torrey, 1993).

The potential for misdiagnosis is clearly great. A misdiagnosis brings with it the possible unnecessary or incorrect use of medication, which is of great concern to people with disabilities, their families, and advocates.

Mental Illness and Substance Abuse

The dual diagnosis of mental illness and substance abuse refers to the presence of a severe psychiatric disorder and abuse of or dependence on alcohol or drugs. People with this dual diagnosis are referred to in a number of ways: for example, dually diagnosed, dually disordered, mentally ill chemical abuser (MICA), mentally ill substance abuser (MISA), chemical abuse and mental illness (CAMI), and others (U.S. Department of Health and Human Services, 1995).

Incidence of Mental Illness and Substance Abuse

This group of individuals appears to make up an astounding percentage of the overall population of people with severe mental illness. Studies indicate that between 17% and 63% of individuals with serious mental illness also abuse substances (Drake, McLaughlin, Pepper, & Minkoff, 1991; Sciacca & Thompson, 1996). Drake and his colleagues (1991) have suggested that the factors contributing to this high incidence are deinstitutionalization and changing societal norms. In short, because people with mental illness spend more time in the community, they have increased access to drugs and alcohol. At the same time, society in general has a greater acceptance of the use of drugs and alcohol.

For many people with this dual diagnosis, the substance abuse predates the onset of mental illness and the reasons for using seem to be the same reasons that nondisabled people use. Some researches hypothesize that the drug use precipitates or induces the mental illness. For other individuals, the reasons for using drugs and alcohol may include self-medication to alleviate psychiatric symptoms or to medicate side effects, the desire to be like their nondisabled peers, or the desire to improve their comfort in social interactions (Drake et al., 1991).

Further complicating this phenomenon, the group identified as dually diagnosed is not homogenous. Individuals with mental illness and substance abuse problems differ from each other in psychiatric diagnosis and severity, type and level of substance abuse, and extent of the impact of either disability on life functioning (Weiss, Mirin, & Frances, 1992). Luke, Mowbray, Klump, Herman, and BootsMiller (1996) identified seven clusters of individuals by examining the type and level of substance abuse and its impact on areas such as medical needs, employment, legal involvement, family/social problems, and psychiatric problems.

Etiology

What is the origin of the strange symptoms described in this chapter? Why do some people get major mental illnesses such as schizophrenia? What is the source of the vulnerability to these disorders?

Although the jury is still out on these questions, we are much closer to a final verdict today than at any time in the past. Mounting biomedical evidence identifies the root cause of these devastating illnesses as biological in nature rather than psychological or **psychodynamic** (i.e., theoretically rooted in past events and the unconscious). Interestingly, much of this progress can be directly attributed to the development of high-speed computers, which have made high-definition medical imaging possible.

Physiological Evidence of the Disease Process in the Brain

The evidence is overwhelming that schizophrenia and similar conditions are due to changes in the structure and functioning of the brain (Buchanan & Carpenter, 1997; Frith, 1997). Today, very sophisticated neuroimaging techniques—such as magnetic resonance imaging (MRI), computerized axial tomography (CAT scan), and positron emissions tomography (PET) scans—provide a window for viewing living, working brains. Developed with the help of high-speed computers, MRI and CAT scans provide pictures of the brain's structure, whereas PET scans provide snapshots of its functioning.

Using these various types of brain scans, the living brains of people with serious mental illnesses have been compared to other individuals of the same age and sex. Based on the differences found between people with serious mental illness and those without it, it has become increasingly clear that the brains of people with serious mental illness have both a different **neuroanatomy** and different neural functioning than people who do not have a major psychiatric disorder (Buchanan & Carpenter, 1997).

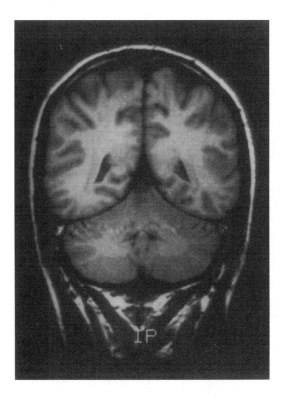 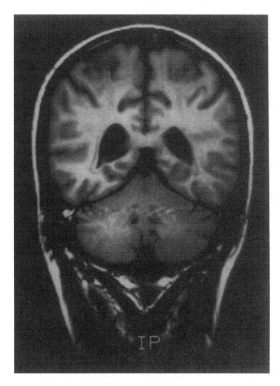

Well twin   Affected twin

FIGURE 2.1   MRI scans of 28-year-old identical twins discordant for schizophrenia showing enlarged cerebral ventricles in the affected twin. Courtesy of Dr. E. Fuller Torrey and Dr. Daniel Weinberger, Clinical Brain Disorders Branch, National Institute of Mental Health.

The magnetic resonance imaging (MRI) scan provides images of the tissue, structure, and spaces (ventricles and sulci) in the brain. In the MRI scans (Figure 2.1), the lighter gray areas are the brain tissue cells or neurons and the two dark black areas near the center of the brain are the ventricles. The **ventricles** are large fluid-filled enclosures, the **sulci** are the spaces or folds in the brain's cortex. These are part of the normal anatomy or structure of the brain. Normally, ventricles and sulci become enlarged as part of the aging process.

The MRI scans are of 28-year-old twins, one has schizophrenia and the other does not. Note that the person with schizophrenia (on the right) has less brain tissue and larger ventricles and sulci compared to her twin on the left. Take particular note of the large black areas, the enlarged ventricles near the center of the brain, in the ill twin.

People with schizophrenia, compared to others their own age, often have larger spaces in their brain in the form of enlarged ventricles and sulci, indicating they have less brain tissue (Gur & Pearlson. 1993). Consistent with the picture above, MRI and CAT scans have consistently found that these spaces are enlarged in the brains of people with schizophrnia (Heckers, 1997). Based on this evidence, it appears that some people with schizophrenia have suffered a type of physical dementia (e.g., enlarged ventricles), perhaps as early as adolescence or young adulthood.

The Case of Dara

Besides demonstrating an important point about the physiological basis of severe mental illness, Dara's case is a good illustration of the importance of educating families and consumers. As you read this case, consider what the family should have known and what the effect of their not knowing has on their attitude about Dara's chances for recovery.

Dara's family was upset enough about her latest "episode," as they called it. A 54-year-old married woman with two children, Dara had been ill for more than 25 years. Dara is a graduate of a 2-year college and worked as an accounting clerk in an insurance agency. Suddenly, for no apparent reason, she stopped going to work. Then one day she jumped out into traffic. Fortunately, she was rescued by a police officer. When she was asked why she had jumped out, she said that voices had been telling her to do this for several hours and she had finally given in. Once in the traffic, she got frightened and yelled for help. At the hospital, she said that President Clinton intervened to save her and had personally sent the police officer. Upon admission, the doctor ordered a CAT scan to rule out a dementia, such as the early onset of Alzheimer's disease, that might have contributed to her seemingly bizarre behavior. Dara did have enlarged spaces (ventricles) in her brain. Her son said "Oh my God, what could be worse? More bad news about mom!" Later, the family members learned, it was the same bad news they had already been living with for many years. Like many people with schizophrenia, there were significant changes in the structure of Dara's brain, perhaps for most of her adult life.

A positron emission tomography (PET) scan provides colored pictures of the brain's activity by measuring blood flow and where the brain is metabolizing glucose. Thus, it detects how the body's sugar (glucose) is being used by cells, in this case in the neurons of the brain.

More use of glucose is related to more nerve cell activity. Figure 2.2 presents black and white examples of PET scans from 31-year-old twins, one with schizophrenia, the other one healthy. The brighter areas in the frontal lobes of the brain are indicative of more brain activity, the darker areas are indicative of less activity. During tasks requiring a great deal of concerntration, the areas of the brain known as the frontal lobes become very active.

Compare the frontal lobes (indicated by the arrows) of the person with schizophrenia (on the right) with those of his twin, the person without schziophrenia (on the left). Both are working on the same task, yet the person with schzophrenia, as indicated by the darker frontal lobe area, has far less activity in that area of the brain than the other individual. This twin has less cerebral blood flow to his frontal lobes is thus considered "hypofrontal."

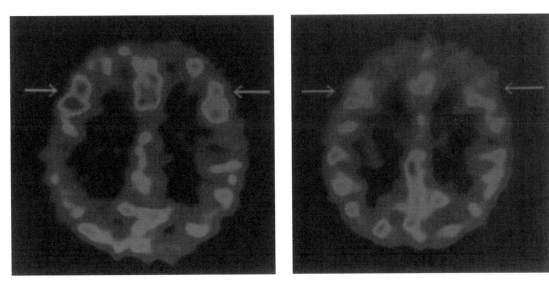

Well twin   Affected twin

FIGURE 2.2   PET scan study of 31-year-old identical twins discordant for schizophrenia. Well twin on left shows evidence of more cerebral blood flow in the area of frontal lobe (arrows). Twin with schizophrenia has less cerebral blood flow to the frontal lobe and is thus "hypofrontal." Courtesy of Dr. E. Fuller Torrey and Dr. Daniel Weinberger, Clinical Brain Disorders Branch, National Institute of Mental Health.

A variety of studies have shown that the frontal lobes are underactive in persons with schizophrenia (Buschbaum & Haier, 1987). Considering the behavioral functions that are mediated there, this disorder in the frontal lobes is likely to result in lack of energy, poor attention and concentration, poor emotional control, flat affect, and restlessness. These problems correspond closely to the negative symptoms of schizophrenia described earlier in this chapter.

Cerebral blood flow studies have found similar results (Buschbaum & Haier, 1987). This technique measures brain activity by tracing where the brain is using blood and oxygen. Once again, the frontal lobes have been found to be underactive. These cerebral blood flow studies have also shown that other areas, such as the temporal and parietal lobes, are receiving more blood and oxygen, compared to people without schizophrenia, indicating overactivity in these areas, perhaps accounting for hallucinations, delusions, and the excessive internal stimulation reported by people with psychoses.

Neurotransmitters

The PET scan and cerebral blood flow studies imply that not only is the structure of the brain different, but the neural functioning or brain's activity is disordered. The brain is an electrochemical organ, and neurotransmitters are literally the chemical messengers of the brain. **Neurotransmitters** ensure the proper functioning of the brain's electrical circuitry, which underlies all of our behavior. Even the simplest actions and thoughts are made up of the functioning of many neurons (cells of the nervous system) in many different areas and systems of the brain, working in collaboration in complex patterns of activity. One brain cell communicates with many other brain cells through the activity of one or more neurotransmitters. Indeed, all of this complex electrochemical interaction is regulated by the chemical messengers of the brain, neurotransmitters. There may be as many as 30 to 40 other neurotransmitters. Each neurotransmitter is involved in many different behaviors or functions. The converse is true as well, the simplest of behaviors entails numerous neurotransmitters.

Some of the major neurotransmitters are the following:

- *Dopamine.* Neurons that use dopamine are involved in all sorts of behavior, especially movement, hearing, and perhaps planning.
- *Norepinephrine.* Also known as Adrenalin, is involved with the circulatory system, the heart, but also affects sleep, appetite, and sexual behavior.
- *Serotonin.* This neurotransmitter affects sleep, impulse control, and other functions.
- *Acetylcholine.* This neurotransmitter affects movement and muscles.

Neurotransmitters and Mental Illness

Two neurotransmitters systems in particular, dopamine and serotonin, seem to be involved in schizophrenia. In persons with this disease, dopamine appears to be overactive and serotonin underactive, although the full explanation for these actions is far more complicated. Nevertheless, the disorders in these systems lead directly to the symptoms of schizophrenia.

Two neurotransmitters, serotonin and norepinephrine, also appear to be involved in mood disorders. This combination would account for the changes in sleep, appetite, and drive seen in these illnesses.

Brain development and brain chemistry are influenced by psychosocial and physical factors. Responses to stress may lead to changes in neurotransmitter functioning. A person who was already vulnerable for genetic or developmental reasons may have abnormal changes in their neurotransmitter system in response to an environmental insult or stressor. Thus, a genetic vulnerability combined with a chain of biological events and environmental stressors may result in the onset of the illness.

The Role of Genetic Factors

What causes these changes in neuroanatomy and neurotransmitter functioning? The evidence suggests that to a large degree these changes are inherited. For quite some time, based on simple observations of a familial incidence of mental illnesses, many researchers, including Sigmund Freud, have hypothesized that schizophrenia and the other major illnesses were inherited. There is no doubt that the risk of developing schizophrenia is greatly increased if one's biological or "blood" relatives have the illness. Numerous studies have found that even if you have never had any contact with your biological relative with schizophrenia, and never shared the same environment, you have an elevated chance of developing this disease (Kendeler & Deihl, 1993).

Risk among Biological Relatives

The probable genetic component of these illnesses is illustrated by examining changes in the probability of contracting these conditions. For persons in the general population who do not have relatives with these conditions, the risk for schizophrenia ranges from about one-half of 1% to 1%. If one parent or sibling has the disorder, the risk is 10 times larger, jumping to from 5% to 10% (Torrey, 1995). If both parents have the disorder, the probability of contracting the illness can be nearly 50%. As illustrated in the Israeli high-risk study, research has demonstrated that these risk increases are independent of environmental factors.

Studying twins has been particularly revealing with respect to the role played by genetics in schizophrenia. Twins can be classified as either monozygotic, coming from one fertilized egg that later splits into two separate zygotes, or dizygotic, coming from two separate eggs fertilized at about the same time. Thus, identical twins are monozygotic and have identical gene sets. Fraternal twins are dizygotic and have gene sets as similar (or different) as brothers and sisters born at different times.

When one of a pair of fraternal twins has schizophrenia, the concordance (or probability) that the other twin will develop the disease is similar to the rate for any siblings: 5% to 10%. For identical twins who have identical genetic heritage, the concordance rate jumps to from 40% to 50% (Torrey, 1995). These figures show that although genetics play a key factor in the etiology of schizophrenia, genetics alone are not a sufficient cause of the disease. If people simply inherited the disorder, the concordance rate between monozygotic identical twins—because they have identical gene sets—would be 100%. Therefore, some developmental or environmental factors must account for why some identical twins do not become ill when their sibling has schizophrenia.

The Israeli high-risk study provides one example from the body of compelling evidence that genetics play a strong role in the etiology of schizophrenia. The exact etiology of schizophrenia has remained one of the major mysteries surrounding this disease. In the past, much of this debate pitted environmental and hereditary factors against each other. Based on a unique environmental characteristic, The Israeli high-risk study (Marcus, Hans, Nagler, Auerbach, Mirsky, & Aubrey, 1987) attempted to help solve this problem. Many Israeli settlements, particularly in formerly unpopulated areas like the Negev Desert, were built on the kibbutz model. One characteristic of a kibbutz is that all the children are raised together by child-care workers rather than being raised in the family. This means that for the children raised in a kibbutz, the environment is basically similar. From a research perspective it was assumed that many environmental factors that might contribute to schizophrenia would also be held constant in the kibbutz. To investigate this phenomenon (among others), researchers identified 100 Israeli children: 50 children from the kibbutz and 50 children from the city where they were brought up in the usual nuclear families. In half the children from the kibbutz (25) and half of the children from the city (25), one or both parents had

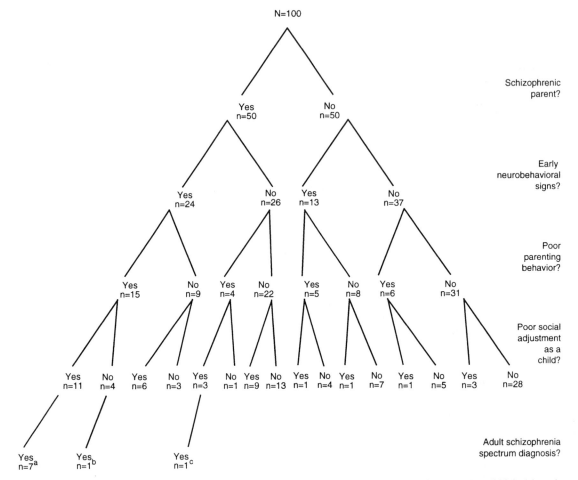

FIGURE 2.3 Decision-tree model for development of schizophrenia: Application to Israeli high-risk study data. Breakdown cases marked "a" = 1 residual-type schizophrenia, 3 paranoid schizophrenia, 2 schizoid personality disorders, and 1 mixed spectrum disorder. Breakdown case marked "b" = 1 residual-type schizophrenia. Breakdown case marked "c" = 1 schizoid personality disorder with dysthymic disorder. From Marcus et al., 1987.

been diagnosed with schizophrenia. The other children's parents were apparently free from mental illness. These hundred children were studied over a 30-year period. Researchers periodically assessed these individuals' neurobiological signs, social adjustment, home life (parenting), and, ultimately, their mental health. One striking finding of this study was that the children who went on to develop either schizophrenia or severe mental illness all had one or more mentally ill parent. The study also found that whether or not the parent with mental illness raised the child did not change the probability of an individual developing the disorder. Similar genetic studies in Europe, particularly in Scandinavia, have confirmed this finding.

Apparently, genetic heritage plays an important part in these diseases. If an individual has no close relatives who have schizophrenia or a major affective disorder, the risk of that person developing such a disorder is minimal (about 1%).

Fetal Development and Early Infancy

Events that occur in vitro may also contribute to the development of schizophrenia. The importance of fetal development in the prenatal environment is highlighted by other findings from twin studies. When twins develop in the same **chorion**—that is, the same sac in their mother's womb—the concordance rate for schizophrenia is higher then when they develop in separate chorions. Birth during the winter months, maternal infections during the second trimester of pregnancy (a time of extensive brain development), lower birth weights, and complications in the delivery of the child are all associated with a higher incidence or likelihood of schizophrenia among those at genetic risk (Torrey, 1995).

Biological factors affect the risk of contracting schizophrenia or other major mental illnesses among people at genetic risk. Their genetic heritage may make the brain more vulnerable to viruses during fetal development or infancy. Obstetric delivery problems such as temporary deprivation of oxygen may be another of these potentially harmful events. All of these are referred to as "insults" to the fetus or infant. These insults, in turn, lead to abnormal development of brain structure or tissue, altering how the person's brain's structure and brain chemistry evolves.

In summary, a host of factors are likely to contribute to injury or insult of the fetal or infant brain. Studies suggest that exposure to these physiological stressors early in life is implicated in the etiology of these illnesses.

CONTROVERSIAL ISSUE
The Chronological and Geographical Incidence of Schizophrenia

Research suggests that prevalence or rate of schizophrenia is affected by what month people are born in and where they live. These differences may or may not provide a clue to the causes of schizophrenia, but they apparently do not occur by chance. Researchers who believe that infectious agents in the environment such as viruses are implicated in schizophrenia have pointed to these differences as possible evidence for their theories.

People born in the winter and early spring have a higher likelihood of contracting schizophrenia than persons born during other seasons. This is true regardless of the hemisphere where the individual is born (when it's summer in the northern hemisphere it's winter in the southern hemisphere). These seasonal variations, which are probably not due to chance, may relate to diet, climate, or other seasonal changes.

Ireland has long been known to have an inordinately high rate of schizophrenia. Some reports found that Ireland had a higher rate of hospitalizations for schizophrenia than any other country in the world (Torrey, 1995). Torrey, who has studied schizophrenia in Ireland, reported that there were large differences in the prevalence of the disease even between different regions in the country. By contrast, countries like Ghana and Botswana in Africa and New Guinea and Taiwan in the Pacific have very low rates of the disease. How can we account for these differences in rate? Some answers may involve how persons with schizophrenia are identified and counted in different settings. Another explanation may deal with the genetic heritage of different groups. Finally, differences in geography relate to climatic differences, which may provide a clue.

The Role of Stress

Despite what the media encourage the public to believe, major mental illness is not caused solely by the stress we encounter in our day-to-day lives. E. Fuller Torrey, a psychiatrist and author who has done extensive research in this area, considers stress a minor cause at best (Torrey, 1995). He has pointed out that illnesses such as schizophrenia are not more prevalent in highly stressful times, such as during wars or large natural catastrophes such as floods, plagues, and famines. Nor is there a higher rate of schizophrenia among people who live in very stressful places, such as prisons or concentration camps. Instead, stress may very well be "the straw that breaks the camel's back," as Torrey has put it. Apparently, when someone has the genetic vulnerability and has suffered the requisite biological insults, high stress may push that person over the edge and bring forth the disease (Torrey, 1995).

Psychosocial and environmental stress may play a part in brain development and brain chemistry. Responses to environmental and psychosocial stress always lead to changes in the brain's chemical messengers—neurotransmitters. However, in individuals who are already vulnerable for genetic or developmental reasons, abnormal changes in neurotransmitter functioning may take place. This is the basic premise of the **diathesis-stress** model, which proposes that a biologically vulnerable person, when exposed to a stress or trigger, then develops the disease (Anthony & Liberman, 1986).

The role of stress in the onset of major depression appears to be significant but not a sufficient cause. The onset of an episode is typically preceded by a serious personal loss of a loved one, a job, a home, or other personal catastrophe. However, while stress has been established as a fairly strong contributing factor, it does not account for why some individuals respond to loss by experiencing a brief period of sadness and hopelessness and others develop a severe condition.

The most obvious example comes from examining responses to the death of a loved one. Most individuals have a period of what is known as uncomplicated bereavement. That is, their mood is depressed, they feel hopeless, maybe even wanting to die for a time, and are unable to sleep or lack appetite. Many may experience this for a period of weeks, or even months, without it markedly affecting their social or occupational functioning. In sharp contrast, individuals suffering from major depression may experience a full-blown episode of depression that severely disrupts their normal functioning, as described in Box 2.3.

Stressful life events also play a role in the onset of episodes experienced by people diagnosed with bipolar disorder. However, research shows that psychosocial and environmental stressors are more evident prior to the onset of the early episodes of this illness. The influence of these stressors seems to play little or no role after the first few episodes (Goodwin & Jamison, 1990). Clearly the etiology of these disorders is a complex one that cannot be explained simply as extreme sensitivity to stress.

The Stress-Vulnerability-Coping-Competence Model

The stress-vulnerability-coping-competence model was proposed by two individuals who are well known in the field of psychiatric rehabilitation, William A. Anthony and Robert Paul Liberman (1986, 1992). The model provides both a theory about the cause of severe

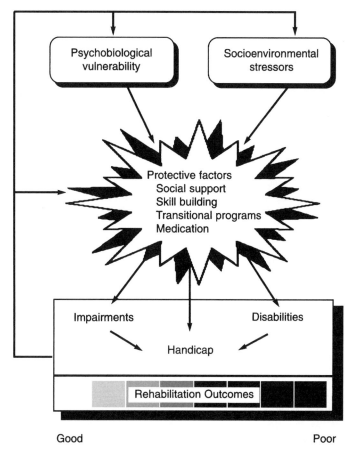

FIGURE 2.4 Vulnerability, stress, coping, and competence model of mental disorders. In this conceptual framework protective factors that facilitate coping and competence can modulate the deleterious effects of psychobiological vulnerability and socioenvironmental stressors. Coping and competence confer protection against impairment, disability, and handicap. Anthony W. A., and Liberman, R. P. (1986). *The Practice of Psychiatric Rehabilitation: Historical, Conceptual, and Research Base. Schizophrenia Bulletin* **12(4)**, 542–559.

mental illness and an explanatory framework for the impact of psychiatric rehabilitation and treatment interventions on the symptoms and functional level of people with psychiatric disabilities.

The model proposes the following: individuals inherit or otherwise acquire a vulnerability (sometimes referred to as diathesis) to major mental illnesses such as schizophrenia, major depression, or bipolar disorder. The illness can be triggered by various stressors, many of which may appear to be of normal intensity but that can lead to the catastrophic symptoms and events of mental illness. Stressors that have the potential to bring on an acute episode include personal losses, developmental transitions, and stressful life events such as marriage, graduation, and moving. Physical illness, injury, substance abuse, and other physiological factors such as sleep deprivation have also been associated with the onset of psychiatric symptoms:

> Even in the absence of a time-limited stressor, vulnerable individuals can succumb to ambient levels of challenge, tension, or conflict in their environment. (Anthony & Liberman, 1992, pp. 6–7)

Fortunately, a number of protective factors can either prevent the onset of an acute episode of illness or lessen the impact of symptoms. These factors include coping skills, supportive resources, competence in relevant life activities, and psychotropic medications. According to this model, the severity and outcome of these disorders have a lot to do with whether or not these protective factors are in place when a stressful event occurs. If an individual does not have adequate coping skills or does not acquire resources or supports that enhance coping, he or she remains vulnerable to the influence of future stressors and more vulnerable to frequent or prolonged relapses. Conversely, a person with well-developed coping skills and a reliable support system is likely to experience fewer acute episodes of mental illness, as well as episodes that are less severe and shorter in duration. Consider the following vignette:

> Cheryl has been coping with schizophrenia for 10 years. For the last 2 years she has been relatively stable, experiencing some negative symptoms but very few positive symptoms. She sees a psychiatrist once a month who prescribes a relatively low dose of antipsychotic medication for her. Sometimes Cheryl forgets to take her medication or chooses to skip her morning dose because it makes her drowsy. She used to attend a peer support group regularly but has gradually lost touch with the group. Cheryl has a part-time clerical job, which she likes. She is not particularly close to friends or family, and when not at her job she prefers to keep to herself. Cheryl was doing well at her job until her supervisor, whom she liked and trusted, left to take another position. About a week later Cheryl began to hear disturbing voices. She also had difficulty sleeping and could not concentrate on her filing duties at work. She missed some days at work and was occasionally late. Her new supervisor criticized her performance and questioned her recent tardiness and absenteeism. Unable to face an increasingly stressful work environment, Cheryl quit her job.

Although Cheryl's job history suggests that she had some coping skills and a certain level of vocational competence, she lacked the problem-solving skills and support system she needed to help her cope with a major change at work. The fact that she was not taking her medication regularly at the time she was exposed to psychosocial stress may also have affected her vulnerability to psychosis and the distressing results.

The role of psychiatric rehabilitation is to aid the individual in the development of coping skills and competence (Anthony & Liberman, 1986). By enhancing coping ability and competence in social and vocational environments, the vulnerability to stress is reduced. Psychotropic medications are also an important protective factor, and PsyR practitioners can play an important role in helping consumers obtain the information and skills they need to utilize medications appropriately. Once individuals who have mastered coping skills, future stressors, which everyone faces, will be much less devastating.

Obsolete Etiological Theories

The scientific community has made real progress in its understanding of the etiology of the major mental illnesses. At the same time, the public is still exposed to a number of discredited or obsolete theories about what causes major mental illness. Most of these obsolete theories center around early childhood psychological trauma or abusive family environments as causal factors. Harding and Zahniser (1994) described the familial role in etiology as one of the great myths about schizophrenia. Although a dysfunctional family environment is clearly unpleasant, often stressful, and may be associated with some psychiatric disorders, it apparently is not the primary cause of severe and persistent mental illness.

One discredited theory traced the cause of schizophrenia to *schizophrenegenic* mothers. Supposedly, these mothers caused schizophrenia in their children by giving them mixed messages, for example, simultaneously encouraging independence and engendering unnatural levels of maternal dependence (Lindz, 1992). Empirical research has provided no support for this theory and others that focus on parentally induced intrapsychic conflict, yet some professionals and members of the general public still subscribe to them.

These theories are not only erroneous, they are harmful. Adherents to these theories have blamed family members for the illness of their loved ones. This, in turn, fostered guilt and animosity among family members, making for tense, counterproductive relationships between family members and professionals (passim Torrey, 1995). This disservice to consumers and their families is also being perpetuated by some educators, who persist in training mental health professionals in these discredited theories despite the lack of evidence for them (Harding, Zubin, & Strauss, 1992; Lefley, 1989).

The Myth of "The Myth of Mental Illness"

The views of Thomas Szasz (1976) were popular in the 1960s and 1970s. He proposed that rather than being an actual disease, mental illnesses, including schizophrenia, were an artifact or creation of psychiatry. In short, he believed that mental illness does not really exist. This theory has been discredited by the extensive biological evidence that an active disease process exists. Szasz built his theory on a single observation, which was undoubtedly true at the time, but he reached a conclusion that was undoubtedly false. Szasz believed that all assertions about human behavior (including diagnoses) by psychiatrists and psychologists are subjective observations based on value judgments, not scientific judgments. In short, judgments like diagnoses and competency were solely matters of opinion rather than scientific facts. There is a body of research that supports this contention (Rosenhan, 1973). Szasz's position was simple, he believed that we should not define mental illness as a disease unless a "brain lesion" can be found. As yet, no specific lesion has been found, nor will it ever be, but a variety of other organic evidence of maladies in the brain have been found. In addition, the symptoms and functional deficits experienced by the millions of people who have schizophrenia are quite real and have a profound effect on their lives.

Other outdated theorists include the late British psychiatrist and author R. D. Laing who believed that psychosis was actually a healing process (Torrey, 1995). Laing believed that through psychosis the individual regresses to the developmental stage at the core of the problem. From this stage, it then becomes possible to bring about a cure. Based on that idea, Laing believed that the professional's task was to encourage regression or psychosis rather than try to stop it. The helper would work with the individuals in such psychotic states to help them mend themselves. To accomplish this for his patients, Laing created a clinic where these individuals could experience their psychosis in a safe environment without interruption. Laing's approach was not only not helpful, it probably was harmful. There is strong evidence that psychosis and regression are accompanied by sometimes irreversible brain tissue atrophy.

The beliefs of Loren Mosher (Mosher & Burti, 1989), formerly of the National Institute of Mental Health (NIMH), were similar to Laing's. He felt people with schizophrenia should not be treated with medication because it deprives patients of "the experience" of their symptoms. He was concerned that they would become out-of-touch with themselves. Given the enormous evidence of the medical-biological nature of mental illness, such thinking is tantamount to saying that people suffering from heart disease should not be treated because it would interfere with their experience of angina (chest pain).

Summary

Individuals who are served in psychiatric rehabilitation programs have various psychiatric diagnoses, including schizophrenia, schizoaffective disorder, bipolar disorder, and major depression recurrent. Generally speaking, within PsyR programs, the most common diagnoses are schizophrenic disorders, whereas in the general population, mood disorders are more common. Details of the criteria of these diagnoses are reported in the American Psychiatric Association's *DSM-IV* manual (APA, 1994). These disorders are long term and are characterized by periods of acute illness followed by episodes of residual symptoms and remission. In the acute phases of these disorders and occasionally at other times, the resulting symptoms have serious behavioral manifestations and often come to preoccupy the sensory and cognitive experience of the individual.

Most people receiving PsyR services have experienced psychotic symptoms, such as hallucinations, delusions, and thought disorders, which are very severe and disruptive to the daily life. The preponderance of evidence is that these major mental illnesses are biological brain disorders. Studies of the structure of the brain through MRIs and CAT scans and studies of the functioning of the brain using PET scans and cerebral blood flow confirm this hypothesis. Indeed, the National Alliance for the Mentally Ill has established a nationwide public relations campaign to replace the term mental illness with *brain disorder*.

Genetic studies, twin studies, and epidemiological investigations all suggest that the vulnerability to schizophrenia and other major mental illnesses is inherited. Stresses, including biological/physical risk factors and psychosocial/environmental events, contribute to further harm already vulnerable individuals. This combination of biological influences, environmental factors, and psychosocial stressors apparently changes the structure and functioning of the brain, which results in symptoms such as hallucinations, delusions, and other serious difficulties. These symptoms have severe cognitive (thinking), psychological, and social consequences for the individual.

Chapter 3 will focus on the persistence of these disorders and will address their treatment, course, and outcome. It will discuss the positive impact of medication, rehabilitation, and other psychosocial interventions, as well as the varied outcomes for persons with these disorders.

Class Exercise

The experience of severe and persistent mental illness raises many questions in the minds of people with the illness. These concerns are shared by loved ones. At times, mental health professionals have been less than forthcoming or honest in their responses to questions. This has often led to misunderstandings and a lack of trust. Sometimes, it has lead to the development of very serious misconceptions and misinformation about mental illness.

Consider how you might respond in the following circumstances.

Scenario 1

A member of the PsyR program you work in has approached you, telling you that he is "not a schizophrenic" because he has only one personality. You say that multiple personalities is not what schizophrenia is all about and try to leave it at that. But he persists by asking you, "what is schizophrenia?" How do you respond?

Scenario 2

The mother of another member of the program you work for approaches you by asking why her daughter should take medication. She says, "For 20 years they have told me she has a mental disease, but they want her to take pills, I think to dope her up. Pills! They can only help if you have a problem with the body, but her problem is with her mind!" How would you clarify matters here?

Scenario 3

Another member of the program and his family believe that the reason he has mental illness is from a curse, a spell put on him by an evil spirit. How do you respond?

References

American Psychiatric Association (APA). (1994). *Diagnostic and statistical manual of mental disorders* (4th ed.). Washington, DC: Author.

Angst, J. (1998). Treated versus untreated major depressive episodes. *Psychopathology*, *31*(1), 37–44.

Anthony, W. A., & Liberman, R. P. (1986). The practice of psychiatric rehabilitation: Historical, conceptual, and research base. *Schizophrenia Bulletin, 12*(4), 542–559.

Arns, P. (1998, June). *Update on using the IAPSRS Toolkit for measuring psychosocial rehabilitation outcomes.* Paper presented at the International Association of Psychosocial Rehabilitation Services conference, Orlando, Florida.

Buchanan, R. W., & Carpenter, W. T. (1997). The neuroanatomies of schizophrenia. *Schizophrenia Bulletin, 23*(3), 367–372.

Buchsbaum, M. S., & Haier, R. J. (1987). Functional and anatomical brain imaging: impact on schizophrenia research. *Schizophrenia Bulletin, 13*(1) 115–132.

DeSisto, M. J., Harding, C. M., McCormick, R. V., Ashikaga, T., & Brooks, G. W. (1995a). The Maine and Vermont three-decade studies of serious mental illness: I. Matched comparison of cross-sectional outcome. *British Journal of Psychiatry, 167*(3), 331–338.

DeSisto, M. J., Harding, C. M., McCormick, R. V., Ashikaga, T., & Brooks, G. W. (1995b). The Maine and Vermont three-decade studies of serious mental illness: II. Longitudinal course comparisons. *British Journal of Psychiatry, 167*(3), 338–342.

Drake, R. E., McLaughlin, P., Pepper, B., & Minkoff, K. (1991). Dual diagnosis of major mental illness and substance disorder: An overview. *New Directions for Mental Health Services, 50*, 3–12.

Frith, C. D. (1997). Functional brain imaging and the neuropathology of schizophrenia. *Schizophrenia Bulletin, 23*(3), 403–422.

Goodwin, F. K., & Jamison, K. R. (1990). *Manic depressive illness.* New York: Oxford University Press.

Gur, R. E., & Pearlson, G. D. (1993). Neuroimaging in schizophrenia research. *Schizophrenia Bulletin, 19*(2), 163–181.

Harding, C. M., Brooks, G. W., Ashikaga, T., Strauss, J. S., & Breier, A. (1987a). The Vermont longitudinal study of persons with severe mental illness: IO Methodology, study sample, and overall status 32 years later. *American Journal of Psychiatry, 144*(6), 718–726.

Harding, C. M., Brooks, G. W., Ashikaga, T., Strauss, J. S., & Breier, A. (1987b). The Vermont longitudinal study of persons with severe mental illness: II. Long-term outcome of subjects who retrospectively met *DSM-III* criteria for schizophrenia. *American Journal of Psychiatry, 144*(6), 727–735.

Harding, C. M., & Zahniser J. H. (1994). Empirical correction of seven myths about schizophrenia with implications for treatment. *Acta Psychiatrica Scandinavica, Supplementum, 384*, 140–146.

Harding, C. M., Zubin, J., & Strauss, J. S. (1992). Chronicity in schizophrenia: Revisited. *British Journal of Psychiatry—Supplement, 18*, 27–37.

Heckers, S. (1997). Neuropathology of schizophrenia: Cortex, thalamus, basal ganglia, and neurotransmitter projection systems. *Schizophrenia Bulletin, 23*(3),525–528.

Kendler, K. S., & Deihl, S. R. (1993). The genetics of schizophrenia: A current genetic-epidemiologic perspective. *Schizophrenia Bulletin, 19*(2), 87–112.

Lefley, H. P. (1989). Family burden and family stigma in major mental illness. *American Psychologist, 44*(3), 556–560.

Lehman, A. F. (1995). Vocational rehabilitation in schizophrenia. *Schizophrenia Bulletin, 21*(4), 645–656.

Licht R. W. (1998). Drug treatment of mania: A critical review. *Acta Psychiatrica Scandinavica, 97*(6), 387–397.

Lindz, T. (1992). *The Relevance of the family to psychoanalytic theory.* Madison, CT: International Universities Press.

Luke, D. A., Mowbray, C. T., Klump, K., Herman, S. E., & BootsMiller, B. (1996). Exploring the diversity of dual diagnosis: Utility of cluster analysis for program planning. *The Journal of Mental Health Administration, 23*(3), 298–316.

Marcus, J., Hans, S. L., Nagler, S., Auerbach, J. G., Mirsky, A. F., & Aubrey, A. (1987). Review of the NIMH Israeli kibbutz-city study and the Jerusalem infant development study. *Schizophrenia Bulletin, 13* (3), 425–437.

Mauch, D. (1991). Separate paths to a common understanding: Treating the human condition of a disability. *The Community Integration of Persons Labeled as Dually Diagnoses: Issues and Models, Selected Conference Proceedings.* Cincinnati: University Affiliated Cincinnati Center for Developmental Disorders, 1–14.

Mosher, L. R., & Burti, L. (1989). *Community Mental Health.* New York: W. W. Norton.

New Jersey Developmental Disabilities Council. (1997/1998). *Resources directory* (8th ed.).

Parsons, J. A., May, J. G., Jr., & Menolascino, F. J. (1984). The nature and incidence of mental illness in mentally retarded individuals. In F. J. Menolascino & J. A. Stark (Eds.), *Handbook of mental illness in the mentally retarded* (pp. 3–43) New York: Plenum Press.

Roberts, M. (Ed.). (1996). *Supported employment training: Competency-based instructional modules* (3rd ed.). University Affiliated Programs of New Jersey, University of Medicine and Dentistry of New Jersey, Piscataway.

Rosenhan, D. L. (1973). On being sane in insane places. *Science, 179*(70), 250–258.

Schwartz, D. B. (1992). *Crossing the river: Creating a conceptual revolution in community and disability.* Cambridge, MA: Brookline Books.

Sciacca, K., & Thompson, C. M. (1996). Program development and integrated treatment across systems for dual diagnosis: Mental illness, drug addiction, and alcoholism (MIDAA). *The Journal of Mental Health Administration, 23*(3), 288–297.

Stark, J. A., McGee, J. J., Menolascino, F. J., Baker, D. H., & Menousek, P. E. (1984). Treatment strategies in the habilitation of severely mentally retarded–mentally ill adolescents and adults. In F. J. Menolascino, & J. A. Stark (Eds.), *Handbook of mental illness in the mentally retarded*, (pp. 189–218). New York: Plenum Press.

Stephens, J. H. (1978). Long-term prognosis and follow-up in schizophrenia. *Schizophrenia Bulletin, 1*(4), 25–47.

Szasz, T. (1976). *Schizophrenia: The sacred symbol of psychiatry.* New York: Basic Books.

Szymanski, L. S., King, B., Goldberg, B., Reid, A. H., Tonge, B. J., & Cain, N. (1998). Diagnosis of mental disorders in people with mental retardation. In S. Reiss & M. G. Aman (Eds.), *Psychotropic medication and developmental disabilities: The international consensus handbook* (pp. 3–17). The Ohio State University Nisonger Center.

Torrey, E. F. (1995). *Surviving schizophrenia.* New York: Harper Perennial.

Torrey, W. C., (1993). Psychiatric care of adults with developmental disabilities and mental illness in the community. *Community Mental Health Journal, 29*(5), 461–473.

U.S. Department of Health and Human Services (1995). Assessment and treatment of patients with coexisting mental illness and alcohol and other drug abuse. *Treatment Improvement Protocol (TIP) Series 9*, Substance Abuse and Mental Health Administration. Washington, DC: Author.

Viguera, A. C., Baldessarini, R. J., & Friedberg, J. (1998). Discontinuing antidepressant treatment in major depression. *Harvard Review of Psychiatry, 5*, 293–306.

Weiss, R. D., Mirin, S. M., & Frances, R. J. (1992). The myth of the typical dual diagnosis patient. *Hospital and Community Psychiatry, 43*, 107–108.

Course, Outcome, and Treatment of Severe and Persistent Mental Illnesses

The course of severe and persistent mental illness can be several years to several decades long. This course is characterized by a significant risk of relapse and may also include persistent symptoms. Psychiatric treatments, both pharmacological and psychosocial in nature, are intended to positively impact the course of mental illness. This may include controlling, eliminating, and reducing symptoms and reductions in the length, frequency, and severity of relapses. For schizophrenia and mood disorders, psychotropic medications are often the primary treatment. These medications, when properly prescribed and taken by the individual, often result in a less virulent course of the illness. Unfortunately, the outcome is rarely a cure, although many individuals experience a great deal of relief.

Responsiveness to treatment and long-term outcome or adjustment may vary widely for individuals with the same diagnostic label. There is wide heterogeneity of outcomes among people with severe and persistent mental illness, ranging from those who deteriorate over time to individuals who have no symptoms at all and no relapses. Although these disorders require biological treatments, they also demand psychosocial interventions such as support and rehabilitation to promote the best possible outcomes. Longitudinal studies, which tracked people with severe mental illness for more than 30 years, have found that in the long run, most people who receive these services cope better, have decreasing symptoms, and function better in the community. Unfortunately, even those who are coping well may suffer occasional relapses. However, these relapses do not preclude other positive outcomes such as the attainment of living, learning, and working goals. Thus, in addition to the heterogeneity of outcomes between individuals, there is a multiplicity of outcomes for each individual. That is, over the course of many years of dealing with mental illness, one individual may experience numerous negative outcomes (e.g., persistence of symptoms or relapses) and positive outcomes (remission of symptoms and achievement of independent living goals).

This chapter will answer the following questions:

1. *Does the functioning of people with severe and persistent mental illness deteriorate or improve over the long term?*
2. *What are the probable long- and short-term outcomes for persons diagnosed with schizophrenic disorders or mood disorders?*
3. *If these illnesses are caused by biological factors, why are psychosocial treatments effective?*
4. *Can support and rehabilitation impact the course of severe and persistent mental illness and bring about positive outcomes?*

Introduction

In understanding the course, outcome, and treatment of severe and persistent mental illness, one must comprehend the interrelatedness of these three areas. The **course** of an illness is its natural history—that is, the sequence of events throughout the length of the illness. For persons experiencing severe and persistent mental illness, this can be a lifelong course marked by a risk of recurrence of severe symptoms. **Outcomes** can refer to specific results, the end of a specific course of treatment, or to the end result of the course of an entire illness. **Treatment** is defined as any action designed to cure a disease or reduce its symptoms.

Treatments are intended to alter the course of these illnesses in a positive manner by reducing the frequency of **relapses** or the intensity of symptoms. If treatments succeed, they are said to have good outcomes. The term *outcome* can also refer to the long-term consequences of having a severe and persistent mental illness on the life of a person with the disease. In general, the course or natural history of severe mental illness is uncertain. As previously stated, its most prominent characteristic is the risk of relapse—that is, the recurrence of acute phases—after periods of **remission** or lack of symptoms. Concomitant with relapse are disruptions in functioning and independent living.

Relapse can lead to the loss of homes, jobs, the disruption of one's education, and familial discord. But the most serious harm a relapse presents may be to the individual's personal health. Each additional relapse may contribute to a further disordering of brain structure and functioning (Torrey, 1995). The costs to the individual of the chronic and recurrent course of severe and persistent mental illness is staggering. Keck and McElroy (1998) cited a U.S. Public Health Service study that projected the devastation of bipolar disorder on an individual's life. As an example, consider a woman who at the age of 25 has the onset of bipolar disorder. She can expect a 9-year reduction in life expectancy based on a 25% chance of attempting suicide, as well as poorer overall health. In the remaining 40 or so years of her life, she can expect 12 years of overt or acute illness and 14 years of reduced productivity (vocationally, scholastically, and as a parent)(Keck & McElroy, 1998).

The personal damage of schizophrenia may be even more severe. Weirsma, Nienhuis, Slooff, and Giel (1998) conducted a **longitudinal study** of 82 people with schizophrenia living in the Netherlands. They periodically assessed these people over a 15-year period. Their findings revealed a pattern of chronicity and relapses consistent with other studies cited later in this chapter, 67% ($n = 55$) of the individuals had at least one relapse. An additional negative finding was that after each relapse, 16% of these subjects (11% of the entire cohort) did not fully recover from the episode. Even more disturbing, 10% of the individuals committed suicide during the 15-year period.

Weirsma et al.'s study highlights the increased risks associated with each additional relapse. That is, with each relapse the individual has a higher likelihood of suicide and of having persistent symptoms that do not remit. Although 21% of the people in this study had very negative outcomes, almost 80% did experience some significant form of recovery. Nevertheless, their findings demonstrate the need for an effective relapse prevention program as part of all psychiatric rehabilitation services.

Course

Short-Term Course of These Diseases

What is the probable short-term prognosis for someone suffering from a severe mental illness? For some, accurate diagnosis and effective treatment take place rapidly. But for others, this process can be difficult, making the time it takes to receive effective treatment extremely lengthy. Certainly, for most persons who develop schizophrenia, the initial phase before effective treatment has begun can be the most devastating and the most frightening. As you will see, determining how to treat these diseases can be a very complicated process. In addition, during the initial stages of the disease the individual is often very unstable, making an accurate diagnosis even more difficult (Chen, Swann, & Johnson, 1998; Wiersma et al., 1998). For example, many people who receive a mood disorder diagnosis will later receive a schizophrenic disorder diagnosis. Those with **schizoaffective disorder** are most likely to have their diagnosis changed on later evaluation (Chen et al., 1998; Wiersma et al., 1998).

The short-term course of these diseases is stormy for several other reasons. Most persons are diagnosed with these conditions during their late teens or early twenties, a time of life when most people feel almost invulnerable to disease. For many of these young people, the most common response to a diagnosis of mental illness, especially if a remission of symptoms is obtained through medication, is denial. Active denial that one has a potentially lifelong, debilitating mental illness is, in some ways, a natural, life-affirming response. Unfortunately, it often leads to noncompliance with medication and severe relapse. For some persons, it takes many cycles of relapse, remission, denial, medication noncompliance, and relapse before they accept the reality of their condition. This cycle is often an important contributor to the high relapse rate among newly diagnosed consumers. It is important for practitioners to be sensitive to the fact that denial in the early stages of severe mental illness is a normal response. Instead, some practitioners tend to interpret behavior related to denial, such as noncompliance with medication, as abnormal or symptomatic.

For many of those with severe mental illness, their first significant treatment experience is hospitalization. There are important reasons why this is often the preferred treatment. In the hospital, a patient can be observed to ensure that he or she is not a danger to themself or others. The hospital is also the best environment to try out different drugs in an attempt to reduce psychotic symptoms. Many of the drugs have side effects, which range from mildly annoying to highly dangerous and, although they are generally not dangerous, these side effects can be very frightening. Side effects are often treated with medication changes or the addition of medicines designed to specifically treat their effects.

After being discharged from the hospital, what is the likelihood of rehospitalization? One of the most illustrative articles on this topic was published by Anthony, Cohen, and Vitalo (1978). By comparing the reported **recidivism** rates from the studies available at the time (see Table 3.1), the authors demonstrated that the probability of relapse in the short term (1 to 5 years) is very high. An examination of Table 3.1 reveals that as the follow-up period increases from 3 months to 5 and 10 years, the corresponding rate of recidivism also increases from 10% to 15% to about 75%. Clearly, if you have been hospitalized because of a major mental illness, the chance you will need rehospitalization at some point in time are very high. This seems to be the case regardless of adherence to a treatment plan and degree of medication compliance. This high risk of relapse is true of schizophrenia, schizoaffective disorder, major depression, and bipolar disorder.

TABLE 3.1

Recidivism Rates by Follow-up Periods

Follow-up Period	Recidivism (%)	Authors
3 months	10	Ellsworth et al. (1971)
	15	Orlinsky and D'Elia (1964)
	16	Johnston and McNeal (1965)[c]
	11 to 22[b]	Moos, Shelton, and Petty (1973)
6 months	14	Angrist et al. (1961)[c]
	27	Johnston and McNeal (1965)
	30	Orlinsky and D'Elia (1964)
	33	Friedman, von Mering, and Hinko (1966)
	33	Miller and Willer (1976)
	35	Morgan (1966)[c]
	40	Fairweather et al. (1960)
9 months	29	Lorei (1964)[c]
6 to 13 months[a]	33	Franklin, Kittredge, and Thrasher (1975)
7 to 10 months[a]	39	Cumming and Markson (1975)
Year	35	Pishkin and Bradshaw (1960)[c]
	36	Wolkon, Karmen, and Tanaka (1966)
	37	Johnston and McNeal (1965)
	37	Michaux et al. (1969)[c]
	37	Katkin et al. (1975)
	38	Williams and Walker (1961)
	38	Freeman and Simmons (1963)
	39	Lorei (1967)
	40	Miller (1966)
	40	Miller (1967)
	41	Schooler et al. (1967)[c]
	42	Bloom and Lang (1970)
	46	Orlinsky and D'Elia (1964)
	48	Savino and Schlamp (1968)
	50	Friedman, von Mering, and Hinko (1966)
1 to 2 Years	20	Lewinsohn (1967)[c]
15 months	45	Wilder, Levin, and Zwerling (1966)
18 months	46	Wolkon, Karmen, and Tanaka (1971)
2 years	51	Johnston and McNeal (1965)
	55	Wolkon, Karmen, and Tanaka (1971)
	55	Katkin et al. (1975)
	75	Mendel (1966)[c]
$2\frac{1}{2}$ years	60	Wolkon, Karmen, and Tanaka (1971)
3 years	56	Johnston and McNeal (1965)
	64	Sherman et al. (1964)[c]
	65	Olshansky (1968)
5 years	67	Friedman, von Mering, and Hinko (1966)
	70	Freyhan (1964)
	70	Miller (1966)
	75	Miller (1967)
10 years	77	Gurel (1970)

[a] Length of follow-up period not the same for every patient in the study.

[b] Data were presented for individual hospital wards.

[c] Recidivism percentages for these studies were excerpted from a review by Clum (1975).

Long-Term Course of These Diseases

Until recently, the long-term prognosis for a person with a severe mental illness such as schizophrenia was considered bleak. Even the American Psychiatric Association manual, *DSM-IIIR* (APA, 1987) reported that in most cases the long-term course of schizophrenia was progressively downward. This was partially due to the fact that for many persons struck with this disease, the initial effects are catastrophic, reducing functioning and leading to marked disabilities. After several years, besides the symptoms of the disease, many individuals are also handicapped by stigmatizing attitudes as well.

Today the picture is much more optimistic. Recent studies have challenged the negative prognosis associated with this disease and given hope to many. Torrey (1995) has summed up the research on the long-term course of schizophrenia by placing outcomes in five possible categories: (a) completely recovered, (b) much improved, (c) improved, (d) hospitalized, and (e) dead. By comparing these tables at both 10 years and 30 years we can see that the long-term prognosis for schizophrenia is generally positive and appears to improve slightly with time. At both 10 years and 30 years, 75% of people stricken with schizophrenia are in a recovered or improved category. It appears that between 10 years and 30 years, an additional 10% improved to the point where they no longer required extensive support and became relatively independent. Thus, after 30 years, whereas more people have died (as would be expected by aging), fewer are hospitalized, fewer require extensive support networks, and a larger number are functioning more independently (see Table 3.2).

The Vermont study conducted by Harding and her colleagues (1987a, 1987b) focused directly on those individuals who might be expected to have the worst prognosis. This study examined a group of 269 patients who had been discharged, literally from the back wards of Vermont's State Psychiatric Hospital 32 years before. Vermont was one of the first states to begin deinstitutionalizing its psychiatric hospital population, starting in the 1950s. This

TABLE 3.2

Outcomes from Vermont Study—Percentages of Individuals with Each Type of Outcome

10 Years after "Backward" Discharge				
25% Completely recovered	25% Much improved, relatively independent	25% Improved, but require extensive support network	15% Hospitalized, unimproved	10% Dead (mostly suicide)
30 Years after Discharge				
25% Completely recovered	35% Much improved, relatively independent	15% Improved, but require extensive support network	10% Hospitalized, unimproved	15% Dead (mostly suicide)

Adapted from Torrey (1995), based on Harding et al. (1987a, 1987b).

TABLE 3.3

Results from the Strauss-Carpentar Levels of Function Scale for the 168 Subjects of the Vermont Study Who Were Alive and Interviewed[a]

Area of Functioning	N	%
Not in hospital in past year	140	83
Met with friends every week or two	111	66
Had one or more moderately to very close friends	128	76
Employed in past year[b]	79	47
Displayed slight or no symptoms	121	72
Able to meet basic needs	133	79
Led moderate to very full life	128	76
Slight or no impairment in overall function	92	55

[a] From C. M. Harding, G. W. Brooks, T. Ashikaga, et al. (1987a). *American Journal of Psychiatry*, *144*, 727–735. ©1987, the American Psychiatric Association. Reprinted by permission.

[b] Quality of work could not be rated; issues of confidentiality prevented visits to subjects' work sites.

was well before the 1963 Community Mental Health Act, which was discussed in chapter 1. The researchers were careful to ensure that the subjects they were following were accurately diagnosed with schizophrenia. They also spent a good deal of time locating people as well as interviewing family members and others who knew the patients. Their findings strongly contradicted the poor prognosis everyone had assumed for those most severely afflicted with schizophrenia. At 10 years postdischarge, 70% of the patients were still out of the hospital, although many required treatment and social supports. At 25 years postdischarge, 50% to 66% were recovered or improved. Table 3.3 provides additional detail on the functional level of the study's subjects. As you can see, many of them attained valued social roles and utilized natural supports within the community.

Course of Mood Disorders

Although there is some evidence that the course of schizophrenia does not progressively worsen for the majority of individuals with that diagnosis, recent studies suggest that the course of chronic or recurrent mood disorders may worsen over time (Kessing, 1998; Kessing, Andersen, Mortensen, & Bolwig, 1998). Outcomes studies of 2 to 5 years duration have found that for individuals with bipolar disorder, recurrent episodes lead to a deterioration in both social and vocational functioning (Keck & McElroy, 1998). This observation may seem unexpected to some mental health professionals. Generally speaking, between acute episodes of mood disorders, there is a greater remission of symptoms than is typically found in schizophrenic disorders (APA, 1994). That is, the person with a mood disorder is likely to be symptom free between acute episodes. Interestingly enough, this does not necessarily imply that the course of a mood disorder is less virulent. Kessing and his colleagues found that the number and frequency of mood disorder episodes increase with age (Kessing et al.,

1998). This is in contrast to schizophrenia where the number and frequency of episodes generally decrease with age.

Described in two articles, Kessing and his colleagues, over a 20-year period, followed all psychiatric admissions in Denmark diagnosed with an affective disorder. In this period, more than 20,000 first-admission patients had been discharged with a diagnosis of affective disorder (mood disorder), depressive disorder, or manic/cyclic type (bipolar) disorder. The results indicated that the rate of recurrence increases with the number of previous episodes for people with depressed and bipolar disorders. The natural history of severe unipolar and bipolar disorder seems to be progressively worse, regardless of gender, age, and type of disorder. This suggests that for some, the course of these disorders is progressive, or worsening, despite treatment. In short, an increasing number of relapses predicts progressively more relapses (Kessing, 1998; Kessing et al., 1998).

The courses of both recurrent major depression and bipolar disorders can be improved through the use of the appropriate psychotropic medications. Still, medication compliance is a problem, particularly among those with bipolar disorder. Indeed, as with schizophrenia, full medication compliance reduces the likelihood of relapse but certainly does not fully eliminate it.

Do Rehabilitation Services Matter?

The results from the Vermont study (Harding, Brooks, Ashikaga, Strauss, & Breier, 1987a, 1987b), which looked at the long-term outcome of schizophrenia, have greatly encouraged the psychiatric rehabilitation community. Regardless of how symptomatic individuals are, there is hope that at some future date they will be able to function independently in the community with reduced symptoms and little or no supports. Is this positive **prognosis** a result of the disease process or is it due to the services that people receive? Some of the researchers from the Vermont study set out to answer this question.

When it began deinstitutionalization, Vermont had a comprehensive rehabilitation system, with elements comparable to today's supported employment and supported living initiatives (see chapters 8 and 9 for details on these programs). A neighboring state, Maine, adopted a more traditional approach for the treatment of its deinstitutionalized population consisting of traditional inpatient treatment and aftercare. Using the same strategy that had been employed in Vermont, DeSisto, Harding, McCormick, Ashikaga, and Brooks (1995a, 1995b) compared 180 deinstitutionalized patients from Vermont with 119 similar patients from Maine. The results were very clear. Individuals from Vermont were more productive, less symptomatic, had better community adjustment and higher levels of functioning.

In both states, the symptomatology and functioning of persons with these illnesses improved over the very long term. However, in Maine, these improvements took much longer. Sometimes it took 10 years longer for people from Maine to achieve the same gains that the Vermonters had attained. Because of this time lag, people in Maine required more mental health services. The authors concluded that these differences were probably the result of Vermont's efforts at community psychiatric rehabilitation. In short, better services produce better outcomes for people with psychiatric disabilities.

Not Just New England

Methodologically sound studies in both the United States and Europe, involving more than 1300 individuals with schizophrenia, found that 46% to 68% either improved or recovered significantly over periods of time ranging from 23 to 37 years (Harding, Zubin, & Strauss, 1992). Thus, one of the basic values of psychiatric rehabilitation, hopefulness, which is discussed in detail in chapter 4, actually has a scientific basis.

Treatment

Categories of Treatment

As defined in chapter 1, treatment seeks to cure a disease or reduce its symptoms. Treatment for serious mental illnesses can be broken into two broad categories: biological (somatic) and psychosocial. The **biological (somatic) treatment** usually involves medications. The **psychosocial treatment** involves attempts to effect change through the manipulation of social or psychological factors.

Biological (Somatic) Treatments

One of the primary approaches in the treatment of severe and persistent mental illness is to use pharmacological agents to treat acute episodes of psychotic or mood symptoms (Lehman & Steinwachs, 1998). In the treatment of schizophrenia, it is clear that antipsychotic or neuroleptic medications are required for any effective symptom reduction to take place (Lehman & Steinwachs, 1998). Thus for a disorder such as schizophrenia or another psychosis, antipsychotic medications, such as Haldol or Risperidol, are often used as the first-line treatment (Lehman & Steinwachs, 1998).

For acute episodes of major depression, the treatment of choice is antidepressant medications, such as Tofranil and Prozac. For bipolar disorder, the treatment of choice is a mood stabilizer, such as Lithobid (lithium) (Keck & McElroy, 1998).

Efficacy of Antipsychotic Medication

There is a large body of evidence supporting the efficacy of antipsychotic medication in the treatment of schizophrenia, with more than 100 well-controlled studies showing that 50% to 85% of persons will improve significantly with reductions in hallucinations, delusions, thought disorders, and bizarre behavior (Lehman & Steinwachs, 1998).

Treatment with antipsychotic medication has become increasingly refined. In most cases, very high doses or exposure to a massive amount of antipsychotics for stabilization is completely unnecessary. Those who experience symptom relief with an antipsychotic medication will typically be prescribed this medication for at least 1 year after the acute symptoms have been reduced (Lehman & Steinwachs, 1998). The purpose of this long-term treatment is to reduce the risk of relapse or the worsening of positive symptoms. More than 30 well-controlled studies have been conducted that show that the annual relapse rate can be reduced from a rate of 55% to 20% to 25% if antipsychotic medication is continued.

Medications are used in the **acute** phases of an illness such as schizophrenia, the **residual** phases to keep symptoms from recurring, and the **prodromal** phases to avert relapse. In the case of most serious mental illnesses, medications are also used in periods of remission.

Course of Schizophrenia When Treated with Antipsychotic Medication

Summarizing studies that looked at the outcomes of more than 2300 patients with schizophrenia, Hogarty (1993) found that medication alone could reduce the rate of relapse from 67% to 39% in the first year. After the first year, by continuing antipsychotic medication, relapse rates were reduced from a level of 65% annually to only 15% annually (Hogarty, 1993).

Hogarty (1993) noted that in many treatment studies about 40% of the people taking antipsychotic medication relapsed anyway in the first year after discharge from a hospital. This was often attributed to suspected medication noncompliance. Many mental health professionals continue to attribute psychotic relapse to medication noncompliance. However, as Hogarty has pointed out, even patients whose compliance was known because they received "depot" or injection medication had approximately the same relatively high rate of relapse.

Besides medication noncompliance, Conley and Buchanan (1997) provided several reasons why people with schizophrenia have a poor response to various psychotropic medications:

- Physical intolerance of medication resulting in serious side effects, bodily adaptations that make the medication ineffective
- Partial compliance of person with the treatment regimen
- Inappropriate dosing or length of trial (most medications require 4 to 6 weeks to determine efficacy)
- True resistance of their disorder to the medication, literally using the wrong medication to bring about a therapeutic effect

According to Hogarty (1993), in addition to medication compliance, appropriate dosage of medication, controlling side effects, promoting a specific type of treatment or home environment, and the development of coping skills are all factors that can contribute to a reduction in the length and frequency of hospitalization.

Pharmacological Treatment of Bipolar Disorder and Mania

Lithium has been used as a treatment for bipolar disorder in the United States since 1970 and was in use in other countries even earlier. It is an effective medication for both the treatment of acute mania and the prevention of the recurrence of both manic and depressive symptoms in bipolar disorders (Keck & McElroy, 1998). At least 12 studies have shown that lithium reduces the symptoms of acute mania.

More than 10 well-controled studies involving more than 500 patients have demonstrated that lithium prevents recurrent affective episodes of both a depressed and manic type (Keck & McElroy, 1998). At the same time, a significant portion of individuals do not respond that well to Lithium maintenance therapy. Poor medication compliance, in large part due to lithium side effects, has interfered with its effective use.

The treatment of mania needs to anticipate the future course of the illness (Licht, 1998). Lithium is still considered the best mood-stabilizing substance although it may be insufficient in mixed episodes and severe mania (Licht, 1998). For those who do not respond to lithium as an ongoing treatment, other medications are available including carbamazepine and valproate. Valproate is preferred for acute episodes, in particular for mixed episodes. Antipsychotics are powerful antimanics, which are particularly beneficial for some clinical presentations of severe mania. However, in general, their use should not be prolonged into the maintenance phase. Antidepressants have also been used for the relief of depressive episodes (Keck & McElroy, 1998).

Freeman and Stoll (1998) reported that polypharmacy, or the use of multiple medications, is common in the treatment of refractory bipolar disorder or conditions that do not respond readily to a single medication. There have been few controlled studies of the use of combinations of mood stabilizers. The interactions of such combinations can be useful but can also be very complicated and are potentially dangerous. The safest and most efficacious mood stabilizer combinations appear to be the mixtures of anticonvulsants and lithium, particularly valproate.

Course of Bipolar Disorder When Taking Lithium

What is the history of events when someone with bipolar disorder takes lithium? Compared to many of the clinical studies described, the results from the field are mixed and disappointing. Lithium does not seem to consistently reduce the risk of recurrence of manic episodes in actual practice as often as might be expected. Silverstone, McPherson, Hunt, and Romans (1998) examined the effectiveness of lithium in preventing recurrences of bipolar disorder over a 2-year period following hospital discharge. Results showed that overall, 67% had a relapse. Although a major reason for this high level of relapses may have been poor compliance by patients, some even discontinuing the lithium, it is clear that this drug is not effective in many cases.

Maj, Pirozzi, Magliano, and Bartoli (1998) collected information on 402 people started on lithium as a maintenance treatment to prevent relapse. Five years after starting treatment, 38% were still taking lithium and had experienced at least one recurrence of the disorder. Twenty three percent were still taking lithium and had experienced no recurrences of disease. Those not taking lithium at follow-up had poorer outcomes than those taking lithium.

Major Depressive Disorders

For depressive disorders, it remains a controversy whether medication or psychosocial interventions are more effective in bringing symptom relief (Craighead, Milkowitz, Vajk, & Frank, 1998; Nemeroff & Schatzberg, 1998). Nevertheless, there is little question that those treated with antidepressants will have a more favorable course than those who do not take these medications (Angst, 1998).

The treatment of choice for the relief of major depressive disorders are the drugs known as selective serotonin reuptake inhibitors, such as the drug Prozac (Nemeroff & Schatzberg, 1998). This class of drugs is named for the nature of the effect they have on the neurotransmitter serotonin. Next, most commonly used are the tricyclic antidepressants such as Tofranil (imipramine), which are named for their chemical structure—three circles. A third group of drugs, monoamine oxidase (MAO) inhibitors, while effective, are rarely used. Typically, it takes at least 3 to 6 weeks to determine whether an anti-depressant is being effective. Tri-cyclic anti-depressants, at full dose, have been found to be effective in reducing the recurrence of major depressive symptoms or episodes (Frank, Kupfer, & Perel, 1990, 1993).

Viguera, Baldessarini, and Friedberg (1998) noted that the benefits of long-term antidepressant treatment in major depression and the risks of discontinuing medication are now well established. Reviewing 27 studies, with more than 3000 patients with depressive symptoms, they compared the course and outcome of the illness between patients whose antidepressants were discontinued and those with continued treatment. Those who had continued treatment showed much lower relapse rates (2% versus 6% per month) and a lower 12-month relapse risk (20% versus 45%). Contrary to prediction, gradual discontinuation (dose tapering or use of long-acting agents) did not yield lower relapse rates. As mentioned earlier, the amount of previous illness, particularly three or more prior episodes or a chronic course, was strongly associated with higher relapse risk after discontinuation of antidepressants. Nevertheless, a chronic course did not negatively affect responsiveness to continued treatment—that is, even those with multiple episodes were likely to respond well to medication.

Does Antidepressant Medication Improve the Course and Outcome of Major Depression?

Can antidepressant medication be used to improve the long-term course and outcome of major depression? Their use appears to have a positive effect on relapse rates. In the first year, those not receiving antidepressants had a 45% chance of relapse, whereas those who did receive these medications had a relapse rate of 20%. Among the groups without antidepressants, 50% had relapsed by the 14-month follow-up. Among those being treated with antidepressants, the 50% relapse rate was not reached until 48 months. More previous episodes were associated with higher relapse. However, more previous episodes did not predict responsiveness to treatment. Although these findings highlight the efficacy of antidepressants, they also pointed out, once again, that like the other illnesses, major depression relapses are a matter of time, even when medication is taken (Viguera, Baldessarini, & Friedberg, 1998).

Reasons Medications Fail

As discussed previously, with the use of antipsychotic medication to treat schizophrenia, there are numerous reasons why medications may fail to achieve their therapeutic purpose.

Medications must be tried for a sufficient length of time and under appropriate circumstances. According to Conley and Buchanan (1997), a systematic approach to the evaluation and characterization of treatment resistance is increasingly important. Since the introduction of many new drugs, patients are more likely than ever to be prescribed a variety of psychotropic medications, if one does not work well. The need for accurate evaluation will continue to increase with the introduction of the new medications. People with severe and persistent mental illness may manifest a poor response to a medication for any variety of reasons, including those enumerated. Psychiatrists facing the decision of when to change from one medication to another must clearly understand the appropriate length of a trial and what target symptoms respond to a particular medication in order to maximize the response in patients with treatment-resistant disorders.

Thus, the challenges for both the physician and the individual usually revolve around a number of questions. First, which psychotropic medication will be most effective? Second, what dosage is needed to be effective without putting the person at unnecessary risk for side effects? Third, how does one cope with the long-term need to take pills regularly, possibly accompanied by frequent blood tests that are required for certain medications such as lithium and clozaril? Further complicating matters, even if the right medication is prescribed, there is some risk of symptom exacerbation and relapse.

Medication Side Effects

Side effects of psychotropic medication are particularly important. They can be very severe and harmful to the individual. Some common side effects are increased appetite, hormonal difficulties (e.g., failing to menstruate), motor difficulties (e.g., shuffling gate), muscular problems (e.g., stiffness), dryness of mouth, blurred vision, impotence, low blood pressure, seizures, and immune system reactions. The burden of side effects can be illustrated by looking at two common and very troubling side effects associated with antipsychotic medication: Parkinsonism and tardive dyskinesia. Antipsychotic medication, because it affects the functioning of the neurotransmitter, dopamine (discussed in chapter 2), interferes significantly with motor functions. Some patients, regardless of age, develop the symptoms (but not the actual disease) of Parkinson's disease: resting tremors, poor control of their own movements, and shuffling movements. Another side effect that may occur from use of these medications is tardive dyskinesia, which results in bizarre and uncontrollable mouth and limb movements. Unlike some of the other side effects, tardive dyskinesia is usually not reversible once it appears. As if it were not enough to endure the bizarre symptoms and behavior associated with psychosis, the involuntary movements of tardive dyskinesia make someone look bizarre, which increases stigma.

Some side effects are eminently treatable with changes in dosage or type of medication. Certain side effects can be treated with other medications, but of course, these medicines can have their own side effects as well. A common remark about these drugs is, "If they were not therapeutic these drugs would be poison."

Table 3.4 is meant to provide an overview of some of the commonly used medications. It is by no means exhaustive, nor would it serve as guide to prescribing medications. It is included solely to share information that mental health consumers and the staff that serve them must know.

TABLE 3.4
Medication Treatment Summary

Broad Diagnostic Categories	Category of Commonly Prescribed Medications	Examples
Schizophrenic disorders	Typical, traditional antipsychotics	Haldol, Mellaril, Prolixin, Thorazine
	Atypical antipsychotics	Clozaril, Risperidol
Mood disorder–depressive disorders	Selective serotonin uptake inhibitors	Prozac, Zoloft
	Tricyclics	Tofranil
	MAO inhibitors	
Bipolar disorder or mania (manic phases only)	Mood stabilizers	Lithium Carbonate Lithobid Valproate
	Anticonvulsant (with mood-stabilizing properties)	Carbamazipine

Today, it is rare that a person with severe and persistent mental illness would go completely untreated with medication, although there are still individuals who receive no care at all. More typical is a large number of individuals who receive inadequate care, and a small number who are served well (Lehman & Steinwachs, 1998).

CONTROVERSIAL ISSUE
Psychotropic Medications versus Alternative Treatments

Should psychiatric rehabilitation (PsyR) practitioners always take a strong promedication stance, prioritizing medication compliance because it is the surest route to stabilization and good community adjustment? Are there situations in which a professional should support a consumer's choice to eschew psychotropic medications in favor of alternative treatments?

As discussed earlier, their is strong evidence that medications are the most effective way to treat the symptoms of severe mental illness. PsyR practitioners should share this knowledge with their clients, assist consumers in accessing good psychiatric treatment, and assist consumers in acquiring the skills and resources needed to take medication as prescribed and communicate effectively with their psychiatrist when problems arise. However, these interventions may become thwarted when clients refuse to take, or stop taking, their medications.

How should PsyR practitioners react when a client is not taking prescribed medication? In some programs, particularly those that adhere in part to the medical model or employ medical personnel, staff may view medication compliance as a primary goal even if the consumer is resistant to the idea of taking medication. In such programs, interventions utilized to increase compliance are sometimes coercive in nature (Diamond & Wikler, 1985), for example, withholding privileges or monetary resources if a client has not taken medication. As you will see in chapter 4, which covers goals, values, and principles of PsyR, both coercive interventions and identification of treatment goals that are not client chosen are inconsistent with PsyR philosophy.

As addressed earlier, there are many reasons for noncompliance, including denial of the illness and discomfort due to side effects. Assisting a consumer in coming to terms with his or her mental illness and eventually accepting psychiatric treatment or working with the consumer and his or her psychiatrist to develop a strategy to reduce side effects are appropriate responses to these issues. Psychoeducational approaches can also be effective in terms of increasing compliance.

Some consumers object to taking medications because of concern about the long-term use of psychotropic medication or because they are opposed to the ingestion of chemical substances for philosophical or religious reasons. Such individuals may explore alternative treatments. Nutritional supplements and special dietary regimens have been used since the 1950s, but thus far there is no solid scientific support for this approach (Torrey, 1995). Others try homeopathic remedies, or relaxation techniques. Patricia Deegan (1995), a consumer advocate, has written a manual on nonmedical strategies for reducing and coping with symptoms called *Coping with Voices: Self Help Strategies for People Who Hear Voices That Are Distressing* (1995). For example, when experiencing aversive auditory hallucinations, some consumers may obtain relief by listening to soothing music with headphones. There is a short biography of Dr. Deegan in chapter 10. The exploration and use of alternative treatments for a variety of physical illnesses is currently widespread in the United States. Some of these approaches have even begun to attain respectability in medical and scientific circles. It is important for practitioners, including those who may not believe in alternative medicine, to recognize consumers' rights to explore other approaches to treatment, just as many nonconsumers might when faced with a chronic disease. Unfortunately, because they have a mental illness the judgment of consumers who may wish to explore alternative approaches is often considered, at best, to be suspect. Instead, such individuals are more likely considered to be in a state of denial regarding their illness.

The questions that this issue raises are numerous. How far should PsyR practitioners go in supporting a client who chooses to utilize an alternative treatment? Should they help consumers gain access to alternative treatment resources? How should they handle a situation in which it seems obvious that a consumer is not benefiting from an alternative treatment approach? Should practitioners continue to counsel clients to reconsider medications, even when a client has expressed resistance to the idea for a number of years? It is important for PsyR practitioners to be thoughtful, to consider ethical implications, and to have an open dialogue with consumers and other professionals when struggling with such questions.

Psychosocial Treatments

In addition to pharmacological treatments, the other broad category of treatment for severe and persistent mental illnesses is psychosocial treatment. To the general public, psychosocial treatment is associated with insight-oriented psychotherapy. This form of psychotherapy is the least useful approach with the major mental illnesses. Instead, psychosocial approaches, which employ strategies for providing support, skill training, and environmental modifications, have been found to be very important in the care of persons with these disorders.

Many experts, such as Craighead, Harding, and Hogarty, believe that most effective impact on the course of severe and persistent mental illness is achieved through a combination of biological and psychosocial interventions. Based on the available evidence, Hogarty (1993) concluded that the right combination of these two categories of treatments resulted in the lowest possible relapse rates.

It is the conventional wisdom that pharmacological interventions are a necessary prerequisite for any psychosocial interventions to be effective. Whereas some experts consider this to be an established fact, others such as Harding and her colleagues, consider this to be a myth. They believe that psychosocial interventions can be effective regardless of the use of psychotropic medication (Harding & Zahniser, 1994).

Some Ineffective Treatments

In the past, some treatments deservedly received a bad name for their ineffectiveness or actual harm in helping people with serious and persistent mental illness. There were efforts to treat people with schizophrenia without antipsychotic medication (available since the 1950s) and with only psychotherapies, such as traditional insight-oriented individual and group therapy. These resulted in very poor outcomes for the patients (Hogarty, 1993; Lehman & Steinwachs, 1998).

Insight-oriented, psychodynamic therapies can be defined as those that use interpretation of unconscious material and focus on therapeutic transference. In the treatment of serious mental illnesses of all types, this form of psychotherapy has been found to be generally ineffective. Actually, some studies have found psychodynamic treatments to be harmful. The consensus is that these should no longer be used to treat schizophrenia (Lehman & Steinwachs, 1998), bipolar disorder (Keck & McElroy, 1998), or major depression (Craighead & Ilardi, 1998). There is, however, a role for providing support through individual counseling, as outlined in the recent recommendations (Lehman et al., 1998) and identified in the research of Hogarty and his colleagues. Effective individual counseling with people who have severe mental illness generally focuses on support, the here and now and problem solving.

Psychodynamic therapy is not the only treatment approach that may have a negative impact. Therapeutic settings that seem very positive might actually promote relapse in some individuals with schizophrenia, especially if they are very high in intensity and expectations (Hogarty, 1993). For example, very high expectation partial care programs, very intensive group therapy, a short length of stay and a high turnover philosophy are associated with more hospitalization and longer relapses (Linn et al., 1979).

Effective Psychosocial Treatments

Another set of treatment strategies, which this entire book is devoted to, are psychosocial interventions that are also rehabilitative in nature. The day programs, assertive community treatment, vocational rehabilitation, residential, and family approaches discussed later in chapters 6 through 11 are all psychosocial approaches, all rehabilitative in nature, and have been found to be effective in helping persons with severe and persistent mental illness.

Psychosocial Treatment of Mood Disorders

Colom, Vieta, Martinez, Jorquera, and Gasto (1998) have reviewed and criticized the different types of psychotherapy in the treatment of bipolar disorder. To date, none have established efficacy in controlled clinical trials regarding outcomes such as hospitalization, relapses, or suicidal behavior. This is in contrast to the numerous controlled studies highlighting the effectiveness of medication. Instead, a psychoeducative approach, either individually or in a group, seems to be the most promising. **Psychoeducation** focuses on illness information, treatment compliance, and illness management skills. These approaches are equally useful for schizophrenia (Anderson et al., 1986).

Soares, Stintzing, Jackson, and Skoldin (1997) explored the effects of an education package on outpatients with bipolar disorder. The primary goals were to determine whether the patients' knowledge of the illness would improve after an educational intervention and whether education would lead to changes in such areas as attitudes toward lithium and psychiatric well-being. The study included 10 patients who were given a six-session education package that covered the following areas: (a) demographics, (b) etiology, (c) illness (course and symptoms), (d) treatment, (e) hospital procedures, and (f) coping with the illness and stress (including problem solving). The results showed significant improvements in knowledge about the illness, attitudes toward lithium, and self-esteem. These effects were maintained several months later.

Psychosocial Treatments of Major Depression

In the treatment of major depression, behavioral therapy, cognitive behavioral therapy, marital therapy, and interpersonal therapy have all been found to reduce depressive symptoms (Craighead & Ilardi, 1998). Discussion of these treatments are outside the scope of this book. Depression that is treated clearly has a better course than depression that is untreated (Angst, 1998). Interventions using behavior therapy, cognitive behavior therapy, and interpersonal therapy have all brought about significant reductions in depressive symptoms. These treatments have also been found to be successful in the sense that the gains of the therapy are maintained.

What We Know about the Course, Outcome, and Treatment of Severe and Persistent Mental Illness

Although schizophrenic and mood disorders often differ markedly in their symptomatology, the medications used to treat them, and to some degree, their course, there are some shared elements. For each disorder, the symptoms can dominate the person's experience, at times to a large extent controlling the person's thoughts and feelings, as presented in some of the vignettes in chapter 2. These symptoms can be harmful to the self-esteem and hopefulness of the individual and put the person at risk for suicide. There are functional deficits associated with these illnesses, specifically in self-care, employment, home making, educational achievements, and independent living. Because of these illnesses, individuals sometimes do not acquire important life skills or are unable to practice the skills they acquired previously.

There is no uniform outcome for all of these disorders. Instead, there are a variety of outcomes. For example, many people with depression, bipolar disorder, and some people with schizophrenia will have only one or two episodes and never relapse again. Alternatively, people with a chronic or recurrent depression or schizophrenia will have both positive and negative outcomes over the course of their lifetime.

All of these conditions are treated with powerful psychotropic medications that, in addition to their therapeutic effects, have numerous side effects. Individuals with these disorders are often prone to relapse, the risk of which is reduced but not eliminated by medication. Because of side effects, the limited efficacy of these medicines, and numerous other reasons, many consumers find it difficult to comply with their medication regimens. The issue of compliance with medication and clear communication between the consumer and his or her psychiatrist is present with all these disorders.

In addition to biological or somatic treatments such as medications, psychosocial interventions are also needed. Only the symptoms of depression seem to be particularly helped by approaches such as cognitive and behavioral therapies. The symptoms of schizophrenia and bipolar disorders are not helped by psychotherapy. Nevertheless, supportive counseling is useful. Psychoeducation—or education about mental illness, its symptoms, and the medications (their therapeutic and side effects)—seems to be helpful for all these illnesses.

The deficits or impairments in functioning caused by these illnesses are best addressed by another psychosocial approach, psychiatric rehabilitation. Psychiatric rehabilitation can eliminate or reduce the impairment the person experiences in his or her living, learning, or working environments. In addition, it can help the individual pursue his or her personal goals, achieve these goals, and maintain these gains.

Over the past decade substantial advances have been made in the psychiatric rehabilitation of persons with severe mental illnesses such as schizophrenia and bipolar disorder. Several areas of interventions that have been found to be effective through extensive research are (a) skills training (discussed in chapter 5), (b) supported employment (discussed in chapter 7), (c) family interventions (discussed in chapter 11), and (d) integrated treatment for people with both severe mental illness and substance use disorders (Mueser, Drake, & Bond, 1997).

The Case of Mary

Mary is a new PsyR worker just learning the ropes. When you read about what happens to Mary and the consumer she is working with, think about how it could have been avoided. Also, consider who was really responsible for the problem. (Hint: There was more than one way to avoid this problem and more than one person responsible.)

Mary always knew that she wanted to work with people. During high school she volunteered at a geriatric home on weekends, reading to some of the residents or helping them with activities like shopping for personal items or just keeping them company. At the small Midwestern college she attended she majored in psychology. Most of the courses she took covered basic psychological theory, research methods, and statistics. Her dream was, someday, to get her Ph.D. and do private therapy. During college she volunteered at

The Case of Mary Continued

a private psychiatric hospital working with the activity therapist. She liked working with the patients. Mary could relate well because many of the patients were her age. She found it very interesting to talk with them about their symptoms.

During her senior year she applied to several doctoral programs in clinical psychology. One of her psychology professors told her that it was harder to get into a clinical psychology program than to get into medical school. She wasn't even contacted for an interview. After graduation Mary went home and searched for a job where she could use her psychology degree. After looking all summer she ended up working as a clerk in a local bookstore.

One day a friend of her mother told Mary about a program for people with mental illness that was looking for people with B.A. degrees to work with the patients. Mary applied, and on the strength of her previous experience and education she got her first psychiatric rehabilitation job. She was really excited. After a weeklong orientation to the program she was assigned to work with Mark. Mark had a master's degree in rehabilitation counseling and more than 4 years experience working in the program. Mark and Mary were responsible for a caseload of 11 clients. Mary quickly got to know the clients and the tasks she had to perform as a case manager. In only a few months she and Mark decided that she would be the primary case manager for John and Helen, two clients with whom she had developed a close relationship. Mary felt that she was really starting to grow as a professional.

When it came to her role as case manager, Mary made sure that she covered all the bases. She genuinely liked John and Helen and she also wanted to prove to Mark that she could do a good job. She reviewed their treatment plans with them and established regular goals for them to achieve. Best of all, they were achieving these goals, and sometimes faster than scheduled. One day Helen was absent on a day when she had an important meeting. That afternoon, Mary called her boarding home, but they said Helen was out, they thought she had gone to the program. The next day Helen was absent again. Mary called the boarding home right away and they said that she had left that morning at her regularly scheduled time; they assumed she had gone to the program. Mary became very worried and went to tell Mark what was happening. That afternoon Helen was brought in by the police. They had found her acting strangely in the park and when they asked if she needed any help she had started screaming and run away. Helen was hospitalized that evening.

When Helen returned to the program, Mary asked her what had happened. Why had she stopped going to the program when she was doing so well. Helen said she knew that she was making real progress with Mary's help. One day she began hearing voices and she became unable to sleep at night. She remembered that Mary had said that if she took her medication and worked on her treatment plan she would get better, but she knew she was getting sick. She knew how much effort Mary put into helping her and what a caring person she was. She felt like she was letting Mary down. When she got too sick to control her symptoms she would go to the park rather than let Mary see her that way after all the work she had done.

Dual Diagnosis Treatments

Service for Persons with Developmental Disabilities and Mental Illness

Historically, medications have been used to sedate individuals or control undesired behavior even when there was no mental illness diagnosed. This problem was portrayed in Ken Kesey's novel *One Flew over the Cuckoo's Nest*, later made into a movie. Kalachnik and his colleagues (Kalachnik et al., 1998) cited a survey done by Lipman in 1967 which revealed that more than 50% of individuals with developmental disabilities in institutions were prescribed psychotropic medication, especially thioridazine and chlorpromazine. These authors further cited an order from a United States District Court judge handed down in 1972, which stated:

> Medication shall not be used as punishment, for the convenience of staff, as a substitute for a habilitative program, or in quantities that interfere with the resident's habilitation program. (p. 47)

In 1980, in response to the overuse and misuse of psychotropic medications for people with developmental disabilities, the Accreditation Council for Services for Mentally Retarded and Other Developmentally Disabled Persons (ACMRDD) recommended the use of interdisciplinary teams for planning and oversight (Davis, Wehmeyer, Board, Fox, Maher, & Roberts, 1998). These teams would include consumers, family members, direct service staff, as well as physicians and other specialists. The team would do more than just monitor medication use. They would provide information to improve the data available for making a diagnosis, help to identify and access needed services, promote self-determination, encourage consumer choice, and aid decision making.

Interdisciplinary teams that developed in the subsequent years varied in makeup depending on whether they were institution based or community based and on the self-perception of the team's purpose. Often they did not include consumers or family members or they operated at times and locations that were not convenient for consumers and families to attend (Davis et al., 1998)

Recognizing that services for people with developmental disabilities are moving from institutions to community settings, Davis and her colleagues (1998) articulated a list of attitudes, skills, and behaviors that should guide interdisciplinary teams. Among other things, these include accessing adequate training on the needs of people with developmental disabilities as well as the use, abuse, and misuse of medications, ensuring the inclusion of consumers and family members in decision making and focusing on community inclusion of consumers.

Stark and his colleagues attempted to describe quality services for people with this dual diagnosis (Stark, McGee, Menolascino, Baker, & Menousek, 1984). They identified seven necessary characteristics of effective alternatives to traditional services. These characteristics, described next, are consistent with many of the principles and values of PsyR. As you read these see if you can identify which PsyR principles are related.

- *Comprehensive community programs.* All learning should take place in real-life situations.
- *A functional, individualized approach.* Training focuses on the individual in a specific environment and develops the skills needed by the individual to be successful there.
- *Training rather than testing.* Observing the individual in the environment helps to assess the person's skills and deficits and informs the training process. Testing merely provides a description of the person's performance at the moment on tasks that often were designed for people with greater cognitive abilities.
- *Unconditional positive regard.* The individual is given the respect, concern, courtesy, attention, and affection that would be afforded any human being. It also means that the person is not blamed for his or her disability or the resulting lack of experiences or skills.
- *Behavioral communication.* Behavior is a means of communication. This is particularly true for people with little or no ability in expressive language. Behavior therefore is viewed as such and rather than being punished is used to understand the person and inform services.
- *Ecological behaviorism.* Behavior is seen as a complex interrelated system that is influenced by the environment rather than a simple example of stimulus-response.
- *A balanced approach.* Both psychotropic medication and behavioral programming are useful tools to help an individual achieve independence.

Services for Persons with Substance Abuse Disorders and Mental Illness

The development of services for people with this dual diagnosis is complicated by the characteristics of the consumers, the providers, and the service systems. These individuals appear to have extensive service and support needs. They have been found to have a high rate of emergency service use, a low rate of responsiveness to services, and a greater risk for suicide and violence (Howland, 1990). Some consumers with this dual diagnosis are reluctant to engage in services that address a mental illness, whereas others are reluctant to engage in services that address substance abuse.

As stated previously, professionals in each system tend to be uninformed about the coexisting disability and therefore may not readily identify its presence. There is evidence that this results in decreases in communication, service effectiveness, and consumer satisfaction (Silverman, O'Neill, Cleary, Barwick, & Joseph, 1992).

Substance abuse services and mental health services often operate out of different bureaucracies and funding streams. They also employ different approaches and philosophies. Substance abuse treatment tends to be more confrontational, expecting the individual to take responsibility for her or his own sobriety and for asking for needed services. These services also tend to adhere strictly to an expectation of abstinence. Mental health services tend to employ more outreach, case management, and support in engaging the individual in services. Mental health services are also more tolerant of a gradual approach to abstinence that includes services provided to individuals who are still using substances (Minkoff, 1991; Sciacca & Thompson, 1996).

In spite of these system differences, there appear to be some important similarities as well. Evans and Sullivan (1990) point out that both services employ a biopsychosocial model of recovery. Both services also work to assist the individual to accept the illness, develop the skills and supports needed to succeed in all areas of life, and prevent relapse.

Three kinds of services, sequential, parallel, and integrated, have been developed to address the needs of people with dual psychiatric disabilities and substance abuse disorders (Minkoff, 1991; U.S. Department of Health and Human Services, 1995).

In the **sequential service model** the consumer receives nonsimultaneous services from both the mental health and substance abuse treatment systems. Which diagnosis (i.e., psychiatric disability or substance abuse) is addressed first depends on the practitioners' beliefs about effectiveness. Some practitioners believe that abstinence must be achieved before mental health services are initiated. Others believe that psychiatric treatment has to be initiated before the person can work on substance abuse recovery. Still others believe that the decision should be based on the severity of the individual's disorder specific symptoms.

In the **parallel service model**, the individual receives substance abuse recovery services and mental health services at the same time from each respective service system. This model uses the resources that are available in each system. With this approach, coordination between systems is critical for effective services but is not always achieved.

The **integrated service model** combines substance abuse services and mental health services into the same system by either cross training professionals in both areas or using integrated treatment teams. Usually, both substance abuse services and mental health services are provided or coordinated by the same person or integrated team incorporating knowledge and expertise in both disability areas.

Both the sequential and parallel service models use services that may already exist. However, they rely on service coordination across systems that is often hampered by systems issues such as conflicting messages and rules about confidentiality. Furthermore, this shuttling between systems to receive services is difficult to manage for some people with dual diagnosis and may interfere with the development of the necessary trusting relationship with staff (Daley, Moss, & Campbell, 1993).

The integrated service model may require the development of new services but has the advantage of a well-coordinated, consistent approach.

Self-Help and Recovery from Substance Abuse and Mental Illness

Substance abuse recovery programs place strong emphasis on self-help, particularly Twelve Step programs such as Alcoholics Anonymous (AA) and Narcotics Anonymous (NA). Twelve Step programs have historically rejected the use of any mood-altering substances. For people using psychotropic medications, this was problematic. More recently, Twelve Step programs have been modified to accommodate people with psychiatric disabilities. Some self-help programs specially designed for persons with substance abuse problems and a mental illness are called Double Trouble groups. These groups incorporate an understanding of the importance of continued use of psychoactive medications for some persons with severe mental illness.

Regardless of which model of service provision is used, recovery from substance abuse or dependency addresses four areas: physical, psychological, social, and spiritual (Daley et al., 1993). As described by Daley and colleagues, the aims of physical recovery include eliminating the substance from one's body, dealing with cravings for the substance, and restoring physical health. Services to accomplish this may include detoxification, ongoing counseling and self-help, and the elimination of environmental reminders (i.e., drug paraphernalia). Psychological recovery addresses issues such as overcoming denial of substance abuse or dependence, establishing a desire for abstinence, restoring emotional stability, identifying personal strengths and weaknesses, examining the impact one's addiction has had on others, developing a substance free identity, and developing a plan for relapse prevention and long-term recovery. Social recovery includes making amends for the impact the addiction has had on others, developing a support network and alternative leisure activities, and dealing with other problems caused by the addiction (e.g., legal or housing problems). Finally, spiritual recovery includes dealing with negative feelings (e.g., guilt or shame), developing a belief in some power greater than oneself, restoring meaning and positive values in one's life, and helping others who are addicted or in recovery.

The psychological and spiritual aspects of this conception of recovery have several important parallels with the concept of recovery from severe mental illness described later in chapter 4. The substance abuser is never really cured but instead is in a constant recovery mode, taking it "one day at a time." When you read about recovery from severe mental illness, which is often a lifelong process, you will see another conception of recovery that is not based on a cure.

Understanding Course, Outcome, and Treatment: What the Staff and Consumers Don't Know Can Hurt Them!

The bewildering and sometimes confusing array of information regarding treatment, course, and outcome highlights the need for consumers and their families, as well as staff, to be informed about medications, symptom relief, and so on. Efforts at education, like those involving mood disorders mentioned earlier, make up an important aspect of the PsyR process.

Consider the issue of continuing medication after someone is symptom free. We know that continuing medication during time periods of remission significantly reduces the likelihood of relapse for people with schizophrenia (Hogarty 1993; Lehman & Steinwachs, 1998), as well as bipolar disorder, manic disorder, and major depression, recurrent (Keck & McElroy,

1998; Nemeroff & Schatzberg, 1998). Still, the need to take medication on a long-term basis presents a major challenge for consumers, their loved ones, PsyR staff, and psychiatrists. Because it may take weeks or months for the effects of the medication to weaken and leave the body completely, the connection between discontinuing medication and a relapse is sometimes difficult for both the individual and for his or her family to recognize. Conveying the knowledge of the importance of continuing medication is imperative.

Knowledge of the facts about the course and outcome of severe and persistent mental illnesses is essential for effective psychiatric rehabilitation services. Practitioners who are unfamiliar with the findings regarding the probability of relapses, especially that relapse is still likely even with treatment compliance, may set inordinately high expectations for consumers and themselves. At the same time, ignorance of the numerous positive outcomes that are possible, indeed likely, also can lead to undue helplessness, inordinately low expectations, and the self-fulfilling prophecy of pessimistic expectations leading to negative outcomes. A realistic understanding of the limited efficacy of treatment, the rocky or stormy course of the illness, and the variety of potential outcomes is more likely to result in high-quality services and better rehabilitation outcomes.

Consider the following. Many well-meaning, enthusiastic staff members lack education specific to the major mental illnesses. Some of these individuals inform consumers that strict adherence to their treatment plans, taking their medication as prescribed, and so on will prevent a relapse. When, despite following a treatment plan, relapse occurs, both the consumer and the staff member may feel that they have failed—that is, they may believe the relapse is their fault rather than a consequence of the disease itself. For the consumer, this might result in hiding or denying symptoms or dropping out of treatment because the individual is so disenchanted with being misled. For the staff person this can produce frustration, a sense of failure, and eventually **burnout**. Consumers and staff members need to know that these illnesses do flare up, requiring medication changes, more intense treatment, support, and sometimes hospitalization. Indeed, most consumers are well aware of this but do not necessarily attribute relapse to the illness itself.

When periodic relapse is seen as a function of the type of illness rather than a personal failure, the chances of a timely intervention are greatly increased. Prompt intervention can sometimes avert severe relapse and help ensure that the consumer is less debilitated. Probably the most important benefit of this knowledge is that relapse is no longer seen as a failure on the part of the consumer or the staff.

At the same time, inordinately low expectations, believing, for example, that the probability of relapse precludes any other positive outcomes, may be just as disenchanting to both staff members and consumers. Deegan (1992) described a "vicious cycle" of disempowerment. She observed that staff expectations of inevitable consumer incompetence leads to learned helplessness on the part of the consumer. In other words, low or negative expectations on the part of staff promote feelings of powerlessness among mental health consumers. Feeling they are unable to affect their own lives, some consumers have learned to become helpless and inadvertently fulfill the staff's expectation of incompetence. Thus, inordinately low expectations for positive outcomes results in the staff not supporting consumers in their educational aspirations, vocational goals, residential goals, or other independent living goals.

Believing that positive outcomes are possible often results in the successful pursuit of a higher quality of life. There is evidence also that successful psychiatric rehabilitation may positively impact the symptomatology. For example, one controlled, random assignment study found that successful vocational rehabilitation actually resulted in lower symptomatology, suggesting that rehabilitation itself may positively affect the course of the illness (Lysaker & Bell, 1995). Other examples of the positive impact of psychiatric rehabilitation interventions on the course of mental illness appear throughout this text.

Summary

The course of severe and persistent mental illness is lengthy and is characterized by a significant risk of relapse. Psychiatric treatments, both pharmacological and psychosocial in nature, often positively change the course of mental illness through reductions in the length, frequency, and severity of symptom relapse. Psychotropic medications are often the primary treatment for both schizophrenic and mood disorders. Unfortunately, although most individuals experience great improvement, the outcome is rarely a full recovery. Indeed, there is a wide diversity of outcomes ranging from those individuals whose condition deteriorates over time to those who fully recover without any residual symptoms. Even though individuals share the same psychiatric diagnosis they do not necessarily share the same response to treatment or long-term adjustment. Although these disorders require pharmacological treatments, psychosocial interventions such as support and rehabilitation are also required to promote the best possible outcomes. Longitudinal studies with follow-up periods of 10 to 30 years have found that over time most people who get these services cope better, gain greater independence, have decreasing symptoms, and function better in the community. Unfortunately, even people who are coping well may occasionally relapse. Nevertheless, these recurrences do not preclude other positive outcomes such as the attainment and maintenance of living, learning, and working goals.

There is also a multiplicity of outcomes in the course of an individual's life. Over the course of many years of dealing with mental illness, one individual will experience both numerous negative outcomes (e.g., persistence of symptoms, relapses) and positive outcomes (e.g., remission of symptoms and achievement of independent living goals). Knowledge of this information is essential for consumers, their families, and their staff. Communication about these issues is critical. To avoid burnout and pessimism on the part of the staff and alienation and learned helplessness on the part of consumers, all stakeholders should be informed in order to develop appropriate and realistic expectations.

Class Exercise

The word *myth* is often taken to mean misconception, but many myths, although essentially fictitious, have a grain of truth. There are numerous myths about severe and persistent mental illness. Consider the following statements. Do you consider them to be myths? Are they complete misconceptions? Do they have any grains of truth? You decide, based on the scientific evidence presented and cited in your text.

Misconception, truth, or a little of both? Explain your answer.

1. Once a person with schizophrenia, always a person with schizophrenia.
2. All people with schizophrenia are alike.
3. Rehabilitation can only happen when someone is completely stable.
4. Psychotherapy is a waste of time for people with severe and persistent mental illness.
5. All people with severe and persistent mental illness must be on medication for the rest of their lives.
6. People with mental illness can only do low-level jobs (maybe peek at chapter 7 before guessing on this one).
7. Families cause mental illness (see chapter 11).

References

American Psychiatric Association (APA). (1987). *Diagnostic and statistical manual of mental disorders* (3rd ed. rev.). Washington, D.C.: Author.

American Psychiatric Association (APA). (1994). *Diagnostic and statistical manual of mental disorders* (4th ed.). Washington, DC: Author.

Anderson, C. M., Reiss, D. J., & Hogarty, G. E. (1986). *Schizophrenia and the family*. New York: Guilford Press.

Angst, J. (1998). Treated versus untreated major depressive episodes. *Psychopathology, 31*(1), 37–44.

Anthony, W. A., Cohen, M. R., & Vitalo, R. (1978). The measurement of rehabilitation outcome. *Schizophrenia Bulletin, 4*, 365–383.

Anthony, W. A., & Jansen, M. A. (1984, May). Predicting the vocational capacity of the chronically mentally ill: Research and policy implications. *American Psychologist, 39*(5), 537–544.

Anthony, W. A., & Liberman, R. P. (1986). The practice of psychiatric rehabilitation: Historical, conceptual and research base. *Schizophrenia Bulletin, 12*(4), 542–559.

Anthony, W. A., Rogers, S., Cohen, M., & Davies, R. (1995). Relationship between psychiatric symptomatology, work skills, and future vocational performance. *Psychiatric Services, 46*(4), 353–358.

Chen, Y. R., Swann, A. C., & Johnson, B. A. (1998). Stability of diagnosis in bipolar disorder. *Journal of Nervous & Mental Disease, 186*(1), 17–23.

Colom, F., Vieta, E., Martinez, A., Jorquera, A., & Gasto, C. (1998). What is the role of psychotherapy in the treatment of bipolar disorder? *Psychotherapy & Psychosomatics, 67*(1), 3–9.

Conley, R. R., & Buchanan R. W. (1997). Evaluation of treatment-reisistant schizophrenia. *Schizophrenia Bulletin, 23*(4), 663–674.

Craighead, W. E., Craighead, L. W., & Ilardi, S. S. (1998). Psychosocial treatments for major depression. In P. E. Nathan & J. M. Gorman, *A guide to treatments that work* (pp. 226–239). New York: Oxford University Press.

Craighead, W. E., Milkowitz, D. J., Vajk, F. C., & Frank, E. (1998). Psychosocial Treatment for Bipolar Disorders. In Nathan, P. E., & Gorman, J. M. *A Guide to Treatments than Work*. New York: Oxford University Press, 240–248.

Daley, D. C., Moss, H. B., & Campbell, F. (1993). *Dual disorders: Counseling clients with chemical dependency & mental illness* (2nd ed.). Center City, MN: Hazelden Foundation.

Davis, S., Wehmeyer, M. L., Board, J. P., Jr., Fox, S., Maher, F., & Roberts, B. (1998). Interdisciplinary teams. In S. Reiss & M. G. Aman (Eds.), *Psychotropic medication and developmental disabilities: The international consensus handbook*, Ohio, Nisonger Center for Mental Retardation and Developmental Disabilities, 73–83.

Deegan, P. E. (1992). The independent living movement and people with psychiatric disabilities: Taking back control over our own lives. *Psychosocial Rehabilitation Journal, 15*(3), 3–19.

Deegan, P. E. (1995). *Coping with Voices: Self-help strategies for People who hear voices that are distressing.* Lawrence, MA: National Empowerment Center.

DeSisto, M. J., Harding, C. M., McCormick, R. V., Ashikaga, T., & Brooks, G. W. (1995a). The Maine and Vermont three-decade studies of serious mental illness: I. Matched comparison of cross-sectional outcome. *British Journal of Psychiatry, 167*(3), 331–338.

DeSisto, M. J., Harding, C. M., McCormick, R. V., Ashikaga, T., & Brooks, G. W. (1995b). The Maine and Vermont three-decade studies of serious mental illness: II. Longitudinal course comparisons. *British Journal of Psychiatry, 167*(3), 338–342.

Diamond, R. J., & Wikler, D. I. (1985). Ethical problems in community treatment of the chronically mentally ill. *New Directions for Mental Health Services, 26*, 85–93.

Evans, K., & Sullivan, J. M. (1990). *Dual diagnosis: Counseling the mentally ill substance abuser.* New York: The Guilford Press.

Frank, E., Kupfer, D. J., & Perel, J. M. (1990). Three year outcome for maintenance therapies in recurrent depression. *Archives of General Psychiatry, 47*(12), 1100–1105.

Frank, E., Kupfer, D. J., & Perel, J. M. (1993). Comparison of full-dose versus half-dose pharmacotherapy in the maintenance treatment of recurrent depression. *Journal of Affective Disorders, 27*(3), 139–145.

Freeman, M. P., & Stoll, A. L. (1998). Mood stabilizer combinations: A review of safety and efficacy. *American Journal of Psychiatry, 155*(1), 12–21.

Harding, C. M., & Zahniser, J. H. (1994). Empirical correction of seven myths about schizophrenia with implications for treatment. *Acta Psychiatrica Scandinavica, Supplementum, 384*, 140–146.

Harding, C. M., Zubin, J., & Strauss, J. S. (1992). Chronicity in schizophrenia: Revisited. *British Journal of Psychiatry—Supplement, 18*, 27–37.

Harding, C. M., Brooks, G. W., Ashikaga, T., Strauss, J. S., & Breier, A. (1987a). The Vermont longitudinal study of persons with severe mental illness: I. Methodology, study sample, and overall status 32 years later. *American Journal of Psychiatry, 144*(6), 718–726.

Harding, C. M., Brooks, G. W., Ashikaga, T., Strauss, J. S., & Breier, A. (1987b). The Vermont longitudinal study of persons with severe mental illness: II. Long-term outcome of subjects who retrospectively met DSM-III criteria for schizophrenia. *American Journal of Psychiatry, 144* (6), 727–735.

Hogarty, G. E. (1993). Prevention of relapse in chronic schizophrenic patients. *The Journal of Clinical Psychiatry, 54*, 3 supplement, 18–23.

Howland, R. H. (1990). Barriers to community treatment of patients with dual diagnoses. *Hospital and Community Psychiatry, 41*, 1134–1135.

Kalachnik, J. E., Leventhal, B. L., James, D. H., Sovner, R., Kastner, T. A., Walsh, K., Weisblatt, S. A., & Klitzke, M. G. (1998). Guidelines for the use of psychotropic medication. In S. Reiss & M. G. Aman (Eds.), *Psychotropic medication and developmental disabilities: The international consensus handbook*, Ohio, Nisonger Center for Mental Retardation and Developmental Disabilities, 45–72.

Keck, P. E., & McElroy, S. A. (1998). Pharmacological treatment of bipolar disorders. In P. E. Nathan & J. M. Gorman *A guide to treatments that work* (249–269). New York: Oxford University Press.

Keck, P. E., McElroy, S. A., Strakowski, S. M., West, S. A., Sax, K. W., Hawkins, J. M., Bourne, M. L., & Haggard, P. (1998, May). 12-month outcome of patients with bipolar disorder following hospitalization for a manic or mixed episode. *American Journal of Psychiatry, 155*(5), 646–652.

Kessing, L. V. (1998). Recurrence in affective disorder: II. Effect of age and gender. *British Journal of Psychiatry, 172*, 29–34.

Kessing, L. V., Andersen, P. K., Mortensen, P. B., & Bolwig, T. G. (1998). Recurrence in affective disorder: I. Case register study. *British Journal of Psychiatry, 172*, 23–28.

Lehman, A. F. (1995). Vocational rehabilitation in schizophrenia. *Schizophrenia Bulletin, 21*(4), 645–656.

Lehman, A. F., & Steinwachs, D. M. (1998). At issue: Translating research into practice: The Schizophrenia patient outcomes research team (PORT) treatment recommendations. *Schizophrenia Bulletin, 24*(1), 1–10.

Licht R. W. (1998). Drug treatment of mania: A critical review. *Acta Psychiatrica Scandinavica, 97*(6), 387–397.

Linn, M. W., Caffey, E. M., Klett, C. J., Hogarty, G. E., & Lamb, H. R. (1979). Day treatment and psychotropic drugs in the aftercare of schizophrenic patients. *Archives of General Psychiatry, 36*, 1055–1066.

Lysaker, P., & Bell, M. (1995). Work rehabilitation and improvements in insight in schizophrenia. *Journal of Nervous & Mental Disease, 183*(2), 103–106.

Maj, M., Pirozzi, R., Magliano, L., & Bartoli, L. (1998). Long-term outcome of lithium prophylaxis in bipolar disorder: A 5-year prospective study of 402 patients at a lithium clinic. *American Journal of Psychiatry, 155*(1), 30–35.

Minkoff, K. (1991). Program components of a comprehensive integrated care system for serious mentally ill patients with substance disorders. *New Directions for Mental Health Services, 50*, 13–27.

Mueser, K. T., Drake, R. E., & Bond G. R. (1997). Recent advances in psychiatric rehabilitation for patients with severe mental illness. *Harvard Review of Psychiatry, 5*(3), 123–137.

Nemeroff, C. B., & Schatzberg, A. F. (1998). Pharmacological treatment of unipolar depression. In P. E. Nathan & J. M. Gorman *A Guide to treatments that work* (pp. 212–225). New York: Oxford University Press.

Sciacca, K., & Thompson, C. M. (1996). Program development and integrated treatment across systems for dual diagnosis: Mental illness, drug addiction, and alcoholism (MIDAA). *The Journal of Mental Health Administration, 23*(3), 288–297.

Silverman, D. C., O'Neill, S. F., Cleary, P. D., Barwick, C., & Joseph, R. C. (1992). Recognition of alcohol abuse in psychiatric outpatients and its effect on treatment. *Hospital and Community Psychiatry, 40*, 644–646.

Silverstone, T., McPherson, H., Hunt, N., & Romans, S. (1998). How effective is lithium in the prevention of relapse in bipolar disorder? A prospective naturalistic follow-up study. *Australian & New Zealand Journal of Psychiatry, 32*(1), 61–66.

Soares, J. J., Stintzing, C. P., Jackson, C., & Skoldin, B. (1997). Psychoeducation for patients with bipolar disorder: An exploratory study *Nordic Journal of Psychiatry, 51*(6), 439–446.

Stark, J. A., McGee, J. J., Menolascino, F. J., Baker, D. H., & Menousek, P. E. (1984). Treatment strategies in the habilitation of severely mentally retarded–mentally ill adolescents and adults. In F. J. Menolascino & J. A. Stark (Eds.), *Handbook of mental illness in the mentally retarded* (pp. 189–218). New York: Plenum Press.

Stephens, J. H. (1978). Long-term prognosis and follow-up in schizophrenia. *Schizophrenia Bulletin, 1*(4), 25–47.

Szasz, T. (1976) *Schizophrenia: The sacred symbol of psychiatry*. New York: Basic Books.

Torrey, E. F. (1995). *Surviving schizophrenia*. New York: Harper Perennial.

U.S. Department of Health and Human Services (1995). Assessment and treatment of patients with coexisting mental illness and alcohol and other drug abuse. *Treatment Improvement Protocol (TIP) Series 9*, Substance Abuse and Mental Health Administration.

Viguera, A. C., Baldessarini, R. J., & Friedberg, J. (1998). Discontinuing antidepressant treatment in major depression. *Harvard Review of Psychiatry, 5*, 293–306.

Wiersma, D., Nienhuis, F. J., Slooff, C. J., & Giel, R. (1998). Natural course of schizophrenic disorders: A 15-year follow-up of a Dutch incidence cohort. *Schizophrenia Bulletin, 24*(1), 75–85.

Part II

Psychiatric Rehabilitation Principles and Methodology

Chapter 4

Goals, Values, and Guiding Principles of Psychiatric Rehabilitation

This chapter reviews the goals, values, and guiding principles of psychiatric rehabilitation (PsyR). Like any new and evolving discipline, the strategies and methods used in PsyR constantly undergo adjustment and change as the field matures and the methods become more refined. These differences are reflected by the wide scope of PsyR practice currently in use. Despite the diversity of practice, there is a great deal of agreement about the core elements that make up this belief system—the goals and values of PsyR. This agreement is clearly demonstrated by the similarity between the many formulations of PsyR principles that have been suggested by different groups and authors.

This chapter will answer the following questions:

1. *How does the concept of recovery inform the goals, values, and philosophy of psychiatric rehabilitation?*
2. *What are the goals of psychiatric rehabilitation?*
3. *What are the defining values held by psychiatric rehabilitation professionals?*
4. *What are the guiding principles that inform state-of-the-art PsyR practice today?*
5. *What are the ethics of PsyR?*

Introduction

This chapter deals with the ideas and philosophy of psychiatric rehabilitation. Because they are shared these goals, values, and principles are what PsyR professionals and services have in common. These concepts are also what make PsyR a unique discipline. A young field, PsyR is actively defining itself by amending its principles as its techniques and skills become more refined. PsyR is one specialty in the broader field of rehabilitation, to which it owes much of its philosophical base.

Physical Rehabilitation as a Model for Psychiatric Rehabilitation

Several authors have suggested that the rehabilitation of persons with physical disabilities provides an apt and instructive model or analogy for understanding the rehabilitation of persons with psychiatric disabilities (e.g., Anthony, Cohen, & Farkas, 1990; Deegan, 1988). An obvious benefit of this comparison is that rehabilitation from physical injury or disease is a relatively common and acceptable phenomenon in modern society. Sports figures recovering from injuries sustained on the playing field and politicians recovering from stress-related diseases such as coronary bypass surgery are common subjects of media coverage. In addition, as medicine improves, life expectancy increases, and the population ages, having family, friends, or acquaintances with physical handicaps is more common today than ever before.

Sadly, it is still true that many people can relate to a physical handicap much better than they can relate to or understand a mental, cognitive, or emotional handicap. On the positive side, as our understanding of the brain and nervous system has increased in the latter part of this century, so has our understanding of mental illness. As understanding increases, fear and stigma about these diseases decrease. Despite this progress, there is still a long way to go to educate the public about mental illnesses and their causes.

The Concept of Recovery

One of the most exciting recent additions to PsyR thinking has been the development of a concept of **recovery.** The idea of recovery represents optimism about the future. Because these conditions are often lifelong, persons with severe mental illness and professionals have not been using the term *recovery*. Today, the concept of recovery from severe mental illness, with its promise of hope for the future, is becoming widely accepted.

Based on models of rehabilitation and recovery from physically handicapping conditions, several researchers have helped to develop a concept of recovery for severe mental illness (Deegan, 1988; Anthony, 1993). For many conditions, recovery refers to a cure. For a lifelong mental illness, recovery refers to a reformulation of one's life aspirations and an eventual adaptation to the disease. The importance of recovery has been recognized by many sectors of the PsyR field. Nationally known consumer advocate, Patricia Deegan, Ph.D., and William Anthony, Ph.D., the director of the Center for Psychiatric Rehabilitation at Boston University, have both spent considerable time and energy spreading the concept of recovery throughout the PsyR community.

Both Deegan and Anthony believe that the first step a person must go through in the recovery or rehabilitation process is acceptance of the handicap or disability. For a person with a cyclical mental illness, this step alone may take years. Deegan believes that in order to achieve an effective recovery the individual has to develop a new worldview that incorporates the handicapping condition as part of his or her reality. Dreams and aspirations may have to be modified to include the mental illness. Deegan has pointed out that helping someone achieve this kind of fundamental change in self-concept is an important aspect of the PsyR practitioner's task.

This fundamental change in self-concept leads to several other important ideas for the recovery process. Deegan (1988) has stressed that one of the most important ideas is that recovery and rehabilitation are not linear processes. People going through these types of changes naturally go through setbacks and temporary failures. When doing better it is very tempting to forget or repress the idea that one has a severe mental illness. Real recovery is a journey that requires exploring new ideas and new self-concepts, and that means being open to failure, disappointment, and possible relapse. PsyR services that do not make realistic allowances for failure do a disservice to their clients.

Another corollary of the recovery concept is that each person's road to recovery is unique. Because recovery is based on developing a new self-image, we might assume that there may be as many roads to recovery as there are people. The uniqueness of each person's rehabilitation has a direct bearing on PsyR services. Effective programs respect diversity and provide many individualized services for their clients. One-size-fits-all services may be easier and more efficient to operate but, especially in the long run, they are inherently less effective at helping people recover.

Because the core task that the recovering person needs to accomplish is the development of a new and positive self-image that incorporates his or her mental illness, other consumers also have an important role to play in the recovery process. Consumers who have achieved a positive self-image despite their illnesses can serve both as role models and as constant reminders that it can be done. This role modeling concept is so fundamental to PsyR services that it is taken for granted in many settings. At the core of many PsyR approaches, role modeling is a powerful tool for providing both hope and specific strategies to achieve goals. The staff of effective PsyR services are also role models for their clients. This is one reason that the PsyR profession believes in reducing the barriers between staff and consumers as much as possible.

The concept of recovery is bolstered by the increasing progress being made in psychiatry and psychiatric rehabilitation. This progress is seen in a number of different developments:

- The results of landmark longitudinal studies on the outcome of schizophrenia (e.g., Harding et al., 1994) (described in chapter 3).
- The recent introduction of improved medications such as clozaril and prozac, which have better results in terms of decreasing both sypmtomatology and side effects for many consumers (described in chapter 3).
- The encouraging outcomes from new developments in psychiatric rehabilitation practice approaches. Supported employment may be the best example of this. Ten years ago most PsyR practitioners still believed in keeping consumers for extended stays in prevocational programs. Today there is strong evidence that this strategy does not work as well as immediate job placement (e.g., Bond, Dietzen, McGrew, & Miller, 1995; Bond & Dincin, 1986) (described in chapter 7).
- The debunking of many of the myths about schizophrenia and mental illness that support continued stigma against people with mental illness (Harding & Zahniser, 1994).

The concept of recovery embodies the optimism and hope that underlie the entire PsyR enterprise. The goal of recovery for every individual with mental illness is an important element in the definition of the PsyR profession.

Goals, Values, and Guiding Principles

This chapter discusses the goals, values, and guiding principles of PsyR. **Values** are deeply held beliefs that may inform specific behaviors, attitudes, and ideas. An individual's values tend to be stable over time. Because they are deeply held, a person may not articulate or question his or her own values. For example, those of us who value the free expression of ideas may not even be aware of that value until we find ourselves coming to the defense of someone who is prevented from expressing her or his opinion at a meeting or gathering. Even then, we may not consider why we felt so strongly about what had just taken place.

Goals represent desired states or objectives to strive for and achieve. Goals are usually identified based on their relationship or presumed relationship with values. Again, if we value free expression we might work hard to achieve the goal of defeating a bill that we believe would stifle free speech on the Internet. Goals are more specific than values. Goals can usually be arrived at by different paths. For example, the goal of an improved quality of life might be achieved in a different manner for each person.

Principles, in contrast to goals, are more specific dictums specifically designed to promulgate values and goals by providing guidelines for addressing specific situations or behaviors. Take the community mental health principle of least restrictive treatment environment, for example. This widely held principle states that an individual should always receive treatment in the most autonomous (least restrictive) setting or environment that is possible but still effective. This means, for example, that no one should be treated in a psychiatric hospital if there is a community-based program available where the person can receive equally effective treatment. We can see that this principle is designed to, among other things, promote the goals of community integration and quality of life, as well as foster the value of respect for the dignity of each human being.

The Goals of Psychiatric Rehabilitation

As stated earlier, the goals of PsyR represent the objectives of PsyR services. These are what all PsyR services strive to achieve for their clients. In that sense, goals are guidelines for service and go hand in hand with PsyR values. The combination of goals and values help determine the guiding principles. Our review of several efforts to identify these ideas (Anthony, Cohen, & Farkas, 1990; Anthony & Nemec, 1983; Cnaan, Blankertz, Messinger, & Gardner, 1988, 1989, 1990; IAPSRS, 1996) suggests that there is near universal agreement on three goals of PsyR (see Table 4.1):

1. *PsyR services are designed to help persons with severe mental illness achieve recovery.* The goal of recovery illustrates both the hope and the difficulty of the PsyR enterprise. Recovery, as discussed earlier, is the defining goal of PsyR. Because recovery is unique for each person, the guidelines of how to achieve this goal may vary. Some of the values and guiding principles outlined in this discussion are designed to promote the idea that each individual must follow his or her own path to recovery. Because recovery is really an abstract idea defined by the individual, it is something that each person must achieve for himself or herself rather than something that we can do for or to someone. Achieving this goal presents the PsyR worker with an important challenge. The worker has to help and encourage the individual to do something that the individual has to accomplish on his or her own.

2. *PsyR services are designed to help persons with severe mental illness achieve maximum community integration.* This goal, for the individual to be able to live with a degree of independence in the community of his or her choice is the most consistently stated goal of PsyR services both nationally and worldwide. In a very real sense, this was the starting point on which all the other goals and values emerged. Residing in the community, instead of in an institution, offers one an opportunity for self-direction, rehabilitation, and recovery. How this goal can be best achieved is still a matter of some contention. A good deal of criticism has been directed at some PsyR services accused of keeping consumers segregated by creating small institutions in the community rather than working toward community integration. Some housing advocates feel strongly that housing facilities should be integrated (a percentage of residences open to the public at large) rather than designated specifically for persons with severe mental illness. Other advocates believe

TABLE 4.1
The Goals, Values, and Guiding Principles of PsyR

Goals (3)
1. Recovery
2. Community integration
3. Quality of life

Values (5)
1. Self-determination
2. Dignity and worth of every individual
3. Optimism
4. Capacity of every individual to learn and grow
5. Cultural sensitivity

Guiding Principles (12)
1. Individualization of all services
2. Maximum client involvement, preference, and choice
3. Normalized and community-based services
4. Strengths focus
5. Situational assessments
6. Treatment/rehabilitation integration, holistic approach
7. Ongoing, accessible, coordinated services
8. Vocational focus
9. Skills training
10. Environmental modifications and supports
11. Partnership with the family
12. Evaluative, assessment, outcome-oriented focus

that there should be no specifically designated housing at all. Instead, people with disabilities should live in regular community residences (e.g., homes or apartments) of their own choosing.

Some PsyR models, such as the Fairweather Lodges, continue to embrace sheltered support for some individuals as an appropriate strategy given the level of stigma that still exists in the community. Regardless of these differences, the maximum degree of community integration possible and feasible continues to be a goal of the PsyR enterprise.

3. *PsyR services are designed to help persons with severe mental illness achieve the highest possible quality of life.* The PsyR practitioner believes in the importance of achieving the highest quality of life possible for every individual regardless of the stage of the illness or the severity of the individual's symptoms. This goal goes hand in hand with optimism about recovery and community integration, despite the presence of a handicapping condition. The presence of symptoms should not detract from the importance of those things that help ensure a reasonable quality of life, such as social support, companionship, employment, recreation, food, shelter, clothing, and an active sex life. For the PsyR worker, quality of life is an important goal regardless of what stage of the illness the person is experiencing. For the individual, symptom reduction can be a quality-of-life issue as much as a treatment issue.

The Values of Psychiatric Rehabilitation

The values that underlie most, if not all, PsyR services relate directly to the goals that PsyR tries to achieve. Values are general attitudes that influence the professional's behavior in many ways. In fact, PsyR workers may hold these values without articulating them, because they are imbedded in the designs of the programs they work in and the service strategies they carry out. As you review the following five PsyR values, consider how they relate to the goals of PsyR.

The PsyR Practitioner Believes That Everyone Has the Right of Self-Determination, Including Participation in All Decisions That Affect Their Lives

In PsyR facilities this value is often referred to as **empowerment**. Although its usage is nearly universal, because the term encompasses so much, there is still no generally agreed upon definition of empowerment. Community psychologist Julian Rappaport (1987) characterized the term *empowerment* as conveying

> both a psychological sense of personal control or influence and a concern with actual social influence, political power, and legal rights. (p. 121)

Consumer involvement and empowerment directly relate to the importance of the recovery process. As Deegan (1988) pointed out, the essence of recovery is the individual's reestablishment of a self-concept that takes the mental illness into account. This is in contrast to the notion that the services provided constitute the rehabilitation itself. Instead, the services help make the rehabilitation process available, attractive, and possible for the individual with a disability who must do the very real work of self-change. As Deegan (1988) put it:

> [P]ersons with a disability do not "get rehabilitated" in the sense that cars "get" tuned up or televisions "get" repaired. They are not passive recipients of rehabilitation services. Rather, they experience themselves as recovering a new sense of self and of purpose within and beyond the limits of the disability. (p. 12)

How can these involvement and empowerment goals be achieved for persons with severe mental illness? Many varied and innovative service delivery strategies have been designed, developed, and refined in an effort to accomplish these goals.

One important aspect of involvement and empowerment concerns consumers' knowledge about their condition and their treatment. A study by Warner, Taylor, Powers, and Hyman (1989) examined the effect of labeling consumers as mentally ill. The authors had hypothesized that consumers who accepted their mental illness diagnosis would have lower levels of functioning. In fact, they found the opposite was true and concluded that empowerment, in the form of shared knowledge, may reduce psychotic disability.

Pratt and Gill (1990, 1993) developed empowerment and involvement strategies for day treatment services that included sharing knowledge, power, and economic resources with consumers. From these starting points, consumers were encouraged to extend their prerogatives to other aspects of their programs. These strategies produced greater consumer involvement with the program, increased acceptance and awareness of mental illness, and improved outcomes (Pratt & Gill, 1990; Gill & Pratt, 1993).

Although everyone uses the term there is still a good deal of debate about how to exactly define empowerment. One way of defining something is to formulate a working definition of it so that it can be measured. With input from several consumer groups around the country, Rogers, Chamberlin, Ellison, and Crean (1997) have begun development of a scale designed to measure empowerment. Based on their efforts they have suggested that empowerment is made up of three parts. The first element of empowerment is self-esteem–self-efficacy combined with optimism and a sense of control over the future. The second element involves possessing actual power. The final element of empowerment is made up of righteous anger and community activism. It is important to recognize that these elements of empowerment describe characteristics of empowered people. Similar to the concept of recovery, empowerment is something that must come from within the individual, rather than something done to or for an individual.

The PsyR Practitioner Believes in the Dignity and Worth of Every Human Being, Regardless of the Degree of Impairment, Disability, or Handicap

This core value underlies every aspect of PsyR practice. People are in no way lessened as human beings by their illness. If asked, most people would personally endorse this position. Despite these socially correct declarations, the persistent stigma against people with mental illness suggests that this is not a commonly held value.

The term *dignity* comes from the Latin *dignitas*, which means worth or merit. A lack of dignity or worth is conveyed in many ways, some of them very subtle. Consider a setting where the clients are addressed by their first names but the staff are only addressed by their titles or surnames. The message in such behavior is very clear—the clients have low status while the staff have high status. This same message may be conveyed in other ways as well, for example, different rules for program staff and clients, nonsensitive (e.g., a lunch or recreation room) program areas where only staff are allowed to congregate, or separate bathrooms for clients and staff. Although individual situations like these are subtle, each sends a message that clients have low status and reduces their dignity. If numerous such situations exist together in an insensitive environment, the message is clear that persons with severe mental illness who require services have less worth than the persons who staff the program.

Most of these situations, when they exist, are unintentional. The concept of staff bathrooms and lunchrooms is relatively common in many settings and does not carry a negative message. Most people address their own doctor as "Doctor." Nevertheless, for persons with mental illness an accumulation of these situations combined with societal stigma conveys a strong message that they are less valued by society. Wolf Wolfensberger's (1983) efforts to develop surveys and scales to identify these dignity-reducing situations are important simply because they are often subtle, unintended, and may be essentially invisible to the staff.

The PsyR Practitioner Is Optimistic Regarding the Improvement and Eventual Recovery of Persons with Severe Mental Illness Who Are Provided Services

The importance of this principle for the provision of effective services to persons with severe mental illness is obvious. In short, every person, regardless of how symptomatic or handicapped the person may be, has the capacity to benefit from services. Real optimism on the part of service providers generalizes to the service recipients. Of course, the ultimate optimistic stance is represented by the concept of recovery described earlier.

At the same time, providers who lack optimism regarding the potential of consumers may be hard pressed to maintain the requisite level of motivation to carry out their functions. Worse, even the most symptomatic client may sense it when a practitioner is doubtful about achieving his or her goals. The practical effects of a lack of optimism were often exemplified by the inadequate and inappropriate treatment provided for persons with severe mental illness by the traditionally trained staff of many community mental health centers. Based on their training, staff members were often pessimistic about the long-term prognosis of persons who lacked appropriate ego functioning and the insight to benefit from treatment. Because of the pervasive belief that these persons could not improve, treatment resources were often allocated to programs providing services for persons with less severe conditions who could benefit from more psychodynamically oriented treatments. Persons experiencing severe and persistent mental illness, labeled *chronics*, were often treated by the least-trained staff and were given minimal psychiatric time and minimal levels of supplies, space, and support staff.

The PsyR Practitioner Assumes That Everyone Has the Capacity to Learn and Grow

Although this value may be considered a corollary of the value of optimism, it is so important that it is constantly emphasized by practitioners. The clear message of this value is that all people, regardless of their level of disability, can benefit from modalities like skill training and education. The presence of a mental illness does not preclude someone's ability to learn and grow.

Consider what happened to a consumer named William who had been in a PsyR day program for five years after spending the previous 13 years in a psychiatric hospital. William, who was always neat and well groomed, was almost entirely noncommunicative. One thing that he did communicate was a desire to work. Previous attempts at getting William to be more outgoing had all ended in failure. Although he did not communicate, William did seem to like to be around people. Reviewing past failures, a new caseworker hit on an idea. If William could learn to use a few phrases and operate the equipment, he could work as an elevator operator, a job for which some openings existed. William responded very positively to this idea. He learned to greet people and ask them what floor they wanted. He also learned to operate the elevator, paying particular attention to the doors and to whether it stopped evenly with the floor at each level. The staff members were amazed that William could learn these things after years of being almost a recluse. William held that job for many years, although he rarely said more than "Good morning!" and "What floor?"

The PsyR Practitioner Is Sensitive to and Respectful of the Individual, Cultural, and Ethnic Differences of Each Consumer

Severe mental illness knows no cultural or ethnic boundaries. Providers of PsyR services must be prepared to aid any individual experiencing these conditions. Sensitivity to cultural and ethnic differences is necessary when we consider that the task of PsyR is essentially reintegration with the consumer's community of choice. To successfully accomplish this goal, it is the responsibility of the practitioner to understand the particular beliefs, mores, and customs of the community in question. In short, the practitioner must become culturally competent and ensure that the services provided are also culturally competent. Tales abound of the kinds of social faux pas that occur when professionals make incorrect judgments about their clients because of a lack of knowledge of a client's culture. For example, in the United States if a person does not look you in the eye she or he is often suspected of having something to hide. However, looking someone directly in the eye may be considered rude or aggressive in some Asian cultures.

This is an especially sensitive area for PsyR practitioners because they must constantly deal with the issue of societal stigma toward their clients. The constant problem of stigma helps to keep the practitioner aware of the importance of correct communication and behavior. In one sense, having a severe mental illness constitutes a unique cultural identity in itself. The struggle to help consumers free themselves from the role of "mental patient" may be aided by increased respect and awareness for the consumer's ethnic and cultural background.

Guiding Principles of Psychiatric Rehabilitation

The guiding principles of psychiatric rehabilitation comprise a set of rules that can be applied to specific situations in order to achieve the goals and reflect the values of the field. In a sense, they constitute rules of thumb that PsyR practitioners can refer to when faced with important decisions. The principles are important tools for providing day-to-day guidance in clinical situations and for systematizing the practice of PsyR.

Although the higher-order values and goals are nearly universally shared, there are still some questions about the application of specific principles. These differences of opinion are reflected in the differences between formulations of PsyR principles that have been put forward in the discipline's short history (Anthony, Cohen, & Farkas, 1990; Anthony & Nemec, 1983; Cnaan, Blankertz, Messinger, & Gardner, 1988, 1989, 1990; IAPSRS, 1996). Rather than actually disagree on these principles, professionals in different settings often prioritize principles differently. This reprioritization is often a response to real differences that exist between settings or unique situations. As an example, to justify billing criteria, in some medical settings staff members are required to focus on the consumers' symptoms and deficits when writing clinical notes, rather than on their strengths. As you will see, this emphasis on symptoms and deficits violates the principle of focusing on an individuals strengths. Regardless, for these workers a refusal to comply with billing requirements might jeopardize the existence of PsyR services in general. In this paradoxical case, for the sake of the consumers, the best response is to avoid an emphasis on strengths when writing chart notes.

As you review the 12 guiding PsyR principles that follow, consider how they relate to the goals and values of PsyR.

Individualization of All Services

This principle means that rehabilitation goal formulation, assessment, and service provision responds to the individual needs and desires of the client. Because it allows each person to develop in the way he or she desires, individualization of services is a very important element of the recovery process. Because many PsyR services are carried out in groups, strict adherence to this principle is very important. Notice how the following supported employment (SE) program is designed to ensure individualization of services and how the curriculum is adjusted depending on the needs of members.

> The SE program at Shore House offers a six week vocational exploration group. The curriculum for this group includes a review of each member's past experiences, including identification of the members' occupational values, skills, interests, and preferences. The final step for each group member is the development of a vocational goal. A new member, Arthur, wants to get a job and believes he will need the support of the job coach to secure and maintain employment. After several meetings, the job coach is satisfied that Arthur knows what kind of job he wants. Rather than spend 6 weeks in the group to gain information he already has, Arthur will immediately begin working with the job coach on job development.

Maximum Client Involvement, Preference, and Choice

This principle is related to the very personal nature of recovery and rehabilitation. Each person has a unique set of preferences, values, and aspirations. Goals or services that are selected for the consumer by the practitioner, or anyone else for that matter, are meaningless. Consider the following situation that confronted Sharon. How would you feel in her shoes?

> Sharon and her counselor, Ann, have completed work on her rehabilitation plan. Sharon's rehabilitation goal is to get a job doing clerical work. All of the interventions described in the plan are related to job acquisition (contacting employers, practicing interviewing, etc.). At her team meeting, Ann shares Sharon's plan with other staff members. Some members of the team believe that before Sharon works on getting a job she needs to become more outgoing. Ann reminds them that there are many clerical jobs in quiet offices where workers are not expected to be outgoing, but the team thinks becoming more outgoing would be good for Sharon, and Ann is pressured to change the plan. When Ann and Sharon meet to review and sign the plan, Ann explains that the team agreed that Sharon should volunteer to run the community meeting three times a week for the next 3-month period, and then, if she's more comfortable socializing, she should resume her work goal. Ann decides not to tell Sharon that she is very much against this plan. She rationalizes this by thinking that Sharon may actually be helped by running the community meeting.

Normalized and Community-Based Services

The term **normalization** was coined by Wolf Wolfensberger, who primarily worked with people who had developmental disabilities. Wolfensberger (1983) described normalization as the promotion of valued social roles. Worker, student, parent, and neighbor are positive social roles that are valued in our society. Psychiatric patient and group home resident are examples of social roles that are devalued. PsyR services are designed to assist people in taking on and succeeding in valued social roles.

Normalized services are appropriate to the person's age, sex, culture, and so on. For example, in an adult program you would not speak to the clients like children or ask them to do finger paintings and then display them on the wall. In normalized residential settings, consumers live in decent, safe neighborhoods; have access to transportation, shopping, and other community resources, and interact with neighbors and participate in community activities. In contrast, institutional settings and group homes in socially isolated locations would not assist consumers in developing valued social roles and would thus be inconsistent with this guiding principle.

Strengths Focus

PsyR services and practitioners recognize and build on an individual's strengths rather than focusing on his or her weaknesses or deficits. This can be a difficult task for both consumer and practitioner. Consumers who have a long history of psychiatric hospitalizations are accustomed to professionals focusing on their symptoms and problems. When asked, "What are your strengths?" they are often at a loss. Initially, practitioners may also have difficulty seeing past psychotic symptoms and social deficits such as extreme withdrawal. However, PsyR programs typically allow consumers and practitioners to develop relationships around work and recreational activities. These experiences encourage practitioners to relate to each consumer as they would to a colleague or friend and to focus on what a consumer can do and likes to do. Perhaps this principle is best illustrated by the following professional descriptions of the same individual:

> Joan is a psychiatric nurse who sees Peter once a month for medication maintenance group. In a chart note she describes Peter as appearing depressed and withdrawn with poor eye contact and constricted affect. Phil is a vocational rehabilitation counselor who is working with Peter in a supported employment program. His chart note, written on the same day as Joan's, describes Peter as a diligent worker who completes assigned tasks and communicates effectively with his supervisor. Both descriptions may be accurate and are appropriate to the professional's function. Joan's note may assist the psychiatrist in making a helpful medication adjustment, whereas Phil's PsyR assessment helps him determine that Peter's vocational rehabilitation goals are being achieved.

Situational Assessments

Doing **situational assessments** rather than overall assessments means that the rehabilitation process focuses on the skills and modifications necessary for the client to function successfully in the environments (i.e., situations) of his or her choice. This is in contrast to doing a **global assessment** unrelated to specific client goals. For example, consumers attending a vocational readiness group may have markedly different employment goals. Sarah wants to get a job as a retail salesperson, whereas Tony would like to pursue work as a laboratory technician. Doing a general assessment of work readiness skills (e.g., ability to follow directions and complete assigned tasks) is not the best way to predict what these clients will need to succeed in their chosen jobs. The best way to assess their abilities to meet the requirements of their chosen careers, is to observe them completing relevant tasks in these very different environments. It is likely that focusing on interpersonal skills will be crucial for Sarah's success. The ability to carry out precise measurements and record results will be important for Tony's chosen line of work.

Treatment/Rehabilitation Integration, Holistic Approach

This means that PsyR services and practitioners do not separate the treatment and rehabilitation processes. Rather, the client is viewed as a complex individual, taking into account all the aspects of his or her life affected by these processes. The term *treatment* usually refers to symptom relief, whereas *rehabilitation* usually refers to overcoming barriers and the pursuit of goals. A modern understanding of PsyR views these as complementary endeavors, although historically medical and rehabilitation professionals have not always seen them as such.

Consider an essential component of the treatment of severe and persistent mental illness—medication compliance. A regimen of psychotropic medication is prescribed by a physician for relief (treatment) of psychotic symptoms. What is the role of rehabilitation in this intervention? On the face of it, one might say it is a simple issue of patient compliance or noncompliance with physician recommendations. Consumers need knowledge and skills to comply with a medication regimen. In addition, they need to monitor their symptoms and side effects to communicate this information to their doctor. This is where rehabilitation can be of assistance to treatment. An individual's ability to monitor and share appropriate information about symptoms, medications, side effects, and so on can be improved through **psychoeducation** (Pratt & Gill, 1990). Explicit training can be implemented to teach or increase these skills, such as instructional curricula developed by various groups, most notably Liberman and his colleagues (1993) at UCLA.

Another important point to consider is that rehabilitation goals may be hampered if treatment efforts are unsuccessful. Conversely, successful treatment should promote rehabilitation goals. Thus, treatment and rehabilitation are complementary and interdependent efforts.

Ongoing, Accessible, Coordinated Services

PsyR services should be unlimited with respect to time (e.g., there should not be a prescribed time length for services). They should be easily accessible and be coordinated to ensure availability and avoid duplication. As discussed in chapter 2 and elsewhere in this book, severe mental illness is not experienced in the same way by everyone. Nor do the resulting service and support needs remain consistent over time. PsyR programs must be designed to accommodate the varied and changing needs of individuals who may require different levels of services during different phases of their illnesses. A clubhouse member may benefit from ongoing involvement with the program even after returning to full-time employment. Such involvement may take the form of a graduate group one evening a week or occasional attendance of clubhouse sponsored recreational activities on the weekends. For many consumers, continuous access to a PsyR program, and practitioners and peers whom they trust, is an essential ingredient for recovery.

Ruth Hughes, executive director of IAPSRS, has pointed out that for many consumers the issue is not membership for life but access for life. This means that "Just as we need to increase services when needed, we also need to facilitate decreasing services and helping people move on when they no longer need us as much" (personal communication, August 31, 1998). Consumers who know that, if needed, they will always be welcome to return will have more courage to explore new opportunities.

Coordination of services is also a crucial aspect of successful community integration. Consumers may be involved with several different PsyR or mental health agencies at the same time or may need to be referred to different service providers as their needs change over time. Case management services (see chapter 8) are one effective strategy for accomplishing this coordination. Consider the problem of service coordination described in the following example:

> Laura is a quiet and somewhat passive young woman who seeks to please both her family and the various practitioners that work with her. She sees a psychiatrist once a month at a community mental health center where she and her family are also involved in a family psychoeducation and support group. Currently, the group facilitator is encouraging Laura and her family to work toward their stated goal of Laura returning to college. Meanwhile, the freestanding clubhouse program that Laura attends three times a week is in the process of placing her in a full-time position through its supported employment program. Laura is ambivalent about her future and is becoming increasingly anxious about working toward conflicting goals.

Clearly the lack of service coordination described in this example can interfere with successful rehabilitation. Even more important, more work needs to be done to help Laura clearly determine what she wants. Such situations usually waste professional resources.

Vocational Focus

Work is an important aspect of life and should be available to everyone who wants it. PsyR practitioners do not question the ability of someone to work but rather assist the individual to acquire the skills, resources, and supports necessary for success. PsyR practitioners know that it is the absence of skills rather than the presence of mental illness that create barriers to successful living.

A good example of this principle is the case study in chapter 7, which covers vocational rehabilitation. Even though Carl had failed repeatedly at his attempts to work, the program continued to support him in pursuing his goal. Rather than focusing on the failures, the job coach focused on Carl's strengths, skills, and interests and explored the supports that might help him to succeed. Maintaining a consistent focus on the vocational goal eventually leads to vocational success.

Skills Training

PsyR services and providers should be capable of helping clients acquire the skills necessary to function successfully in the environments of their choice.

Skills training often encompasses much more than the specific skills one needs to work on a job. We are often unaware of the skills we employ to negotiate everyday situations. Consider the set of skills one must master just to get through a job interview. The effective PsyR practitioner identifies the skills his client needs to succeed and helps him or her acquire them. Role-playing the interview might reveal that the client speaks too softly and does not make eye contact. The practitioner might role-play these skills for the client, teach the skills and then provide opportunities for practice until the practitioner and the client feel the skill is mastered.

Environmental Modifications and Supports

PsyR services and providers help clients access or negotiate the environmental modifications and supports necessary to function successfully in the environments of their choice. Environmental modifications and supports can take many forms. For someone in a wheelchair, providing a ramp into a building is an important modification. For someone with mental illness, a change in working hours to accommodate a public transportation schedule might be a very important modification.

Partnership with the Family

Families are, in many cases, the most important and stable support system for persons with severe mental illness. State-of-the-art psychiatric rehabilitation includes family members as partners whenever possible if it is acceptable to the consumer. Thus, the best PsyR programs will have family members, together with consumers, on advisory and governing boards of directors. At the same time, consumer involvement is promoted among any services offered to families. If a family psychoeducation initiative is offered, the best practice of PsyR requires the inclusion of mental health consumers themselves. PsyR professionals and agencies promote communication with interested family members, with the consent of consumers. For example, family members who inquire about a family member who is receiving PsyR service are often denied information for reasons of confidentiality and lack of a signed release. Best practice in this case means having an appropriate release of information or consent signed prior to a family member asking for information. Given that numerous consumers live with their families, it is critical that family members are engaged as partners in the processes of rehabilitation and recovery. For more information about the role of the family in PsyR, see chapter 11.

Evaluative, Assessment, Outcome-Oriented Focus

To ensure that services are effective, providers must continuously evaluate and assess the outcomes they achieve and the quality of their services on both an individual and a systemwide level. Continued evaluation and assessment is very important, for instance, to identify changes in the needs of the population that programs are designed to serve. These population changes are much more common than might be imagined. Consider the case of the emergence of the mentally ill chemical abuser (MICA) client. Services for MICA clients were not seen as a top priority for the population that went through deinstitutionalization. Long periods of hospitalization may have precluded the possibility of substance abuse for many of these people. After deinstitutionalization, when most persons with major mental illness were in the community, professionals began to become aware of increasing numbers of clients with substance abuse problems. Facilities that employed program evaluation strategies and regularly monitored their outcomes were the first to identify this new need in their treatment population and begin to devise specifically designed services for them.

BOX 4.1
IAPSRS, Core Principles of Psychiatric Rehabilitation

As a first step toward professional certification and licensing, in 1996 the International Association of Psychosocial Rehabilitation Services (IAPSRS) established the national Registry for Psychiatric Rehabilitation Professionals. The registry sets standards and reviews applications from individuals who wish to be nationally registered as PsyR professionals. One of the criteria for registry is an understanding of and adherence to the 12 principles of PsyR which IAPSRS has put forth. As you review these you will see that the IAPSRS principles are really a combination of values, goals, and principles.

1. The ultimate goals of PsyR are recovery, re-establishment of normal roles in the community, development of a personal support network and increased quality of life.
2. All people have the capacity to learn and grow.
3. People have the right to direct their own affairs, including the services they receive, related to their psychiatric disability.
4. All people are to be treated with respect, dignity, and with a conscious and consistent effort to eliminate labeling or discrimination of any type, including discrimination based on disabling conditions.

5. PsyR practitioners recognize and appreciate culture and/or ethnicity as a source of strength and enrichment to the person and the services and [are aware that they] play an important role in a person's recovery.
6. PsyR interventions build on the strengths of each person and facilitate the process of recovery and the re-integration into community life.
7. Services are to be integrated, coordinated, accessible and available as long as needed.
8. All services and assessments are to be designed to address the unique needs of each individual, consistent with the individual's cultural values and norms.
9. Services are normalized, community centered and encompass the whole life of the individual.
10. The PsyR practitioner actively encourages and supports the involvement of the person in normal community activities, such as school and work, throughout the rehabilitation process.
11. The involvement and partnership of persons receiving services and family members are essential to effective operation, evaluation and governance of PsyR services.
12. PsyR practitioners should constantly strive to improve the services which they provide.

CONTROVERSIAL ISSUE
Self-Determination versus Quality of Life

Today, for all practical purposes, deinstitutionalization is an established fact. In addition, in many areas it is relatively rare for any but the most psychiatrically disabled individual to be hospitalized for any length of time. The era of long periods of treatment in psychiatric institutions is clearly at an end, and a period of community treatment is well underway. Nearly all providers of community treatment are in agreement with the goals of deinstitutionalization. The principal of least-restrictive treatment environment is also widely supported. Through the courts, the right of a person not to be hospitalized against one's own will has been greatly strengthened during the past 3 decades. Consumer rights and consumer empowerment are on the increase. These changes appear to support the values, goals, and principles of PsyR that have been presented in this textbook.

In a recent book titled *Out of the Shadows: Confronting America's Mental Illness Crisis*, E. Fuller Torrey (1997) made a strong argument for both maintaining beds in psychiatric hospitals and liberalizing involuntary commitment (the ability to hospitalize someone with severe mental illness against the person's wishes). He began with the fact that persons with severe mental illness frequently need hospitalization, if only for a short time, as part of their treatment. The goal of deinstitutionalization, he went on to argue, tends toward the reduction of too many hospital beds through hospital closing and reduced funding, which in turn keep people in the community when they should be in the hospital. In addition, he believes that the legal profession has gone too far in its campaign to "liberate" psychiatric patients. This effort has resulted in legal policies that dictate that a people can only be hospitalized against their will if they are a clear danger to themselves or others and the right of hospital patients to refuse medication. Torrey pointed out that courts have ruled that living on the street and eating your own feces does not constitute a threat to the individual or others. He quoted a psychiatrist, Donald Trefert, commenting on a case where a judge found that a man was within his rights to refuse psychiatric treatment:

> The liberty to be naked in a padded cell in a county jail, hallucinating and tormented, without treatment that ought to be given is not liberty, it is another form of imprisonment—imprisonment for the crime of being ill. (Torrey, 1997, p. 143)

It would be difficult for anyone to make an argument that, whether right or wrong, Torrey does not have the best interests of persons with severe mental illness in mind. He has dedicated his professional life to their cause, taking many difficult and unpopular stands along the way.

Another Viewpoint

Some advocates for the rights of people with severe mental illness have firsthand experience as psychiatric inpatients. As such, they have been victims of (or witnesses of) atrocities carried out in the name of involuntary psychiatric treatment. Patricia Deegan, a psychologist and activist diagnosed with schizophrenia, described watching a fellow inpatient suffer:

> Quietly I slipped past the mental health worker and looked inside the seclusion room. An old man, probably about 60 or so, with white hair and very thin, was strapped down on a green rubber mattress. Heavy leather cuffs lashed his wrists and ankles to the cold steel of the metal bed frame. He was stripped naked except for his underwear. When I saw that mental health worker sitting in casual comfort outside of the room in which the man was restrained, humiliated and crying out for help, I froze in terror and disbelief. For a moment I could not move. I felt numb. Then I felt a tearing inside my heart. (Deegan, 1990, p. 304)

Deegan has helped to form a campaign against the use of both seclusion and restraint in psychiatric hospitals. Her fellow advocates include people who witnessed similar experiences with involuntary treatment and some who "talked of being stripped naked and being left in their own urine and feces" (Stevens, 1991, p. 20). It is hard to imagine such individuals as being better off than those described by Dr. Torrey.

A basic premise of activists in the ex-patient movement (also called the ex-psychiatric inmate movement) is that much of what the mental health system calls treatment is experienced by service recipients as unwanted control over their lives and in some cases as abuse. Individuals who are suffering from physical illnesses are rarely forced to take medication or remain in a hospital against their will, even despite the fact that a decision not to follow a doctors orders can have serious consequences. Consider the following case:

Jack is a 59-year-old man (with no apparent mental illness) who has been suffering from adult onset diabetes for more than 10 years. One symptom of his disorder is ulcers on his hands and feet, which take many months to heal. His doctor has warned him that if he does not take his medication regularly, alter his dietary habits, and keep regular medical appointments for ongoing wound care, he runs the risk of a gangrenous infection that could result in amputation or death. Jack does not heed his doctor's advice. His wife is extremely concerned and consults the doctor. They both come to the conclusion that there isn't much that can be done, as Jack is an extremely stubborn man who mistrusts the medical profession. Forced treatment, such as commitment to a medical facility, is never considered as an option because Jack has a legal right to refuse treatment. It is very unlikely that a court would assume the parens patriae (parental) role and order medical treatment in the case of an adult not assumed to have a mental illness. A few months later Jack develops a severe enough infection to require amputation of both his legs.

Although involuntary treatment was never considered in Jack's case, people diagnosed with mental disorders are committed by the courts to psychiatric hospitals on a regular basis. According to ex-patient movement activist Judi Chamberlin, this constitutes discrimination. She and other advocates maintain the following perspective:

The basic principle of the [ex-patient] movement is that all laws and practices which induce discrimination toward individuals who have been labelled as mentally ill need to be changed, so that a psychiatric diagnosis has no more impact on a person's citizenship rights and responsibilities than does a diagnosis of diabetes or heart disease. To that end, all commitment laws, forced treatment laws, insanity defenses, and other similar practices should be abolished. (Chamberlin, 1990)

Although we may wish that there was some way to force both an acutely psychotic individual who is living in squalor and Jack to accept treatment, there are some real issues we must grapple with before accepting Dr. Torrey's recommendations. One concern is the kind of help that a psychiatric inpatient is likely to receive, particularly in large state institutions. Another issue is basic civil rights.

Who is right? Has deinstitutionalization and the movement for patients' rights gone too far, as Torrey suggests? Or are individual civil rights paramount in all cases?

Psychiatric Rehabilitation Ethics

A code of ethics is an intellectual framework that is consistent with the principles and values of a profession and that helps us analyze and make decisions when faced with moral choices. All professions (e.g., medicine, law, psychology) follow a specific code of ethics. An important step in the evolution of PsyR from a service-provision approach to a distinct profession was the development and adoption in 1996 of a Code of Ethics for Psychiatric Rehabilitation Practitioners by IAPSRS. The IAPSRS code has five sections, each of which addresses a different aspect of professional practice. They are conduct and comportment, ethical responsibility to people receiving services, ethical responsibility to colleagues, ethical responsibility to the profession, and ethical responsibility to society.

The IAPSRS code of ethics addresses issues that often arise in day-to-day practice, such as client confidentiality, dual relationships with consumers, and a consumer's right to make decisions about the services he or she receives, including the right to refuse services. What a code cannot do, however, is provide definitive answers for all situations that have ethical implications. Sometimes practitioners are faced with difficult ethical dilemmas. For example, relationship boundaries between consumers and PsyR practitioners can be difficult to determine. The IAPSRS code clearly states that it is unethical for a practitioner to have a sexual relationship with a client. It also cautions practitioners not to otherwise exploit their relationships with consumers. So it would be inappropriate for a practitioner who had a side business selling health care products to solicit sales to clients. Otherwise, there is a great deal of controversy in the PsyR field about what are the appropriate limits of relationships between practitioners and consumers. Although practice guidelines call for reduced professional boundaries and staff members are generally encouraged to develop friendly and informal relationships with consumers, some agencies have strict policies forbidding staff members to socialize with consumers outside of the program environment. Other PsyR programs do not discourage the development of outside friendships with consumers, as long as the relationship is in the best interest of the consumer. Thus, in certain social situations PsyR providers have to make difficult decisions. Is it appropriate to take a consumer out to lunch to celebrate a birthday or achievement of a goal? Should one accept a Christmas gift from a client? Is it acceptable to attend a consumer's wedding reception?

Practitioners need to be aware of possible ethical dilemmas in their everyday activities. Familiarity with the IAPSRS code of ethics is a good starting point. First of all, it can help practitioners recognize when they are grappling with an issue that has ethical implications. Second, it assists them in determining whether or not a considered solution is consistent with PsyR standards for ethical behavior. Practitioners also need to be aware of specific agency policies and with state laws that may apply to practice issues such as client confidentiality. Finally, good practitioners who recognize that they are on the horns of an ethical dilemma seek out supervision or team discussion of the situation to reach the best possible solution.

BOX 4.2
IAPSRS Code of Ethics

The following is taken from the code of ethics adopted by IAPSRS in 1996.

Major Ethical Principles

The following principles should guide Psychiatric Rehabilitation Practitioners in their various professional roles, relationships and levels of responsibility in which they function professionally.

Conduct and Comportment

A. Practitioners maintain high standards of personal conduct in their capacity or identity as a Psychiatric Rehabilitation Practitioner.
B. Practitioners strive to be proficient in Psychiatric Rehabilitation and in the performance of service delivery.
C. Practitioners regard as primary the obligation to help individuals achieve their needs and wants.
D. Practitioners promote multi-cultural competence in all places and relationships in the practice of Psychiatric Rehabilitation.

Ethical Responsibility to People Receiving Services

A. The primary responsibility of Practitioners is to persons receiving Psychiatric Rehabilitation Services.
B. Practitioners refrain from entering into dual relationships with persons receiving their services.
C. Practitioners act with integrity in their relationships with colleagues, families, significant others, other organizations, agencies, institutions, referral sources, and other professionals so as to facilitate the contribution of all resources for achieving optimum benefit for persons receiving their services.
D. Practitioners make every effort to support the maximum self-determination of the person served.
E. Practitioners respect the privacy of consumers and hold in confidence all information obtained in the course of professional service.

Ethical Responsibility to Colleagues

A. Practitioners treat colleagues with respect, courtesy, fairness and good faith.

Ethical Responsibility to the Profession

A. Practitioners uphold and advance the mission, ethics and principles of Psychiatric Rehabilitation.
B. Practitioners assist the profession by promoting Psychiatric Rehabilitation services as a primary service modality.
C. Practitioners take responsibility for identifying, developing and fully utilizing knowledge in professional practice.

Ethical Responsibility to Society

A. Psychiatric Rehabilitation Practitioners promote the general welfare of society by promoting the acceptance of persons with mental illness.

Researching the Principles of Psychosocial Rehabilitation

In an important set of studies, Cnaan and colleagues (1988, 1989, 1990) addressed the lack of clarity about the definition of psychosocial rehabilitation (PSR). (Note: PSR and PsyR are different terms for the same practice.) They believed that the lack of agreement on the definition of PSR causes several problems. Lack of a clear definition tends to render the term *psychosocial rehabilitation* meaningless, because anything might be termed or labeled PSR. This all inclusiveness also hinders the development of an agreed on body of knowledge that represents PSR. Finally, because there is little agreement as to what constitutes PSR, there is no way to evaluate a program regarding how well it is carrying out PSR. In response to these issues, the researchers attempted to identify, clarify, and confirm some of the definitional issues surrounding PSR.

In two initial studies (Cnaan et al., 1988, 1989), they identified 15 principles derived from the PSR and PsyR literature. Then, in the most recent study (Cnaan et al., 1990), the research team translated each principle into two or three specific PSR activities or practices. The presence of these practices indicated that the corresponding principle was adhered too. In other words, if an activity was deemed important in a particular PSR setting, the researchers assumed that the principle that the activity represented was supported. From this work a survey instrument composed of activities and practices representing the 15 principles was created. Next, using a Delphi method as described in chapter 1, the researchers identified a large group of PsyR experts from (a) authors of PsyR research literature, (b) the board of directors of IAPSRS, and (c) recent presenters at IAPSRS conferences. Seventy-two of these experts responded to the survey consisting of items about the importance of different activities PSR practitioners perform (that were presumed to relate to the 15 principles). Results from a statistically sophisticated factor-analytic technique revealed support for 13 of the original 15 principles.

In another recent effort, also based on an extensive literature review, Cook and Hoffschmidt (1993) reviewed models (treatment strategies) of psychosocial rehabilitation (PSR). Their review uncovered 11 principles of PSR that are found, in different degrees, in nearly every PSR service.

The Future of PsyR Thought and Practice

It should be clear that some values, goals, and principles were derived from humanistic ideals that seemed right to practitioners at the time. Other ideas where borrowed from more established fields like psychiatry, psychology, and social work. Regardless of where these values, goals, and principles come from, their continued use will be based on (a) their utility as guides to effective rehabilitation and (b) their ability to withstand testing through empirical research and evaluation.

No one should be surprised if some of the concepts put forth in this chapter are modified or even discarded over time. Consider, for example, how attitudes about hospitalization have evolved over time. Before deinstitutionalization a person diagnosed with a major mental illness who experienced continuous psychotic symptoms had a very good chance of spending most of his or her life in a psychiatric institution. With deinstitutionalization the goal was to get people out of the institutions and into the community. This policy was embraced with such a fervor by some workers that one might have suspected that the community itself was a therapeutic agent. Once in the community, the primary goal changed to the prevention of rehospitalization. Many services considered any client who did not require rehospitalization a success. Today, as our understanding of these illnesses has matured, we have adopted the goals of recovery, community integration, and quality of life. In this new conception hospitalization, if it is necessary, is seen as a manifestation of the disease and treated as a minor setback.

Will our attitude toward hospitalization change again? We should not be surprised if it does. Each of these changes reflects a better understanding of persons with mental illness and the conditions themselves. These changes represent progress.

Summary

Psychiatric rehabilitation shares many similarities with physical rehabilitation. The most important advance is PsyR has been the development of a concept of recovery. Recovery in PsyR means that the individual establishes a new self-image that incorporates the fact that the person has a mental illness, not absence of disease. The primary goals of PsyR are to achieve recovery, maximum community integration, and the highest possible quality of life. These goals are supported by values including self-determination, respect for human dignity, optimism, and the belief that all people have the capacity for growth. PsyR goals and values are actualized in practice by following specific guiding principles. IAPSRS, the national professional organization, has established practice guidelines and ethical principles to help guide the field. These goals, values, and guidelines may change as the field advances and new knowledge is created.

Class Exercise

The following vignette describes a situation that has ethical implications. Carefully read the vignette and then consider the questions that follow.

Eric is a 29-year-old man with a history of many psychiatric hospitalizations. He has been referred to a number of PsyR programs in the past, but he has been difficult to engage. Eric's symptoms typically include restlessness, confusion, and paranoia, and although he seems to respond well to antipsychotic medications, he frequently refuses to take them. Following a hospital discharge, Eric returns home to live with his mother and is assigned to an assertive community treatment program in which a team of staff provide services for Eric at his home. Eric is reluctant to talk with the team members when they visit and more often then not, despite pleas from his mother, refuses to take medication. The team decides to implement the following plan: Eric's mother, who is the payee for his monthly disability check, will give him a weekly allowance of spending money if he complies with the following conditions: (a) taking his medication as prescribed twice a day and (b) talking with the team members when they visit. Each time Eric refuses to take a dosage or talk to the staff he will be docked a specific amount of money. The staff's rationale is that coercion is necessary to both prevent exacerbation of symptoms and to establish a relationship with Eric. At first Eric resents the plan, but because he needs money for cigarettes eventually goes along with it.

Questions

1. From the team's point of view, how can its plan help Eric achieve the PsyR goals of recovery, community integration, and a better quality of life?
2. From Eric's point of view, what are the negative implications of the team's plan? Can the plan interfere with the achievement of the PsyR goals?
3. Is the plan consistent with PsyR values such as self-determination?
4. If the answer to Question 3 is no, what type of plan would be helpful to Eric and be more consistent with PsyR values?

References

Anthony, W. A. (1993). Recovery from mental illness: The guiding vision of the mental health service system in the 1990's. *Psychosocial Rehabilitation Journal, 16*(4), 11–23.

Anthony, W. A., Cohen, M. R., & Farkas, M. D. (1990). *Psychiatric rehabilitation.* Boston: Center for Psychiatric Rehabilitation, Boston University.

Anthony, W. A., & Nemec, P. B. (1983). Psychiatric rehabilitation. In A. S. Bellack (Ed.), *The treatment and care of schizophrenia,* New York: Grune & Stratton.

Bond, G. R., Dietzen, L. L., McGrew, J. H., & Miller, L. D. (1995). Accelerating entry into supported employment for persons with severe psychiatric disabilities. *Rehabilitation Psychology, 40*(2), 91–111.

Bond, G. R., & Dincin, J. (1986). Accelerating entry into transitional employment in a psychosocial rehabilitation agency. *Rehabilitation Psychology, 31,* 143–155.

Budson, R. D. (Ed.). (1981). New directions for mental health services: Issues in community residential care (Vol. 11). San Francisco: Jossey-Bass.

Campbell, M. (1981). The three-quarterway house: A step beyond the half-way house toward independent living. *Hospital and Community Psychiatry, 32,* 500–501.

Carling, P. (1995). *Return to community.* New York: Guilford Press.

Chamberlin, J. (1990). The ex-patient movement: Where we've been and where we're going. *Journal of Mind and Behavior, 11,* 323–336.

Cnaan, R. A., Blankertz, L., Messinger, K. W., & Gardner, J. R. (1988). Psychosocial rehabilitation: Towards a definition. *Psychosocial Rehabilitation Journal, 11*(4), 61–77.

Cnaan, R. A., Blankertz, L., Messinger, K. W., & Gardner, J. R. (1989). Psychosocial rehabilitation: Towards a theoretical base. *Psychosocial Rehabilitation Journal, 13*(1), 33–55.

Cnaan, R. A., Blankertz, L., Messinger, K. W., & Gardner, J. R. (1990). Experts assessment of psychosocial rehabilitation principles. *Psychosocial Rehabilitation Journal, 13*(3), 59–73.

Cook, J. A., & Hoffschmidt, S. J. (1993). Comprehensive models of psychosocial rehabilitation. In R. W. Flexer & P. A. Solomon (Eds.), *Psychiatric rehabilitation in practice,* (pp. 81–97). Boston: Andover Medical Publishers.

Deegan, P. E. (1990). Spirit breaking: When the helping professions hurt.*The Humanistic Psychologist, 18*(3), 301–313.

Deegan, P. E. (1988). Recovery: The lived experience of rehabilitation. *Psychosocial Rehabilitation Journal, 11*(4), 11–19.

Fairweather, G. W. (Ed.). (1980). *New directions for mental health services: No. 7.* The Fairweather Lodge: A twenty-five year retrospective. San Francisco: Jossey-Bass.

Gill, K. J., & Pratt, C. W. (1993). Profit sharing in psychiatric rehabilitation: A five-year evaluation. *Psychosocial Rehabilitation Journal, 17*(2), 33–41.

Harding, C. M., & Zahniser, J. H. (1994). Empirical Correction of seven myths about schizophrenia with implications for treatment. *Acta Psychiatrica Scandanavica, 90* (Suppl 384), 140–146.

IAPSRS (1996). *Code of ethics for psychiatric rehabilitation practitioners.* Columbia, Maryland: Author.

IAPSRS (1996). *Core principles of psychiatric rehabilitation.* Columbia, Maryland: Author.

IAPSRS (1998). *The registry for psychiatric rehabilitation practitioners.* Columbia, Maryland: Author.

Liberman, R. P., Wallace, C. J., Blackwell, G., Eckman, T. A., Vaccaro, J. V., & Kuehnel, T. G. (1993). Innovations in skill training for people with serious mental illness: The UCLA social and independent living skills modules. *Innovations & Research, 2*(2), 46–59.

Pratt, C. W., & Gill, K. J. (1990). Sharing research knowledge to empower people who are chronically mentally ill. *Psychosocial Rehabilitation Journal, 13*(3), 75–79.

Rappaport, J. (1987). Terms of empowerment/exemplars of prevention: Toward a theory for community psychology. *American Journal of Community Psychology, 15*(2), 121–144.

Ridgway, P., & Zipple, A. M. (1990). The paradigm shift in residential services: From the linear continuum to supported housing approaches. *Psychosocial Rehabilitation Journal, 13*(4), 11–31.

Stevens, K. (1991, November). The mental health liberation movement. *Sojourner: The Women's Forum, 17,* 20–21.

Torrey, E. F. (1997). *Out of the shadows: Confronting America's mental illness crisis.* New York: John Wiley & Sons.

Warner, R., Taylor, D., Powers, M., & Hyman, J. (1989). Acceptance of the mental illness label by psychotic patients: Effects on functioning. *American Journal of Orthopsychiatry, 59*(3), 398–409.

Wolfensberger, W. (1983). Social role valorization: A proposed new term for the principle of normalization. *Mental Retardation, 21*(6), 235–239.

Chapter 5

Psychiatric Rehabilitation Methods

This chapter outlines the basic strategies involved in the rehabilitation of persons with severe psychiatric conditions. Many of these ideas had their origins in the efforts to rehabilitate persons with physical disabilities because until very recently most professionals did not even consider the possibility of successful psychiatric rehabilitation. The inability to effect a cure and in some cases even arrest the symptoms of the major mental illnesses has been a barrier. The constant presence of the illness and the subsequent emphasis on symptom reduction often relegated the rehabilitation process to a lower priority in the eyes of professionals and sometimes even consumers. Today, as evidenced by the concept of recovery championed by Deegan, Anthony, and many others, there is general acceptance that rehabilitation must begin as soon as possible. There is encouraging evidence that there are numerous social, vocational, emotional, and psychological benefits to the rehabilitation process.

   This chapter will answer the following questions:

1. What elements make up a successful psychiatric rehabilitation intervention?

2. What is the role of the professional in the rehabilitation process?

3. What is the role of the consumer in the rehabilitation process?
4. Can consumers learn skills and can they apply the skills they have learned?
5. What role do environmental supports and modifications play in the rehabilitation process?

Introduction

William Anthony and the staff of the Center for Psychiatric Rehabilitation at Boston University have been at the center of the psychiatric rehabilitation (PsyR) movement in this country for some time. Formulating and field-testing strategies based on the scientific evidence provided by the PsyR literature, this group developed a PsyR technology, a systematic strategy for rehabilitation. In addition, the Center for Psychiatric Rehabilitation has put a great deal of effort into training professionals in its PsyR technology, both at Boston University and through off-campus correspondence courses on a nationwide and international basis. For many reasons, including misunderstandings about how the technique worked, and perceived threats to cherished beliefs and philosophies such as an adherence to psychodynamic principles, its efforts have often been met with resistance. Today, by any objective analysis it must be recognized that the importance of the center's contribution to the successful rehabilitation of persons with severe mental illness has been incalculable. Many others have also made important contributions in this area. For example, Robert Paul Liberman and his colleagues at UCLA have been strong proponents of a skills training approach for some time (Liberman et al., 1985; Liberman, DeRisi, Mueser, 1989). Still, a great deal of this body of knowledge must be directly credited to the work done at Boston University.

A successful rehabilitation process must be preceded by a thorough assessment of the consumer's readiness to participate in rehabilitation activities, his or her skill use, and the environments in which he or she operates or wishes to operate. Next, using the information from this assessment, a rehabilitation plan that outlines and prioritizes specific goals and objectives is formulated. Finally, the specific strategies to accomplish each goal or objective are defined. The Center for Psychiatric Rehabilitation characterizes these steps as the diagnostic phase, the planning phase, and the intervention phase. This chapter will cover each of these phases in more detail.

Consumer Choice

Consumer involvement in each and every aspect of the process is a basic ingredient of any successful rehabilitation. Consumer involvement is essential to ensure that the individual is ready to take action. Unlike a medical problem for which the doctor defines what is wrong and, therefore, what should be done, the rehabilitation process is designed to achieve the goals selected by the consumer. Goals that are set by the staff without real input from the consumer, even if they are made with the very best intentions, are not likely to be motivating. This may even be true in cases in which a staff person selects the same goal the consumer would have if given the chance. Instead, the very act of its selection signifies ownership of a goal and helps to motivate us to work toward its accomplishment.

A lack of involvement in the planning process might also cause problems later on due to incomplete information. For example, a person who likes animals and has some clerical and medical education might not be a good candidate for working in a veterinary hospital if the person is highly allergic to cats.

The most important reason for maximum consumer involvement in the PsyR process may be recovery. As Deegan (1988) described this process, the task for the individual is the creation of a new self-image that incorporates the fact that the person has a mental illness. This topic is covered in chapters 4 and 10. The re-creation of a new self-image demands that the individual be included in every aspect of the PsyR process from setting goals, to determining the time frames for achieving goals, to setting the criteria for success. Recovery, after all, must be the ultimate goal of the PsyR process.

BOX 5.1
William A. Anthony

William Anthony is probably the psychiatric rehabilitation professional with the greatest name recognition. During the more than 31 years he has worked in the field he has received numerous awards including a Distinguished Service Award from the president of the United States (1992) and the Distinguished Service Award from NAMI (the National Alliance for the Mentally Ill), and he has appeared on *Nightline* with Ted Koppel. Dr. Anthony has published more than 100 articles and more than a dozen books on psychiatric rehabilitation. He has been the director of the Center for Psychiatric Rehabilitation at Sargent College of Health and Rehabilitation Sciences since its inception. Dr. Anthony is currently coeditor of the *Psychiatric Rehabilitation Journal*. To paraphrase both Laurie Flynn, the executive director of NAMI and his presidential award:

> *Dr. Anthony's efforts have challenged ideas which have limited the potential of persons with mental illness. The innovative programs created through his leadership offer hope and opportunity by promoting the dignity, equality, independence and employment of people with disabilities.*

Environments of Choice

Unlike a medical evaluation, which assesses a person's overall health, PsyR interventions are targeted toward the consumer's environments of choice. In short, what will enable the consumer to function in the specific environments where he or she chooses to live, work, and socialize. By targeting specific environments, the rehabilitation task is made both more relevant and more manageable. Only the skills and resources necessary for success in the environments of choice are developed. Symptoms or negative behaviors that are not problematic in the environments of choice may not be given high priority. This strategy represents a clear difference from the emphasis of some prevocational training efforts, which were designed to help make the consumer vocationally ready in all areas without regard for the specific needs of a particular job.

An important goal of the PsyR process is to help people to become successful and satisfied in the environments of their choosing. Rather than just focusing on the individual and his or her disability, PsyR includes an assessment of the requirements and characteristics of the environment and may attempt to modify these as part of the overall plan. Such modifications might consist of flex hours, more frequent breaks, more obvious environmental cues, and so on. The importance of environmental assessment and modification was highlighted by the 1990 Americans with Disabilities Act, which calls for "reasonable accommodations" to assist individuals with disabilities on the job. These reasonable accommodations often take the form of environmental modifications or policy adjustments that aid the consumer in performing his or her job.

Psychiatric Rehabilitation Readiness

Psychiatric rehabilitation **readiness** refers to an individual's desire and motivation to pursue some aspect of psychiatric rehabilitation. Without desire or motivation an individual will not act to achieve a goal. Some degree of readiness is, therefore, a necessary element for rehabilitation success. This focus on readiness is in sharp contrast to much of medical and psychological practice. When a treatment is seen as superior for a particular condition, it is often prescribed without offering the patient any alternatives, because in the doctor's view there are no real alternatives. In the case of psychiatric rehabilitation, the success of the process depends on the readiness of the individual to work toward the rehabilitation goals.

Rehabilitation is essentially carried out through a partnership between the individual and psychiatric rehabilitation professional. As several theorists have pointed out "a service (psychiatric rehabilitation) that must be done *with* a person never *to* a person" (Cohen & Mynks, 1993). Working together is one of the hallmarks of psychiatric rehabilitation.

Why would a person not want to pursue goals of his or her own choosing in order to improve one's situation in life? Several possible factors may impede psychiatric rehabilitation readiness. As is often the case, when several of these negative factors are combined in one individual, the probability of psychiatric rehabilitation readiness is very low.

Many candidates for psychiatric rehabilitation have experienced numerous and repeated failures in their attempts to improve their lot. These failures may come about because of relapses, lack of necessary skills, inadequate environmental supports, ineffective training, poor planning, and from setting goals inappropriate to the individual. Individuals often experience several of these problems at once, particularly if they are working with poorly trained or overworked PsyR staff. After several failures in a row, it might seem smarter to avoid getting one's hopes up and just to accept one's lot in life. For these persons positive change may not seem to be a real possibility. In short, they may lack the confidence necessary to participate in rehabilitation.

Some individuals become so habituated to the role of psychiatric patient that they do not want to change roles. Whether they are fearful of change or just stuck in their ways, these individuals would rather stay in their present situations than work for change.

An important factor working against psychiatric rehabilitation readiness for many persons is their lack of knowledge about themselves, about their environment, and about the supports that are available. As an example, when looking for a career most people typically do not know enough about their own likes and dislikes, about the kinds of jobs that might be available, and about the kinds of skills that are required for various jobs. For example, how many of your friends know about PsyR, the kinds of skills required, and what a PsyR professional would do all day? If the typical person lacks this vocational and self-knowledge, consider someone who has been coping with a major mental illness all her or his adult life. A lack of knowledge of who we are and what is possible can narrow our choices and reduce our motivation.

Readiness Assessment

Several researchers (Cohen, Farkas, & Cohen, 1992; Cohen & Forbess, 1992; Cohen & Mynks, 1993) have stressed that one of the first steps in the psychiatric rehabilitation process should be a **readiness assessment**. The goal of a readiness assessment is to evaluate the individual's readiness for entering a psychiatric rehabilitation process that has a good chance of success. If the individual is not ready for such a process, the researchers recommend that services be targeted toward improving or developing the person's readiness for rehabilitation. These readiness activities, such as exploring goals, values, and family expectations, would be targeted at the kinds of problems mentioned earlier.

Cohen, Farkas, and Cohen (1992) recommended that a readiness assessment should look at five distinct factors:

- *Need for change.* This asks the question, how motivated is the individual for change or, conversely, how dissatisfied is the individual with his or her current situation? This may also involve environmental issues such as how successful he or she is in the environment and whether or not the environment is forcing a change (e.g., being evicted from an apartment).
- *Commitment for change.* This assesses the person's belief that change is (a) necessary, (b) positive, (c) possible, and (d) will be supported. Can the person see him or herself making the change or will someone else or the circumstances have to change?
- *Environmental awareness.* This assesses the persons knowledge, including previous experiences, about the environments in which she or he plans to operate.
- *Self-awareness.* This assesses the individual's knowledge about herself or himself. For example, his or her likes and dislikes or personal values.
- *Closeness to practitioner.* This evaluates the relationship with the PsyR professional on dimensions such as trust.

A person with high scores on each of these five dimensions is considered ready for rehabilitation and, more important, has a very good chance of success. If, on the other hand, a person has low scores on one or more of these dimensions, services need to be targeted toward improving those areas.

Rehabilitation Diagnosis

The **rehabilitation diagnosis** is based on the consumer's choice of the environments in which he or she wishes to function. Identifying an **overall rehabilitation goal** and conducting both a **functional assessment** and a **resource assessment** are all part of the rehabilitation diagnosis. The first step in the diagnosis process is setting the overall rehabilitation goal. One aspect of setting this goal is looking at the range of choices within the environment. For example, a person may consider several different housing arrangements (single apartment, shared apartment, group home, etc.) for a living environment. The requirements for each of these housing choices is then compared to the person's resources and characteristics. Once the possible options are determined, the individual's needs and preferences are considered in making the final choice of the goal. This goal-setting process is designed to increase the chances of success and to ensure satisfaction once the goal is achieved. This process can by synthesized into three stages: (a) developing decision-making skills, (b) determining the requirements of the environment, and (c) determining what the individual needs to be successful in the environment. Once these factors are determined the matches between the environment and the individual will be evident and an appropriate goal can be set. It is important to remember that the goal is based on the individual's preferences, not on the individual's skills.

Once a goal has been established, the PsyR worker and the consumer need to determine the skills and resources that the consumer will need to be successful and satisfied. These skills need to be described in behavioral terms, which allow for an objective evaluation of how well the consumer performs them and the necessary level of performance for success on the job or in the environment. Once the skills and behaviors required for a certain environment or job are listed, an assessment of the consumer can take place.

The diagnostic process can be carried out in several ways. Most typically it is carried out through individual meetings between the PsyR worker and the consumer. Some programs employ group meetings in which several consumers work together with a staff person or a team of PsyR professionals to arrive at rehabilitation goals and assessments. When outside funding organizations such as the state vocational rehabilitation agency are involved, consumers may be referred for standardized skill and interest testing. These tests, which are usually expensive to administer and score, can provide detailed profiles of a consumer's basic areas of interest, skills, and skill deficits. Some of these tests employ task simulation strategies to evaluate skills such as dexterity, following directions, and problem solving. For example, a consumer who has expressed interest in studying to become an electrician might be given the tools, material, and instructions to build an electric circuit. His or her ability to follow directions, use the tools properly, and finish the task in a timely manner would be assessed. Although these tests are designed to achieve a clear assessment of a person's skills and abilities, they are hampered by the fact that they are not carried out in the actual job setting. Their principle advantage is that they can produce a fairly systematic and objective evaluation of specific skills.

Functional Assessment

At this stage the PsyR professional and the consumer can determine which skills and behaviors constitute either strengths or weaknesses for each environment of choice—in short, how well the consumer is functioning with respect to his or her environments of choice. Strengths obviously are tasks that the consumer does well, meaning at or above the required level. Weaknesses are areas that need improvement or development. Because it is often more important to reinforce strengths than to emphasize weaknesses, the PsyR practitioner should focus first on the consumer's strengths.

Areas where the consumer's performance does not match the required level are identified for further assessment and future intervention. For example, Jane, who is the receptionist at her PsyR day program, wants to be a receptionist in a law office. To be successful she needs to take clear messages listing who the call was for, the caller's name, the time of the call, and the message. A review of her work as the program receptionist indicates that of the twenty or so messages Jane takes on her 2-hour shift, one or two omit some of the needed information. For her new job Jane will have to be able to take messages without omitting the required information.

You may have noticed that before we can help Jane correct these messages, we need to determine why she is omitting information. It could be, for example, that Jane has a slight hearing problem. Or it may be that Jane is distracted by either having to field several calls at once or by other people speaking to her when she is trying to record a message. Whatever the case, Jane's message taking won't be improved unless the problem can be clearly identified.

Resource Assessment

The availability of resources that can help the consumer achieve his or her goals must also be assessed. These resources, such as transportation, housing assistance, or special training, might relate either to a specific environment such as a job situation or to the needs of the individual. For example, its not uncommon because of scheduling constraints for a consumer to have to change his or her case manager, therapist, or psychiatrist when the individual gets a job. Such a resource adjustment should be planned for in advance to ensure that it does not cause unnecessary problems for the consumer. The goal of the resource assessment is to identify resource strengths, deficits, or problems so that they can be dealt with in the rehabilitation plan.

Rehabilitation Plan

The **rehabilitation plan** sets forth the skill and resource goals and objectives that consumers must achieve to operate in the environments they choose. An important aspect of the rehabilitation plan is that the consumer prioritizes these goals and objectives. Obviously, some skills need to be acquired before other skills. For example, someone who wants to do word processing should acquire some ability at keyboarding before learning the intricacies of a word processing program. Another important aspect of this prioritization process is how it is experienced by the consumer. All of us like and need to experience some success regarding our efforts. For persons that have gone through many previous failures, starting with the most difficult or longest tasks first might not be the best strategy. Instead, it might be more motivating to start with a task that can provide some success in the short term and build up to the more difficult tasks. Unlike more traditional therapies, decisions about this kind of motivational issue is the responsibility of the PsyR professional and consumer working as a team.

The rehabilitation plan is essentially an integration of (a) the decisions the consumer has made about what environments he or she wish to operate in, (b) the functional and resource assessments, and (c) knowledge about the consumer and the best path to take to achieve his or her goals.

Rehabilitation Interventions

The **rehabilitation interventions** are the specific strategies for acquiring needed skills, behaviors, and resources. This is the information that is usually recorded in an individual service plan or treatment plan. As such, these interventions need to be specific, objective, **quantifiable**, and time delineated. In short, it needs to be very clear to everyone concerned, particularly the consumer. When behaviors and goals are described in quantifiable ways they can be easily interpreted. For example, Jane may be maintaining a rate of 85% accuracy per week taking messages at the program. A goal might be that Jane will improve her accuracy to a rate of 95% per week. By giving the goal a time frame, say 2 months, Jane and her PsyR worker will be able to objectively evaluate her progress.

The Case of Paul (continued from chapter 1)

We first met Paul in chapter 1. The following aspect of Paul's case covers his attendance at a program and his efforts, with the aid of his counselor Ruth, to achieve his goals. As you read the following case, look for the strategies that Ruth uses to help Paul move toward recovery.

Paul was nervous about what to expect on his first day at the program. After getting a short tour of the program from one of the members, he was directed to his counselor, Ruth. Ruth invited Paul to have a seat and then chose a seat for herself across from him rather than behind her desk. "You know, Paul, you and I have some important and exciting work to do. We have to figure out what you want your life to look like, what your goals are, and how to reach those goals. But before we get started on that, I wonder if you have some questions or concerns? I know the first day here can be confusing."

The Case of Paul Continued

Paul was reluctant at first to ask questions but Ruth encouraged him to be honest with her, so he talked about the people who looked like they'd been at the program forever, about schizophrenia, and about his terrible experience at college. Finally, Paul said "I can't believe my life is over. I don't want to come here for the rest of my life."

"Good," said Ruth, "then lets talk about where you do want to be." During the meetings that followed, Paul and Ruth talked about all areas of his life. Paul decided that he was happy living with his parents for now. They got along okay, and he couldn't afford to pay rent anyway. They seemed happy to have him there even though they worried a lot about him and he wished they wouldn't. His social life was dismal. He'd pretty much alienated everyone he knew when he was "getting sick." Most important to Paul, though, was that he'd dropped out of school. His first love was still anthropology. He couldn't imagine doing any other kind of work. Ruth and Paul agreed that going back to school was the area to start with.

Paul felt hopeful and scared at the same time. His goal of graduating with a degree in anthropology had seemed out of reach a few months ago. Paul wondered if he was kidding himself. He imagined his professors seeing him back in class after he'd failed the first time and remembered the hurtful things he'd said to his friends. But Paul trusted Ruth. When he told her about these concerns she didn't dismiss them or accept them as evidence that he couldn't go to school. Instead she talked about making sure Paul had the supports and resources he would need to succeed in this goal.

Paul and Ruth listed the critical skills for him to reach this goal. Naturally, he'd have to meet all the requirements of the courses. This was of some concern to Paul because both his concentration and stamina were diminished because of the illness and the medication. He'd have to get some kind of transportation to school because he wouldn't be living on campus this time, and he'd have to learn to manage the symptoms he was still experiencing: hearing voices and feeling withdrawn.

With Ruth's encouragement, Paul contacted the registrar at the college he'd been attending. He found out that he'd withdrawn from some classes and failed others. In any case, he'd have to start over. He decided to take one course and he and Ruth agreed it should be Introduction to Anthropology because this was his interest and he'd be more likely to do well. There was one month until the start of the next semester. During this time, Ruth taught Paul how to use the public transportation system. To practice, Paul took the bus to the school a few times to help him feel less anxious about the trip. A few weeks before the course started, Paul contacted the professor and got permission to audiotape the class lectures. This way he could listen to the tapes to help organize his notes. He also got the reading assignments for the semester to help him plan his study schedule. He knew that his problems concentrating meant he'd have to start early because he'd need lots of breaks.

Ruth helped Paul set up a schedule that included study time, relaxation time, and meetings with her for support and problem solving. Paul's parents were skeptical about his plan to return to school. They were convinced that the stress of school is what had "pushed

The Case of Paul Continued

him over the edge." However, with Ruth's help, Paul was able to tell them how important school was for him and how important their support would be to his success. Paul's parents agreed to support his plan as long as they could figure out what to do if Paul got sick again. Paul, his parents, and Ruth made a list of things that would indicate that he was experiencing another episode of his illness and the things people could do to help.

Paul and Ruth had a meeting scheduled the day the midterm grades were posted. Paul arrived looking worried. "You look like your grade wasn't what you'd hoped for," Ruth offered.

Paul looked surprised. "Oh, no," he chuckled, "I got a B! It's just that, well, some of the guys in my class invited me out to sort of celebrate, you know. It means I'd have to cut our meeting short."

"Go!" Ruth laughed. "Go and have fun! I'll see you next week. Call me if anything comes up before then. Oh, and by the way, Paul, good work!"

Skill Acquisition and Development

As you can see from Paul's case, a skill is the ability to successfully perform a behavior at a certain level, in a specific context. Acquiring and developing skills refer to teaching and refining specific behaviors so that they can be performed both correctly and frequently enough for success in the individual's environment of choice (Nemec, McNamara, & Walsh, 1992).

Effective skills teaching is much more involved than the kinds of didactic lectures that high school and college students usually experience. This is particularly true when persons have been discouraged by repeated failures or when they have to simultaneously cope with other issues such as psychiatric symptoms.

Skills Training and Direct Skills Teaching

The two major proponents for a skills training approach to PsyR have been the Center for Psychiatric Rehabilitation at Boston University led by William Anthony and the Clinical Research Center for Schizophrenia and Psychiatric Rehabilitation at the University of California at Los Angeles led by Robert Paul Liberman. The UCLA group has simply titled its strategy **skills training**. Liberman's group has put a great deal of effort into the development of modules for teaching specific skills, for example, medication maintenance. The researchers at the Center for Psychiatric Rehabilitation call the technology they devised for teaching skills **direct skills teaching** (DST). The term *technology* conveys the importance this group places on the systematic application of the DST method.

Nemec, McNamara, and Walsh (1992) created an informative table to illustrate the subtle differences between skills training and direct skill teaching. The similarities should be

TABLE 5.1
Skills Training versus Direct Skills Teaching

	Skills Training	Direct Skills Teaching
Purpose	Skills development	Skill development
Foundation	Learning theory, behavior therapy	Education, teaching as treatment
Components	Assessment—determination of skill deficits in a targeted area (e.g., social skills)	Assessment—determination of skill performance requirements of client's performance in relation to environmental requirements
	Acquisition—person can perform target behaviors	Acquisition—person can perform the skill as needed
	Generalization—person can perform target behaviors in the natural environment	Generalization—person can perform the skill as needed in his or her preferred environment
	Maintenance—person can continue to perform target behaviors over time	Maintenance—person can continue to perform skills as needed over time
	Impact—the new skill plays a meaningful role in improving the person's life	Impact—the new skill increases the person's success and satisfaction in his or her preferred environment
Techniques	Instructions—specific directions or requests to elicit behavior	Orient person to process Tell—comprehensive explanations and descriptions of skill performance
	Modeling—demonstrated performance of skill and competent behaviors	Show—demonstrations of performance of skill and competent behaviors
	Role play—practice of skill	Do—practice of competent behaviors and performance
	Feedback—strengths and weaknesses of performance presented with encouragement and reinforcement	Critique—interactive discussion about strengths and weaknesses of skill performance, with encouragement and reinforcement
	Homework—assigned practice with feedback and reinforcement	Skill programming—identification of barriers to successful skill performance, of action steps, and of self-rewards to use to eliminate barriers to skill performance

From Nemec, McNamara, & Walsh, 1992, pp. 15–16. Reprinted with permission.

apparent as you review the comparison between the two strategies presented in Table 5.1. Keep in mind that this table was formulated by researchers from the Boston University (DST) group.

Role Modeling

One of the most important and most common ways people learn is through role modeling. All of us have used role modeling at one time or another to shape our behaviors. Consider a time when you were entering a new environment, say a new school, a new club, or some

---

BOX 5.2
Social Learning Theory

Albert Bandura (1977) formulated a social learning paradigm that defines the five learning steps an individual goes through when effectively acquiring a new skill. These steps are very similar to the strategy adapted for skills training by both the Boston University (DST) and UCLA (skills training) rehabilitation research centers. As you review the following steps notice how each one builds on the previous step so that the skill or behavior is approached gradually.

1. *Instruction.* This is the didactic part of the process (you get the bus on the corner of Main and 2nd Streets; you need to have the exact change; etc.).

2. *Modeling.* Here the consumer watches the instructor perform the skill (e.g., the instructor takes the bus with the consumer, demonstrating how it is done and essentially taking care of everything).
3. *Role playing.* Here the consumer role-plays the situation and skill in question (the consumer role plays getting on the bus, paying the fare, etc.).
4. *Behavioral rehearsal.* Here the consumer actually carries out the skill (e.g., The consumer takes the bus, with the instructor present or not).
5. *In-vivo practice.* Here the consumer practices doing the skill in the real situation (e.g., the consumer uses the bus on a regular basis for practice).

---

other place where you were not exactly sure how to behave, dress, speak, and so on. Your probable response to this situation was to observe others to see how they were acting, how they dressed, and who they spoke with. After observing for a time, you probably began to feel more confident about how to behave in the new environment. You could model your behavior on the behavior you had observed. You can see how several of the steps in Bandura's learning theory (Box 5.2) utilize role modeling.

Role modeling is also part of the reason that many PsyR professionals attempt to reduce obvious differences between themselves and consumers or members. It is easiest to role-model if we perceive that the people we are modeling our own behavior on are like ourselves. It is unlikely that a consumer in a PsyR program would model his or her behavior on a staff person wearing a name tag and an expensive suit who keeps his professional distance. It is more likely that a staff person who eats lunch with the consumers, pitches in on some of the chores, and attends some of the social events will be seen as a good role model.

A Client-Centered Approach

Client-centered therapy, introduced by Carl Rogers in the 1940s, was a substantial departure from the traditional psychoanalytic therapies. Sometimes called nondirective therapy, client-centered therapy proposed that the role of the therapist was not to direct or instruct the client based on the therapist's theoretical beliefs but to assist the client in understanding his or her own experience of the world and promote positive change through a trustworthy relationship (Brammer, Shostrom, & Abrego, 1989; Krech, Crutchfield, & Livson, 1969). To accomplish this the therapist has to hold the client in positive regard. In other words the therapist has to respect the client and empathize with him or her.

The basic tenets of client-centered therapy are highly compatible with psychiatric rehabilitation and have had an important influence on the field. Client-centered therapy is based on the belief that people will engage in activities leading to positive growth and development if given the opportunity (Krech et al., 1969). This belief is consistent with the PsyR value of optimism or hope. The practitioner believes that everyone has the potential for growth. Client-centered therapy asserts that the opportunity for growth exists within relationships that offer empathy, positive regard, and genuineness (Brammer et al., 1989). In PsyR we know that the quality of the client-practitioner relationship is crucial to recovery and rehabilitation. Here, too, the relationship is an egalitarian one, based on empathy, positive regard, and acceptance.

Client-centered therapy focuses on the client's perception of his or her present circumstances and assists the client in identifying his or her own answers to problems or barriers (Brammer et al., 1989). A major strategy in client-centered therapy is reflecting back to the client the feelings, thoughts, and behaviors the client has communicated to the therapist but may not be fully aware of. Psychiatric rehabilitation also focuses on the here and now and uses active listening and reflection to assist clients in understanding their experiences.

Finally, client-centered therapy places the major responsibility for successful change on the client (Krech et al., 1969). PsyR practitioners recognize the value of self-determination in achieving personal life goals. The work of counseling psychologist Robert Carkuff (1987), author of *The Art of Helping*, has been a great help to many PsyR professionals. Carkuff's writings reduce the helping process into comprehensible steps that the practitioner can easily understand.

Behavioral Strategies

One of the basic ways to teach skills is through the application of behavioral strategies. Popularized by B. F. Skinner, **behaviorism** has often been accused of being an essentially inhuman or insensitive approach to education. In reality, some form of behaviorism underlies almost every teaching strategy or style.

A basic principle of behaviorism is to encourage behaviors by reinforcing them and to extinguish behaviors by not rewarding them or punishing them. We accomplish this by using either positive or negative rewards or positive or negative punishments. In this case, think of positive or negative as adding something or taking something away, respectively, the same way you think of positive (something added) or negative (something lost or taken away) symptoms of schizophrenia. Behavior can be encouraged using positive rewards. For example, a teacher might say, "If you complete this project, you will receive a higher grade." A behavior can also be reinforced using negative rewards. For example, a teacher might say, "If you complete this project, you will not have to take the final exam." A positive punishment means that something negative is added: "If you do not do well on this test, you will have to write an additional paper." A negative punishment means that something positive is taken away: "If you do not do well on this test, you will not be allowed to go on the class trip."

This theme of reward and punishment is a common element in education. One point that behaviorists stress is that reward is almost always preferable to punishment. Even though both strategies may be equally effective at either encouraging or extinguishing a particular behavior, the use of punishment often causes unwanted negative effects. People do not like to be punished and often feel resentment toward the person or source of their punishment. This resentment often expresses itself in other negative behaviors that can cause unexpected problems.

Rewards are more important when they are granted correctly. You may have noticed that you are less interested in playing a game when you know you will always win. When games are difficult to conquer, we consider them a challenge and work harder for the reward of winning.

Rewards are very important in the context of rehabilitation. When staff members are uneducated about the importance of rewards they often give rewards too freely in an effort to encourage their client or to be liked. When a reward (e.g., praise) is given too freely, or at times when criticism is more appropriate, it loses its value. Rewards need to be given out after careful evaluation to ensure that they are timely and appropriate. People feel rewards are meaningful when they believe they represent real achievement. When handled carefully, providing rewards can be an important form of communication about a person's progress and can reinforce positive behavior.

Skill Generalization and Skill Maintenance

Skill generalization and skill maintenance are two important factors that need to be considered for any successful rehabilitation plan. Skill generalization refers to the fact that behavior (or skill performance) is situation specific. In simple terms, just because a person can perform a skill in one environment does not mean that the person can or will perform the same skill in a different environment. This problem has been one of the main drawbacks to the prevocational training strategy practiced for so long by PsyR services trying to get people back into the workforce. Individuals who demonstrated successful acquisition of prevocational skills (proper grooming, punctuality, attention to detail, etc.) at a PsyR program often did not maintain these skills when they started regular employment. This failure to generalize skills to other environments appears to be a common human failure rather than a characteristic of individuals with mental illness. More recent strategies for vocational rehabilitation that have taken this factor into account, most notably supported employment (which will be discussed in chapter 7), have demonstrated much higher rates of successful job placement.

Skill maintenance is another important consideration for successful rehabilitation. You have probably noticed that when you do not perform a complex or difficult task for some time your performance level goes down. You might have experienced this if you used to be a fast typist, a chess player, a golfer, or if you performed any task in which higher levels of practice and experience have a direct effect on performance. The common saying describing this effect is "use it or lose it." For the individual going through rehabilitation, it is just as important to maintain skills that the person already has as it is to acquire new ones. Persons attending PsyR programs that mainly focused on therapy, recreation, and prevocational skills—instead of work skills and practice—often had fewer skills when leaving the program than they had when they entered.

The PsyR principle of emphasizing strengths rather than deficits helps to identify and highlight the skills consumers possess. An awareness that these skills must be reinforced through regular practice will help to ensure that they are not lost. Lastly, most people take pride in the things they do well. Maintaining skills as a source of pride for individuals is an important element in the rehabilitation process. The fact that a person can do some things very well gives one confidence that, with some time and effort, she or he can do other things well.

Principles of Skill Development

Cohen, Ridley, and Cohen (1985, as cited in Anthony, Cohen, & Farkas, 1990) formulated 11 principles that should be considered in the development of skill intervention strategies. Notice how these suggested principles incorporate the ideas behind Bandura's social learning theory as well as behavioral strategies. In addition, Anthony, Cohen, and Farkas (1992) pointed out that the application of these principles may increase the individual's ability to generalize learned skills to new environments.

1. Use the natural reinforcers present in the relevant environment to reward appropriate responses in the training environment.
2. Provide support services to the client in the relevant environment.
3. Teach support persons to use the skill of awarding selective rewards in the relevant environment.
4. Teach the client to identify intrinsic motivation (enjoying the task) as a replacement for extrinsic reward (pay or benefits).
5. Increase the delay of reward gradually.
6. Teach skill performance in a variety of situations.
7. Teach variations of skill use in the same situation.
8. Teach self-evaluation and self-reward.
9. Teach the rules or principles that underlie the skill.
10. Use gradually more difficult homework assignments.
11. Involve the client in setting goals and selecting intervention strategies.

Resource Development

One important area of the rehabilitation process is resource development or acquisition. Resources might be thought of as any person or thing that can help one to achieve goals or be successful in environments of choice. A basic example of resources are public entitlements that provide one with financial assistance to meet living expenses. A PsyR practitioner might assist someone in applying for Social Security benefits, rental assistance, a prescription plan to purchase medications at reduced rates, or any number of other financial programs. A resource might also be an item that improves someone's ability to function in a particular setting, such as a bus schedule or a watch that can be set to beep when it is time to take medication. Sometimes resources are people. A job coach who provides work support, a peer counselor at a drop-in center, or a friend who provides transportation to the program might all be considered resources.

In the rehabilitation planning process, the client and the PsyR practitioner will identify any needed resources. In some cases, a client may choose to access a resource instead of developing a skill if the individual is unable to develop that skill or doing so would take too long. For example, instead of learning the skills of job acquisition, someone might rely on a job coach to make contact with potential employers. After identifying needed resources, the client and practitioner will assess whether or not the resources are currently available and articulate a plan to acquire those that are not.

Environmental Modifications

Another important set of elements in rehabilitation are modifications to the environments in which the consumer wants to operate. Environmental modifications share some similarities with resource development, because they can include supports such as the presence of a job coach. In the workplace, environmental modifications might include assistance such as the job coach, changes in policy that make allowances for the medical needs of consumers, and communication with supervisors and coworkers so that they have a clear understanding about mental illness.

Since passage of the Americans with Disabilities Act (ADA) in 1990, reasonable environmental modifications are the law. Some of the more visible results of this law are handicapped parking spaces, cutouts on curbs, and building ramps for wheelchairs. ADA will be explained in more detail in the chapter on vocational rehabilitation.

CONTROVERSIAL ISSUE
Independence, Dependence, or Interdependence

Independence versus dependence has been an issue in PsyR since deinstitutionalization. Because of their disabilities, many persons with severe mental illness require ongoing support to reside comfortably in the community. As demonstrated by the effectiveness of case management programs (described in chapter 8), without effective supports many individuals would be hospitalized more often and for longer periods of time. At the same time, efforts to achieve community integration, self-determination, and

empowerment suggest that independence is an important goal for the individual. Recovery itself is based on the individual determining what he or she wants in life, which cannot happen without a degree of independence.

Anthony, Cohen, and Farkas (1990) dealt with the issue of independence versus dependence in their formulation of PsyR principles. One principle states:

———————————————

The deliberate increase in client dependency can lead to an eventual increase in the client's independent functioning.

———————————————

On the first read this may seem like a contradiction. This is the same contradiction that has troubled the PsyR community for years. Further consideration reveals that for a client to gain the benefits of rehabilitation he or she must be willing to go through the process. Hence, the client must follow the lead of (be somewhat dependent on) the rehabilitation worker in order to achieve the eventual goal of acquiring independence.

In one way, this conception of independence versus dependence may be too simplistic. Who among us is truly independent? In fact, although we all achieve degrees of independence, we all have some areas of dependence. We may be dependent on a spouse or loved one, an institution like a school or a job, or anything else in our life that we rely on. At the same time, these people and institutions may be depen-dent on us. In fact, the issue is more correctly defined as one of interdependence—that is, being simultane-ously dependent on others while they are dependent on us. This balance, which is both normalizing and empowering, is often absent in the lives of people with disabilities. To complicate matters further, our degree of interdependency with elements in our en-vironment may go through constant changes. Con-sider the parents who want to protect their child and help her to grow up and be self-reliant. Or the couple who want to support each other in their different ca-reers while being dependent on one another. The real goal seems to be much more complicated than sim-ply achieving independence. Instead, we must learn to be simultaneously comfortable with a degree of de-pendence and comfortable with a degree of indepen-dence.

Evaluating Rehabilitation Progress

An important step in the process of rehabilitation service planning is the periodic evaluation of progress toward rehabilitation goals and objectives. Typically PsyR service providers evaluate the progress of their clients about every 3 months, although the length of the time period between evaluations often varies quite a bit depending on agency policy and the individual needs of a particular client.

Evaluating whether goals are achieved is a much simpler task when the goals are ob-jective, time framed, and easily measured. For example, a client's goal may be to improve punctuality. As it stands, this goal is rather nebulous and it would be difficult to evaluate the client's progress. This goal can be made specific and measurable by stating it this way: The client will arrive at the PsyR program location at 9:30 A.M., five times a week. In a program where the arrival time of clients is logged, it is easy to keep track of progress toward this goal. More important, the evaluation results would be unequivocal. When all the goals and objectives specified on an individual's rehabilitation plan are written in an easily measurable form, determining whether or not progress has been made can be an easy task.

If a practitioner and client have determined that progress has been made toward a goal, the progress should be acknowledged in a positive way. Once a goal is achieved, a new goal may be specified. However, if progress has not been made or is too slow, the crucial task is to determine why. Sometimes practitioners do not ask this question and instead assume that more time is needed to work toward the existing goal. Although this may be the case, one should not jump to such a conclusion until the practitioner and client have thoroughly explored possible reasons for lack of progress. It may be that the basis for a particular deficit was not clarified to begin with. For example, a practitioner could assume that the reason a client often arrives late to program is because he is not used to taking responsibility for being someplace on time. The actual reason could be that the client does not own an alarm clock. When practitioners make inaccurate assumptions about the cause of a problem it is very unlikely that the intervention they devise to solve the problem will be successful. In the above mentioned example, the practitioner's original intervention might have been to give the client positive reinforcement. This might consist of praising the client each time he arrived on time and rewarding him with a cup of coffee at the end of the week if his punctuality showed improvement. However, if the root of the problem is actually the lack of an alarm clock, positive reinforcement may have no discernable effect. The appropriate intervention is helping the client purchase an alarm clock, which happens to be a good example of resource acquisition.

A lack of progress is often very frustrating for the client as well as the staff. Sometimes it is difficult to determine why progress is not being made. There are several reasons why a client might be unmotivated to achieve a goal. The client may feel that the goal is not really what he or she wants. It may be that the client has lost interest in working toward a particular goal. Or it could be that although the client wants to achieve the goal, he or she is not ready to work on it. This last issue relates to the section on rehabilitation readiness presented earlier in the chapter.

Staff members need to be very thoughtful and empathic when progress is eluding a client. Too many staff members automatically associate lack of progress with lack of motivation and then fail to productively address the motivation/readiness issue. Frustrated practitioners tend to place blame on the client and think, if she only would try harder she could do it. The reality is often that practitioners need to make a greater effort to gain a clearer understanding of their client's situation. In some cases, the answer may be to abandon an unrealized goal and return to the initial stage of the service planning process: helping the client to choose a rehabilitation goal that is consistent with his or her hopes and dreams (and rehabilitation readiness).

Summary

Rehabilitation methodology begins with consumer choice. The first task of the PsyR worker is often to help a client understand what her or his choices are and how to make decisions that will satisfy the client. Before rehabilitation takes place, a consumer's readiness to begin a rehabilitation process can be assessed. Increasing rehabilitation readiness can be an important first step for someone who lacks the confidence to work toward a goal. Once a goal has been established, the PsyR worker helps the client evaluate the skills that will be required, the environmental supports that will be required, and the resources that can be made available. This approach provides the greatest chance for success. This is in contrast to strategies that focus on a client's deficits without regard for the specific skills needed for success in a specific environment. Instead, only those skills required for success in the environments that the client chooses to operate in are addressed. Skill teaching and modification can be achieved through a number of strategies including role modeling, direct skills teaching, and behavioral techniques. The basic philosophy used by the PsyR professional is a client-centered approach that respects the consumer.

Class Exercise

This exercise is designed to give you some familiarity with the PsyR service planning process. You will begin by doing a mock functional assessment, and then you will chose critical skills on which to focus. Finally, you will identify appropriate PsyR interventions aimed at the achievement of an overall rehabilitation goal.

Read the following, and then answer the questions posed.

Anne is a 27-year-old woman who has a severe mental illness. She has spent much of the last 8 years in and out of psychiatric hospitals. In between hospitalizations, Anne had lived with her parents. However, the last time she was discharged she was placed in a boarding home, where she now resides. Although Anne is currently stable and doing well in her part-time job as a receptionist in a dentist's office, she is unhappy with her living situation. She would like to move to her own apartment.

Anne shares her desire to live independently with Bill, her PsyR practitioner. Bill assists her in the process of researching local housing opportunities that are affordable for Anne. They have determined that even with her monthly social security check and the salary from her part-time job, it will be difficult for Anne to afford a one bedroom apartment. However, they are able to place her on a waiting list for a federally subsidized housing complex. A few months later Anne gets a call. An efficiency apartment will become available in 3 months! Anne is both excited and apprehensive, as she is not sure she is prepared to live successfully on her own. She is particularly concerned about money, as she has very limited experience with managing her own finances. She is also unfamiliar with the location of the apartment complex. She has grown comfortable with the neighborhood her boarding home is in, in part because she can catch a bus on the corner that takes her to her job and the mental health center.

Anne sits down with Bill to plan for the move. They begin by writing an overall rehabilitation goal: "Anne will move into an efficiency apartment at the Cedar Hill Apartments in May 1999." Their next steps are to complete a functional assessment of Anne's independent living skills, to choose critical skills to begin working on and to determine strategies for helping Anne acquire the skills and resources she will need.

Question 1

From the following list of "independent living skills," determine which skills are critical to Anne's success in her new apartment. It may be helpful to think about what skills you actually use if you live independently. However, keep in mind that some of these skills may be necessary for some people to be successful and satisfied in their own home but are not necessarily critical to Anne's success. Be prepared to discuss the rationale for your choices with the class.

Independent Living Skills

- Creating a monthly budget
- Paying bills
- Maintaining a bank account
- Applying for Social Security/other entitlement programs
- Maintaining entitlements
- Shopping for food
- Shopping for clothing and household items
- Preparing meals
- Maintaining a healthy diet
- Cleaning bathrooms
- Cleaning kitchen appliances
- Vacuuming and mopping floors
- Using the telephone
- Using public transportation
- Driving a car
- Maintaining a car
- Taking medication
- Starting a conversation with neighbors
- Forming and maintaining friendships with neighbors
- Structuring leisure time

Question 2

Keeping in mind that Anne may already be proficient in some of the critical skills you have chosen, identify the two skills that you think are most important to begin work on. Provide a clear rationale for your choices.

Question 3

What specific strategies would you use to help Anne to develop the two skills you identified?

References

Anthony, W. A., Cohen, M. R., & Farkas, M. D. (1990). *Psychiatric rehabilitation*. Boston, MA: Center for Psychiatric Rehabilitation.

Bandura, A. (1977). *Social learning theory*. Englewood Cliffs, NJ: Prentice Hall.

Brammer, L. M., Shostrom, E. L., & Abrego, P. J. (1989). *Therapeutic psychology: Fundamentals of counseling and psychotherapy* (5th ed.). Englewood Cliffs, NJ: Prentice Hall.

Carkuff, R. R. (1993). *The Art of helping VI*. Amherst, MA: Human Resource Development Press.

Cohen, M. R., Farkas, M. D., & Cohen, B. (1992). *Training technology: Assessing readiness for rehabilitation*. Boston: Center for Psychiatric Rehabilitation.

Cohen, M. & Forbess, R. (1992). *Training technology: Developing readiness for rehabilitation*. Boston, MA: Center for Psychiatric Rehabilitation.

Cohen, M. R., & Mynks, D. (1993). *Compendium of activities for assessing and developing readiness for rehabilitation services*. Boston: Center for Psychiatric Rehabilitation.

Deegan, P. E. (1988). Recovery: The lived experience of rehabilitation. *Psychosocial Rehabilitation Journal, 11*(4), 11–19.

Krech, D., Crutchfield, R. S., & Livson, N. (1969). *Elements of psychology* (2nd ed.). New York: Knopf.

Liberman, R. P., DeRisi, W. J., & Mueser, K. T. (1989). *Social skills training for psychiatric patients*. Elmsford, NY: Pergamon Press.

Liberman, R. P., Massell, H. K., Mosk, M., & Wong, S. E. (1985). Social skills training for chronic mental patients. *Hospital and Community Psychiatry, 36*, 396–403.

Nemec, P. B., McNamara, S., & Walsh, D. (1992). Direct skills teaching. *Psychosocial Rehabilitation Journal, 16*(1), 13–25.

Part III

Applications of Psychiatric Rehabilitation Principle and Methodology

Chapter 6

Psychiatric Rehabilitation Day Programming

Much of the development of psychiatric rehabilitation has taken place in community-based settings where groups of consumers gather during the day for friendship, support, recreation, rehabilitation, and treatment. These settings are most effective when their environments are designed to promote recovery for their clients. This chapter explores the historical roots of these programs. Starting from two distinctly different program types, each emphasizing different philosophies, characteristics, and program elements, the chapter traces their eventual synthesis into today's state-of-the-art psychiatric rehabilitation day program. Finally, the chapter examines how these programs may be designed and operated to help facilitate specific rehabilitation outcomes.

This chapter will answer the following questions:

1. What is psychiatric rehabilitation day programming?
2. When did day programming begin and how did it develop?

3. What are the common elements that make up a day program?
4. What is milieu therapy and how does it work?
5. How can programs be designed to produce specific outcomes?

Introduction

Psychiatric rehabilitation day programs are based on the premise that an environment can be created that will contribute to the rehabilitation and recovery of persons with severe mental illness. This type of setting is not meant to be an institution or a residence. Rather, people attend the program several times per week and engage in a variety of activities.

These programs have their roots in at least three separate philosophies or movements, which will be described in this chapter: the clubhouse movement, partial hospitalization, and milieu therapy. Within the community mental health field, these three program types are peceived as being quite different. For example, traditional therapy is a common element in many partial hospital programs. Clubhouses, on the other hand, are not viewed as treatment programs and do not perform therapy. Milieu therapy represents a treatment style or philosophy rather than a specific program model. In a sense, milieu therapy is what happens during the program, and both the clubhouse and partial hospitalization movements are based on principles of milieu therapy. Despite these differences, each of these movements shares the belief that by working together, people can help each other promote rehabilitation and recovery.

The **clubhouse** movement began in the 1940s and 50s as a natural human response to the needs and wants of ex-psychiatric patients living in communities around the country. Facing stigma, rejection, unemployment, and poverty, these individuals began to band together for mutual support and comradeship. As these groups became established, they became recognized community support networks for persons with mental illness. This chapter will describe the development of Fountain House in New York City, one of the first clubhouses in the country. From that modest beginning, what is today a worldwide network of clubhouses was established. The ex-patients attending these programs are known as members rather than patients and have a real say in how the clubhouse is operated. In turn, clubhouses are very responsive to the needs of their members.

As the deinstitutionalization movement grew in the late 1960s and 1970s, the treatment of many persons with severe and persistent mental illness began shifting to community mental health center (CMHC) programs called partial hospitals. The partial hospital label reflects these programs' initial similarity to inpatient psychiatric hospitals. At a typical partial hospitalization program, groups of patients received various types of service, such as group and recreation therapy, socialization, medication monitoring, and activities of daily living skills training.

At their inception, both of these community-based psychiatric rehabilitation program models represented important treatment innovations for persons with severe and persistent mental illness. Much of the growth of psychiatric rehabilitation (PsyR) from the late 1960s until today has taken place in these settings. This chapter covers the history and development of these day programs.

The Origins of Day Programming in the United States

Today's state-of-the-art day treatment program combines elements from two distinct and very different treatment elements and philosophies: the clubhouse movement and the partial hospitalization movement. The clubhouse movement started as a grassroots movement. With extensive support from private charities, ex-hospital patients in several major cities around the nation developed clubhouses as everyday places to congregate for social support, recreation, and to address community living needs and problems. Partial hospitalization programs were part of a large, federally funded program. Initiated by the federal government, numerous partial hospitalization programs were developed as elements of community mental health centers. These essentially medical model programs typically provided deinstitutionalized consumers with therapeutic and medication monitoring services from Monday through Friday. As it turns out, both the clubhouse movement and the partial hospitalization movement had a great deal to offer persons with severe mental illness.

The Development of Clubhouse Programs

During the late 1940s a group of ex-patients from Rockland Psychiatric Center in New York state formed a support group that met on the steps of the New York City Public

Library in Manhattan. The support group members called themselves WANA (We Are Not Alone). A private social welfare group, the National Council of Jewish Women, became aware of the WANA group and began supporting their cause. In 1948, with the help of Elizabeth Schermerhorn, a building on West 47th Street in New York City was purchased as a clubhouse for WANA (Dincin, 1975; Flannery & Glickman, 1996; Propst, 1992a). Because it had a small fountain in the backyard, the group named it Fountain House. Fountain House, initially staffed and operated solely by its members and volunteers, was designed to provide social supports and serve as a meeting place for ex-patients. People who joined Fountain House were called members rather than patients and, like a club, they could remain members for as long as they wished.

As Fountain House grew, the members decided to hire a professional, nonconsumer staff to operate the program. The first professional, nonconsumer mental health staff members were recruited in 1955. Even with the addition of professionally trained staff, Fountain House retained its clubhouse atmosphere and philosophy. After trying out several directors with unsatisfactory results, a social worker named John Beard was hired. Beard helped to change Fountain House from what was essentially a social club into a truly comprehensive psychiatric rehabilitation facility that became the model for the clubhouse movement in the United States.

The National Council of Jewish Women played a major role in the development of the clubhouse movement and psychiatric rehabilitation nationwide. During the 1950s this philanthropic group focused its attention on the plight of ex-mental patients. Capitalizing on the success of its efforts at Fountain House, the group supported and encouraged the development of clubhouse model programs nationwide, including Thresholds (Chicago, Illinois), Hill House (Cleveland, Ohio), Council House (Pittsburgh, Pennsylvania), and Bridge Haven (Louisville, Kentucky) (Dincin, 1975).

As awareness of the benefits of clubhouses grew, other centers were developed around the country, including Horizon House (Philadelphia, Pennsylvania), Fellowship House (Miami, Florida), Center Club (Boston, Massachusetts), and the Social Rehabilitation Center (Fairfax, Virginia), to name but a few. Most importantly, using a strategy similar to the mythical Johnny Appleseed, Fountain House and programs like it vigorously trained their staff members and then sent them out to develop new clubhouses around the country (Propst, 1992; Vorspan, 1992). Today, literally hundreds of clubhouse programs can trace their roots back to either Fountain House or one of the other early clubhouse programs.

The clubhouse existed and still exists primarily to improve the quality of life of its members, and that is what is emphasized. Clubhouses began as places where ex-hospital patients could gather to socialize and to give and receive support. As such, nothing designated as treatment took place there. Members were accepted without regard to their symptoms and did not have to "improve" in order to continue their member status. This emphasis on quality of life led to an emphasis on members basic needs: housing, work, socialization, and recreation. Length of stay, the time an individual is in a program, is a good example of the difference in how a clubhouse operates compared to a partial hospitalization program. Clubhouse members can stay as long as they like regardless of their clinical state; they are considered members for life. By contrast, many partial hospitalization programs have prescribed lengths of stay and clients are discharged if their clinical state improves.

Probably the most important difference between clubhouses and the partial hospitalization programs developed through the CMHC initiative is their emphasis on work (Jackson, 1992; Vorspan, 1992). Clubhouse philosophy stresses the importance of work for providing a sense of meaning in life and a sense of belonging to a community. Performing meaningful work endows the worker with purpose and meaning. For clubhouse members, work begins with the day-to-day operation of the clubhouse itself, from custodial tasks and record keeping to paying bills and hiring new staff. The clubhouse emphasis on work leads to several other important outcomes, such as member empowerment and the development of a sense of self-efficacy and self-esteem. Clubhouse members and staff emphasize many ways that their programs differ from other types of psychiatric rehabilitation services. The following section about clubhouse standards highlights some of the most important ideas behind these programs and some of the ideas that make them different.

BOX 6.2
John H. Beard

John Beard was the father of the worldwide clubhouse movement. Beard, who earned his master's degree in social work from Wayne State University in Detroit, Michigan, had worked at Wayne County General Hospital in Michigan as a social worker. In 1955, Elizabeth Schermerhorn and the board of directors of Fountain House hired Beard as their executive director. He led Fountain House until his death in 1982.

Beard focused on the members' strengths rather than on their illnesses. An excerpt from a video made in 1978 captures his attitude about working with members.

> I had no interest in why he was sick. That was not my job . . . I wasn't interested in trying to review his . . . psychopathology. I had no interest in it at all. I was terribly interested in how normal we might get him to function. (Flannery & Glickman, 1996, p. 28)

Almost single-handedly at first, Beard's vision and efforts were the guiding force behind the creation of the clubhouse movement. Today there are over 300 clubhouses worldwide and the number is growing. Each of these programs is, in some small way, a symbol of Beard's caring and efforts. In 1982 he recieved the Extraordinary Service Award for Exceptional Commitment and Dedication in Serving the Mentally Ill of New York. The award reads as follows:

> His leadership has provided:
> Dignity where there was shame,
> Belonging where there was alienation,
> Empowerment where there was helpessness,
> Self-respect where there was self-denigration,
> Hope and opportunity where once there was only despair.

Clubhouse Standards

In 1988 the Robert Wood Johnson Foundation, Pew Charitable Trusts, and the Public Welfare Foundation funded the National Clubhouse Expansion Program (NCEP). One of the tasks of the NCEP was the development of standards for clubhouse programs. Starting in 1989, the staff of the NCEP and a group designated the Faculty for Clubhouse Development made up of 50 members and staff from clubhouse programs around the country set out to involve the entire clubhouse community in the development of standards (Propst, 1992a).

This group identified 35 standards that should be adhered to by programs considering themselves to be clubhouses (Propst, 1992b). The following are a select group of standards, which outline some of the aspects of clubhouses that set them apart from the more traditional psychiatric day programs.

Some Selected Standards for Clubhouse Programs

Program standards can tell us a great deal about the places they describe. As you read the following standards for clubhouse programs, imagine what such a place would feel like. You might also consider how these policies might be received in a highly professional, formalized environment such as a hospital. More importantly, consider what attitudes about psychiatric treatment and rehabilitation are reflected by these standards. Finally, although most clubhouses reject the notion of therapy, decide whether you think the clubhouse can be a therapeutic environment for its members.

Membership
- Membership is voluntary and without time limits.
- Members choose the way they utilize the clubhouse and the staff with whom they work. There are no agreements, behavioral contracts, schedules, or rules intended to enforce participation of members.
- Members, at their choice, are involved in the writing of all records reflecting their participation in the clubhouse. All such records are to be signed by both member and staff.

Relationships
- All clubhouse meetings are open to both members and staff. There are no formal member-only meetings or formal staff-only meetings where program decisions and member issues are discussed.
- Clubhouse staff members have generalist roles. All program staff members share employment, housing, evenings and weekends, and unit responsibilities. Clubhouse staff members do not divide their time between the clubhouse and other responsibilities.

Space
- All clubhouse space is member and staff accessible. There are no staff-only or member-only spaces.

Work-Ordered Day

- The work-ordered day engages members and staff together, side by side, in the running of the clubhouse. The clubhouse focuses on members' strengths, talents, and abilities: therefore, the work-ordered day is inconsistent with medication clinics, day treatment, or therapy programs within the clubhouse.
- All work in the clubhouse is designed to help members regain self-worth, purpose, and confidence; it is not intended to be job-specific training.

Employment

- The clubhouse enables its members to return to the normal work world through **transitional employment** and independent employment; therefore, the clubhouse does not provide employment to members through in-house businesses, segregated clubhouse enterprises, or sheltered workshops.

The Case of Jill R., Affinity House Member

A great deal goes on each day in a typical day program. As you read about Jill R.'s day consider how she carries out her role as a program member and the apparent role of the staff. Is attending the program having a positive effect on Jill? Would she be better off returning to college? Far from being obvious, these kinds of questions trouble PsyR practitioners every day. What is the right plan for someone like Jill? Is the day program the right place for her at this stage?

Jill R., 27 years old, has been a member of Affinity House for 7 months. Diagnosed with schizophrenia at 17, Jill has been in and out of the hospital numerous times, all the while trying to earn a college degree in English and journalism. Two years ago, still a sophomore, she was hospitalized again for 6 months. While Jill was getting ready for discharge, a liaison worker suggested that she might try Affinity House because at the hospital she would be discharged in the middle of the spring semester and could not return to school until the fall semester some 7 months away. Affinity House would be different. While still in the hospital, Jill made a visit to Affinity House and because it seemed like a warm place with friendly people she decided to give it a try.

Today, Jill is the assistant supervisor of the clerical unit and is mainly responsible for putting out the weekly Affinity House newsletter All Things Considered. The members and staff at Affinity House were really excited when Jill told them about her studies in journalism. Even though Jill hadn't always been able to complete her courses, she had learned a great deal about creating effective newsletters. Now she had the chance to put her knowledge to good use. Helping improve the newsletter was exciting and fun. She found that her ideas were well received and really made a difference in the quality of the publication, which over the weeks grew better and better.

The hardest part of this job for Jill was that as more and more of her ideas were put into practice she became the one responsible for supervising other members working on the newsletter. This responsibility was something she had not experienced before or been

The Case of Jill R., Affinity House Member Continued

trained for. The clerical unit supervisor, Emil (also a member of Affinity House), and the staff assigned to the unit were important sources of support for Jill in her new role as supervisor. Jill found it difficult to supervise people, mainly because her first impulse was not to say anything that would upset anyone. She wanted to be liked, but she also took great pride in the newsletter. She spent some time every week speaking to Emil or a staff member about how to motivate her workers or how, when someone had made a mistake, she could correct the person but be supportive and encouraging at the same time. After several months of supervising the newsletter, Jill was gaining some confidence in her ability to supervise and be a leader.

The first scheduled event at Affinity House each morning is the unit meeting which starts at 9:30 sharp. Unit members meet to plan the tasks of the day, see how other unit members and staff are doing, and evaluate how things are going. Unit meetings are also the time when new members who might be trying out the unit as part of their orientation are introduced. When a new member is introduced, Jill always remembers how nervous she was when she first came to the clerical unit for her orientation. Today a new member named Bob was introduced to everyone. Jill suggested that Bob might work with her on the initial layout of the next newsletter.

At 10:00 the unit work begins. Most unit members are clear about the tasks they have to perform, and Jill and Emil spend most of their time supervising the members and helping out when problems arise. Staff members are usually present and either working on clerical projects or doing case management with members. With the members preparing the newsletter, writing outreach letters, and preparing mailings, the unit generally has a very busy, productive feeling in the morning.

Lunch, prepared by members in the food service unit, is usually from 12:00 to 12:30. Jill often eats with other members from her unit or with a staff person who she had met several years ago in one of her classes in college. After lunch several of the members and staff go outside to smoke.

In the afternoon, in addition to the unit work, there are meetings to attend concerning both program operations and things of interest to members. Jill attends a 2 P.M. vocational readiness meeting. This meeting is designed to orient members who are planning to get a supported employment position. Members learn about supported employment, share some of their past experiences at work, talk about what kind of jobs they would like, and find out about jobs that may be available. Jill has only attended this meeting once in the last 2 weeks, so she is still getting to know the members and working up her courage to really talk about her concerns about work. Her work in the unit has built up her confidence in her ability to hold down a regular job. During the meeting a staff person invites anyone who is interested to attend that evenings supported employment (SE) support group. The SE support group is for members who are out working in the community. The staff person believes that attending this group will give everyone a better idea of the issues they will face when they get a supported employment job. Jill isn't sure if she wants to attend the evening group. She is still debating whether she should return to college or try to work, and the idea of going to the group feels too much like she is ruling out college.

> **The Case of Jill R., Affinity House Member Continued**
>
> Back in the unit, Jill sees that Bob, the new member on orientation, has left early and has not finished cutting out some of the illustrations that must be pasted into the next newsletter. Jill enlists another unit member, Herb, and they finish the task together. Other members report that Bob said he was going out for a cigarette but didn't return.
>
> At 3:30 the day is over and members head out to their rides or the van. Jill has made sure the computers are turned off and the supplies locked up for the night. Jill decides not to attend the SE support group this evening. It's her favorite TV night and she's tired. Maybe she will attend next month.

Partial Hospitalization

It is ironic that the first published reports on the principal treatment strategy employed for the massive deinstitutionalization of persons in the United States came from Stalinist Russia (Dzhagarov, 1937). During the early 1930s, after a revolution followed by a bitter civil war, there were too few psychiatric beds in Moscow to meet the demand. Out of necessity, Dzhagarov, the director of a psychiatric hospital, had some of the patients attend the hospital during the day but return to their own homes at night. Dzhagarov reported that his "half hospital" served more than 1200 patients and achieved results equivalent to those produced by full-time hospitalization. Necessity, often the mother of invention, led to an important innovation in psychiatric treatment and rehabilitation.

Shortly after World War II, similar programs emerged in Canada (Cameron, 1947, 1956) and the United Kingdom (Bierer, 1948). Cameron, who established a program at the Allen Memorial Institute of Psychiatry in Montreal in 1946, is generally credited with introducing the term *day hospital* to describe this emerging treatment modality (Luber, 1979). In the United States, programs were reported at the Yale University Clinic and the Menninger Clinic as early as 1948. Many of these early programs were organized from a **psychoanalytic** perspective, emphasizing individual and group therapy as well as expressive therapies such as dance and art. These pre-deinstitutionalization programs provided services to patients who were generally less symptomatic and less disabled than those relegated to continued institutionalization. Possibly, these "healthier" patients were deemed more appropriate for an insight-oriented therapeutic approach.

By 1963, according to a National Institute of Mental Health (NIMH) report, there were 168 operating day treatment programs in the United States (Taube, 1973). With the passage of the 1963 Community Mental Health Construction Act, the number of programs grew by over 700% in 10 years. By 1973 there were 1280 programs in operation treating approximately 186,000 patients. This phenomenal growth helped make community treatment available to thousands of deinstitutionalized patients. At the same time, the meteoric development of this new treatment modality presented some very real challenges and problems. No one was completely sure how these programs should operate, who should staff them, or what kinds of services they should offer the patients. Because there was no clear definition of what a day hospital or day treatment program was, many programs began formulating their own strategies for the community treatment of persons with severe and persistent mental illness.

The Development of Partial Hospitalization Programs

The Community Mental Health Centers Construction Act (PL 88-164), passed in 1963, designated partial hospitalization as one of the five essential service modalities each CMHC must provide to be eligible for funding. The requirement that each CMHC must offer partial hospitalization was responsible for the tremendous increase in the number of these services around the country described earlier. The partial hospital programs were intended to be the main community-based treatment element for persons deinstitutionalized from state psychiatric hospitals.

This initiative represented a major change in policy regarding responsibility for persons with major mental illness. Up to that time the states were responsible for providing treatment for this population. With this act, the federal government began providing the states with some of the resources required to move the treatment of persons with severe mental illness from state hospitals into the community. This initiative was also supported on the federal level with the passage of Medicaid and Medicare, which helped to pay for the services for a large proportion of this population.

To foster the continued development of CMHCs around the country, despite limited resources, the centers were placed on 8-year funding cycles. The plan was that with the help of Medicaid, Medicare, and other sources of funds, these centers would learn to become financially self-sufficient. During the first 2 years of their existence, CMHCs were federally funded at 100% of their cost for providing services. From the third year to the eighth year their funding was reduced, and by the ninth year when they would receive nothing. The money that was saved as funding was reduced was earmarked for the funding of new CMHCs in identified areas of need around the country. This highly logical funding plan only worked for a time. The cost of the war in Vietnam, combined with rising medical costs, helped to scuttle the plan financially. In the CMHCs themselves, many staff and administrators focused their efforts on their higher-functioning clients. In these centers people with severe mental illness were either ignored or assigned to poorly funded treatment programs operated by staff with little or no training. In short, in many centers the mission of treating people with severe mental illness was abandoned in favor of working with higher-functioning clients.

These partial hospitalization programs were (and still are) essentially medical model programs. In order to bill Medicaid, Medicare, or other sources, program clients had to have a psychiatric diagnosis (ICD or DSM) conferred by a licensed psychiatrist. By government regulation, psychiatrists also had to supervise or prescribe many of the treatments provided. Medication, medication monitoring, group, individual, and expressive therapies were emphasized, as well as recreation and socialization.

Milieu Therapy

Day programs were largely based on a treatment strategy for providing services called milieu therapy. *Milieu*, a French term which literally means *environment*, refers in this case to the physical, social, and cultural setting of the program. **Milieu therapy** is a technique based on the idea that every aspect of a treatment setting or environment can be used to help achieve therapeutic or rehabilitation goals or results. Milieu therapy is a very powerful tool for shaping behavior, encouraging self-awareness, and increasing self-confidence. In everyday terms, milieu therapy uses phenomena like peer pressure, social support, public recognition, and social mores to help improve a participants' social functioning, self-confidence, and ability to check their perceptions of reality (reality check). Some examples of the implementation of milieu therapy strategies are structuring a day around work tasks, community meetings, and skills training; ensuring that the physical environment is comfortable, inviting, and clean; and planning a recreational event that will encourage high levels of participation and interaction between people. Each of these tasks helps to shape the environment in order to make it conducive to achieving the goals of the individuals receiving services.

- *Milieu therapy.* The use of the whole physical, social, and cultural environment in the therapeutic process. In milieu therapy the environment is the essential treatment component.

Milieu therapy had its roots in inpatient treatment, where all aspects of the patient's life were under the control of treatment professionals. For persons with disorienting conditions (e.g., psychosis), varied aspects of their surroundings and environmental cues can be very important. We have all experienced these environmental effects. Messy, hectic environments accompanied by loud noise tend to make people either anxious or withdrawn. Peaceful, calm environments accompanied by soft music tend to make people relaxed. For persons with severe mental illness, attention to all aspects of the milieu is critical because these effects can be greatly magnified.

Gunderson (1978) described five basic elements of successful treatment that were helped by milieu therapy: containment, support, structure, involvement, and validation. As you review these terms, consider what it might feel like if each of these elements were absent. Then consider how important it is to an individual's sense of well-being to help restore these elements:

- *Containment.* A sense of being controlled by the environment.
- *Support.* A sense of being supported or affirmed by the environment.
- *Structure.* An ordered environment, where who, what, and where are predictable.
- *Involvement.* Participation and belonging to the social environment.
- *Validation.* Affirmation of the individual in the environment.

The benefits of these therapeutic effects for persons with severe mental illness were first observed in inpatient settings, but they are equally beneficial and important for persons in the community programs where milieu strategies are employed.

Washburn and Conrad (1979) suggested that a sixth important treatment element of milieu therapy is negotiation. Negotiation refers to the process a consumer goes through with treatment staff to determine treatment goals and plans. As PsyR has developed, so has the emphasis on client choice and involvement, making negotiation a very important skill for the consumer. Numerous other benefits of milieu therapy have also been suggested by practitioners and researchers. Today there is general agreement among professionals that milieu therapy can be a powerful tool for reducing anxiety, improving self-awareness, and shaping and maintaining behavior.

Components of a PsyR Day Program

The following are general components or characteristics of almost any PsyR day program: members, clients, or patients, staff, space, program ingredients, and scheduling. By understanding these you will understand the core elements that make up these programs. As you read their descriptions, notice that there is room for a good deal of variability within each component, characteristic, or element. This variability and the lack of universally agreed on principles of PsyR have helped create a situation in which its seems that no two programs are truly alike. Many professionals regard the idiosyncratic nature of day treatment programs as a major strength. These different program types are seen as the laboratories where new PsyR strategies are developed and refined. Others point out that program differences create nearly insurmountable problems for program evaluation and research. If no two programs are alike, how can we determine which are superior or even which program elements are effective?

Clients or Members

- Clients or members of a program should be diagnosed with a severe and persistent mental illness that warrants participation in such a program. This relates to the mental health principle of least-restrictive setting. This principle states that all consumers of mental health services should be treated in the least-restrictive setting that can provide effective services for them. For example, clients should not be hospitalized if they are not a danger to themselves or others and they can receive comparable treatment in the community.
- Clients or members of a program should have a history of either long or repeated hospitalization or have repeatedly failed to function in the community without substantial structure or support. This also relates to the principle of least-restrictive treatment setting. Clients who function well in the community should not be referred to such a program in most cases, despite symptoms or diagnoses.
- Clients or members of a program should not be a danger to themselves or others. Persons judged to be a danger to themselves or others are usually more appropriate for a hospital setting where their behavior can be closely monitored.
- Clients or members of a program should be able to tolerate the milieu. The milieu of a PsyR day program, no matter how it is designed, can be a stressful place for some people.

For such people the amount of stress generated by the milieu may offset any gains that the program has to offer.

Staff

* *Director.* The program director sets both the administrative and philosophical tone for the program. The specific tasks of the director may typically include supervising the daily operations of the program, setting the program design, supervising the staff, and recruiting staff members. Program directors usually have years of experience in PsyR and at least a master's degree in an appropriate field, such as psychiatric rehabilitation, social work, psychology, or a related human service field.

* *Supervisory level staff.* These staff members typically are responsible for specific program staff, program elements (vocational units, intake, etc.), or client caseloads. These staff members often hold master's degrees in an appropriate field (psychiatric rehabilitation, social work, psychology, etc.). Supervisory-level staff may also be direct service workers such as case managers, team leaders, clinical supervisors, or unit leaders. These staff members may also function as administrators responsible for elements of the program, such as intake or hospital liaison.

* *Counselors, case managers.* These workers, sometimes referred to as line staff, spend most of their time working directly with consumers. Their academic training may range from a high school education to a master's degree. These workers typically make up staff teams supervised by more experienced staff.

* *Mental health aides or paraprofessionals.* These workers typically have little relevant education or experience in the field. There are numerous tasks that aides can carry out effectively in the milieu. These staff members often work in prevocational units, help out with activities, drive vans, and conduct outreach, to name just some of their roles.

* *Auxiliary and support staff.* A number of other staff members are critical for the operation of a successful PsyR program. Auxiliary staff often include medical staff such as psychiatrists and nurses, specialized therapists such as art and dance therapists, and other specialized professionals such as vocational counselors, job developers, and residential counselors. Support staff include roles such as secretary, file room clerk, and accountants.

Space

The program should have enough square footage to allow staff and members to function in groups and carry out different kinds of activities. It is usually necessary for there to be at least one space big enough for the entire program to meet. The program area should be safe and clean. It should be well lighted, have proper ventilation (including heating and cooling), and have the necessary equipment and furnishings to carry out designated functions. There should also be appropriate auxiliary facilities such as toilets, washrooms, and kitchens. Most important, the program should be located in a safe, **normalized** environment and have reasonably easy access by public transportation. A program located on the locked ward of a hospital, for example, would not be in a normalized environment, even if the clients returned home every afternoon.

Program Ingredients

Program ingredients refer to the kinds of activities that take place during the program day. Typical program ingredients are recreation; socialization; skills training including social skills, activities of daily living, prevocational, and vocational; education including basic remedial education and symptoms, illness and medication education; medication monitoring; case management; and vocational services such as transitional employment or supported employment. Sadly, despite years of progress, programs still exist where one might observe clients doing simple arts and crafts or playing BINGO when they are not in individual or group therapy. Better programs have a rational mix of skills training, vocational activities, support, and recreation depending on the individual needs of the program members. These programs also conduct periodic or ongoing needs assessments to ensure that their efforts are in line with the needs of their clients.

Scheduling

Scheduling refers to issues such as what time the program opens, when activities take place, and whether members have to be on time. Programs frequently have evening hours for recreation, graduates, or clients who work. What happens during the hours the program is operating is a matter of scheduling clients and staff. Scheduling may reflect a regular work environment or the looseness of a social club. A program's scheduling should be in line with its philosophy, goals, and ingredients. For example, a program designed to help its clients enter the work world should maintain a regular worklike schedule and have strict rules about arriving on time, absences, and so on. Last, how schedules are set and who sets them can be an important **empowerment** issue.

The schedule in Figure 6.1 attempts to capture the broad scope of services provided by Prospect House, a PsyR Program in East Orange, New Jersey. Many Prospect House members spend their time working in units such as Food Service, Member Services, or Clerical/Research. A schedule for the Clerical/Research Unit appears in Figure 6.2. Note the variety of special groups offered, and that activities are regularly offered two evenings a week and on Saturdays.

Evaluating PsyR Day Programs

A PsyR Day Program Taxonomy

Several researchers have suggested that partial hospitalization programs and PsyR programs in general are most effective when they are designed to produce a specific outcome for a particular type of client (Astrachan, Flynn, Geller, & Harvey, 1970; Neffinger, 1981). For example, if a program's primary purpose is to help its clients return to regular community

Name: _____   **Date:** _____

TIME	MON	TUE	WED	THU	FRI	SAT
8:00 AM						
8:30 AM	←		Breakfast (Optional)		→	
9:00 AM	←		Unit Meetings		→	
9:30 AM	←	Fresh Start (MICA Members Only) →				→
	←	Unit Activities →				
10:00 AM	Unit Activities (Cont'd.) ← →		Clubhouse Committee	Voice of Prospect House	Unit Activities (Cont'd.)	
10:30 AM	← Coffee Break		↓	↓	→	SOCIAL
11:00 AM	MICA Education		Member Reps. Meeting		MICA Relapse Prevention	(OPTIONAL)
11:30 AM	← ↓		Unit Activities		↓ →	10:00 AM
12:00 PM	←		Lunch		→	TO
12:30 PM	←		Community Meeting		→	4:00 PM
1:00 PM	Continuing Education		Unit Activities (Cont'd.)			
1:30 PM	↓	←	→			
2:00 PM	Case Mgmt.	← Unit Activities →			Unit Activities s	
2:30 PM	↓			Case Mgmt.		
3:00-7:00 PM			Social (Optional)		Social (Optional)	

Assigned Unit: _____   **Days in Program:** _____

SPECIAL GROUPS:

☐ MICA	☐ Continuing Education	☐ Member Reps	☐ Voice of PH
☐ TE	☐ Coping Groups	☐ Fresh Start	☐ Clubhouse Committee
☐ SE	☐ Other	☐ Clerical Research	☐ Food Services
☐ House Services	☐ Member Services	☐ Seniors	

FIGURE 6.1

CLERICAL/RESEARCH UNIT SCHEDULE

MONDAY	TUESDAY	WEDNESDAY	THURSDAY	FRIDAY
9:00-9:30 MORNING MEETING	*9:00-9:30* MORNING MEETING	*9:00-9:30* MORNING MEETING	*9:00-9:30* MORNING MEETING	*9:00-9:30* MORNING MEETING
9:30-10:30 CLERICAL DUTIES	*9:30-10:30* CLERICAL DUTIES	*9:30-10:30* CLERICAL DUTIES	*9:30-10:30* CLERICAL DUTIES	*9:30-10:30* CLERICAL DUTIES
10:30-10:45 BREAKTIME	*10:30-10:45* BREAKTIME	*10:30-10:45* BREAKTIME	*10:30-10:45* BREAKTIME	*10:30-10:45* BREAKTIME
10:45-12:00 CLERICAL DUTIES	*10:45-12:00* COPING W/ MENTAL ILLNESS GRP.	*10:45-12:00* CLERICAL DUTIES	*10:45-12:00* CLERICAL DUTIES	*10:45-12:00* CLERICAL DUTIES
12:00-12:30 LUNCH	*12:00-12:30* LUNCH	*12:00-12:30* LUNCH	*12:00-12:30* LUNCH	*12:00-12:30* LUNCH
12:30-1:00 COMMUNITY MEETING	*12:30-1:00* COMMUNITY MEETING	*12:30-1:00* COMMUNITY MEETING	*12:30-1:00* COMMUNITY MEETING	*12:30-1:00* COMMUNITY MEETING
1:00-2:00 CLERICAL DUTIES	*1:00-2:45* NEWS BULLETIN	*1:00-2:45* TUTORIALS	*1:00-2:30* STATS TRAINING	*1:00-2:15* UPBEAT TIME *2:15-2:30* WRAP-UP
2:00-3:00 CASE MGT.	*2:45-3:00* WRAP-UP	*2:45-3:00* WRAP-UP	*2:30-3:00* CASE MGT.	*2:30-3:00* COFFEE SHOP

FIGURE 6.2

life as quickly as possible, that program might emphasize skills training and supportive therapy. Alternatively, if a program's primary purpose is to keep people from going back to the hospital, it might emphasize support and medication maintenance. This idea might be summed up by the question, "What type of program is effective for what type of client?"

In 1981 Neffinger proposed a taxonomy of partial hospitalization (PH) programs (see Table 6.1). Neffinger's taxonomy identified three different primary purposes or functions for PHs: (a) an alternative to inpatient treatment, which he labeled *day hospital*; (b) a supplement to traditional outpatient treatment and vocational rehabilitation, which he labeled *day treatment*; and (c) functional maintenance in the community, which he labeled *day care*. Many programs today can still be classified using this taxonomy, although they would probably employ different terms to describe themselves. For example, today programs designed to function as an alternative to inpatient treatment are typically called acute partial hospitals.

It is instructive to closely review the details of Neffinger's taxonomy in Table 6.1. Notice that the term *chronic*, which is no longer acceptable, is used. Also, review the variables or program characteristics Neffinger used to distinguish between program types. These variables are still important considerations when evaluating these programs, but their content

TABLE 6.1

A Schematic Presentation of the Theoretical Spectrum of Partial Hospitalization Programs Subdivided into Three Parallel Continua Representing (A) General Taxonomy, (B) Primary Function, and (C) Differential Characteristics[a]

		Day Hospital	Day Treatment	Day Care
A.	General Taxonomy	Day Hospital	Day Treatment	Day Care
B.	Primary Function	Alternative to inpatient transitional setting	Supplement to traditional outpatient treatment, vocational rehabiliation	Functional maintenanace
C.	Differential Characteristics			
	Treatment Goal	Stabilize acute episode	Catalyze rapid improve-ment Minimize Subsequent treatment	Prevent further deterioration and rehospitalization
	Treatment Modality	Psychopharmacology/ supportive therapy	Intensive psychotherapy and struture	Activity therapy, and advocacy
	Symptom Intensity	Acute	Pre/post acute	Chronic
	Age	Mixed	Younger	Older
	Staffing Pattern	Medical mental health professionals	Nonmedical mental health professionals	Predominantly paraprofessionals
	Patient/ Staff Ratio	4	6	15+
	Maximum Census	12	20 to 40	50+
	Treatment Duration	2 to 4 weeks	3 to 4 months	Indefinite
	Organizational Relationships	Closely allied to emergency and/or inpatient unit	Separate from but available to inpatient or emergency unit	No necessary relationship to inpatient or emergency unit

[a] From Neffinger, G. G. (1981). Partial hospitalization: An overview. *Journal of Community Psychology,* 9, 263. ©1981, John Wiley & Sons, Inc. Reprinted by permission.

has changed somewhat as the field has evolved. For example, intensive psychotherapy has been replaced by supportive psychotherapy. In addition, the characterization of day-care patients as older is probably an artifact of the deinstitutionalization movement and is certainly less true today. The original exodus included many middle-aged and elderly patients who had spent the better part of their adult lives in institutions.

The Effectiveness of PsyR Day Programs

The first reports of effective day hospitals (Bierer, 1948; Cameron, 1947; Dzhagarov, 1937) stressed the innovative strategy of using these programs in place of inpatient treatment. This strategy had several obvious benefits in addition to the fact that it is much less expensive to provide day treatment than inpatient hospitalization. Day treatment allowed patients to stay in the community, which reduced stigma and helped maintain normal contacts and supports. Day treatment also eliminated the need for what was often a difficult transition back to the community after a long inpatient stay.

The first evaluations of day treatment in the United States focused on the question of how this treatment strategy compared with inpatient hospitalization. This research was nearly unanimous in finding that day hospitalization was both clinically superior and more economical than inpatient hospitalization. In a 1971 study, Herz, Endicott, Spitzer, and Mesnikoff randomly assigned patients to either inpatient treatment or day hospitalization and found that day treatment was superior on each of their outcome measures.

A similar study by Washburn, Vannicelli, Longabaugh, and Scheff (1976) found that initially, day hospitalization was superior to inpatient hospitalization in reducing subjective distress, improving community functioning, and reducing family burden, total hospital cost, and length of stay in the program. At a 24-month reassessment, they found that there was no longer a difference between the day hospital and inpatient hospital groups. It is interesting to speculate why the differences between the day programming and inpatient groups fade after 2 years. The most likely explanation is that for many of these individuals the disease process may have reasserted itself, blurring the advantages gained by attending day programming.

As the advantages of day hospitalization became clear, the focus of research moved toward determining which elements of the day hospital were most effective. Neffinger's work cited previously is one example of this effort. Probably the most important study in this area to date was done by researchers working for the Veterans Administration (VA). Taking advantage of the large number of day hospitals operated by the VA, Linn, Caffey, Klett, Hogarty, and Lamb (1979) randomly assigned patients from 10 different hospitals to receive either psychotropic drugs plus day treatment or psychotropic drugs alone. The positive results of day programming were not immediately apparent. At the initial 6- month follow-up the researchers found no difference between the two groups. But at the 18-month follow-up they found that medication plus day treatment were superior to medication alone. Patients who had received day treatment plus medication had fewer episodes of hospitalization, spent less time in the hospital, and had better social functioning. Day treatment plus medication was found to be clearly superior on almost every outcome measure. Interestingly, they also found that the overall treatment cost of day treatment plus medication was not higher than the treatment cost of medication alone. This might be considered a surprising result, because the day treatment patients with better outcomes were receiving more services than those receiving medication alone. The lower cost of their treatment was due to the fact that they used fewer inpatient services, which have very high cost.

Analyzing the results further, the researchers found some sharp differences between programs on the outcome variables under study. They found that six of the day hospitals produced positive outcomes, whereas the other four day hospitals produced outcomes no better than medication alone. They proceeded to study which program factors were associated with both positive and negative outcomes. One important finding was that the six centers producing positive outcomes had costs that were not much greater than the cost of drugs alone, whereas the costs of the four centers with poor outcomes were significantly higher.

After reviewing their findings the authors concluded that

> High patient turnover and brief but more intensive treatment, particularly in terms of psychotherapeutic counseling by professionals, may lead to relapse for some schizophrenic patients. (Linn et al., 1979, p. 1061.)

In short, group psychotherapy, which costs more because it requires more professionally trained and higher paid staff, also produced poorer outcomes. In contrast to more traditional therapy, this evidence supports a more practical, supportive, skills-training approach, which is one of the hallmarks of PsyR.

Beigel and Feder (1970) had similar results, finding that patients with more persistent conditions do poorly in programs designed to provide treatment more appropriate for acute patients. This indicates that certain types of programs are effective for certain types of patients and ineffective or even harmful for others. These findings also imply that different client types have different treatment needs and goals, the attainment of which may best be achieved in specifically designed programs.

CONTROVERSIAL ISSUE

Day Programming: An Effective Treatment Strategy or Institutions in the Community?

In day treatment programs without specific length of stay requirements it is not uncommon to find that quite a few of the clients or members have been attending the program for 10 or more years. The level of functioning among these individuals does not appear to improve, nor do they become more integrated with the community from year to year. Instead, they seem to function at about the same level regardless of the services they receive. Many voices have been raised questioning whether we have traded large, state-operated, psychiatric institutions for a series of small institutions in the community that receive some federal funding through Medicaid and Medicare. Those debating this issue continue the argument by pointing to the inadequate and inconsistent treatment available in the community compared to an institution. This, in turn, has led to a large increase in the number of homeless people who are mentally ill on the streets and in jails.

Deinstitutionalization advocates argue that despite long lengths of stay, community programs are keeping people out of the hospital while improving their quality of life and, it is important to note, accomplishing this at less cost. They argue that these disabling illnesses are often lifelong and require constant care. Essentially, because there is no cure, it is better for a person to be in the community than to be in an institution.

Clearly, on an economic efficiency or cost basis deinstitutionalization advocates have a strong advantage. Finances aside, the argument must hinge on the quality of the treatment provided, the quality of life of the individuals with severe mental illness, and the impact of different strategies on society. With any issue of real controversy there is a large gray area. For those people who are homeless and mentally ill or those that remain unaided by medication, community treatment may be a disaster for the individual and society. For those who can function with some degree of independence but still need regular services, community treatment can be liberating.

State of the Art PsyR Day Programming

One of the most important contributions of organizations such as the International Association of Psychosocial Rehabilitation Services (IAPSRS) and publications such as the *Psychiatric Rehabilitation Journal* is that they bring together professionals, consumers, family members, and others from all philosophies of PsyR. This coming together, which has grown year by year, has helped to synthesize the best elements of these different program types into what we consider today's state-of-the-art program. PsyR services are still idiosyncratic, but the best programs contain many of the same elements, though in differing amounts.

From the clubhouse movement we get a strong respect for each individual's quality of life and those things that support quality of life: employment, housing, social supports, and membership in the community. This translates into many support initiatives that go far beyond treating the mental illness itself. State-of-the-art programs are instrumental in securing housing for their members, have one or more vocational rehabilitation elements (see chapter 7), support their members' efforts to further their education, and help provide opportunities for building social supports and networks. Clubhouses, for example, tend to be open in the evenings and on weekends because their members' social lives and recreation are important.

The development of a nationwide network of clubhouse programs helped give birth to the psychosocial rehabilitation movement. The clubhouse network was also instrumental in the creation of IAPSRS. Today, many clubhouses belong to both IAPSRS as institutional members and to the national clubhouse movement.

From the partial hospitalization movement, our state-of-the-art program gets its emphasis on medication, medication management, and symptom and medication education for consumers and their families. This aspect is important because the major mental illnesses are biologically based diseases and their symptoms can be controlled with medication. It is also believed that the best long-term outcomes are achieved if psychotic episodes are dealt with effectively and in a timely fashion.

Although it would be wrong to give the impression that there is universal agreement about how things should be done, PsyR is no longer divided between groups with totally different philosophies and strategies. Rather, the field has matured to the point where PsyR professionals agree on the general goals, values, and some principles but still debate the proper mix of these elements to achieve our objectives. Take the idea of empowerment, for example. Many people use this term and many professionals believe it is an important PsyR element. But there is still little agreement as to just what the term *empowerment* means and whether it is a good idea in every situation. Consider the issues spelled out in Box 6.3.

BOX 6.3
Empowerment: Will We Know It If We See It?

Empowerment is something that comes from within a person, rather than something that is done to a person. People who are empowered may have a sense that what they think and feel counts, that their wishes are important, and that they have choices to make. The best a program can do is create an environment that encourages empowerment. In a PsyR day program, member empowerment might manifest itself in many ways. There might be a strong client committee or governing body, members might hold supervisory positions, and they might help to collect data to evaluate the program. The staff at some programs try to engender some of these activities but find that they are rejected by their clients. Empowerment, like recovery, is a personal and complicated phenomenon.

Can you tell whether a program milieu empowers its members? In many programs the clients and staff give a great deal of lip service to the importance of empowerment. In other programs the issue of empowerment is not discussed unless it is raised by a visitor. Does speaking about empowerment indicate that a program is empowering? Apparently not. A study done by students of the first author of this text found an inverse relationship in programs between consumer empowerment and talking about empowerment. In short, programs that claimed to be empowering tended to be less empowering than programs that didn't mention the term at all.

Some strategies have been devised to evaluate the program milieu (Moos, 1974; Wolfensberger, 1983). These scales do not claim to measure empowerment directly. Instead, they touch on many similar issues, such as normalization and control. Although empowerment is considered an important ingredient of PsyR programming, there is still no agreement on an objective way to measure it. Recently, working hand in hand with consumers, researchers have been devising a scale to address this problem (Rogers, Chamberlin, Ellison, & Crean, 1997).

The Future of Day Programming

The future of day programming depends on many factors including the decisions made by funding sources as to what kinds of treatment they will pay for and at what rate. Putting these practical considerations aside, the real issue that will determine the future of day programming is its ability to aid consumers in recovery. Regardless of other developments or issues, day treatment will ultimately survive and flourish if it meets the needs of its clients. If it does not meet those needs, it will be replaced by other, more effective services.

Day treatment is often one element of a comprehensive continuum of services. Many state-of-the-art programs today provide nearly comprehensive services for their clients or members. For example, a program might provide its members, on an as-needed basis, with (a) case management services for advocacy and supports, (b) skills training, (c) medication evaluation and monitoring, (d) socialization and recreation, (e) transitional or supported housing, (f) several types of vocational programs, (g) supported education, and (h) MICA services. Programs typically provide other services if they identify a need for them. For example, many programs provide transportation to help clients get to work, doctors, shopping, and so on.

The advantage of one program providing all these services is very clear. Coordination of services is carried out more effectively and efficiently. The need for the client to negotiate the system is reduced almost to zero. Therefore, client stress is kept at a minimum.

The disadvantage is that opportunities for community integration may be lost. For example, relying on a program for recreation may mean participating in activities that are agreeable to a majority of people at a time that is convenient for the staff. Pursuing personal interests by accessing community recreational activities increases the opportunity to meet new people and reduces stigma.

Summary

Psychiatric rehabilitation day programming has roots in the clubhouse movement, the partial hospitalization movement, and milieu therapy. These programs were the principle treatment facilities for many of the people deinstitutionalized during the 1960s and 1970s. These programs are characterized by the belief that people coming together facing the same problems and issues can create an environment that is conducive to treatment, rehabilitation, and recovery. Research has demonstrated that some program designs (a focus on the here and now, less formal therapy, etc.) produce outcomes that are superior to medications alone (Linn et al., 1979). Research has also demonstrated that these programs are economically efficient. Today's state-of-the-art program is a combination of elements of the partial hospitalization movement (emphasis on medication, treatment, etc.) and the clubhouse movement (emphasis on quality of life, consumer empowerment, etc.). Many of the programs have grown into large multiservice agencies that attempt to provide for all, if not most, of the needs of their clients or members with severe mental illness.

Class Exercise

The following are nine variables or characteristics of day treatment programs that help to determine how the program functions: member/staff ratio, program size, staffing, staffing pattern, attendance requirements, scheduled program time, treatment focus, program ingredients, and empowerment.

Member/Staff Ratio

May range from low (2/1 to 6/1) to high (16/1 or more) depending on the type and philosophy of the program.

Program Size

May vary from small (20–40 members) to very large programs with hundreds of members.

Staffing

May vary from being predominantly paraprofessional to predominantly professional depending on the goals and type of program.

Staffing Pattern

May vary from being a generalist pattern, in which staff carry out multiple roles with little regard for academic or professional credentials, to a specialist staffing pattern, in which staff carry out specified organizational or professional roles.

Attendance Requirements

May vary from laissez faire (consumers attend when they wish) to strict and mandatory, similar to a regular work environment.

Scheduled Program Time

May be loose, varied, and flexible or may approximate a typical work environment.

Treatment Focus

May vary from no treatment other than concrete feedback about the task at hand to intensive and frequent group and individual therapy.

Program Ingredients

Programs may offer differing amounts (from none to all day) of recreation, socialization, supportive individual or group therapy, expressive therapies (art, dance, etc.), prevocational skills training, specific skills training, work units, and transitional or supported employment. These ingredients should be offered in an internally consistent pattern with respect to program type and philosophy. Some of these grouping variables might be vocational (work-like) versus nonvocational (supportive), high therapy versus no therapy, or skills training versus social learning theory.

Empowerment

Programs range from being run by consumers to being totally controlled by the staff. Clues to the degree of empowerment in a particular program might be the degree of authority wielded by a member government, the presence of members in important meetings, and the ability of members to shape both their individual treatment plans and the program in ways important to them.

Instructions

Based on Neffinger's taxonomy of day treatment programs and using the program-type-by-program-variables matrix that follows, fill in the value of each variable (e.g., member/staff ratio = low, staffing pattern = general, empowerment = high) under each program type. You should have a clear rationale for each decision.

Program Variables	Program Type		
	Maintenance	Movement	Acute
Member/staff ratio			
Program size			
Staffing			
Staffing pattern			
Attendance requirements			
Scheduled program time			
Treatment focus			
Program ingredients			
Empowerment			

References

Astrachan, B. M., Flynn, H. R., Geller, J. D., & Harvey, H. H. (1970). Systems approach to day hospitalization. *Archives of General Psychiatry, 22,* 550–559.

Beard, J. H., Propst, R. n., & Malamud, T. J. (1982). The Fountain House model of psychiatric rehabilitation. *Psychosocial Rehabilitation Journal, 5, 1,* 47–53.

Beigel, A., & Feder, S. L. (1970). Patterns of utilization in partial hospitalization. *American Journal of Psychiatry, 126,* 1267–1274.

Bierer, J. (1948). *Therapeutic social clubs.* London: H. K. Lewis.

Cameron, D. E. (1947). The day hospital: Experimental forms of hospitalization for patients. *Modern Hospital, 69* (3), 60–62.

Cameron, D. E. (1956). The day hospital. In A. E. Bennett, E. A. Hargrove, & B. Engle, (Eds.), *The practice of psychiatry in general hospitals.* Berkeley: University of California Press.

Dincin, J. (1975). Psychiatric rehabilitation. *Schizophrenia Bulletin, 13,* 131–147.

Dzhagarov, M. (1937). Experience in organizing a half hospital for mental patients. *Neuropathologia Psikhatria,* 137–147.

Flannery, M., & Glickman, M. (1996). *Fountain House: Portraits of lives reclaimed from mental illness.* Center City, MN: Hazelden.

Gunderson, J. G. (1978). Defining the therapeutic process in psychiatric milieus. *Psychiatry: Journal for the Study of Interpersonal Process, 41,* 327–335.

Herz, M. I., Endicott, J., Spitzer, R. I., & Mesnikoff, A. (1971). Day versus inpatient hospitalization: A controlled study. *American Journal of Psychiatry, 127,* 1371–1382.

Jackson, R. (1992). How work works. *Psychosocial Rehabilitation Journal, 16*(2), 49–54.

Linn, M. W., Caffey, E. M., Klett, C. J., Hogarty G. E., & Lamb, H. R. (1979). Day treatment and psychotropic drugs in the aftercare of schizophrenic patients. *Archives of General Psychiatry, 36,* 1055–1066.

Luber, R. F. (1979). The growth and scope of partial hospitalization. In R. F. Luber (Ed.), *Partial hospitalization: A current perspective* (pp. 3–20). New York: Plenum.

Moos, R. (1974). *Evaluating treatment environments: A social ecological approach.* New York: John Wiley & Sons.

Neffinger, G. G. (1981). Partial hospitalization: An overview. *Journal of Community Psychology, 9,* 262–269.

Propst, R. n. (1992a). Introduction special issue: The clubhouse model. *Psychosocial Rehabilitation Journal, 16,* (2), 25–30.

Propst, R. n. (1992b). Standards for clubhouse programs: Why and how they were developed. *Psychosocial Rehabilitation Journal, 16* (2), 25–30.

Rogers, E. S., Chamberlin, J., Ellison, M. L., & Crean, T. (1997). A consumer-constructed scale to measure empowerment among users of mental health services. *Psychiatric Services, 48*(8), 1042–1047.

Taube, C. A. (1973). Day care services in federally funded community mental health centers. *Statistical Note No. 96,* Survey and Reports Section, Biometry Branch, National Institute of Mental Health, Rockville, Maryland.

Vorspan, R. (1992). Why work works. *Psychosocial Rehabilitation Journal, 16*(2), 49–54.

Washburn, S. L., & Conrad, M. (1979). Organization of the therapeutic milieu in the partial hospital. In R. F. Luber (Ed.), *Partial hospitalization: A current perspective* (pp. 47–70). New York: Plenum.

Washburn, S. L., Vannicelli, M., Longabaugh, R., & Scheff, B. J. (1976). A controlled comparison of psychiatric day treatment and inpatient hospitalization. *Journal of Consulting and Clinical Psychology, 44,* 665–675.

Wolfensberger, W. (1983). The definition of normalization: Update, problems, disagreements and misunderstandings. In R. J. Flynn & K. E. Nitsch (Eds.), *Normalization, Social Integration and Community Services.* Baltimore: University Park Press.

Chapter 7

Vocational and Educational Rehabilitation

Many people respond to questions about who they are by talking about their job, position, or profession. Whatever a person does that is productive or meaningful contributes greatly to his or her sense of identity. Such information often conveys the individual's socioeconomic status, interests, values, and, particularly in the case of education, aspirations. A person without a job or profession who has a major mental illness is relegated to the role of mental patient. This chapter outlines some of the problems associated with helping these individuals achieve their vocational and educational goals and some of the strategies that have proven to be effective. Persons with major mental illness can complete school, be effective workers, and have professions. When they accomplish these goals their condition becomes something that they have overcome rather than defining who they are.

This chapter will answer the following questions:

1. *What are the barriers to employment for people with a psychiatric disability?*
2. *What skills, resources, or experiences are related to vocational success?*
3. *What constitutes quality vocational services?*
4. *What kinds of vocational services have been developed?*

Introduction

Employment is an essential adult activity. If we are fortunate, the work we choose to do reflects our interests, skills, and talents. Working, especially working and earning a paycheck, promotes self-confidence, self-esteem, status in the community, and economic well-being. Because of all these obvious advantages, our culture puts great value on the role of worker. In addition, the role of worker provides access to other valued social roles, including that of friend, spouse, parent, homeowner, neighbor, customer, and taxpayer (Carling, 1995). For most adults, having a job or profession is an essential element in defining who they are and for achieving a positive quality of life.

Does work have some additional benefits for people with mental illness? It certainly seems logical that successful employment would have a positive impact on other areas such as symptom reduction, community integration, and improved functioning. The results of a number of studies hint that this may be true (Arns & Linney, 1993; Bell, Milstein, & Lysaker, 1993; Drake, McHugo, Becker, Anthony, & Clark, 1996; Lysaker & Bell, 1995). One study that specifically looked at this issue was conducted by Mueser and his colleagues in 1997 (Mueser, Becker, Torrey, Xie, Bond, Drake, & Dain, 1997). In this study, the researchers examined the relationship between competitive employment and nonvocational domains. Data were taken at the beginning of the study, and at 6, 12, and 18 months. The results indicate that

> formerly unemployed psychiatric patients who obtained competitive employment while participating in a vocational program tended to have lower symptoms, better overall functioning, higher self-esteem, and higher satisfaction with vocational services and finances. (p. 423).

More studies on this topic are needed to confirm and further illuminate these findings.

Persons with major mental illness, however, rarely get to experience the positive results of having a regular job. Employment rates for people with a psychiatric disability are very low, ranging from 0% to 30% (Anthony & Blanch, 1987; Anthony, Cohen, & Danley, 1988; Anthony, Cohen, & Farkas, 1990). More problems than the mental illnesses themselves contribute to the high unemployment rate among people with severe mental illness.

Barriers to Employment

Stigma

One of the greatest barriers to employment for people with a psychiatric disability is stigma. This stigma has several sources. The most obvious source of stigma, which we have all experienced, is the frequently negative characterization of people with mental illness by the mass media. This is reflected in many of the attitudes about mental illness held by laypersons. Media reports often leave the false impression that a person with mental illness is usually emotionally unstable, irrational, and dangerous.

Another, more subtle source of stigma is reflected in the beliefs (both conscious and unconscious) of professionals regarding the ability of people with psychiatric disability to work or to work in any but the most menial jobs. These beliefs are reflected in some of the vocational services and choices made available for persons with major mental illnesses.

Finally, the most insidious form of stigma may exist within persons with mental illness themselves. When society reduces access to good jobs and staff people give subtle or overt messages of doubt about a person's ability to perform on the job, these negative beliefs can be internalized (Department of Education, 1993). This self-stigma may be the hardest form of stigma to detect and is often the most difficult form of stigma to overcome.

An informal review of articles about mental health issues appearing in a large newspaper over a period of a year may be instructive on the issue of stigma in the media (Roberts & Rotteveel, 1995). The review found that more than 60% of the articles portrayed people with mental illness as criminals or in other undesirable roles, whereas only 4% of the articles presented a positive image of any kind. This kind of portrayal, as well as many seen in movies and advertisements, have a profound effect on the attitudes of both members of the community at large and of the business community. A recent Harris poll regarding attitudes of the general public toward people with disabilities found

---

BOX 7.1
The Disclosure Dilemma

When a person with a psychiatric disability decides to seek employment, he or she may be faced with the question of whether or not to disclose the disability to the employer. The decision is often a difficult one.

On the one hand, the results of disclosure can be very negative. The applicant who discloses might not be hired. The worker who discloses might be discriminated against in explicit ways, such as not being considered for advancement, or more subtly, such as being treated as less capable or fragile. On the other hand, not disclosing may leave the individual feeling vulnerable about someone discovering the illness at a later time. Any supports the person may need would also be unavailable if the person had not disclosed their illness.

On the positive side, disclosure allows one the opportunity to request and gain accommodations that may be essential for the worker's success. Some workers feel more comfortable if their employer knows about the disability and they do not have to hide it. In some workplaces, informal support among coworkers on personal issues is common and workers with psychiatric disabilities may benefit from accessing it.

How would you assist someone in deciding whether or not to disclose? What would be the important factors in deciding when, to whom, and how much to disclose?

an overall improved acceptance of people with disabilities in the community, but it also found a continued feeling of uneasiness about people with mental illness (Chapman, 1992).

Misguided Services

Uninformed beliefs on the part of professionals about the abilities, desires, and needs of people with a psychiatric disability have resulted in both unnecessarily delayed access to vocational services and unnecessarily limited vocational options (Bond, Dietzen, McGrew, & Miller, 1995; Department of Education, 1993). Concerns about stress, symptomatology, medication compliance, and rehospitalization have caused providers to withhold access to vocational services until the client or member has demonstrated successful participation in a setting that is segregated from the regular community, even though studies show that functioning in one setting is not predictive of functioning in other settings (Anthony & Jansen, 1984). Additionally, studies show that direct entry into competitive employment does not result in increased rehospitalization or homelessness, as was feared. Instead, direct entry may result in "increased involvement in other community activities; . . . increased general supports; and . . . increased independence of consumers" (Torrey, Becker, & Mowbray, 1995, p. 72). Similarly, Bond, and Dincin (1986) and Bond et al. (1995) found increased rates of full-time competitive employment as a result of "accelerated entry into community jobs" (Bond et al., 1995, p. 106). In this latter study, Bond and his colleagues also found that delayed entry into employment because of participation in prevocational activities, including sheltered work, may decrease one's likelihood of ever entering competitive employment and lower the participant's self-expectations (p. 106). In a similar vein, Blankertz and Robinson (1996) pointed out that although wages have been found to be an important motivator, many programs expect people to demonstrate motivation prior to accessing paid employment opportunities.

Often the employment options offered by providers are restricted to low-skill jobs with little if any chance of advancement, even when the worker has advanced academic degrees, a strong work history, or simply greater aspirations.

Lack of Vocational Experience

Another barrier to employment for many people with a psychiatric disability is their own limited experience and understanding of themselves as workers and of the world of work (Danley & Anthony, 1987). Early experiences in employment provide us with important information about our skills, preferences, interests, and aspirations. These experiences also help us learn about the expectations in the world of work. Over time, multiple experiences in employment contribute to our ability to make appropriate career choices and, ultimately, to be successful in a career. For people who experience a psychiatric disability, these employment experiences and the crucial vocational information they contain have often times been missed (Danley & Anthony, 1987; Department of Education, 1993; Russert & Frey, 1991). People entering vocational services after long periods of psychiatric disability often have considerably less knowledge of their own skills, interests, and preferences than would be expected from comparable persons their own age. Typically, vocational service programs are evaluated by how many persons they place in jobs and how long the people hold these jobs. Because of this, they are usually neither able nor willing to provide the multiple employment experiences that may be needed to provide someone with the knowledge necessary to select a vocational direction that is appropriate for that person.

Psychiatric Disability

Other barriers to employment may be the result of the mental illness itself—the impact of the mental illness on thought and affect as well as the episodic and cyclical nature of the disability (Department of Education, 1993; Russert & Frey, 1991; Rutman, 1994). This means that some people at some times may experience difficulties with memory, concentration, organization, or even interpersonal interactions. Some effects of the mental illness may be what Jansen (1988) called "psychological problems," such as a lack of self-esteem and self-confidence, fear of failure, anxiety, and difficulty getting along with others (p. 36). Finally, the obvious physical side effects of medications can be severe and pose a significant barrier to employment (Braitman et al., 1995; Rutman, 1994).

Less obvious but no less important are the social side effects of medications. For example, a medication that increases one's sensitivity to the sun may also interfere with the user's ability to play on the company softball team and put the person in the uncomfortable position of having to disclose personal information or be seen as "not part of the gang." Similarly, a worker who cannot drink alcohol because of his or her medication may feel awkward when invited to join coworkers for a beer after work. In fact, any medication side effect that has an impact on the person's social activities can increase the person's appearance of differentness and make it harder for the person to fit in (Roberts, 1997, p. 83).

Possible Loss of Benefits

For individuals who receive Supplemental Security Income (SSI) or Social Security Disability Insurance (SSDI), the Social Security Administration regulations regarding the effect of earned income on benefits may be seen as posing a substantial barrier to employment. Most people with mental illness are aware that their illness can flair up at any time. In the event of a relapse, Social Security may be the only source of income available. The fear of losing one's benefits, coupled with the fear that one may not be able to sustain employment, makes the risk of attempting employment very great (Ford, 1995).

The regulations governing Social Security benefits are complicated and often difficult to understand. They are also subject to change. Currently they are as follows.

The regulations for SSI employ a formula for determining specific reductions in cash benefits as a result of earned income. The person's cash benefit will be reduced by $1 for every $2 the person earns in excess of any exclusions to which the person is entitled. Those exclusions may include an Earned income exclusion and a general income exclusion. These exclusions or disregards ($20 and $65, respectively) are earnings that Social Security allows without effect on benefits.

The SSDI recipient is entitled to a trial work period during which his or her SSDI cash benefit is protected even though the person is earning wages. This period is followed by an extended period of eligibility during which time the person's entitlement to the cash benefit will depend on whether or not the person's earnings exceed the amount that is considered to be substantial gainful activity. There is no formula to reduce the SSDI amount. Instead, it is an all-or-nothing proposition. The person either receives the SSDI cash benefit or he or she does not.

Both of these programs include work incentives that can be used to reduce the person's countable earned income and maintain some or all of the cash benefit at least for a time.

For most recipients of Social Security benefits, the greatest fear is the loss of medical coverage. SSI recipients are covered by Medicaid and may continue to be covered until their earnings reach a particular amount, even after their earnings have resulted in the cessation of their cash benefit. SSDI recipients are eligible for Medicare and may continue to be covered for a period after their SSDI cash benefit ends (Roberts, 1996). Currently, there are bills in Congress that would further secure the medical care benefits after the person becomes employed.

Despite what seems like an overwhelming list of barriers, people with psychiatric disabilities can and do experience success and satisfaction in employment. Informed psychiatric rehabilitation (PsyR) practitioners understand that the relevant question is not "Can people with psychiatric disabilities work?" but rather "What is needed for this individual to be successful in his or her chosen job or career?"

Developing Vocational Services

Several researchers have attempted to guide effective vocational services by identifying which characteristics, circumstances, or experiences are related to or predictive of vocational success. This has proven to be a difficult task.

In an extensive review of the literature, Anthony and Jansen (1984) concluded that past work experience is the best predictor of employment success. They also found that, counter to what is often believed, factors such as diagnosis and level of symptomatology were not related to vocational success. This finding makes sense based on our previous discussion of how persons tend to prepare for making vocational choices. Employment success is influenced by learning from past experience. In a later review of the literature, Anthony (1994), found consistent results. Again, past work history, number and length of hospitalizations, marital status, race, and previous occupational level all had been found to be correlated to vocational outcome as had work adjustment skills (i.e., work readiness, attitudes and quality, and interpersonl relations). Diagnosis, symptomatology, and functioning in other life domains were not found to correlate to vocational outcome with a few exceptions. A study done by Boston University Center for Psychiatric Rehabilitaion in which all subjects were individuals who had identified a vocational goal found the only predictors of vocational outcome to be symptomatology, criminal justice involvement, and marital status. Anthony suggested that the fact that the subjects had selected a vocational goal and were receiving a vocational intervention may distinguish this group from previous research groups.

Futhermore, in at least a few studies, diagnosis has been found to be related to vocational outcome (Anthony, 1994, Mowbray, Bybee, Harris, & McCrohan, 1995). Some studies suggest a possible relationship between medication and work performance in that medication appears to impair work performance. The fact of receiving Social Security benefits has correlated with vocational outcome in some studies and not in others.

Blankertz and Robinson, in a 1996 study that examined the integration of vocational rehabilitation services with typical mental health services, suggested that those things that predict positive vocational outcomes are not characteristics of individuals but characteristics of programs. These authors have asserted that "vocational rehabilitation should be an integral part of the mental health rehabilitation process" (p.1222). Bond, Drake, Mueser, and Becker (1997) also identified the integration of clinical and vocational services as an essential feature of quality services.

Although there is still some debate about the predictors of success, it is safe to say that, given supports and reasonable environmental adjustments, persons experiencing major mental illness can be successful workers in jobs of their choice.

Features of Effective Vocational Services

Some individuals have examined the question, "What are the features of effective vocational services?" *The Rehab Brief* (Department of Education, 1993) summarized the outcome of a Consensus Validation Conference convened by the National Institute on Disability and Rehabilitation Research (NIDRR) to examine employment for people with psychiatric disabilities. This document describes the features of effective vocational rehabilitation in four areas: the practitioner, the process, the programs, and the principles. Its basic findings are summarized as follows:

Practitioner
- "There is evidence that the most effective practitioners demonstrate respect for clients and their individual experiences of illness; they not only establish partnerships that allow clients to lead but also provide information and direction, and they are knowledgeable about psychiatric disabilities and the larger service system." (p. 2)

Process
- "The vocational rehabilitation process must be comprehensive, dynamic and adaptable, not limited to standard programming." (p. 2)

Programs
- Effective programs "emphasize 'real work for real pay' in community settings." (p. 2)

Principles
Effective services operate on several shared principles:

- *Consumer choice.* Consumers direct their rehabilitation process and choose those services and supports that best meet their needs.

- *Integrated settings*. Services support people in entering regular community settings.
- *Service linkages*. People are connected to needed services in all areas of their lives, not just employment.
- *Natural supports*. People with disabilities are helped to access those supports that exist within the setting itself.
- *Rapid placement*. People are helped to move quickly into employment and receive the supports needed to be successful.
- *Job accommodations*. People with disabilities receive effective and appropriate accommodations.
- *Seamless services*. Services are provided with continuity and without changes in counselors, agencies, or other providers.
- *Employer education*. Service providers understand the needs of employers and view the worker with a disability as a valuable member of the workforce who is able to meet the employer's needs, rather than asking employers to offer employment as a charitable or therapeutic thing to do. (p. 3)

Other researchers in this area have examined the elements necessary for a successful vocational service. Among features that should be a part of any high-quality vocational service, both Toms Barker (1994) and Ford (1995) listed what some might consider obvious: a focus on and commitment to employment outcomes. Bond and Boyer (1988) agreed, stating that programs without an explicit focus on vocational outcomes may inhibit clients from seeking work. For example, programs in which employment is viewed as something to be achieved after a client has acquired a degree of stability and good personal adjustment skills may be less effective than a program in which obtaining a job is viewed as the primary goal.

A strong, overt belief on the part of the agency and the staff in both the right and ability of people with a psychiatric disability to work is a very important element in any successful service. This may seem obvious on the face of it, but vocational service agencies and staff can also hold stigmatizing beliefs about the ability of people with mental illness to achieve vocational success. Such beliefs may be unconsciously represented in an agency's policies or in the attitudes staff hold about the ability of their clients to perform certain jobs. The staff person plays an important role as the principle liaison between the community mental health system and the business community. A staff person who can communicate clearly with the business community can help to reduce stigma, provide supports, and arrange for the environmental modifications necessary to ensure that an individual with psychiatric disability can work successfully.

Toms Barker (1994) also emphasized the need for program administrators to be willing to continually evaluate the effectiveness of their services. It is not sufficient to provide services in a particular way without considering whether or not good outcomes are being achieved. Furthermore, in vocational services, like everything else, things change. Job opportunities in the community change and important characteristics of the people who need help getting the jobs may also change. Programs that do not recognize change and adjust to it become increasingly less effective at helping their clients secure appropriate jobs. Thus, self-awareness in the form of periodic evaluations can help vocational services continue to be both efficient and effective in their employment efforts.

CONTROVERSIAL ISSUE
Is Prevoc Really No Voc?

A week after an interesting class discussion about the future of vocational services in PsyR, one of our graduate students (with many years of PsyR experience) reported having an interesting altercation at work. It seems that during a staff meeting at the partial care program where he worked, he had questioned whether it was really helpful to work on prevocational skills with the clients if the goal was to prepare them for regular jobs. Instead, he had suggested that maybe "prevoc was really no voc." He was very surprised by how upset some of the staff became by his remark. Yet today there is a growing body of research that suggests he may be right.

The case for prevocational training is very straightforward. For a number of very sound reasons, many of the first vocational services, which were set up in response to the deinstitutionalization movement, focused on teaching prevocational skills. These programs were designed to help individuals entering the community after years of psychiatric institutionalization. Members of this institutionalized population had spent much of their adult lives in settings where even the simplest decisions were made for them. There was no question that many of them lacked the prevocational skills—such as grooming, punctuality, and socialization—that are necessary to function effectively in the workplace. In addition, program staff could readily identify and work with the prevocational skill deficits of their clients but had scant information about the more specific job skills they might need at particular jobs. A subtle but possibly no less important reason for the emphasis on prevocational training, especially in community mental health centers, was how services were (in some places still are)

reimbursed. In most cases programs could not bill for off-site services. That meant that any work the staff might do outside the center in the community would not be reimbursable. This created a barrier to the staff doing realistic kinds of skill training and job development work. Instead, most staff members focused on what they felt they could do best while surviving financially—prevocational skills training.

Since the advent of supported employment (SE), the idea of forgoing prevocational training in favor of direct placement and the provision of support services on the job has received increasing support from researchers. As previously mentioned in this chapter, a number of researchers (Bond et al., 1995; Bond & Dincin, 1986; Torrey, Becker, & Mowbray, 1995) have found that direct placement is superior to prevocational training with respect to vocational outcomes. In their 1995 study, Bond and his colleagues suggested that during the time the client spends in prevocational training, he or she may become dependent on the program, develop a support network there, and lose some of the motivation to work a regular job. This makes sense if we consider the recovery theories put forth by Pat Deegan (1988) and William Anthony (1993b). These theories suggest that the recovery task involves creating a new self-image that incorporates the fact of the mental illness. Consider the development of this new self-image after spending a year at prevocational training versus spending a year at a regular job.

Opponents of direct placement SE still argue that this strategy causes higher stress and higher hospitalization rates. Research has not supported these claims. It is very possible that there is a subpopulation of individuals for whom each of these strategies is superior. Clearly, this represents an area of PsyR where our knowledge may be moving faster than our attitudes about what constitutes good service.

Vocational Rehabilitation: The Federal Initiative

In 1918 the federal government established the Office of Vocational Rehabilitation to assist the returning veterans of World War I in finding employment. This title was subsequently changed to the Rehabilitation Services Administration (RSA). The scope of vocational rehabilitation has been expanded several times from its original mission to assist veterans.

In 1920 Congress decided that civilians with physical disabilities should also be eligible for vocational rehabilitation services. In 1943 services were expanded again to include persons with mental retardation and mental illness (Ledbetter & Field, 1978; Neff, 1988; Roberts, 1996). During the Great Society instituted by President Johnson in the 1960s, services were expanded to recipients of Social Security Disability Insurance (SSDI) and later to "the disadvantaged or socially and culturally deprived" (Ledbetter & Field, 1978, p. 36).

Prior to the 1970s, vocational rehabilitation services were not readily accessible to people with a psychiatric disability (Anthony & Blanch, 1987). In 1973 Congress overrode a presidential veto and passed the Rehabilitation Act. This act established the Rehabilitation Services Administration (RSA) and authorized it to do several things including, but not limited to, providing vocational rehabilitation services to people with the most severe disabilities and to those people who had been underserved in the past and to "develop new and innovative methods" to achieve vocational rehabilitation (PL93-112, p. 3) (Ledbetter & Field, 1978; McGurrin, 1994; Roberts, 1996). This new emphasis on serving people with the most severe disabilities helped to make services more accessible to people with a psychiatric disability. The Rehabilitation Act also allowed for funding to be allocated to states to provide vocational rehabilitation services. This funding is based on the per capita income of the state (PL93-112). Each state has a state agency that corresponds to the federal RSA. This state agency, which has different names in different states (Division of Vocational Rehabilitation, Office of Vocational Rehabilitation, VESID, etc.), employs vocational rehabilitation counselors in local offices throughout the state.

In addition, the 1973 act established the Individual Written Rehabilitation Plan (IWRP) (Ledbetter & Field, 1978). The IWRP identifies the desired rehabilitation outcome and the services and activities that will be provided to achieve it. Each vocational rehabilitation (VR) client is required to be actively involved in the development of his or her rehabilitation plan to ensure that it reflects the desires of the individual. The vocational rehabilitation counselor works with individuals with disabilities to establish the IWRP and then to access the needed services. In some states the vocational rehabilitation agency provides those services and in other states the services are purchased from authorized vocational rehabilitation vendors such as many psychiatric rehabilitation providers. These services include assessments of the worker's capacity, skills, and interests, work adjustment such as attendance, grooming, and productivity; education or training; job acquistion; and initial support. Once a VR client is employed and stable on the job, VR will continue to be involved for a brief period of time (currently 90 days) and then will close the person's case.

Access to services was further improved in the 1970s when the National Institute of Mental Health (NIMH) established the Community Support Program (CSP) initiative. The CSP stressed vocational rehabilitation services as an important element of support for deinstitutionalized psychiatric patients. In 1978, partly based on the CSP initiative, the NIMH entered into a collaborative agreement with RSA establishing two rehabilitation research and training centers focused on psychiatric disability (Anthony & Blanch, 1987; McGurrin, 1994).

In 1980 NIMH, RSA, the National Institute on Handicapped Research, and the Council of State Administrators of Vocational Rehabilitation entered into a cooperative interagency agreement that led to the development of a work group focused on improving services for people with psychiatric disabilities. This work group was instrumental in bringing about the 1986 amendments to the Rehabilitation Act (Anthony & Blanch, 1987). In response to strong advocacy efforts, the 1986 amendments to the Rehabilitation Act defined supported employment (SE), a newly emerging vocational service of great promise, established a category of funds to pay for supported employment (Title VI[C]), and made it possible for vocational rehabilitation counselors to use regular case service funds to pay for supported employment (Roberts, 1996).

Most recently, in response to testimony from people with disabilities and advocates, the 1992 amendments to the Rehabilitation Act modified the definition of supported employment, increased the emphasis on consumer choice and mandated "a 'presumption of employability' for all people" (Roberts, 1996, p. 19).

In spite of these developments, it appears that vocational rehabilitation services for people with psychiatric disability in some places remain elusive and inadequate. Noble (1998), in a review of reports generated by the General Accounting Office of the federal government, reported that although the amount of money allocated to vocational rehabilitation has increased substantially since 1975, the percentage of that money being used to purchase services for clients has declined. Furthermore, vocational rehabilitation agencies repeatedly have been found to ignore recommendations of best practice by continuing instead to use tests and assessments that are not good measures of vocational capacity for people with mental illness, failing to develop a specialization in mental illness among vocational rehabilitation counselors, and continuing to use outdated diagnostic nomenclature and categories. Noble stated, "The traditional vocational rehabilitation process is insufficient and top-heavy with personnel who stubbornly adhere to outdated methods and a time orientation that is insensitive to the intermittent or ongoing needs of people with severe mental illnesses" (p. 778). Although these criticisms may be warranted in general, it is also true that in some places the vocational rehabilitation agency has been instumental in the development of vocational services for people with mental illness.

BOX 7.2
Americans with Disabilities Act

The Americans with Disabilities Act (ADA) passed by Congress in 1990 is designed to protect people with disabilities from discrimination in five areas: employment, transportation, telecommunication, public accommodation, and the business of local and state government (Mancuso, 1990; National Alliance of Business, 1991; Roberts, 1996). The ADA is not the first law to prohibit discrimination in employment against people with disabilities nor to refer to reasonable accommodations. The Rehabilitation Act of 1973 prohibits discrimination by federal agencies or employers who receive federal funds. Additionally, all but a few states have laws protecting people with disabilities from discrimination as does the District of Columbia (Lee, n.d.).

In the area of employment, the ADA prohibits discrimination against any qualified person because of their disability in all areas of employment including hiring, firing, advancement, compensation, and training. The ADA requires that employers consider whether a qualified applicant is able to perform the "essential functions" of the job with or without accommodations. A "qualified applicant" is one who has the experience or credentials required for the job. For example, if a job requires that the worker have a certain number of years of experience or a particular academic degree or training and the applicant does not have those things, the employer does not have to consider that applicant because the person does not have the qualifications. The "essential functions" are tasks that are integral to the job. In deciding which tasks are integral, employers usually consider if the job exists to perform those tasks, how many people are available to perform those tasks, or what the result would be if the tasks were not performed. Employers are required to make reasonable accommodations for applicants or employees with disabilities. An accommodation is considered "reasonable" if it is not an "undue burden"—that is, if the cost is not excessive given the business' resources and the accommodation does not change the nature of the work performed (Jones, 1993, Lee, n.d.; National Alliance of Business, 1991; Roberts, 1996). The ADA holds employers to a higher standard than previous laws regarding the definition of "undue burden." According to Lee (n.d.) the ADA "requires the employer to prove that an accommodation would be significantly difficult or expensive" (p. 3).

The Job Accommodations Network, JAN, is a service of the President's Committee on Employment of People with Disabilities and is set up to provide technical assistance in selecting or designing accommodations (Jones, 1993). JAN reports that most accommodations cost less than $500. In fact, they estimate that the "average cost of accommodation is less than $100 per person" (Jones, 1993, p. 8).

Accommodations for people with psychiatric disabilities are usually not costly because they are not usually structural. These accommodations are sometimes referred to as "soft accommodations." Jacqueline Parrish and Laura Mancuso have identified accommodations that have been helpful to people with psychiatric disabilities (in Jones, 1993). They identify four categories of accommodation as follows:

- *Human Assistance*, including a job coach, additional training, coworker support, or mentoring.
- *Changes in workplace policy*, such as allowing telephone calls for support, using sick leave for emotional illness, allowing someone to work at home, and setting up a quiet workplace for someone whose concentration is impacted by distractions. Other policy changes might include holding a job for someone who is out for an extended period because of the mental illness, advancing paid or unpaid sick leave, flexibility in scheduling due to medical appointments, job sharing (in which two people share one job), or allowing the worker to set his or her own workpace.
- *Supervision*, including providing training to supervisors on management skills and topics such as the ADA.
- *Shaping coworkers' attitudes*, including sensitivity training and information about mental illness.

Although the ADA is not the first law to prohibit employment discrimination, it is a far-reaching law and a strong statement about the rights of people with disabilities to be included in the community.

Vocational Service Modalities

Perhaps the first PsyR community services that included work as an integral component took place at Fountain House in New York City, one of the original psychosocial rehabilitation clubhouses. Established in the 1950s, Fountain House provides work units in which clubhouse members work alongside staff completing the tasks necessary to operate and maintain the clubhouse. These activities give members the opportunity to contribute, to build self-esteem and confidence, and to develop relationships (Beard, Propst, & Malamud, 1994). Partly through the efforts of Fountain House, the clubhouse and other versions of psychosocial rehabilitation services that incorporate the use of prevocational work units have been established throughout the world.

Although the purpose of the work unit activities is the benefit one derives from making an important contribution, some also thought that the activities of the work units would provide the skill development necessary for regular employment. This has not been the case. As Marrone (1993) stated, "Work units are not

- Volunteer work (any more than cooking for your family is)
- Specific skills training (any more than cooking meals at home helps you learn to run a restaurant)
- A means of assessing or achieving 'generic' work adjustment (p. 45).

Additionally, some researchers have suggested that the more time an individual spends in prevocational activities, the less likely it is that the person will move into regular employment in the community (Bond et al., 1995).

Transitional Employment

Perhaps the greatest contribution Fountain House has made to the development of specific employment services for people with psychiatric disabilities is the development of transitional employment (TE). TE provides program members with experiences at real jobs, in real employment settings, earning competitive wages. A TE job is acquired from the employer by the vocational services agency. The agency takes full responsibility for the job, which is initially managed by agency staff. Once the staff members have learned the job, they are ready to place program members in the job and to provide them with the training and support they need to succeed. A program member works the job for a specified period of time (usually 3 to 9 months, but this varies) before being replaced by another program member. The agency continues to be responsible for the job at all times. In fact, if the program member is unable to work on a certain day, it is the staff member's responsibility to take his or her place on the job. Obviously, the staff members are very motivated to thoroughly train and provide all the necessary supports so that the program member can do the job successfully.

TE jobs are typically part time and require minimal skills so that they can accommodate a variety of members with a wide range of skill levels. Members have the opportunity to develop real work skills, gain regular work experience, and earn a paycheck. The employer is assured that the job will be continuously filled with trained workers (or by staff members).

Program members may go though a series of TE jobs. In fact, the Fountain House philosophy is that members will experience as many transitional employment jobs as needed to eventually achieve permanent employment in jobs of their own (Beard et al., 1994). Transitional employment has been an important forerunner to supported employment, which will be discussed later.

Fairweather Lodges

A very different approach to employment services, Fairweather Lodges, was developed by George Fairweather in the 1950s. Fairweather Lodges are programs where people with a mental illness live together and work together operating a member-run business.

Fairweather observed that the only social status available to psychiatric patients who were leaving the hospital and entering the community was an inferior one. He believed that a new subsystem in which people with mental illness could occupy valued roles, advance in social status, and challenge the image of people with mental illness held by the larger society, was necessary (Fairweather, 1980).

The lodge community was organized around a set of principles which addressed issues such as the importance of meaningful work, autonomy, advancement, tolerance, support, and similarity to the larger society (Fairweather, 1980).

The lodge community offers its members the opportunity to access valued societal roles in a mutually supportive, albeit segregated, environment. Members of the lodge occupy positions of responsibility within the business. The amount of responsibility one assumes is commensurate with one's ability at that time. Experts, such as accountants, are hired from outside the lodge when needed on a temporary basis.

Historically, referrals for lodge membership came directly from psychiatric hospitals and the training in preparation for entry into the lodge was provided by the hospital. This training included topics such as group decision making, problem solving, and conflict resolution. More recently, referrals are accepted from a variety of sources. Lodge members are allowed to continue to participate in the work program even after moving out of the residence and some members are accepted to the work program without ever being in the residence (Ford, 1995; Onaga, 1994; Toms Barker, 1994).

Hospital-Based Work Programs

On-site vocational opportunities have been developed at some hospitals giving patients the chance to do work for pay within the hospital setting during periods of hospitalization. These programs have been less successful than anticipated in improving postdischarge employment outcomes for patients. In fact, there is evidence that such programs result in the development of dependency in some patients (Bond & Boyer, 1988). According to Bond and Boyer (1988), "Most reviewers have concluded that there is no relationship between successful adjustment to work programs within the hospital and post hospital employment" (p. 235).

Job Clubs

A job club provides the structure and resources necessary to assist participants to conduct their own job search. The club provides training and resources, such as instruction in job-seeking skills (resume writing, interviewing, etc.), access to telephones to call employers, and clerical support (McGurrin, 1994). An important feature that the job club supplies its members is peer support. This unique approach to job development may be less successful for many people with severe mental illness. Many individuals need a greater level of support in accomplishing the tasks of job acquisition (Bond et al., 1997).

Sheltered Workshops

Sheltered workshops solicit manufacturing jobs from local business and industry and provide support and supervision to people with disabilities in a factory-like setting owned or operated by the agency. Workers in the shop are usually paid a piece rate based on their productivity. This piece rate is based on the number of pieces that a nondisabled worker could produce in a given period of time.

For some, sheltered work is expected to be a step toward competitive employment, whereas others see it as permanent placement (Bond & Boyer, 1988). According to Bond and Boyer (1988), even when sheltered employment is expected to be short term, "there is a tendency for clients to remain indefinitely" (p. 241). Sheltered workshops have come under much criticism in recent years as new vocational strategies such as supported employment have demonstrated that even people with the most severe disabilities can be successful in community employment. With regular employment an individual is more likely to earn better wages, enjoy greater status in the community, develop relationships with nondisabled peers (Murphy & Rogan, 1995), and work for longer periods of time (Bond et al., 1997).

Affirmative Industries

Affirmative industries represent another way agencies offer supervised employment opportunities to clients or members. These businesses are owned, managed, and operated by the agency. Affirmative industries, which can range from commercial cleaning or landscape crews to bakeries and caterers, provide services to the community at large. The mental health agency secures contracts with local citizens and businesses to provide products or services. The workers are clients who are supervised by agency staff and are paid by the agency. This strategy provides members with a mix of support and a regular work experience. There are, however, a number of disadvantages to this approach. Consumer choice is quite limited. Clients must work in the business the agency runs. People with disabilities, working as a group, tend to generate stigma. This may be particularly true if the work crew is used as an employment opportunity for people with severe and more obvious disabilities. Finally, crew members wages tend to be very low (Marrone, 1993). Similar to affirmative industries is client-employing businesses (Marrone, 1993). These businesses employ nondisabled workers as well as people with psychiatric disabilities and may be profit generating.

Supported Employment

"Supported Employment is really part of a social movement. It represents inclusion [of people with disabilities] into the fabric of community settings" (DiLeo in Roberts, 1996, p. 12). With the advent of supported employment, people with the most severe disabilities, who were thought to have no vocational potential and were therefore denied access to vocational services, would finally have a chance in the workplace.

Initially designed for people with severe developmental disabilities, supported employment (SE) emerged in the early 1980s as a response to unsatisfactory employment opportunities (Anthony & Blanch, 1987; Bond et al., 1997). A small number of university-based projects demonstrated that even people with the most severe disabilities could work successfully in community settings if they were placed in jobs and provided the necessary training and support (Roberts, 1996). This new place-train approach reversed the traditional train-place approach whereby clients would attend day programs or simulated work settings—segregated from the regular community—to prepare for employment (Anthony & Blanch, 1987; Danley & Anthony, 1987). Although the vocational and skill deficits produced by severe psychiatric disability made the train-place strategy seem logical, it resulted in very little actual employment and tended to screen out people with the most severe disabilities who were considered too low functioning to be successful in the workplace (Ford, 1995).

SE gained a great deal of attention in the field of psychiatric rehabilitation as well. In 1987, Danley and Anthony articulated the Choose-Get-Keep model of supported employment for people with a psychiatric disability. Danley and Anthony asserted that rather than being placed in a job, people with a psychiatric disability needed to be involved in the process of achieving employment outcomes and that the process needed to include choosing a job that matched an individuals interests, preferences, and skills. Reviewing studies of supported employment, Bond and his colleagues (1997) found that when workers were in jobs that matched their preferences, they stayed twice as long as when the job did not match the worker's preferences.

This combination of choice and support, available either on or off the job site for the duration of the person's employment tenure, has become the hallmark of quality-supported employment for all people with disabilities (Carling, 1995; Department of Education, 1993; Roberts, 1996).

A critical feature of SE is the underlying philosophy that given adequate supports everyone is capable of competitive employment (Anthony & Blanch, 1987; Ford, 1995; Roberts, 1996). The Rehabilitation Act defines SE as

---

BOX 7.3
Karen S. Danley

Karen Danley, Ph.D., was one of the founding members of the Center for Psychiatric Rehabilitation at Sargent College of Health and Rehabilitation Sciences, Boston University. Focusing on vocational rehabilitation, Dr. Danley was largely responsible for the development of the Choose-Get-Keep model of supported employment, which set the tone and standard for this service for PsyR and ultimately the entire field of supported employment. As the first director of Career Achievement Services she established many new program initiatives for the Center for Psychiatric Rehabilitation as well as many innovations for the field. An experienced and successful grant writer, Dr. Danley's efforts have helped to fund much of the important research and training carried out at the center. Some of her recent work included outreach to the inner-city youth of Boston who experience serious mental illness and using the Choose-Get-Keep strategy with veterans who have psychiatric disabilities.

Sadly, Karen Danley passed away in April 1998. Her passing is a great loss for psychiatric rehabilitation. Perhaps her most important legacy is all the individuals she has helped to achieve vocational and educational success.

competitive work in an integrated work setting, with ongoing support services, for individuals with severe handicaps for whom competitive employment has not traditionally occurred or has been interrupted or intermittent as a result of severe handicaps. (Federal Register, 1992, p. 28438)

The Case of Carl

The story of Carl's frustrations and failures at his first attempts to get into the workforce and his eventual success illustrates some of the vocational problems people face. Carl's story also illustrates some of the differences between transitional employment and supported employment. As you read this case, consider the following questions:

1. Why did Carl's first attempts at employment fail?
2. What were the differences between Carl's TE and SE experiences?
3. Is SE the best strategy for every person like Carl?
4. What will be required for Carl to continue to succeed as he moves on to college and more demanding jobs?

Carl is a 32-year-old diagnosed with schizophrenia. Carl experienced his first psychiatric hospitalization at age 18, during his senior year in high school. The first symptoms he was aware of were hearing voices and feeling depressed. Carl's involvement in school activities had been minimal but his grades were good and he was expecting to go to college. After being discharged from the hospital, Carl had to really struggle to finish high school, but he did manage to graduate with his class.

A month after graduation Carl was hospitalized again. This time the voices were more persistent and his depression was more pervasive. When Carl returned home he still felt confused, unmotivated, and lethargic and spent a great deal of time either sleeping or watching television. His dream of going to college and becoming an art teacher seemed remote. His friends from high school had stopped calling; they were busy getting ready for college. During the next 4 years, Carl was hospitalized five times. At his mother's urging, he attempted to take an art class offered by the local YMCA on Saturday mornings, but he felt too groggy in the morning and ended up missing most of the classes.

After Carl's seventh hospitalization, and in response to his parents' complaints that all he did was hang out at home, Carl's psychiatrist recommended that he attend the local partial care program. The program didn't seem right for Carl. He was usually late in the mornings and only participated minimally in the work units and recreational activities. He thought he would like the arts and crafts group but complained that the projects were too simple.

When a position opened for the program's transitional employment job at the local Kmart, Carl's counselor asked him if he'd like to try working. Carl lasted for 1 week at the Kmart. He was almost always late, the voices were making it hard for him to concentrate, and he was reprimanded by his supervisor when he failed to hear a customer ask for help. Carl's counselor said Carl would get another chance to try TE but first he needed to improve his punctuality within the program and learn to accept feedback from his supervisor.

The Case of Carl Continued

Six months later, Carl was given another TEP job. This time Carl worked as a dishwasher in the cafeteria at the local high school. Carl's counselor thought this would be a good job for him because his punctuality had not improved and he would not have to be at this job until 11 A.M. The counselor also thought that because Carl knew people at the school he'd feel less stress. This was Carl's high school. In reality, Carl felt defeated ending up back at his school as a dishwasher. He worked there for 2 weeks before he ran into his former art teacher. Her surprise at seeing him working in the cafeteria highlighted his own feelings of disappointment and failure, and he quit the job.

Carl's program received funding for a new employment strategy, supported employment (SE). Shortly after the program started, Sharon, the SE specialist found Carl outside her office reading the program description on the bulletin board. When she asked Carl if he was interested in work, he told her that he was not able to work because he couldn't get to most jobs on time, couldn't get along with people, and couldn't concentrate on even the simplest things like stocking shelves. Undaunted, Sharon said she was willing to give it a try if he was, and they agreed to meet the next day.

Sharon started by asking Carl to describe his ideal job, and Carl talked about being an art teacher. He described his love for art and how important his high school art teacher had been to him. He talked about the lost opportunity for college and his present inability to succeed at anything. They researched the necessary credentials to be an art teacher and talked about the possibility of college. Carl insisted that he did not have the concentration necessary to pass college courses right now and he was not even confident about his artistic abilities anymore.

Sharon and Carl examined his past experiences. They discovered many examples of Carl's ability to help others use their artistic abilities both in high school, where he worked with younger students, and at the program, where he helped other members in the arts and crafts group. They saw that even when he had to meet deadlines for his art projects, Carl didn't experience the same kind of stress that made him lose concentration when doing simple tasks. They looked at his work history to figure out why he wasn't successful on his jobs and what kinds of supports might have helped him at the time.

Sharon suggested that they contact Carl's high school art teacher because he liked and trusted her and he had worked for her informally by helping other students when he was in school. Sharon thought the art teacher could give them some ideas about jobs that were related to art but that didn't require a college degree. Carl was a little embarrassed and nervous but agreed to let Sharon set up the meeting.

The art teacher met with Carl and Sharon and told them that the after-school program at the elementary school was looking for someone to work part time. She thought that Carl would be allowed to start an art program for the kids and she would be willing to help him plan it. She also agreed to talk to the program director and recommend Carl.

For the first time in a long time, Carl felt hopeful. He knew the morning grogginess from his medication would not interfere because this job started late in the day. He was excited about being involved in art again and felt confident that he could do it. Sharon helped Carl prepare for the interview and select pieces of Carl's artwork that he could show

> **The Case of Carl Continued**
>
> *the program director. They reviewed bus schedules and figured out what bus Carl should take. At the interview, Carl told the program director that he hadn't worked for a while and was hoping someone would be nearby at first in case he felt overwhelmed. Carl and Sharon had agreed that knowing who to go to for help might keep Carl from feeling like he had to quit if he was feeling stressed. They also agreed that at first Sharon would drive Carl to work and stay outside in the car in case he needed her.*
>
> *Sharon drove Carl to work for the first 3 days. At the end of his third day, Carl told Sharon that he'd take the bus the next day and that he'd call her if he needed help or at the end of the day if he managed okay. During the first month Carl called Sharon several times to talk through his nervousness about work. He never missed a day. When the school year ended, the program director offered Carl a job working in the summer recreation program. Sharon was surprised when Carl reported that he was thinking of turning it down. He told her he wanted to talk to her about going to college.*

The Job Coach

SE has led to the emergence of a new kind of practitioner, the job coach. In the early days of SE, the job coach typically arranged for the worker to be placed in a job and then provided training and support to the worker at the job site. The job coach often educated the employer about disabilities and effective ways to teach the new employee and also tried to facilitate the development of relationships between the new worker and his or her coworkers. The job coach may have also assisted the supported employee with money management, transportation, social security benefits monitoring, and other needed supports.

Over the years there has been increasing recognition of the highly professionalized role that the job coach plays. Working without direct supervision, the job coach must successfully accomplish many different tasks. With the emphasis on career choice, the job coach has to know about career planning and development. Taking a broad view of potential careers for people with a psychiatric disability, the job coach has to know about marketing, job development, and effectively interacting with the business community. The job coach has to understand the needs of the business community in general and the needs and work culture of specific work settings.

Gervey and Kowal (1995) reported that it takes an average of 42 job development contacts to generate one job offer. Obviously, the job coach has to be persistent. The job coach may interact with family members, community members, doctors, and other service providers in assisting the supported employee to access needed supports. Perhaps the most important characteristic of a job coach is flexibility. An active job coach may have to provide these services in an executive office, on a loading dock, and in a restaurant kitchen all on the same day.

Reflecting the complex nature of the task, the job coach title has undergone some changes as well. Titles like employment specialist, employment consultant, and human resource consultant among and others, reflect the sophistication and professional nature of the job and the person doing that job.

Supported Employment Program Models

In the relatively brief time that SE has been available to people with mental illness, a variety of approaches have emerged. In part, this is because one of the critical features of SE is the individualized nature of services. Some feared that premature standardization of SE would eliminate the innovative thinking that led to the development of SE to begin with. Another complication is that SE is sometimes added on to more traditional vocational services already being offered by the agency. This may result in an uncomfortable mix of values and competition for resources. Geography may also play a part in the design of services as agencies in rural areas, where jobs are fewer, may be inclined to develop group employment models. Nevertheless, in an update on the status of SE for people with mental illness, Bond and colleagues (1997) identified features of SE that appear to be common across many programs. These include

> a goal of permanent competitive employment, minimal screening for employability, avoidance of prevocational training, individualized placement instead of placement in enclaves or mobile work crews, time-unlimited support, and consideration of client preferences. (p. 336)

Some of the main forms SE programs have taken are described below including the job coach model, the enclave or work crew model, and assertive community treatment.

Job Coach Model

The job coach model is the most individualized approach to SE. In this model, a job coach works with an individual to identify and achieve the person's vocational goal. The services used to achieve this goal will differ depending on the client's needs and wishes as well as the agencies' method.

The best-defined examples of the job coach model for people with mental illness are the Choose-Get-Keep model articulated by Boston University Center for Psychiatric Rehabilitation (Danley & Anthony, 1987; MacDonald-Wilson, Mancuso, Danley, & Anthony, 1989) and the individual placement and support model (IPS) articulated by the New Hampshire-Dartmouth Psychiatric Research Center (Becker & Drake, 1994). These models are highly compatible. Both emphasize competitive employment based on the preferences of the individual and the importance of ongoing support.

Both the Choose-Get-Keep model and the IPS model engage the client and the significant people in the client's life in identifying the person's skills, preferences, interests, resources, and support needs and match these to a job and work setting. In the Choose-Get-Keep model, this is done in the choose phase. By examining past experiences in all areas of the person's life, he or she is helped to identify and objectify those personal values and skills that will impact on the person's success and satisfaction in employment. Clients are helped to identify the skills they've developed through previous experiences and also their reactions to those experiences to illuminate their likes and dislikes, preferences, interests, and support needs. This leads to the development of a career goal and a plan for developing or acquiring the skills and resources necessary for success. (In some cases, the chosen career requires more credentials than the person has and may lead the person to seek of training or education. Supported education, a strategy to provide people with the educational background they need, will be discussed later in this chapter.) Job development, which also occurs in the choose phase, is based on the skills and values of the individual. Significant people in the client's life are engaged in supporting the goal that the client has articulated (MacDonald-Wilson et al., 1989).

In the IPS model this is done in the engagement and vocational assessment stages. This model emphasizes rapid entry into employment and the need to do continual assessment after the client has gotten her or his first job, using each job to gain new information about skills, preferences, and personal style.

In both the get phase of the Choose-Get-Keep model and the obtaining employment stage of the IPS model, the client is given whatever support is needed and desired to obtain a job. In some cases the job coach or employment specialist will teach the skills of job acquisition and the clients will do the actual tasks of job development themselves. Many clients prefer not to disclose their disabilities to potential employers and so prefer to do their own job development. In other cases clients need more direct support in this area and the job coach will be more directly involved in contacting the employer, presenting the candidates qualifications, and perhaps even accompanying the client to the job interview. The job coach also assists in the other tasks of job acquisition such as resume preparation and practicing interviewing. According to Becker and Drake (1994), job development stategies include time spent on the part of the job coach, getting to know the particular operations, needs and hiring practices of potential employers, tapping into personal networks for job leads, and creating jobs where a task and setting match the skills and interests of a client but the job doesn't currently exist. This is sometimes referred to as job carving (DiLeo & Langton, 1993) and is a strategy often used when the severity of a person's disability prohibits the individual from performing all of the duties associated with existing jobs.

The keep phase of the Choose-Get-Keep model and the job support stage of the IPS model involve activities that identify and ensure access to adequate and ongoing support to promote successful and satisfying employment. Some supports may be in the area of learning new skills, learning to use skills in a new setting, accessing needed services, or arranging for environmental modifications. Supports are available on or off the job site and address not only meeting the requirements of the new job or adjusting to the workplace but also coaching and support in the area of interpersonal interactions. In some cases the job coach accompanies the new worker to the job for a period of time. In this case, the job coach may be providing support in mastering the job, negotiating accommodations, and also in fitting into the workplace and developing relationships with coworkers. If the job coach provides some of the job training for the worker, it is usually because the worker requires more training than the employer typically provides. It is least stigmatizing for the supported employee to access the same training that is available to all workers in that setting. Often the support is provided off the job site. This may include supportive counseling, problem solving, and even role-playing difficult interactions. Support provided is not limited to work issues but includes any area of the person's life that affects succcessful employment.

Ideally the job coach is not the sole means of support but has worked with the supported employee to identify and develop a support network. This network may include family, friends, counselors, coworkers, or anyone the client chooses. In fact, there has recently been greater emphasis placed on using "natural supports"—that is, those people or things that are naturally present in the setting. Not only is this usually less stigmatizing, but it is also frequently more effective. Most workplaces and workers in that setting have developed ways of supporting each other. The supported employee should be assisted in accessing those supports and in contributing support to others. It is important that the supported employee hold a valued role as a participant and contributor in the work setting.

The level, type, and frequency of support needed by the supported employee may change over time and the support provided should change accordingly.

According to Bond (1998), the IPS model operates from a set of six principles for which there is direct or indirect empirical support. These principles are consistent with the philosophy of SE and the values of PsyR. The six principles are as follows:

1. Competitive employment is the goal
2. Rapid job search
3. Integration of rehabilitation and mental health
4. Attention to consumer preferences
5. Continuous and comprehensive assessment
6. Time-unlimited support (p. 12)

The Enclave or Work Crew Model

Instead of focusing on an individual, the enclave model of SE places a small group of workers with disabilities in a community employment setting. The group usually works as a separate unit within the business or industry and is trained and supervised by a job coach who is present with the enclave or work crew for the entire work day. In some cases the workers who make up the enclave are dispersed throughout the business or industry. The Rehabilitation Act specifies that an enclave or work crew must include no more than eight individuals with disabilities in order to satisfy the definition of "integrated setting" (Federal Register, 1992). This part of the regulation reflects the PsyR principle of normalization. By keeping work crews or enclaves small, the opportunity for contact with nondisabled workers increases. As with other group models of employment services discussed previously, there are disadvantages to this model of supported employment. Although the enclave or work crew is located in a place of business, it is usually separate from the "regular" employees, which reduces chances for interaction and increases stigma. Furthermore, consumer choice is quite limited as consumers must be willing to do whatever work the enclave or work crew was hired to do.

SE in Assertive Community Treatment

Assertive Community Treatment (ACT) programs, which are described in depth in chapter 8, often include a vocational component. This strategy combines vocational rehabilitation services with other treatment services provided by the ACT team. Using an individualized placement approach, the service is based on the belief that employment is both an outcome and a treatment. "A basic assumption is that a complex relationship exists between symptoms and vocational functioning; thus the ACT model of treatment views work as a critical competing process to symptoms" (Russert & Frey, 1991, p. 342). In other words, the person who is concentrating on performing work tasks is less likely to be preoccupied with his or her symptoms and may be better able to develop coping strategies for symptom management.

Quality Features of SE

Features of SE have been shown to improve employment outcomes. In a review of studies that measured the outcomes of SE, Bond and colleagues (1997) identified three principles that consistently resulted in better outcomes. "First, clients need direct assistance in finding and keeping jobs" (p. 342). It is not enough to provide case managment, skill, or prevocational training. There needs to be a clear expectation of competitive employment as an outcome. "Second, direct approaches to finding and attaining employment, that is place-train models, increase rates of competitive employment more than do gradual, stepwise approaches" (p. 342). Assisting people to become employed quickly rather than going through a step-by-step process of skill development or demonstration had better results. "Third, integration of vocational and clinical approaches is more effective than brokered approaches" (p. 342). The provision of both clinical and vocational services from the same team or agency results in better outcomes than when the client has to deal with two distinct systems.

Vocational Exploration Services

In addition to a review of past experiences, many programs utilize community experiences to improve one's knowledge of oneself as a worker or one's perception of the world of work. This knowledge can facilitate the career-choice process. Some examples of these experiences are as follows:

- *Tours of businesses.* For someone with extremely limited knowledge of the world of work, sometimes just observing the variety of jobs that exists in the community can be the beginning of identifying preferences.
- *Volunteering.* For some individuals, paid employment seems too big a risk or responsibility at first. Volunteering for a short time may help to build self-confidence.
- *Job sampling.* Job sampling programs are usually very brief (a few hours to a few days) work experiences in a variety of real work settings. The person doing the sampling may or may not be paid. If the person is paid, it is ususally by the rehabilitation agency rather than the employer. Job sampling may help someone with very limited knowledge of work begin to identify preferences.
- *Job shadowing.* Accompanying someone else as he or she does a job may give one a clearer idea of the tasks involved.
- *Informational interviews.* Interviewing someone who is currently employed in a job or field of interest may help one get a clearer picture of what that career is like.
- *Worksite interactive internships.* This innovative employment service is a comprehensive career education and planning strategy to assist consumers through an occupational self-discovery process. Based on the Career Planning Curriculum from the Boston University Center for Psychiatric Rehabilitation, this service is designed for people who are interested in going beyond selecting a job and want to explore an occupational area. Consumers are assisted in exploring their own general occupational values and interests, nonvocational activities of interest, and a self-rating of aptitudes, abilities and skills to produce a worker profile. A comparison of the person's profile with characteristics of occupational areas results in the selection of an occupation or field of interest. This interest is then field tested through an internship in that occupation. The internship is arranged by the agency that is providing the service, and it may or may not be paid. At the end of the internship a consumer may decide to pursue this occupation by looking for a job or accessing training or education as required, or the person may decide that he or she is not interested and return to the exploration process (Fishbein, personal communication).

Supported Education

Services to assist people with psychiatric disabilities to access postsecondary educational opportunities emerged in many places around the country in the 1980s. These efforts were in response to the expressed dissatisfaction of younger clients with traditional services and their desire for better futures that education and training promised (Anthony, 1993a; Unger, 1993).

Supported education (SEd), a term coined by the Boston University Center for Psychiatric Rehabilitation (Anthony, 1993a), recognized the importance of postsecondary education in enhancing quality of life, social mobility, career options, career advancement, and self-improvement for anyone while also recognizing the supports that may be critical to success for people with psychiatric disabilities (Cook & Solomon, 1993; Dougherty, Hastie, Bernard, Broadhurst, & Marcus, 1994; Unger, 1990; Unger, 1993).

Borrowing from the definition of supported employment, Unger (1990) defined SEd as follows:

> Education in integrated settings for people with severe psychiatric disabilities for whom post secondary education has not traditionally occurred or for people for whom post secondary education has been interrupted or intermittent as a result of a severe psychiatric disability and who, because of their handicap, need ongoing support services to be successful in the education environment. (p. 10)

In addition to the benefits that continued education and training offer everyone, supported education offers a person with a psychiatric disability services that are desirable in a setting that is normalized and nonstigmatizing. Cook and Solomon (1993) pointed out that the role of student is a valued one and that the college or university setting is not only nonstigmatizing but also offers increased opportunities for social interaction and community integration.

Barriers to Education

In developing SEd programs, practitioners and researchers have identified a number of barriers to overcome. These barriers are similar to those faced in employment.

Stigma

The beliefs held by many mental health and rehabilitation professionals about the abilities of people with psychiatric disabilities to be successful in postsecondary education has resulted in a reluctance to refer clients to or support clients in this effort (Cook & Solomon, 1993; Frankie et al., 1996; Mowbray, Moxley, & Brown, 1993).

Faculty, administration, and staff at postsecondary educational institutions have expressed fears that students with psychiatric disabilities will be disruptive, violent, dangerous, or unable to meet the academic standard (Frankie et al., 1996; Housel & Hickey, 1993).

People with psychiatric disabilities have expressed their own fears of failure, discrimination, and isolation (Cooper, 1993; Dougherty et al.,1994; Mowbray et al., 1993).

Psychiatric Disability

Some barriers are caused by the experience of having a mental illness, such as reduced self-esteem or confidence. Often, the individual's educational career was interrupted by the mental illness and the person may need remedial work in courses such as math and English. Other barriers may be caused by the mental illness itself, such as recurring symptoms, reduced ability to concentrate or process information, susceptibility to anxiety, or stress. Barriers may be caused by medication, such as slowed movements (Cooper, 1993; Mowbray et al., 1993; Dougherty et al.,1994; Frankie et al., 1996).

Availability of Resources

For many students with psychiatric disabilities, securing the financial resources to pay for school, living expenses, child care, and accessing transportation poses significant challenges (Frankie et al., 1996).

Systems Management

Supported education adds, to the sometimes incompatible systems of Vocational Rehabilitation and Mental Health, a postsecondary education institution with its own complicated systems of admission, financial aid, registration, and other factors. Managing these systems may require tenacity, creativity, flexibility, and support (Cooper, 1993; Dougherty et al.,1994; Frankie, et al., 1996).

Models of Supported Education

Supported education has taken many forms. Although some models are well defined, in practice many services modify or combine features of these to meet the needs of the people they serve or to accommodate the circumstances in which they operate.

Unger (1990) described three models of supported education: the self-contained classroom, on-site support, and mobile support.

In the self-contained classroom model, students take a fixed curriculum in a class of students, each of whom has a psychiatric disability. The curriculum focuses on career planning and skill building. The class is held on the school campus and students can access other school activities and resources. At the completion of the curriculum, students may choose to enter postsecondary education or employment. Students who move on to regular college classes continue to access support from the supported education staff (Mowbray et al., 1993; Unger, 1990). This is the least integrated model of supported education.

The On-Site support model assists students in utilizing resources that already exist within the college community. The supported education staff may work to make existing services, such as disabled student services or student counseling services, more relevant or accessible for students with a psychiatric disability (Mowbray et al., 1993; Unger, 1990).

The most individualized approach to supported education is the mobile support model. In this model, SEd staff, sometimes called mobile education support workers (Cook & Solomon, 1993) provide support on or off the education site as needed by the student (Cook & Solomon, 1993; Mowbray et al., 1993; Unger, 1990).

Sullivan, Nicolellis, Danley, and MacDonald-Wilson (1993) applied a Choose-Get-Keep approach to supported education. This approach assists people with psychiatric disabilities to access and examine relevant information so that they can make informed choices about going to or returning to school, develop the needed skills, and secure the supports necessary to be admitted to school and to maintain enrollment.

Quality Features of SEd Programs

Unger (1990) described the values that should be inherent in SEd programs. These are consistent with the values and principles of PsyR and include the following:

- *Self-determination.* The goals, environment, and supports are selected by the student (Sullivan et al., 1993; Unger, 1990).
- *Individualization.* The supports and services are designed to meet the unique needs of the student.(Sullivan et al. 1993; Unger, 1990).
- *Normalization.* The services are integrated and "consistent with the routines of the setting" (Unger, 1990, p. 13). Attention is given to achieving a good match between the student and the setting (Sullivan et al., 1993).
- *Support.* Support is available indefinitely and is flexible to match the changing needs of the student (Unger, 1990).
- *Dignity.* Supports and services protect the privacy and dignity of the individual (Unger, 1990).
- *Hope.* There is an evident belief in the capability of the individual to grow (Unger, 1990).

In addition to these values, Mowbray and colleagues (1993) offered six principles that should guide the development of supported education programs. They are as follows:

1. Integration into normalizing social and interpersonal environments, which can provide diverse socialization experiences
2. Access to leisure, recreational, and cultural resources available to all students on college campuses
3. Skill building of educational competencies, including study skills, attendance, time management, and stress management
4. Opportunities to identify and explore individual vocational interests
5. Support in mastering the educational environment, troubleshooting stress situations, and connecting to natural support networks within the educational setting
6. Peer support from other consumers in the supported education program or through concurrent membership in a clubhouse or other psychoocial rehabilitation alternative (Mowbray et al., 1993, pp. 133–134).

Summary

The barriers to both employment and postsecondary education for people with mental illness include stigma, the experience of mental illness, the disabilities brought about by the illness, and concern about the loss of benefits. Stigma reduces community acceptance of people with mental illness. The stigma that exists among mental health professionals results in reduced quality services and fewer options offered to program clients. A client's internalized stigma reduces the individual's belief in their his or her potential and may be the hardest stigma to overcome. Many people with mental illness, have missed out on important vocational experiences. The illness itself may affect many areas such as memory, concentration, interpersonal interactions, self-esteem, and anxiety. Medication may have overt physical side effects and less obvious social side effects. Individuals with mental illness who rely on public financial assistance may be reluctant to jeopardize this income and medical benefit by attempting employment.

There is strong evidence that past work history is the best predictor of vocational or educational success. Some innovative vocational services were developed for people with psychiatric disabilities as early as the 1950s. Fountain House, one of the original club-houses, introduced transitional employment, a program of real jobs in community settings. Fairweather lodges provide a combination of residential and employment programs. Lodge members live together and work together running a small business. Services such as sheltered workshops and mobile work crews are more segregated and therefore more stigmatizing then regular community employment.

In the 1980s, supported employment (SE) was introduced for people with severe developmental disabilities, and it was adopted in the field of psychiatric rehabilitation as well. SE assists individuals to become employed in jobs that match their skills, interests, and preferences and provides whatever supports are needed to ensure success and satisfaction.

Supported education (SEd), introduced in the 1980s, provides individualized and ongoing services to assist an individual to be successful and satisfied in postsecondary education or training.

Consumer choice, individualized services, self-determination, rapid entry into employment, and time-unlimited support have all been identified as quality features in vocational and educational programs.

The Rehabilitation Act, which established the Rehabilitation Services Administration, provides federal funding for vocational rehabilitation services. It also defines supported employment and emphasizes consumer choice and a presumption of employability for all people with disabilities. The Americans with Disabilities Act, passed in 1990, protects people with disabilities from discrimination in a number of areas including employment and education. This act is a far-reaching statement about the right and ability of citizens with disabilities to be fully included in all aspects of community life.

Class Exercise

The partial care program where you have been a case manager for 3 years, has just been notified that funding to develop supported employment (SE) services is going to be available soon. The director of your agency would like to apply for this funding and has brought together the staff members who are primarily responsible for the transitional employment program (TEP) to design the SE program. It becomes evident immediately that there are many different opinions about how to structure the SE program. Some think that SE should be completely separate from the rest of the program so that clients who want to can access SE without being involved in partial care at all. Others want to use SE as the next step after TEP. Their reasoning is that people have to demonstrate commitment, motivation, and good work behavior before you can convince an employer to hire them. Still others want to develop a multistep program, in which clients spend 8 weeks in a work unit demonstrating attendance, punctuality, good grooming, adequate productivity, ability to work as a team member, and ability to accept feedback from a supervisor. At the same time, clients will attend a work-readiness group where they will discuss reasons for wanting to work. This will be followed by 3 months on a TEP and then the client can go into a SE job.

1. Considering what you've read about predictors of vocational success and quality vocational services, evaluate each of these ideas.
2. Describe an SE program design that incorporates what you have learned about vocational issues and quality services.

References

Anthony, W. A. (1993a). Editorial. *Psychosocial Rehabilitation Journal, 17*(1), 1.

Anthony, W. A. (1993b). Recovery from mental illness: The guiding vision of the mental health service system in the 1990's. *Psychosocial Rehabilitation Journal, 16*(4), 11–23.

Anthony, W. A. (1994). Characteristics of people with psychiatric disabilities that are predictive of entry into the rehabilitation process and successful employment. *Psychosocial Rehabilitation Journal, 17*(3), 3–13.

Anthony, W. A., & Blanch, A. (1987). Supported employment for persons who are psychiatrically disabled: An historical and conceptual perspective. *Psychosocial Rehabilitation Journal, XI* (2), 5–23.

Anthony, W. A., Cohen, M. R., & Danley, K. S. (1988). The psychiatric rehabilitation model as applied to vocational rehabilitation. In J. A. Ciardiello & M. D. Bell (Eds.), *Vocational rehabilitation of persons with prolonged psychiatric disorders.* (pp. 59–80). Baltimore: The Johns Hopkins University Press.

Anthony, W. A., Cohen, M., & Farkas, M. (1990). *Psychiatric Rehabilitation.* Boston: Center for Psychiatric Rehabilitation.

Anthony W. A., & Jansen, M. A. (1984). Predicting the vocational capacity of the chronically mentally ill: Research and policy implications. *American Psychologist, 39,* 537–544.

Arns, P. G., & Linney, J. A. (1993). Work, self, and life satisfaction for persons with severe and persistent mental disorders. *Psychosocial Rehabilitation Journal, 17*(2), 63–79.

Beard, J. H., Propst, R. n., & Malamud, T. J. (1994). The Fountain House model of psychiatric rehabilitation. In Spaniol et al. (Eds.), *An Introduction to Psychiatric Rehabilitation* (pp. 42–52). Columbia, MD: International Association of Psychosocial Rehabilitation Services.

Becker, D. R., & Drake, R. E. (1994). Individual placement and support: A community mental health center approach to vocational rehabilitation. *Community Mental Health Journal, 30*(2), 193–206.

Bell, M., & Lysaker, P. (1996). Levels of expectation for work activity in schizophrenia: Clinical and rehabilitation outcomes. *Psychiatric Rehabilitation Journal, 19*(3), 71–76.

Bell, M. D., Milstein, R. M., & Lysaker, P. H. (1993). Pay and participation in work activity: Clinical benefits for clients with schizophrenia. *Psychosocial Rehabilitation Journal, 17*(2), 173–176.

Blankertz, L., & Robinson, S. (1996). Adding a vocational focus to mental health rehabilitation. *Psychiatric Services, 47*(11), 1216–1222.

Bond, G. R. (1998). Principles of the individual placement and support model: Empirical support. *Psychiatric Rehabilitation Journal, 22*(1), 11–23.

Bond, G. R., & Boyer, S. L. (1988). Rehabilitation programs and outcomes. In J. A. Ciardiello & M. D. Bell (Eds.), *Vocational rehabilitation of persons with prolonged psychiatric disorders* (231–263). Baltimore: Johns Hopkins University Press.

Bond, G. R., Dietzen, L. L., McGrew, J. H., & Miller, L. D. (1995). Accelerating entry into supported employment for persons with severe psychiatric disabilities. *Rehabilitation Psychology, 40*(2), 91–111.

Bond, G. R., & Dincin, J. (1986). Accelerating entry into transitional employment in a psychosocial rehabilitation agency. *Rehabilitation Psychology, 31*, 143–155.

Bond, G. R., Drake, R. E., Mueser, K. T., & Becker, D. R. (1997). An update on supported employment for people with severe mental illness. *Psychiatric Services, 48*(3), 335–346.

Braitman, A., Counts, P., Avenport, R., Zurbinden, B., Rogers, M., Clauss, J., Kulkarni, A., Kymla, J., & Montgomery, L. (1995). Comparison of barriers to employment for unemployed and employed clients in a case management program: An exploratory study. *Psychiatric Rehabilitation Journal, 19*(1), 3–8.

Carling, P. J. (1995). *Return to community: Building support systems for people with psychiatric disabilities.* New York: The Guilford Press.

Chapman, B. (1992). Poll shows support for disabled. *Orlando Sentinel.* In D. DiLeo (Ed.), *Supported employment training competency-based instructional modules* (1st ed.), p. 55. Piscataway, NJ: University Affiliated Program of New Jersey, University of Medicine and Dentistry of New Jersey.

Cook, J. A., & Solomon, M. L. (1993). The community scholar program: An outcome study of supported education for students with severe mental illness. *Psychosocial Rehabilitation Journal, 17*(1), 83–97.

Cooper, L. (1993). Serving adults with psychiatric disabilities on campus: A mobile support approach. *Psychosocial Rehabilitation Journal, 17*(1), 25–38.

Danley, K. S., & Anthony, W. A. (1987). The choose get keep approach to supported employment. *American Rehabilitation, 13*(4), 6–9, 27–29.

Deegan, P. E. (1988). Recovery: The lived experience of rehabilitation. *Psychosocial Rehabilitation Journal, 11*(4), 11–19.

Department of Education. (1993). *Rehab brief: Bringing research into effective focus* (Vol. XV, No. 10, pp. 1–4) Washington, D C: Author.

DiLeo, D., & Langton, D. (1993). Get the marketing edge. St. Augustine, FL: TRN.

Dougherty, S., Hastie, C., Bernard, J., Broadhurst, S., & Marcus, L. (1994). Supported education: A clubhouse experience. In Anthony, W. A., & Spaniol, L. (Eds.), *Readings in Psychiatric Rehabilitation* (pp. 404–422). Boston: Center for Psychiatric Rehabilitation.

Drake, R. E., McHugo, G. J., Becker, D. R., Anthony, W. A., & Clark, R. I. (1996). The New Hampshire study of supported employment for people with severe mental illness. *Journal of Consulting and Clinical Psychology, 64*(2), 391–399.

Fairweather, G. W. (Ed.). (1980). New Directions for Mental Health Services: No. 7. The Fairweather Lodge: A twenty-five year retrospective. San Francisco: Jossey-Bass.

Federal Register. (1992). Department of Education, 28432–28442.

Fishbein, S., Director, Office of Human Resource and Rehabilitation Development, NJ Division of Mental Health Services. Personal Communication, 7/21/98.

Ford, L. H. (1995). *Providing employment support for people with long-term mental illness.* Baltimore: Brookes Publishing.

Frankie, P. A., Levine, P., Mowbray, C. T., Shriner, W., Conklin, C., & Thomas, E. R. (1996). Supported education for persons with psychiatric disabilities: Implementaion in an urban setting. *The Journal of Mental Health Administration, 23*(4), 406–417.

Gervey, R., & Kowal, H. (1995). Job development strategies for placing persons with psychiatric disabilities into supported employment jobs in a large city. *Psychosocial Rehabilitation Journal, 18*(4), 95–113.

Housel, D. P., & Hickey, J. S. (1993). Supported education in a community college for students with psychiatric disabilities: The Houston community college model. *Psychosocial Rehabilitaion Journal, 17*(1), 41–50.

Jansen, M. A. (1988). The psychological and vocational problems of persons with chronic mental illness. In J. A. Ciardiello, & M. D. Bell (Eds.), *Vocational rehabilitation of persons with prolonged psychiatric disorders* (pp. 35–46). Baltimore: Johns Hopkins University Press.

Jones, T. L. (1993). *The Americans with Disabilities Act: A review of best practices.* New York: American Management Association.

Ledbetter, J., & Field, T. F. (1978). A brief history of vocational rehabilitation legislation. *Psychosocial Rehabilitation Journal, II*(3), 35–42.

Lee, B. A., (n. d.). *Reasonable accommodation under the Americans with Disabilities Act.* Bureau of Economic Research, New Brunswick: Rutgers University.

Lysaker, P., & Bell, M. (1995). Work rehabilitation and improvements in insight in schizophrenia. *Journal of Nervous & Mental Disease, 183*(2), 103–106.

MacDonald-Wilson, K. L., Mancuso, L. L., Danley, K. S., & Anthony, W. A. (1989). Supported employment for people with psychiatric disability. *Journal of Applied Rehabilitation Counseling, 20*(3), 50–57.

Mancuso, L. L. (1990). Reasonable accommodations for workers with psychiatric disabilities. *Psychosocial Rehabilitation Journal, 14*(2), 3–19.

Marrone, J. (1993). Creating positive vocational outcomes for people with severe mental illness. *Psychosocial Rehabilitation Journal, 17*(2), 43–62.

McGurrin, M. C. (1994). An overview of the effectiveness of traditional vocational rehabilitation services in the treatment of long-term mental illness. *Psychosocial Rehabilitation Journal, 17*(3), 37–54.

Mowbray, C. T., Bybee, D., Harris, S. N., & McCrohan, N. (1995). Predictors of work status and future work orientation in people with a psychiatric disability. *Psychiatric Rehabilitation Journal, 19*(2), 17–28.

Mowbray, C. T., Moxley, D. P., & Brown, K. S. (1993). A framework for initiating supported education programs. *Psychosocial Rehabilitation Journal, 17*(1), 129–149.

Mueser, K. T., Becker, D. R., Torrey, W. C., Xie, H., Bond, G. R., Drake, R. E., & Dain, B. J. (1997). Work and nonvocational domains of functioning in persons with severe mental illness: A longitudinal analysis. *The Journal of Nervous and Mental Disease, 185*(7), 410–425.

Murphy, S. T., & Rogan, P. M. (1995). *Closing the shop: Conversion from sheltered to integrated work*. Baltimore: Brookes Publishing.

National Alliance of Business. (1991). *ADA sourcebook, what you need to know about the Americans with disabilities act: A guide for small and medium-sized businesses*. Washington, D.C.: Author.

Neff, W. S. (1988). Vocational rehabilitation in perspective. In J. A. Ciardiello & M. D. Bell (Eds.), *Vocational rehabilitation of persons with prolonged psychiatric disorders* (pp. 5–18). Baltimore: Johns Hopkins University Press.

Noble, J. H. (1998). Policy reform dilemmas in promoting employment of persons with severe mental illness. *Psychiatric Services, 49*(6), 775–781.

Onaga, E. E. (1994). The Fairweather lodge as a psychosocial program in the 1990s. In Spaniol et al. (Eds.), *An introduction to psychiatric rehabilitation* (pp. 206–214). Columbia, MD: International Association of Psychosocial Rehabilitation Services.

Rehabilitation Act of 1973, Pub. L. No. 93-112, 87 STAT. 358 (1973).

Roberts, M. (Ed.). (1996). *Supported employment training: Competency-based instructional modules* (3rd ed.). Piscataway, NJ: University Affiliated Programs of New Jersey, University of Medicine and Dentistry of New Jersey.

Roberts, M. (1997). Supported /Transitional employment program design and implementation. In *Integrated employment for persons with psychiatric disabilities: A rehabilitation and recovery-based approach, Module II* (pp. 78–84). Ithaca, NY: Cornell University and Rehabilitation Support Services.

Roberts, M., & Rotteveel, J. (1995). Stigma in the workplace. Presented at the Sixth Annual APSE Conference, Denver, Colorado.

Russert, M. G., & Frey, J. L. (1991). The PACT vocational model: A step into the future. *Psychosocial Rehabilitation Journal, 14*(4), 7–18.

Rutman, I. D. (1994). How psychiatric disability expresses itself as a barrier to employment. *Psychosocial Rehabilitation Journal, 17*(3), 15–35.

Sullivan, A. P., Nicolellis, D. L., Danley, K. S., & MacDonald-Wilson, K. (1993). Choose-get-keep: A psychiatric rehabilitation approach to supported education. *Psychosocial Rehabilitation Journal, 17*(1), 55–68.

Toms Barker, L. (1994). Community based models of employment services for people with long term mental illness. *Psychosocial Rehabilitation Journal, 17*(3), 55–65.

Torrey, W. C, Becker, D. R., & Mowbray, C. T. (1995). Rehabilitative day treatment vs. supported employment II: Consumer, family and staff reactions to a program change. *Psychosocial Rehabilitation Journal, 18*(3), 67–75.

Unger, K. V. (1990). Supported postsecondary education for people with mental illness. *American Rehabilitation, 14*(10), 10–14, 32–33.

Unger, K. V. (1993). Creating supported education programs utilizing existing community resources. *Psychosocial Rehabilitation Journal, 17*(1), 11–23.

Chapter 8

Case Management Strategies

Psychiatric rehabilitation (PsyR) responds to the variety of needs of persons with serious and persistent mental illness. Given the multifaceted nature of the disability caused by these illnesses, and the fragmented systems of care, it is necessary to coordinate services and resources. This coordination is called case management and it is an essential ingredient of psychiatric rehabilitation.

This chapter will answer the following questions:

1. What is case management?
2. Why do psychiatric rehabilitation services require so much coordination?
3. What are the different approaches to case management?
4. Why is case management essential to psychiatric rehabilitation?
5. What is the evidence that case management is effective?

Introduction

Deinstitutionalization, the national policy of discharging institutionalized psychiatric patients back to the community, reached its peak during the early 1970s. Moving the site of
treatment from large, long-term institutions to the community was an important milestone
for persons with severe and persistent mental illness. In a 5-year period between 1970 and
1975, more than 100,000 patients were discharged into the community for treatment. By
1985 the number of patients in state and county psychiatric hospitals around the country
had been reduced by 450,000.

As they deinstitutionalized, psychiatric hospitals also began to reduce the length of stay
of newly admitted patients. Unlike the previous era, when long-term hospitalization was the
rule, psychiatric hospitals began discharging patients after very short stays. Sadly, many of
those discharged returned to the hospital after equally short stays in the community. This
created a new set of problems for these people and the psychiatric treatment system that
was supposed to serve them.

The number of patients returning to the hospital, known as **recidivism**, also grew. This
problem of frequent discharge and readmittance to the hospital became known as the revolving door syndrome. Warehousing patients in large psychiatric institutions was a thing
of the past, but community treatment still had a long way to go to meet the needs of people
with psychiatric disabilities. Compounding these problems was the fact that most of the
money spent for hospital treatment stayed at the hospitals rather than following the patients
into the community to provide treatment for them there.

Mental health planners found that the concept of "cheaper by the dozen" has a flip side.
As the number of patients in the hospital decreased, most hospital costs tended to remain
the same. In fact, it cost almost as much to run a hospital at 30% of its capacity as it had to
operate that same institution at 110% of capacity.

As these problems became apparent, considerable criticism of the national policy of
deinstitutionalization was raised by lay persons, professionals, and consumers. One critical
report questioned a policy that "releases mental patients into community facilities that don't
exist" (Santiestevan, 1975).

In 1986 *Newsweek* magazine wrote an expose on the effects of deinstitutionalization.
Labeled "abandoned," the article pointed out that despite the good intentions of the deinstitutionalization reforms, thousands of people with mental illness were left to fend for
themselves on the street.

> Todd had his first psychotic episode at 20, after a prep-school career marked by bril-
> liance in science, baseball and the piano. His family spent his college tuition on private
> psychiatric care—and when their savings were exhausted, transferred him to a state
> mental institution. In and out of the hospital for years, Todd, now 37, recently was re-
> leased to a boarding home in Worcester, Mass. Three weeks later he was mugged—an
> event which precipitated yet another psychotic breakdown. "He tried so hard to make
> it," his mother says. "They all try so hard, and they fail because they receive no care.
> Its torture for the families to watch that. These people are too sick to be let out into

the community without any help. Its a national disgrace." (*Newsweek*, January 6, 1986, pp. 14–15)

Several researchers at the time (Aviram & Segal, 1973; Kirk & Therrien, 1975; Klerman, 1977; Kohen & Paul, 1976) saw the deinstitutionalization movement as essentially an overambitious, unrealistic plan driven by rhetoric and myth but lacking any real planning. Planners had underestimated the difficulties of recently released patients. In fact, patients were often "ghettoized" or socially excluded (Aviram & Segal, 1973). One consumer wrote that the conditions she saw in the community were often worse than those in the hospital and that it was a myth that one treatment setting (i.e., community) was better than another (i.e., hospital) (Allen, 1974). In fact, for many of the people who were deinstitutionalized, the movement that was heralded as bringing important (legal) rights to psychiatric patients was actually a major catastrophe in terms of their **quality of life**.

The Need for Continuity of Care

As with any broadly disabling condition, the person coping with major mental illness often requires a wide scope of services. These include basic needs such as food, shelter, and clothing. Various type of treatment and rehabilitation are also required. Ideally, these services are delivered in an uninterrupted flow over time until the disability is corrected or compensated for. This issue of receiving all the services necessary for the length of time they are required is called **continuity of care**. The continuity of care issues for people experiencing severe and persistent mental illnesses are critically important and, because of the nature of the disability, often difficult to solve. Major continuity of care problems first arose as patients moved from the centralized, institutional environment of the psychiatric hospital to the decentralized, multiagency environment of the community. Hospital environments had been designed to meet the basic needs of their patients.

Some researchers believed that the continuity of care needs of the patients was an important hospital benefit that was inadvertently lost with the rush to deinstitutionalize (Kirk & Therrien, 1975). The hospitals usually included medical staff, housekeeping staff, and recreation workers, all integrated within one large institution. In contrast, community services have often been provided by different agencies and programs that rarely communicated with one another. This situation still exists today.

On returning to the community, a typical consumer might find herself attending a partial care program or clubhouse during the day, receiving her medication from a private physician, and living in a private boarding home. Moving from one organization, the hospital, where the smallest details of her life were orchestrated by the staff, she now has to deal with three or more separate organizations. In the hospital her modest economic needs for food, clothing, and shelter were met. Now, in the community, she has concerns about maintaining her income through disability or welfare payments. In addition, she now needs medical benefits, from Medicaid or a similar program, in order to pay for her physician, medication, and treatment services. Worse still, if she failed in any of these community settings she might find herself on the street, out of medication, or back in the hospital. In one sense, at the very moment she is trying to reestablish herself in the community, her opportunities for failure have been tripled. Paradoxically, improvements in her life might prove to be equally troublesome. A large reduction in symptoms or obtaining regular employment might make her ineligible for her disability benefits or medical coverage.

The service delivery systems available for these newly released patients in the community were new and usually uncoordinated. With several agencies or programs responsible for different aspects of a patient's treatment, a systemic kind of *diffusion of responsibility* problem arose. Diffusion of responsibility occurs when shared responsibility for an issue leads each responsible party to assume that another party will take care of the situation (Darley & Latane, 1968). This social and psychological phenomenon can be observed in large cities where bystanders will literally step over someone lying on the sidewalk or when drivers pass a broken down car by the side of the road, each driver thinking that someone else has called for help. In effect, although everyone was responsible for some aspect of a patient's treatment and care, no one was responsible for the whole patient. Staff at one agency would assume some other agency or person should be taking care of issues that his or her own agency was not designed or funded to deal with. This increased jeopardy created a situation by which consumers were said to fall through the cracks of the service delivery system. These consumers would often return to the hospital, end up living on the streets, or become homebound recluses.

In addition to the difficulty of connecting with needed services in the community, the newly discharged patient often found that certain services did not exist (Test, 1979). Partly because of a lack of affordable housing, in many areas patients were given bus tickets and literally discharged into the streets. Vocational programs were also in very short supply during the early stages of the deinstitutionalization process. In these situations, continuity of care could not be achieved because there were no available services.

To appreciate the vast scope of this problem we must multiply the plight of each individual consumer by the hundreds of thousands of deinstitutionalized patients. The increased stress associated with dealing with a complex, often disorganized and unconnected treatment delivery system contributed to the high rates of recidivism experienced by the deinstitutionalized population.

The risk of rehospitalization is highest during the first 6 months after a person is discharged from the hospital. People are hospitalized during **acute phases** of their illness and this instability may extend past their discharge. The obvious stress related to psychiatric relapse, or **decompensation**, and then returning to the community may also add to high rates of recidivism in the 6 months following discharge.

Probably the most important single cause of recidivism is failure to connect with needed services and supports in the community. Everyone is aware of the difficulties and frustrations involved in dealing with large, impersonal bureaucratic systems. The newly discharged consumers often have to connect with new agencies, doctors, and staff persons. They have to make these connections at the very time when they may be least likely to cope with the frustrations and stress that we all experience dealing with large organizations or new situations. It is little wonder that persons with stress-related disorders become ill during the months directly after discharge.

BOX 8.1
An Innovation in Psychiatric Rehabilitation

Just as with other sciences, many of the innovations in psychiatric rehabilitation have emerged from seemingly casual observations and the initiatives of regular staff members "doing what comes naturally." The "discovery" of what would emerge as the assertive community treatment model describes such an event:

> About the fall of 1970, soon after Dr. Arnold Marx had assumed leadership of the Special Treatment Unit [STU] (a research unit of the Mendota Mental Health Institute), and after Mary Ann Test had been at the STU for two of what had become rather standard six-month long studies, a critical event happened at the traditional staff party held to celebrate the end of each study and to generate ideas about what type of study to do next. Few staff came. Those present pulled their chairs into

> a circle and began to discuss why others did not show up. Some staff did not come, it was observed, because their morale was low. They were discouraged because, despite their energetic efforts to create innovative inpatient treatments enabling discharge (Mendota is a Wisconsin state psychiatric hospital), discharged patients kept coming back to the hospital. Some aides suggested that they would not do another similar study.
>
> In this discussion, one aide observed that when a social worker, Barb, followed patients into the community and provided aftercare, these patients tended not to come back to the hospital. As the evening wore on, they talked about how Barb did this. Someone suggested that the STU should do what Barb did and abandon the inpatient interventions. Eventually, it was agreed that this is what they would do, and the STU leadership, Drs. Marx and Test, stuck to this decision in the morning and thereafter. The next STU study was to be one about caring for persons with severe mental illness in the community. (Greenley, 1995, pp. 9–10)

Awareness of the Need for Case Management at the National Level

As the negative effects of massive deinstitutionalization became more widely known, the need for case management for the mentally ill population in the community became a concern at the national level. The U.S. Congress passed PL99-660 (1973), the Comprehensive Mental Health Services Act, which required each state to develop a plan for providing community-based services for persons suffering from severe and persistent mental illness. This act required each state to include case management services as an element of its plan.

In an effort to respond to the obvious unmet needs of the newly deinstitutionalized, in 1977 the National Institute of Mental Health (NIMH) created the Community Support Program (CSP). This program provided for nationwide demonstration projects to improve services to persons experiencing chronic (today we would say persistent) mental illness (Turner & TenHoor, 1978). CSP projects employed state-of-the-art solutions and strategies to meet client needs in the community. One strategy the program managers employed to meet the comprehensive needs of people with a chronic mental illness was case management.

Case Management

The term *case management* can mean widely different things to PsyR workers around the country. Despite the varied treatment procedures these differences usually represent, there is fairly good agreement about the goals of a case management system. Case management refers to any "process or method for insuring that the consumer is provided needed services in a coordinated, effective and efficient manner" (Baker & Intagliata, 1992, p. 215).

Baker and Intagliata (1992) have done extensive research on case management. They define four basic service objectives that are common to successful case management services. These programs ensure the following:

1. *Continuity of care.* The client receives comprehensive services over an appropriate period of time.
2. *Accessibility.* The client can enter or utilize the services he or she needs.
3. *Accountability.* The system accepts responsibility for the services it provides the client.
4. *Efficiency.* Services are provided in an appropriate and economical fashion.

Providing consumers with needed services in a coordinated, effective, and efficient manner actually requires many distinct case management functions. Agranoff (1977) suggested that a good case management system should carry out five basic functions for its clients:

1. *Assessing.* Identifying the client's needs,
2. *Planning.* Developing a comprehensive service plan for the client
3. *Linking.* Connecting the client with services to be delivered
4. *Monitoring.* Ensuring that the services are actually delivered to the client
5. *Evaluating.* Assessing the client's response to services and providing follow-up

Furthermore, Baker and Intagliata (1992) suggested that a good case management system may also (a) reach out to clients who are service resistant, (b) advocate for clients so that they receive services at other agencies and programs, and (c) provide direct services to clients.

The Case Manager

The case manager is both a psychiatric rehabilitation Jack-of-all-trades and the single point of responsibility at the core of the case management service. This PsyR *generalist* carries out the functions listed by performing many different roles, including but not limited to "case manager, integrator, expediter, broker, ombudsman, advocate, primary therapist, patient representative, personal program coordinator, systems agent and continuity agent" (Baker & Intagliata, 1992, p. 217).

At its best, case management is the epitome of individualized service. Each consumer is met on her or his own ground and dealt with individually. The case manager's first task is to comprehend the needs and aspirations of the individual consumer. To accomplish this, the case manager must form a close working relationship with the consumer based on trust. With this assessment also comes a clear understanding of the aspects of the psychiatric disability that must be dealt with through the case management process to achieve the consumer's goals. Working together, the next step for the consumer and case manager is to develop a comprehensive plan. The plan should take into account strengths and weaknesses as well as environmental contingencies that will help the consumer reach his or her desired goals. Consumer input at this planning stage is critical for future success. Goals that are not *owned* by the consumer probably won't be achieved by the consumer. This concept is explained in more detail in chapter 5.

The next step is for the case manager to help the consumer link up with the agencies, services, or organizations necessary for achieving the goals of the plan. This phase might be carried out by the case manager or by the consumer depending on the types of services needed and the ability of the consumer. Regardless of who makes the initial contact, it is important for the case manager to form and maintain an ongoing professional relationship with each of the services the consumer is utilizing. This will allow the case manager to perform other functions such as monitoring, advocating, and evaluating if they are needed. Some level of monitoring should take place even if no problems exist. If carried out unobtrusively, this process can have important benefits. The consumer may be reassured that someone is watching out for his or her interests. The agency or service will be reminded that the case manager is an available resource and support if the need arises.

Some case management systems, such as assertive community treatment, are designed with the idea that the case manager will provide many of the services the consumer requires.

One of the most difficult tasks for the case manager is evaluating the consumer's progress toward his or her goals. Working with the consumer, the case manager needs to help assess progress and develop priorities for services and goals. Premature advancement to the next phase of a plan can be as great a threat as failure to advance to the next step when the consumer is ready. Because of the difficulties inherent in assessing others and in being evaluated, the level of trust established in the working relationship between the consumer and the case manager is often tested at this stage of the process.

Finally, achieving goals may not signal the end of the process. Often, new needs and aspirations emerge as goals are achieved. An effective case management process is prepared to provide support for the consumer indefinitely.

The Case Management Team

Many case management models actually employ teams rather than individual case managers to provide services (Test, 1992). The use of teams, rather than solo practitioners, to provide services is one of the hallmarks of PsyR. A typical case management team is interdisciplinary, made up of professionals and workers from several distinct rehabilitation and treatment professions. A team might consist of PsyR professionals working with a vocational rehabilitation specialist, a case manager who is also an identified consumer, a psychiatrist, and a nurse. The ideal case management team can provide almost the entire range of services needed by the consumer in the community. Highly mobile, these teams provide services to the consumer where they are in the community. Operating 24 hours a day, 7 days a week, the team is ready for crisis intervention when it is needed. Around-the-clock continuity of care is available if it is needed.

Teams also have the advantage of providing reliable case management over the long term. Some case management programs have experienced high rates of staff turnover. Staff members work round the clock in the community, often on the streets. They are often responsible for a large and challenging caseload. All this can lead to **staff burnout**. When a staff person leaves the team, other team members who have also formed a good working relationship with the consumer can take his or her place.

Teams can have important effects on their members. Team members can help keep one another's motivation and morale high and provide support for each other when problems arise and the going gets tough. This spirit of comraderie and support can help make teams much more effective than the same workers would be if they were carrying out their roles as individual practitioners.

Models of Case Management

A large number of case management programs around the country are composed of program elements and philosophies borrowed from different program models. Despite this confusion, a number of identifiably unique models of case management exist and can be defined.

Solomon (1992) identified four types of commonly practiced case management:

1. Expanded broker model
2. Rehabilitation model
3. Personal strengths model
4. Full support model

A short explanation of each of these models is provided next. Most of these models have many common characteristics. For example, in each model the assessment and treatment planning process is individualized rather than being based on available services. When actually applied to the real world, program administrators and staff may combine one or more of these models. On the other hand, they may choose not to employ a particular element of a given model.

The full support model is given the most attention. Also referred to as **assertive community treatment (ACT)**, the full support model is the most comprehensive case management approach and probably has had the most influence on subsequent case management program designs.

Expanded Broker Model

Staff working in the expanded broker model, also called the generalist model, depend on referrals to other agencies and services in the community for most of the basic services provided to their clients. This traditional case management model uses its staff primarily for assessment, planning, linking, and advocating. In general, the staff of the expanded broker model program acts as an agent for the client rather than a service provider. Staff members become resource persons steering their clients to different agencies or services to meet specific needs. Staff members also function as liaisons, advocates, and troubleshooters for their clients. For example, if a consumer was experiencing problems at her or his boarding home, the case manager might meet with the boarding home manager to discuss the problem and arrange for additional services, such as personal skills training (personal hygiene, clothes washing, etc.). It should be obvious from this example that for the staff member working in the expanded broker model, direct experience with existing community services (including knowing key staff persons, program rules and hours, etc.) is a must.

Although its influence on the quality and emphasis of services provided is necessarily reduced, this model has the advantage of allowing for much larger caseloads than do the other three models. Obviously, the effectiveness of the expanded broker model depends on the comprehensiveness and effectiveness of existing community services. The case management task in such an environment is to ensure that the consumer takes advantage of the services that are available.

Rehabilitation Model

This model follows a traditional rehabilitation approach. Emphasis is on helping the clients to achieve success in the environments of their choice rather than emphasizing a comprehensive program for improvement. Clients are given a **functional assessment** from which a rehabilitation plan is developed. Under this model, the case manager focuses on skill development until the client establishes a support network (Goering, Wasylenki, Farkas, Lancee, & Ballantyne, 1988). In a sense, the rehabilitation model is case management within the context of the overall PsyR approach (Hodge & Drain, 1993). Chapter 5 provides a detailed overview of the PsyR assessment and service planning process.

Personal Strengths Model

The personal strengths model, also known as the development-acquisition model, is based on two assumptions (Modrcin, Rapp, & Chamberlin; 1985). The first assumption is that to be a successful person you must be able to use, develop, and access your own potential and have the resources to do this. The second assumption is that a person's behavior is dependent on the resources the person has available. A focus on the individual's strengths, as opposed to the individual's pathology, is the defining element of this model, making it consistent with PsyR principles. In this model, the case manager acts as a mentor who assists the client in problem solving and resource development (Hodge & Draine, 1993).

Full Support Model

In addition to providing the five basic case management functions, the full support model attempts to directly provide most or all of the necessary services for its clients. Thus there is much less emphasis on referring clients to other existing community services. In other words, case managers utilizing the full support model are providing basic case management services plus a variety of rehabilitative and treatment services. Typically, an interdisciplinary team composed of specialists from different services areas such as housing, nursing, and vocational rehabilitation is employed to ensure that clients have everything they need to make a good adjustment in the community.

The Development of Training for Community Living

In the early 1970s Mary Ann Test, Ph.D., and Leonard Stein, M. D., working at the Mendota Mental Health Institute in Madison, Wisconsin, began developing strategies to solve the revolving door problem at their hospital and hospitals around the country. Test and Stein set out to reduce recidivism rates by supporting their patients in the community so effectively that they would not need to be continually readmitted for inpatient treatment. They started with the assumption that high readmission rates came about because patients needs were not being met in the community (Stein & Test, 1980). They believed that discharged patients had the following needs, which had to be met for them to be able to remain in the community:

1. Material resources, such as food, shelter, clothing, medical care, and recreation
2. Coping skills to meet the demands of community life
3. Motivation to persevere and remain involved with life
4. Freedom from pathological dependent relationships
5. A supportive system, which assertively helps the patient with the previous four requirements

The model they developed was called training in community living (TCL). They implemented it in a program where they could conduct ongoing research, which eventually became known as the program for assertive community treatment (PACT). TCL introduced to psychiatric rehabilitation, an important innovation and a support system that takes an assertive stance in helping consumers to stay out of the hospital. TCL staff members visited clients in the community, wherever and whenever they needed assistance, rather than asking them to come to a particular site. This approach has been referred to as "a hospital without walls" (Harron, 1993), because it was designed as an alternative to inpatient treatment.

Test (1992) reported that the Madison TCL program team consisted of 13 staff members providing services for 115 persons with schizophrenic disorders. The team's main goal was to meet the needs necessary to maintain the patient in the community. To accomplish this, the team developed individualized service plans for each patient. Whenever possible the team also carried out most aspects of the treatment plan. The interdisciplinary team, which was made up of specialists such as mental health technicians, nurses, and vocational rehabilitation counselors, worked together in a generalist staffing mode to meet each client's needs. A generalist staffing pattern implies that each staff person can and did do each task. A psychiatrist was also a part-time member of the team.

TCL services were provided in the community, at the patient's home, recreation, or job site. This is sometimes referred to as **in vivo**, or in the client's environment. There are many advantages to this approach—for example, teaching a client a skill in the location where it will be used is a highly effective intervention (see chapter 5 for more on this concept). Perhaps most important, staff used a very assertive outreach strategy to assure that services were provided when and where they were needed. For example, if a client had difficulty remembering to take the correct dosage of medications, team members might visit him at home once or twice a day to deliver and monitor the medications. When appropriate, the TCL team also worked with families, community agencies, landlords, or whoever was involved in a client's support system.

Providing services to patients in the community ensures that these services are individualized rather than watered down to meet the needs of a large group. The team provides patients with symptom management in the form of medication, round-the-clock on-call services for crises intervention, and brief hospitalization if necessary. The team also helps patients obtain basic needs like food and shelter, social supports, and assistance with family relations. Finally, the team helps patients secure and maintain regular employment positions in the community. Initially, TCL was designed as a time-limited program. Follow-up research studies indicated that many patients regressed when the program supports were removed. Rather than being time limited, the current program is designed to provide services indefinitely on an as-needed basis.

The revolving door process of readmitting patients for short-term hospitalizations and then returning them to the community for aftercare services, was both ineffective and very costly. Test and Stein believed that it would be better for the patient, and less costly for the system, to provide intensive case management services and keep the patient in the community. Research study results (Stein & Test, 1985; Test, 1992) supported their beliefs, and TCL was soon replicated in other parts of Wisconsin and eventually in other states and countries as well.

When implemented in different locations, some agencies began to modify the TCL model to address the unique needs of their client population or to compensate for limited resources. For example, a program serving a high percentage of individuals with a MICA diagnosis might require several team members to be substance abuse specialists; or a program that lacks the financial resources to include psychiatrists and nurses on its teams might contract with another agency to provide medical and psychiatric services. Although not strictly adhering to the full range of services provided by the original TCL program, these programs were strongly influenced by the work of Test and Stein. Today, most PsyR professionals refer to the TCL model, and its many variations, as assertive community treatment (ACT).

CONTROVERSIAL ISSUE
Program Standardization versus Program Diversity

Some consumer advocates have called for increased vigilance on the part of state and federal funding sources to ensure that programs are operated strictly as designed. Other advocates, sometimes represent-

ing the same groups, have lauded programs that have experimented with new strategies and methods.

Many researchers have commented on the great diversity to be found among programs labeled case management (Bond, McGrew, & Fekete, 1995; Chamberlin & Rapp, 1991; Solomon, 1992). These differences in implementation, methodology, and philosophy, in turn, affect the outcomes that these programs achieve. The

Bond research team suggests that the ultimate question is "What program characteristics lead to which client outcomes for which clients, and at what cost." Clearly, it is hard to judge the effectiveness of a treatment strategy such as case management if programs implement the strategy differently. This problem is compounded when we consider the problems raised by differences in the client populations served by these programs. Program clients may have different diagnoses, different levels of symptomatology and disability, diverse cultural backgrounds, varying levels of social and economic support, and may live in widely different geographic and environmental settings, to name just some of the more obvious differences. Programs often try to adjust to this diversity by altering their methods, strategies, and, ultimately, their philosophies.

Increased program standardization could be mandated by funding sources. States mandate how many days public schools stay open each year, what classes students must take, and the credentials and training of teachers. The amount of time someone spends in the hospital for a specific condition, such as a tonsillectomy, and the appropriate treatment procedure is also mandated. State and federal funding sources could write strict guidelines describing how a case management program is staffed and operated. Instead, state and federal guidelines for these programs, when they exist, tend to be very broad.

This lack of clarity has distinct advantages. The diversity among programs holds out the possibility of discovering improved methods for achieving positive outcomes for program clients. Partly because PsyR is such a young discipline, knowledge about which techniques and strategies produce the best outcomes for clients is constantly growing and changing. This opportunity for the creative development of new treatment strategies helps make PsyR an exciting profession.

The Case of Micky

The situation described in this case study is a good example of the day-to-day challenges that face a PsyR professional working in case management. As you read, consider the strategies represented by the different models of case management.

1. What services did the case management team employ to help Micky?
2. What do you think they could have done differently?
3. What could they have done that might have been more effective?
4. What model of case management does this team most resemble and how can you tell?

At 23 years old, Micky had been hospitalized six times since her 19th birthday. A bright student who got only average grades, Micky had spent most of high school writing poetry and smoking marijuana. She had her first full-blown psychotic episode a month after graduation and was hospitalized the next year with a diagnosis of schizophrenia, paranoid type.

Her psychotic episodes followed a predictable pattern. After being stabilized on medication in the hospital, Micky would be discharged to a residential program. Initially, Micky would exhibit an unusually high level of functioning for a recently discharged person with her diagnosis. For several months she would make excellent progress toward the educational or vocational goals she had set with the help of her caseworker at the mental health center.

The Case of Micky Continued

Then, as she neared her goal, Micky would typically stop taking her medication, because she was free from any symptoms and accomplishing a great deal. This was followed in several weeks by a psychotic episode, during which Micky usually blamed her caseworker for all her problems, dropped out of her job or school, and ran away. When she was found, frightening hysterical outbursts followed, which usually led to Micky being put out of her residence and hospitalized. Her doctors had tried long-acting, injectable medication, but this did not break Micky's cycle of decompensations.

After discharge from the hospital Micky was always very grounded in reality and rational. Because she was friendly and had a good vocabulary many of her caseworkers scheduled individual therapy sessions with her. During these sessions Micky exhibited good insight about her cycle of decompensation. Many of her caseworkers believed that Micky's insight regarding the obvious pattern of her behavior would ensure that the same events would not happen again.

Now, being discharged for the sixth time in 4 years, Micky was being referred to a case management team. She first met two of the team members in the hospital. They had talked to her about where she wanted to live and what she wanted to do when she left the hospital. Before discharge, one of the team members drove her to a garden apartment complex to meet a woman named Sylvia who she might share an apartment with there. Micky and Sylvia got along fine. Sylvia had been hospitalized once, 2 years ago. Since then she had completed her schooling and worked for a small company putting documents on microfilm for storage. Sylvia had been with the case management team since her discharge.

Micky had decided to go to work after discharge rather than go back to school. With the aid of one member of the case management team who seemed to know where to find jobs, Micky got a job as a billing clerk in a local heating oil company. The same team member visited Micky on the job for several weeks until she was sure that everything was going well. After discussing it with her caseworker, Micky decided to tell her fellow workers and the boss that she had been in the hospital. She was nervous about admitting her mental illness but pleased when she found that they were accepting rather than rejecting. Several days after she had told the others about her mental illness, one of the other clerks called Micky aside. Swearing her to secrecy, she told Micky that she had been to a psychiatrist after her divorce and that he had given her pills to take. Micky felt accepted.

She got along well with Sylvia. Team members visited the apartment frequently when Micky first moved in. They helped arrange for special services like bank accounts and a telephone in her room. They also set up meetings so she and Sylvia could devise ways of sharing the household bills like the rent, telephone, gas, and electric. They divided the household chores like cooking, cleaning, shopping, and washing clothes between them. At the end of each week, a team member would visit and ask how things were going, if there were any problems, and if there was anything special coming up during the following week. Micky and Sylvia became friends.

The Case of Micky Continued

As the members of the case management team knew, rapid initial success after discharge was Micky's typical pattern. Their goal was to identify signs of decompensation and intervene as quickly as possible to prevent another decompensation and hospitalization. They informed Micky and Sylvia about this plan. They told Micky that if and when she began to decompensate, they would arrange for her to see the team psychiatrist for evaluation and a possible increase or change in medication. They also told her that if necessary they would arrange for a leave of absence at her work and that they had a respite bed available if she needed more structure than she had at the apartment. Rather than try to elicit insight regarding her part in the pattern, the team members told Micky that her pattern of decompensations was caused by her illness. They stressed that she had a biological disease like diabetes or arthritis and that one of the symptoms of her illness was periodic psychotic relapses. Her job was to recognize when she was becoming ill and to inform them so that they could help her get more treatment.

Eight months after moving in with Sylvia, Micky decided to stop taking her medication. After a week, Sylvia noticed that Micky's medication had not been touched and asked her about it. Micky got very angry at first but Sylvia reminded her of what the team had said about her decompensations. Sylvia told Micky that it wasn't her fault but that she needed to get more help. Micky called a team member and explained what had happened. An hour later the psychiatrist was at the apartment. After evaluating Micky, he changed her medication, adding something to help her sleep better. He asked her to come to see him the next day at the office to see how the new medications where doing. When the team members left, Micky thanked Sylvia for helping her.

Micky continued to get worse for several days. She had several fights with Sylvia and got into a fight with a coworker. One evening she felt so agitated that she asked to sleep at the respite bed where there was a 24-hour nurse. A team member came to the apartment every evening during this crisis time to see how things were going and monitor Micky's progress. A week and a half after she had seen the psychiatrist, Micky began to feel better. She felt the same way she had each time she had been discharged from the hospital. But this time she hadn't been in the hospital, she still had her job and her apartment and Sylvia was still talking to her.

Evaluating Case Management

Since its development, numerous research studies have been carried out to evaluate the effectiveness and efficiency of case management. Partly because of the differences between case management programs, the results of these studies have been mixed and sometimes contradictory. Nevertheless, there is clear consensus that case management is effective for achieving certain results. This research literature answers specific questions about the effectiveness of specific types of case management programs (Bond, McGrew, & Fekete, 1995; Chamberlin & Rapp, 1991; Mueser, Bond, Drake, & Resnick, 1998; Solomon, 1992).

Evaluating Training for Community Living

As the success of TCL (Training for Community Living) became apparent, Test and Stein (1978) conducted research to test the effectiveness of their program compared with the traditional services offered in Madison. Their research design consisted of randomly assigning new psychiatric hospital intakes to either the TCL program or traditional treatment, which consisted of hospitalization and referral to a community agency. By the end of the first year, 130 patients, evenly divided between those receiving TCL and those receiving traditional treatment, were included in their study. Of the 65 patients assigned to TCL, only 12 were hospitalized. This compared to 58 of the 65 traditional treatment patients who were hospitalized. In addition, TCL patients spent an average of 11 days in the hospital compared with the control group's average of 37 days in the hospital.

Evaluating Case Management Outcomes

Chamberlin and Rapp (1991) reviewed what they considered the relevant research literature on case management. They began by evaluating the quality of the research represented by each paper. Applying very stringent criteria, they selected a small number of research papers on case management that were appropriate for review. Chamberlin and Rapp concluded that the primary focus of the intervention in a case management program (except when employing an expanded broker program model) is usually successful. In other words, whatever the program sets as its first or primary priority will probably be achieved. Or as they state it,

> defining a principal focus seems sufficient to insure achievement on that dimension.
> (p. 185)

Solomon (1992) examined 20 studies and came to the conclusion that case management is effective in reducing recidivism rates as well as the number of days that are spent in the hospital. She also concluded, but with somewhat less certainty, that case management often improved the client's quality of life. Solomon went on to make a very insightful point about the impact of case management, which is supported by the previous study by Chamberlin and Rapp. She suggested that because case management is essentially more of a system management service than a clinical service, it affects system outcomes, such as recidivism rates, more than clinical outcomes, such as level of functioning. In short, it produces outcome effects such as reducing hospitalization by ensuring that necessary services are provided in a timely manner. But because case management does not represent an improvement in services, the clinical and functioning state of the consumer is no more affected than it would be by traditional services.

A study by Bond, McGrew, and Fekete (1995) used meta-analysis, a technique for combining data from several studies into one large study, to evaluate the assertive outreach model of case management. First developed at Thresholds, a psychiatric rehabilitation agency in Chicago, this model is similar to the TCL model described earlier. The Bond team combined the results of nine separate studies from Illinois, Indiana, and Pennsylvania, all designed to evaluate the assertive outreach model of case management. The meta-analytic

---

BOX 8.2
Gary Bond

The research and writing of Gary Bond, Ph.D., professor of rehabilitation psychology at Indiana University-Purdue University Indianapolis, has contributed immeasurably to the field of psychiatric re-

habilitation. Since entering the field as director of research at Thresholds, a large PsyR agency in Chicago, he has worked to understand how services can be more effective and to train professionals to work in the field.

When he went to Thresholds for the first time, Dr. Bond found that the practical and egalitarian orientation appealed to him, as did the real-world relevance of the research questions. Does psychiatric rehabilitation help people get jobs? Does it help them to live independently? His interest in the answers to such questions has a personal side as well. Having watched his sister deal with the symptoms of schizophrenia and his father deal with the results of a stroke, Dr. Bond was convinced that people with disabilities can and should live independent lives.

Dr. Bond's research has focused on finding effective approaches for helping people with severe and persistent mental illness achieve full integration in the community. He has conducted groundbreaking research and evaluation studies in supported employment, assertive community treatment, mental health consumers working as human service professionals, and many other areas. Gary Bond's work is some of the most frequently cited research in the psychiatric rehabilitation literature.

---

technique has the advantage of increasing the number of subjects under study, which increases the researchers ability to detect results.

Using the nine studies combined, the Bond study examined (a) the effect of assertive case management on how long clients received services, (b) how many days clients spent in the hospital, (c) their quality of life, and (d) their level of functioning. Results indicated that clients receiving assertive outreach were much more likely to continue in treatment longer than clients receiving more traditional services. Similar to most evaluations of case management, this research found that assertive outreach clients spent significantly fewer days in the hospital than other clients. Results regarding quality of life and level of functioning were less clear. This is not surprising because these factors are more difficult to measure and may not change as rapidly in the short period of time usually afforded these type of studies.

What Are the Important Program Elements?

McGrew and Bond (1995) looked at which program ingredients are most important for a successful assertive community treatment (ACT) program. With National Institute of Mental

Health funding, McGrew and Bond conducted an extensive review of the literature. The two authors identified important ACT elements, which they included in the Critical Components of Assertive Community Treatment Interview (CCACTI). Next, they employed a **Delphi technique** to identify important ACT ingredients. Twenty persons, who they identified as ACT program experts, were surveyed about the importance of 73 specific program elements. Each of the interviewees was asked to rate each ACT element listed on the CCACTI on a scale from 1 (*very unimportant*) to 7 (*very important*). Despite the numerous differences between program models and differences due to factors such as geographic setting, funding, and program auspices (e.g., freestanding programs or hospital-based programs), this study found surprisingly high levels of agreement on important ACT ingredients among the 20 experts.

Interestingly, McGrew and Bond's experts also identified which workers they believed would make up an ideal staffing pattern for an ACT team. Using an assumed caseload of 50 clients, 84% of the experts selected a psychiatrist, nurse, and social workers as ideal staff persons. Only 58% of the respondents identified a vocational specialist and 37% an addictions counselor as ideal staff persons.

Somewhat surprisingly, staff members who also happened to be consumers, sometimes known as **prosumers** or **consumer providers**, were not included as members of this ideal team. The concept of including identified mental health service consumers on ACT teams has been receiving support in several new state initiatives. The authors feel that every ACT team should contain consumer members who are psychiatric rehabilitation professionals. Chapter 10 provides more information about utilizing prosumers in a variety of PsyR practitioner roles.

Evaluating the State of the Art in Case Management

The most comprehensive and up-to-date assessment of case management research was carried out by Mueser, Bond, Drake, and Resnick (1998). Selecting on the basis of scientific merit, from the now extensive literature on case management, these researchers identified 75 controlled studies for review. Most of these 75 studies examined assertive community treatment (ACT) programs or intensive case management (ICM) programs. Because other models of case management were less well represented in the research literature, the authors focused most of their results on ACT and ICM. These two program models are very similar with respect to design (see Table 8.1). The major difference between them is that ACT program staff share caseloads, whereas while ICM program staff do not. This review provided clear evidence that these programs were effective at reducing time spent in the hospital and increasing clients' housing stability in the community. They also provided some modest evidence for improvements in quality of life and symptomology. The review did not suggest that ACT or ICM were effective at improving social functioning, vocational functioning, or reducing arrests or time spend in jail. Most important, the authors concluded that when case management services were reduced or withdrawn—for example, when programs had a designated length of service—consumers showed reduced levels of functioning. This has very important implications for funding as well as for the design of

TABLE 8.1

Features of Different Community Care Models

Program Feature	Community Care Model					
	Brokered Case Management	Clinical Case Management	Strengths Model	Rehabilitation Model	Assertive Community Treatment	Intensive Case Management
Staff : patient ratio	1:50?	1:30+	1:20-30	1:20-30	1:10	1:10
Outreach to patients	Low	Low	Moderate	Moderate	High	High
Shared caseload	No	No	No	No	Yes	No
24-hour coverage	No	No	No	No	Often	Often
Consumer input	No	Low	High	High	Low	Low
Emphasis on skills training	No	Low	Moderate	High	Moderate?	Moderate?
Frequency of patient contacts	Low	Moderate	Moderate	Moderate	High	High
Locus of contacts	Clinic	Clinic	Community	Clinic/ Community	Community	Community
Intergration of treatment	Low	Moderate	Low?	Low?	High	High?
Direct service provision	Low	Moderate	Moderate	Moderate	High	High
Target population	SMI	SMI	SMI	SMI	SMI high service utilizers	SMI high service utilizers

From Mueser, K. T., Bond, G. R., Drake, R. E., & Resnick, S. G. (1998). Models of community care for severe mental illness: A review of research on case management. *Schizophrenia Bulletin, 24*(1), 40.

future case management services. For example, the authors of this study found very little information on vocational outcomes and concluded that getting clients to work was a low priority for most case management systems. If time limited services prove less effective, vocational services, which reduce service requirements in the long run, may be more widely utilized.

The Mueser, Bond, Drake, and Resnick (1998) article contains a table (Table 8.1) that does a good job of clarifying the differences between different case management models for the reader.

The Future of Case Management

It is not surprising that the use of case management strategies for the community treatment of severe mental illness has steadily increased. There are obvious economic advantages to case management. Although case management is more expensive than traditional community-based services, it is considerably cheaper than psychiatric hospitalization. Planners on the state and national levels see increasing evidence that employing case management strategies reduces hospital usage. Numerous states have adopted case management strategies in an effort to reduce hospitalizations and close some of state hospitals. These new strategies, especially assertive community treatment, have also proven to be effective for reaching those consumers who have fallen through the cracks in the system. Whether because of their illness, underlying personality issues, past experiences that have alienated them from the system, or any number of other reasons, a large number of consumers are unconnected with the mental health system. Today we know that treatment and psychosocial interventions have a positive effect on the long-term outcome of these conditions. Assertive community treatment, and other intensive case management approaches have proven to be one of the most effective strategies for reaching out to this group and getting these consumers the treatment and services they need.

Finally, and most important, case management models that provide services to consumers in the community are a more normalized form of treatment delivery than the traditional partial care program or supervised residence. Such case management strategies allow the consumer to reside and work in the environment of the individual's choice and to receive services there. Consumers are not stigmatized by frequently attending a mental health center or vocational workshop. The services provided have a direct relationship to the here and now issues involved with coping with their illnesses and succeeding in the community. This consistency with the PsyR principle of normalization makes case management attractive to many consumers and PsyR professionals.

Summary

Case management programs were developed in response to the high rate of hospital re-cidivism often caused by substandard, underfunded, and uncoordinated community-based services. These programs are characterized by the fact that services are provided in the community where the consumers live, rather than in a mental health center, clinic, and so forth. The role of the case manager may vary according to the model of program for which one works. Some case managers act as brokers or agents arranging services for their clients. Others may be direct service providers working one-to-one with their clients in the community to help meet their needs. By either arranging for or directly providing services, case management systems strive to ensure that client needs are met in an appropriate and timely manner. Evaluation of these programs has demonstrated that they are effective at reducing both the number and length of hospital stays. They have also been used effectively to reach out to those segments of the population with severe mental illness who are most resistant to treatment.

Class Exercise:
The Role of the Case Manager

Who is today's case manager? She or he is an advocate, broker, continuity agent, educator, employment counselor, evaluator, expeditor, integrator, ombudsman, patient representative, personal program coordinator, primary therapist, systems agent, and trainer. In other words, the effective case manager needs to wear many hats. What kinds of hats may depend on what case management model is being followed. The following exercise is designed to make students aware of the different roles case managers play while also helping them to appreciate how different models of case management may affect these roles.

1. Have the class generate a list of possible roles case managers might play similar to those listed. Encouraged students to think very broadly on this subject, and clarify the importance of the roles they suggest for others in the class.
2. Next, discuss the case management programs models that the class has reviewed. Select two models that have fairly different philosophies about the staff's role. For example, compare the expanded broker model of case management to the assertive community treatment model. Raise the following questions with the class: What are the typical roles that staff members must play in each of these models? In what way are the models similar and how are they different?
3. Divide the class into small discussion groups and ask them to generate a list of staff roles for each of these models. Some student groups might generate lists of roles for one model while other students generate a list for the other model.
4. Finally, compare the lists generated for each model. How much do they have in common? What do the differences between these lists tell us about the individual models? What do the commonalities between these lists tell us about case management in general?

References

Abandoned. (1986, January 6). *Newsweek*, p. 14–15.

Agranoff, R. (1977). Services integration. In W. F. Anderson, B. J. Frieded, & M. J. Murphy (Eds.), *Managing human services*. Washington, DC: International City Management Association.

Allen, P. A. (1974). A consumer's view of California's mental health care system. *Psychiatric Quarterly, 48*, 1–13.

Aviram, U., & Segal, S. P. (1973). Exclusion of the mentally ill: Reflection on an old problem in a new context. *Archives of General Psychiatry, 29*, 126–131.

Baker, F., & Intagliata, J. (1992). Case management. In R. P. Liberman (Ed.), *Handbook of psychiatric rehabilitation*. General Psychology Series (Vol. 166). Boston: Allyn & Bacon.

Bond, G. R., McGrew, J. H., & Fekete, D. M. (1995). Assertive outreach for frequent users of psychiatric hospitals: A meta-analysis. *The Journal of Mental Health Administration, 22*(1), 4–16.

Chamberlin, R., & Rapp, C. A. (1991). A decade of case management: A methodological review of outcome research. *Community Mental Health Journal, 27*(3), 171–188.

Darley, J. M., & Latane, B. (1968). Bystander interventions in emergencies: Diffusion of responsibility. *Journal of Personality and Social Psychology, 8*, 377–383.

Goering, P., Wasylenki, D., Farkas, M., Lancee, W., & Ballantyne, R. (1988). What difference does case management make? *Hospital and Community Psychiatry, 39*, 272–276.

Greenley, J. R. (1995). Implementation of an innovative service in Madison, Wisconsin: The program of assertive community treatment (PACT). *Research Paper Series 49*, Mental Health Research Center, Madison, WI.

Harron, B. (Producer/Director). (1993). *Hospital without walls* [videotape]. (Available from Duke University Medical Center, Durham, NC)

Hodge, M., & Draine, J. (1993). Development of support through case management services. In R. W. Flexer & P. L. Solomon (Eds.), *Psychiatric rehabilitation in practice*. Boston: Andover Medical Publishers.

Kirk, S. A., & Therrien, M. G. (1975). Community mental health myths and the fate of former hospitalized patients. *Psychiatry, 38*, 209–217.

Klerman, G. (1977). Better but not well: Social and ethical issues in the deinstitutionalization of the mentally ill. *Schizophrenia Bulletin, 3*(4), 617–631.

Kohen, W., & Paul, G. L. (1976). Current trends and recommended changes in extended-care placement of mental patients: The Illinois system as a case in point. *Schizophrenia Bulletin, 2*, 575–594.

McGrew, J. H., & Bond, G. R. (1995). Critical ingredients of assertive community treatment: Judgments of experts. *The Journal of Mental Health Administration, 22*(2), 113–125.

Modrcin, M., Rapp, C., & Chamberlin, R. (1985). *Case management with psychiatrically disabled individuals: Curriculum & training program*. University of Kansas School of Social Welfare, Lawrence.

Mueser, K. T., Bond, G. R., Drake, R. E., & Resnick, S. G. (1998). Models of community care for severe mental illness: A review of research on case management. *Schizophrenia Bulletin, 24*(1), 37–74.

Santiestevan, H. (1975). *Deinstitutionalization: Out of their beds and into the streets*. Washington, DC.: American Federation of State, County, and Municipal Employees.

Solomon, P. (1992). The efficacy of case management services for severely mentally disabled clients. *Community Mental Health Journal, 28*(3), 163–180.

Stein, L. I., & Test, M. A. (1980). Alternative to mental hospital treatment: I. Conceptual model, treatment program, and clinical evaluation. *Archives of General Psychiatry, 37*, 392–397.

Stein, L. I., & Test, M. A. (1985). The evolution of the training in community living model. *New Directions for Mental Health Services, 26*, 7–16.

Test, M. A. (1979). Continuity of care in community treatment. *New Directions for Mental Health Services, 2*, 15–23.

Test, M. A. (1992). Training in community living. In R. P. Liberman (Ed.), *Handbook of psychiatric rehabilitation* (General Psychology Series, Vol. 166). Boston: Allyn & Bacon.

Test, M. A., & Stein, L. I. (1978). Training in community living: Research design and results. In L. I. Stein and M. A. Test (Eds.), *Alternatives to mental hospital treatment*. New York: Plenum.

Turner, J. C., & TenHoor, W. J. (1978). The NIMH community support program: Pilot approach to a needed social reform. *Schizophrenia Bulletin, 4*(3), 319–344.

Chapter 9

Residential Services
and Independent Living

Helping people with psychiatric disabilities to choose and maintain safe and affordable housing is an important goal of psychiatric rehabilitation (PsyR) practitioners. It is also one of the toughest challenges facing the field today. Where we live is an integral part of our lives. Having a home that we are generally satisfied with and where we feel safe and secure has a positive impact on the quality of our lives. Residing in a place where we do not feel comfortable, where our safety and security may be threatened, can be very stressful and have a negative impact on our sense of well-being.

Many consumers reside in environments that are not of their own choosing. Those living in supervised residential programs may be uncomfortable with certain program policies such as curfews or mandatory attendance at day programs. Another source of consumers' discomfort may be sharing their living space with other consumers whom they do not know well and may not like. Some consumers live in substandard housing, which may be in neighborhoods characterized by a degree of poverty and high crime rates. In addition, a sizable percentage of people who have a severe mental illness spend some period of their lives counted among the homeless (Carling, 1994; Torrey, 1995). These and other difficult living arrangements are endured by a substantial number of consumers because they do not have access to other options.

This chapter will answer the following questions:

1. *Why is it such a struggle for consumers to find a decent place to live in their communities?*
2. *Where did ex-psychiatric patients go once the era of deinstitutionalization began?*
3. *What are the current models of residential service provision?*
4. *Can people with severe functional deficits live in regular housing in the community?*
5. *How can people with psychiatric disabilities achieve the goal of independent living?*

Barriers to Housing

Affordability

There are many barriers to the acquisition of housing for consumers. The primary barrier to acceptable housing is economic. The United States is currently undergoing a nationwide housing crisis that affects everyone with a limited income, not just PsyR consumers. Basically there are two reasons that safe, decent, and affordable housing is difficult to find. The first is that there is less affordable housing available. Part of the decline in low-income housing is due to the **gentrification** of many inner-city neighborhoods and expanding suburbs. The second economic factor that reduces housing availability is cuts in the funding earmarked for federally assisted low-income housing (Carling, 1993). Both of these factors are aggravated by the fact that the cost of both rent and home purchase has risen, while, for many people, incomes have not risen at a comparable rate. Many consumers rely on entitlements as their sole income, which typically keep them well below the poverty level and unable to afford most housing options. For example, according to federal guidelines, people who receive a monthly Supplementary Security Income (SSI) check cannot even afford an efficiency apartment in the United States (Carling, 1995).

Stigma

A second key barrier to housing for people with psychiatric disabilities is stigma. Many landlords refuse to rent to people with a known history of mental illness. Consider the case of Ellen:

> After losing an apartment because her building was about to be demolished to make way for a minimall, Ellen finally located an apartment she could afford, a third-floor walk-up in a building in which the landlord also resided. Ellen made a good impression during her initial meeting with the landlord. He noticed she was a smoker, which wasn't a problem as he smoked cigarettes as well. However, when the landlord called one of her references and discovered her psychiatric history, he became wary. He discussed

the situation with his wife, who was quite blunt in her assessment: "I don't want some crazy woman who smokes cigarettes in our building, she'll be sure to burn the place down!" When Ellen stopped by the next day she was told the apartment was already rented.

Community opposition to living near mental health consumers has been referred to as the NIMBY ("Not in my backyard!") syndrome. When community residents learn that people with psychiatric disabilities have moved or are planning to move to their neighborhood, they may have an overt negative reaction. This is particularly true with **congregate care** residences. The residents' typical concern is for the safety of their children, family members, and themselves. This situation is often aggravated by the common myth portrayed in the media that mental illness equates with dangerousness. Another common concern often voiced is that the presence of people with psychiatric disabilities will have a negative effect on real estate values. Research shows that this is an unfounded assumption (Carling, 1995; Cook, 1997) but one that has been known to fuel organized efforts to rid a neighborhood of unwanted individuals.

The NIMBY attitude not only creates a barrier to housing, but it can be hurtful in other ways as well. Negative actions taken by resistant community members include lawsuits, exclusion from community activities, and verbal and physical harassment. Housing advocates have cited examples of extreme reactions, such as group homes that were burnt to the ground, allegedly by angry neighbors. All these actions clearly convey to people with psychiatric disabilities that they are unwanted and undesirable.

The social welfare and mental health systems may have perpetuated the housing crisis for consumers by refusing to focus on the problem in productive ways. Instead, some researchers believe that each group has attempted to pass the buck to the other (Carling, 1993). The mental health system has historically seen its role as providing residential treatment rather than permanent housing options. However, residential treatment programs (which will be discussed later in the chapter) do not provide what many consumers want and need from a place of residence (Collaborative Support Programs of New Jersey, 1991,1996; Tanzman, 1993; Yeich, Mowbray, Bybee, & Cohen, 1994). They are also available to only a small percentage of consumers (Carling, 1993). On the other hand, from the social welfare system's point of view, public housing programs are not equipped to meet the special needs of people with disabilities (Carling, 1994).

As addressed earlier, the lack of decent and affordable housing has a negative effect on the quality of many consumer's lives. It has other negative effects as well (Carling, 1993). Families frequently take in relatives with psychiatric disabilities who have nowhere else to go, even though the family is ill-prepared for the emotional and financial burdens that may accompany such a living arrangement. Psychiatric institutions often extend the stays of people ready for discharge simply because these patients have no place else to go. Considering the high costs of inpatient treatment, this is a huge waste of resources that could be used to support people in more productive ways.

As we will see, the field of psychiatric rehabilitation currently has a number of effective strategies to help people attain the type of housing that they want. However, these barriers continue to thwart efforts to provide many consumers with appropriate housing options.

History of Residential Services

From the mid 1950s to the mid 1970s several hundred thousand people were discharged from psychiatric institutions throughout the United States (Torrey, 1995). Where did these people go after they were discharged? Unfortunately, the community mental health system did not create a clear plan or allocate funding for postdischarge housing. Some people went back to their families (for more on family involvement in the care of relatives who have a mental illness, see chapter 11), many went to live in boarding houses or single-room occupancy hotels, others were transferred to nursing homes. Increases in the numbers of homeless people were also associated with deinstitutionalization (Torrey, 1995).

Although some residential service models with rehabilitation goals were developed during this first phase of deinstitutionalization, implementation was scattered and reached only a small percentage of people. Among mental health professionals, there was little agreement on what ideal residential services looked like and "the mental health system did not develop a coherent and widely accepted model for residential services in the first few decades of deinstitutionalization" (Ridgeway & Zipple, 1990, p. 12). Still, it is informative to examine some of these early residential options as many of them are still widely utilized today.

Boarding Homes and SROs

A 1981 study by Goldman, Gattozzi, and Taube estimated that in the United States, 300,000 to 400,000 people with a severe mental illness were living in boarding homes, or what are also called board-and-care facilities. Boarding homes have existed in this country, as a residential option for many kinds of people, for hundreds of years. They generally include the provision of a room, meals, and other services, such as laundry and housekeeping, for a weekly or monthly fee. They are typically used by people on the lower levels of the socioeconomic scale, and often house those living a transient lifestyle. Some boarding home operators rent out a few rooms in their own homes; others own one or more large facilities each housing dozens of people.

It is not an accident that entrepreneurs throughout the United States responded to the deinstitutionalization movement by opening boarding homes that exclusively catered to people discharged from psychiatric institutions. Some converted old hotels or apartment buildings into single room occupancy residences (commonly referred to as SROs), which might house up to 100 or more people. The financial incentive for these entrepreneurs was the establishment of Aid to the Disabled (ATD) in 1963, a monthly check provided by the federal government to people with disabilities who were not eligible for Social Security Disability (SSD) benefits due to the lack of a substantial work history. ATD is now called Supplemental Security Income or SSI. Boarding home operators are able to establish themselves as payees for the people residing in their facilities. They are allowed to keep most of the money as payment for room and board and give the remainder to residents in what amounts to a small monthly allowance—barely enough to buy coffee and cigarettes or a few personal items. Although some boarding home operators viewed deinstitutionalization as an opportunity to make a decent living and to provide residents with a caring, homelike environment, others focused solely on the ways they could maximize their profits. Horror stories abound of residents subsisting on cold cereal and bologna sandwiches, sharing cramped quarters, living in filthy conditions, and dealing with physical and verbal abuse at the hands of operators, staff, and roommates.

Many boarding homes are located in dangerous inner-city neighborhoods, where large old homes can often be purchased inexpensively. It is not unusual for residents, particularly those discharged directly to a boarding home after a lengthy hospital stay of 10 years or more, to rarely venture out in neighborhoods that were both unfamiliar and crime ridden. The result was a sort of "transinstitutionalization" (Carling, 1995, p. 33), since being discharged to what some referred to as "psychiatric ghettos" in no way resembled normalized community existence. Thus for many consumers life in a boarding home was not much better, and in some cases worse, than hospital life, particularly in terms of issues such as privacy and safety. In a 1982 study done by Lehman, Ward, and Linn, boarding home residents described a quality of life that was significantly less satisfying than the general population and somewhat less satisfying than other socially disadvantaged groups.

Access to psychiatric treatment and rehabilitation for boarding home residents varies. Some operators contract with psychiatrists and other mental health professionals to provide services in-house, making these facilities even more like mini-institutions. Other operators establish a relationship with local community mental health centers or PsyR programs. These situations typically involve sending residents, often by the vanload, to programs on a regular basis. In fact, sometimes boarding home operators require residents to attend day programs or be away from the facility for significant portions of the day.

Family Foster Care

In some parts of the country, programs were developed that placed one or more consumers with a family other than their own. In the early 1980s it was estimated that the Veterans Administration, probably the largest utilizer of foster care for disabled adults, had approximately 11,000 ex-psychiatric patients in **family foster care** at any one time (Linn, Klett, & Caffey, 1980). Typically, families received payment and some level of professional support. The arrangement could either be transitional or long term. Family foster care in the United States has its roots in Geel, Belgium, where people with psychiatric disabilities have been cared for in private homes for centuries (Lamb, 1982; Linn et al., 1980).

Ideally, family foster care seeks to incorporate consumers in all aspects of family and community life. For consumers who desire an active family life but are estranged from their family of origin, this may be a viable residential option—if a mutually satisfying match can be made between the consumer and an interested family. Research suggests that several aspects of the family home environment may be associated with positive outcomes in the area of social functioning. Specifically, consumers may function better in foster families which care for fewer consumers, are not large in terms of total number of people residing in the home, and that have more children living at home (Linn et al., 1980). When several consumers reside in a foster care setting it is sometimes hard to distinguish from a boarding home.

Carling (1994) has cautioned that in many family foster care settings only minimal supports are provided and true integration into the community is not realized. He did however cite the more recent development of some creative ways to utilize family foster care. One is as a short-term alternative to hospitalization. Such an arrangement is temporary, allowing an individual to stabilize during a period of crisis. Family foster care has also been used as a transition from the hospital to independent living. Such programs can "provide a caring home on a short term basis for individuals who are leaving a hospital, and who are trying to establish roots in a particular community" (Carling, 1994, p. 92).

Fairweather Lodges

During the early years of deinstitutionalization, a social scientist named George Fairweather recognized the difficulties that discharged people were having with community adjustment. He started an experimental program designed to provide a long-term supportive residential environment while at the same time addressing work and social needs. What began as a research study evolved into a distinct PsyR approach known as the **Fairweather lodge** model, which is still widely used in some parts of the country.

Fairweather began his research at a California Veterans Administration Hospital in the mid-1960s (Onaga, 1994). Initially, he established small problem-solving groups of patients preparing for discharge. Each group was responsible for the individual progress of its members. These experimental groups were able to meet the criteria for discharge sooner than the control group who received traditional hospital treatment (Lamb, 1982). However, following discharge, recidivism rates were basically the same for both the experimental and the control groups.

> The crucial factor in remaining in the community was found to be the amount of support the patient received from the people with whom he or she lived. When these facts became clear, Fairweather's group decided to move these problem-solving patient groups as units from the hospital to the community. The new phase of the program involved setting up the Community Lodge program: a dormitory for patients and a sheltered workshop situation—a janitorial service owned and operated by the ex-patients themselves. (Lamb, 1982, p. 50)

Professional staff acted as consultants to the lodge, initially providing a high level of support and assistance in dealing with both work and daily living issues. Eventually the consultation needs of the lodge members decreased and they were able to maintain the lodge and the business with minimal staff assistance. Members did receive psychiatric care from a private physician. The original Fairweather lodge was a resounding success in terms of recidivism rates and vocational outcomes (all of the lodge members were employed). Many members also reported an increase in self-esteem. The model was soon replicated in other parts of the United States, as well as in foreign countries (Lamb, 1982).

A number of essential principles guide the operation of community lodges. They were outlined by Fairweather, Saunders, Maynard, and Cressler(1969) in the book *Community Life for the Mentally Ill*. Onaga (1994) noted the similarity of these principles with some of the basic PsyR principles as stated by Caan, Blankertz, Messinger, and Gardner (1988). Some examples of Fairweather lodge principles are as follows:

1. Lodge members must have meaningful roles in the lodge/business and be given as much autonomy as possible. (These tenets are compatible with the PsyR principles of normalization and self-determination.)
2. Lodge members should have upward mobility within the lodge community. (This principle adheres to the PsyR value that people have the capacity to grow and change.)
3. The role of professional staff associated with Fairweather lodges is that of a consultant who bases his or her level of involvement on the current needs and abilities of lodge members. Staff must be available to lodge members when they are having difficulties, yet ready to step back when members are able to solve their own problems. (This approach is in agreement with PsyR attitudes about staff commitment and deprofessionalization of the staff role.)

As the PsyR field moves away from segregated, facility-based approaches and toward more integrated community living, the Fairweather lodge approach becomes questionable. Essentially lodges become subsocieties, in which members may spend their time living, working, and socializing primarily with other people who have psychiatric disabilities. Fairweather viewed the lodges as a long-term alternative to institutionalization and doubted whether members could maintain good community adjustment outside of the sheltered lodge environment (Lamb, 1982). More recently we have recognized that people with psychiatric disabilities can live and work independently given the right opportunities and continued support. From our current orientation, the Fairweather lodge might be viewed as stigmatizing. Proponents of the model hold a different view. According to Onaga (1994):

> Lodge principles reflect a value to de-stigmatize the psychiatrically disabled by enabling them to hold new roles in society that are valued, and to remove them from association with traditional systems that further stigmatize them. (p. 206)

Thus if a lodge can establish a successful business and a good rapport with the community in which it is located, it has the potential to break down stigmatizing attitudes about mental illness.

Today Fairweather lodges are still flourishing in some parts of the United States, particularly in Michigan and Texas (Onaga, 1994). The model has made some adaptations since its inception more than 30 years ago. Due to the changing nature of the psychiatric hospital system, potential lodge members cannot always be prepared for discharge in small, hospital-based, problem-solving groups. Instead, training lodges have been developed in some areas. These short-term facilities prepare individuals coming from both the hospital and the community for entry into a Fairweather lodge community. Potential members can then interview with existing lodges to ensure a mutually satisfying fit. Some lodges no longer require members to live and work in the lodge community. In some instances, members leave the lodge to live independently but continue to work in the lodge business. In other situations, individuals who never resided in a particular lodge can find employment there. Finally, some lodges employ people who do not have psychiatric disabilities but have skills needed to enhance the business (Onaga, 1994). For more on the vocational aspects of Fairweather lodges, see chapter 7.

Residential Treatment Facilities

Whereas boarding homes, SROs, and family foster care are typically nonprofessional ventures, a variety of residential programs run by mental health professionals emerged during the early years of deinstitutionalization (the 1960s and 1970s) and continue to exist today. Unlike the Fairweather lodges, most of these programs were not based on a clearly articulated model of service provision, but they still had a number of similarities. The most prolific approach to residential service provision has been segregated, congregate care facilities (Carling, 1994). These programs utilize various names, most commonly *group homes* and *halfway houses*. Like the partial care programs discussed in chapter 6, most **residential treatment facilities** seek to establish a therapeutic milieu—in other words, an environment carefully crafted to encourage clinical and functional improvements (Ridgway & Zipple, 1990). Some of these programs have rehabilitation goals, striving to provide residents with independent living skills so that they can eventually move on to a less protected setting or into their own homes. Other programs focus on long-term care in a small homelike environment rather than a large institutional setting.

The number of consumers residing in a group home can vary, although 6 to 12 is probably the most typical range. However, some professionally run programs may house large numbers of consumers and resemble SROs, and some may accommodate just a few individuals and resemble foster care settings. In most programs, staff are present, or readily available, 24 hours a day. Typical program activities include staff-assisted group menu planning and meal preparation, individual or small-group activity of daily living (ADL) skills training (budgeting, hygiene, laundry, etc.), social and recreational activities, assistance in utilization of local transportation and other community resources, community meetings, individual and group counseling, and symptoms and medication education. In some programs residents spend weekdays outside of the residential facility either at day programs, workshops, school, or jobs. Other programs have on-site treatment and rehabilitation groups.

Stigma and Residential Treatment Programs

Many residential treatment programs are located in urban and suburban residential neighborhoods. Ideally, program residents become an integral part of the local community life (e.g., developing friendly relationships with neighbors, attending block parties, and joining religious congregations). Unfortunately, NIMBY attitudes mentioned earlier often create a barrier to true community integration. In fact, a key issue faced by residential treatment program administrators is whether or not to notify neighbors of their intention to open a group home. Some programs approach the issue collaboratively, notifying neighbors early on in an attempt to establish positive relationships. However, some studies have indicated that this approach can backfire and help fuel community opposition (Zippay, 1997). Other programs refrain from notifying neighbors in an effort to protect consumers' civil rights and to avoid a stigmatizing confrontation. This latter strategy has been criticized for its potential to create resentment and mistrust as neighbors begin to realize that a group home exists (Zippay, 1997). A third approach is to publicly announce intentions to open a residential facility, but rather than attempting to collaborate with a community that is expected to be resistant, some programs act offensively and threaten to sue the community (Carling, 1995). How would you feel if a group home for people with severe mental illness opened in your neighborhood? If you were a consumer living in a group home would you want neighbors to be notified before you moved in? What do you think would happen if neighbors were not notified beforehand or if a lawsuit was threatened?

Carling (1995) suggested that community members who oppose the presence of residential treatment facilities should not automatically be labeled as the bad guys. Although people with disabilities should have the right to live wherever they choose, mental health professionals and consumer advocates must be sensitive to community members' concerns about having a group home in the neighborhood. Sometimes these concerns are based on a lack of accurate information. However, one cannot ignore the fact that sometimes facility-based residential programs do alter the character of a neighborhood. In some cases, neighbors cite practical concerns such as parking and increased traffic problems (Cook, 1997). Carling stated that in his experience, "most mental health professionals do not want a group home or other treatment program sited next to their own homes" (Carling, 1995, p. 116).

Despite the fact that numerous instances of community opposition to the siting of residential treatment facilities have been reported, this is not the whole story. In many communities, group homes and single or multifamily residences coexist peacefully. In some instances a substantial percentage of neighbors were not even aware that a group home for people with disabilities was in their neighborhood (Cook, 1997). Presumably this occurs most often when program staff and residents make an effort to keep a low profile. In other communities, positive relationships have developed between group home residents and their neighbors. One study found that neighbors cited the benefits associated with living near a group home (e.g., learning more about disabilities) about as often as they cited problems and concerns (Cook, 1997).

Emergence of the Linear Continuum Paradigm

As mentioned earlier, some programs place no time limits on consumer residency and thus can be considered long term. Other facility-based residential programs are designed to be a transition between psychiatric hospitalization and independent living. In the 1970s programs began to add steps to the transition between the hospital and independent living (Carling, 1994). This approach to residential treatment has been called the linear continuum paradigm (Ridgeway & Zipple, 1990). Throughout the 1980s (and into the 1990s in some places), "the linear residential continuum has remained the dominant conceptual framework in the field of residential services" (Ridgway & Zipple, 1990).

Thus the halfway house approach became augmented by the addition of different housing situations, each offering varying amounts of staff support, structure, and supervision. These steps may consist of quarterway houses, typically located on the grounds of state psychiatric institutions (Carling, 1994); three-quarterway houses, in which staff were no longer present round the clock (Campbell, 1981); supervised apartments; semisupervised apartments; and other residential options that represented steps toward the eventual goal of fully independent living. Some residential continua also include crisis alternative residences, also called respite care, designed to help acutely symptomatic consumers avoid a hospitalization (Carling, 1994).

Exactly what is offered along a particular residential continuum varies, as do the names given to the different types of programming. It is therefore difficult to compare these residential approaches, and a clear idea of the ideal continuum has never emerged (Ridgway & Zipple, 1990). However, some basic concepts characterize programs that adhere to this linear residential service continuum approach (Ridgway & Zipple, 1990):

1. The existence of several residential settings, which offer different levels of service provision, staff supervision, and restrictiveness.
2. Program participants are expected to move, in an orderly fashion, from the most-restrictive level to the least-restrictive level.
3. Participants in each setting are similar in terms of clinical stability and functional ability. They are expected to make progress before graduating to another level on the continuum.
4. If a program participant decompensates and ends up back in the hospital, the person often reenters the continuum at the most restrictive level (i.e., he or she has to start over again at the bottom).
5. The ultimate goal is to move on to independent living and no longer require services from the program.

Research conducted on the efficacy of the residential continuum model is somewhat scant and inconclusive. As indicated earlier, it is hard to study an approach in which the nomenclature varies and clearly defined, consistent intervention strategies do not exist. In addition, most of the studies that have been done in this area did not use rigorous experimental methods and thus are not very useful. The literature available on transitional residential treatment suggests that the approach is not particularly successful in helping people to achieve the PsyR goal of community integration (Carling, 1994).

It is also important to keep in mind that residential programs of this type only serve a small percentage of the people in need. The housing resources available in local mental health systems (such as money earmarked to buy houses, rent apartments, and staff residential continuum programs) are providing services for fewer than 5% of the people with psychiatric disabilities (Carling, 1994).

Although the linear continuum approach seems to be a coherent strategy for helping consumers become gradually reintegrated into the community, we should question the current use of this approach when 30 or more years later there are no strong research findings to back it up. At the same time, the monetary resources are not available to provide the service to the vast majority of consumers. In addition, consider some of issues raised in the following case study.

The Case of Joanna

Joanna is a 32-year-old woman who has never had a home of her own as an adult. She was diagnosed with a severe mental illness in her senior year of high school and spent the next 10 years shuffling back and forth between psychiatric hospitals and her parents' home. When Joanna was 28, and residing at a state institution, her parents informed her and the hospital staff that when she was ready for discharge they could not take her back home. They were in the process of selling their house and moving to a retirement community and felt it was an appropriate time for Joanna to become less dependent on them. Joanna was put on a waiting list for a residential program that ran three types of facilities: group homes (with staff supervision 24 hours a day), a supervised apartment complex, and semisupervised scattered site apartments.

Six months later Joanna moved into a group home where she was one of eight residents and where she shared a bedroom with another woman. She liked the program better than being at the hospital, although she missed the privacy of her own room at home. She grew quite attached to some of the program staff who were supportive and seemed to truly care about her. However, her relationship with her roommate was not so good. They had little in common and some of the roommate's behaviors, such as pacing back and forth in the middle of the night, made Joanna uneasy.

After 10 months in the group home, the staff told Joanna she was ready to move to the next level in the agency's housing continuum: the supervised apartment complex where staff members were usually on site just a few hours a day. An opening was expected within a few months. Joanna had ambivalent feelings about the impending move. On the one hand, she was happy that the staff thought she had made progress and she liked the idea of having her own room. On the other hand, she wasn't convinced she was ready to live more independently. She had learned to contribute to shopping and cooking for eight people, although the staff was always on hand should something go wrong. Besides, in the new place she would be living with two other people. She wasn't sure if she would be cooking for herself or sharing meal preparation with roommates. What if she didn't like the roommates or got into an argument? The staff wouldn't be as available to intervene. She had many other concerns as well, such as housecleaning routines, sticking to a budget, using public transportation instead of the agency van, getting used to a new neighborhood, and so on. She also felt uneasy about the fact that her stay in the new apartment would also be temporary. She knew that one of the group home graduates, who lived for less than a year at the apartment complex where Joanna would be living, was already being pressured to move on to the semisupervised apartments.

The Case of Joanna Continued

As the weeks went by and she came closer to her moving date Joanna began to spend more and more time worrying about the impending changes. She began to get symptomatic again but did not tell the staff because she feared they would be disappointed in her. One week before moving, Joanna ended up back in the hospital. When a staff member from the group home visited with her several weeks later, Joanna said she was feeling better and would like to discuss some of her concerns about the new apartment. The staff member told her not to worry about it. Another group home resident had been moved in her place. When she was ready for discharge she could come back to the group home again and work on her ADL skills so that she could be ready for the apartment the next time. Joanna felt both relieved and disappointed. She was back to square one again, as if the progress she had made in the group home had never happened.

The Case against the Linear Continuum Approach

The preceding case study illustrates a number of reasons why the linear continuum approach to residential treatment has been criticized in recent years. An inherent flaw in this approach is the requirement that consumers frequently change their living situation. For most people, moving from one home to another is a stressful event. It means abandoning routines and settings that have become comfortable and getting used to a whole new place. Such changes are often hard to deal with for people without psychiatric disabilities. For people who have a severe mental illness, change can be disastrous. As explained in chapter 2, mental illness is episodic in nature and stressful life events can exacerbate symptoms. Considering these facts, mental health professionals should not be surprised when people like Joanna end up back in the hospital just as they are about to make a major life transition. In this sense, the linear continuum model and severe mental illness is not a good fit. Even if a consumer is able to make it through all the levels of programming and graduate to independent living, the individual is often short-changed by the program structure. In the linear continuum model, independent living typically means that the consumer will no longer have access to program supports at a time when he or she may most need them. It is not uncommon for a person who has finally achieved a long sought after goal of obtaining his or her own apartment to lose it when faced with a crisis situation because the needed support was no longer available.

Another reason that the linear continuum approach may be ineffective was addressed in chapter 5. Skills needed to function successfully in living, learning, working, and social environments are best learned in the specific places where they will be used. It is hard for people to generalize what they learn in one setting (e.g., meal planning and preparation for the eight residents of a group home) to another setting (e.g., meal planning and preparation for oneself in an efficiency apartment). Thus Joanna's concerns about how prepared she was to make a move were quite realistic.

Probably the best reason to question the linear continuum model, or any approach that utilizes facility-based congregate care settings, is that they do not provide the type of housing that most consumers want. Arguably people with psychiatric disabilities may not always know what type of treatment is best suited to their particular illness. However they certainly know a great deal about where they feel comfortable residing! In a society that places high value on personal freedom, everyone should have the right to pursue a home life of their own choosing. Prior to the mid-1980s the idea of asking consumers what kind of housing they wanted was not widely considered, but in recent years a number of studies have examined consumers' housing preferences (Tanzman, 1993). A literature review that analyzed the results of 26 such studies found that the majority of the people surveyed preferred living independently in either a house or an apartment. Not surprisingly, only a small percentage of respondents in most of the studies had a preference for living in a residential treatment facility (Tanzman, 1993). Similar results were found in a subsequent studies (Collaborative Support Programs, 1996; Yeich et al., 1994).

Some housing preference studies have also explored the question of preferred housemates. In the case study, one of the things Joanna liked least about the group home was her roommate. Wondering who she would be placed with in the supervised apartment was one of her major concerns. Most of us can appreciate Joanna's apprehension about living with strangers. Imagine a living situation in which the only thing you know about your roommates is that they were all recently discharged from a psychiatric hospital. Even if you are an open-minded person who does not buy into stigmatizing myths about mental illness, you would probably have some concerns. Many consumers have concerns as well. Some find it hard to have to deal with both their own illness and the symptoms and problems experienced by roommates (Carling, 1994).

When given a choice, most consumers would rather live by themselves or with a spouse, friend, or family member (Tanzman, 1993). This is not a surprising finding. The vast majority of nondisabled persons would probably identify similar preferences. However, it is important to know that some consumers do choose to live with other people who have a mental illness. In 2 out of 16 studies that examined this issue, "more consumers preferred to live with other mental health consumers than with non-consumers" (Tanzman, 1993, p. 453). It may be that some people accustomed to living, learning, working, and socializing in facility-based programs feel most comfortable being with people who have had similar life experiences.

Considering the criticisms outlined earlier, there are strong reasons to question whether the mental health system should continue to allocate limited resources to programs that adhere to the linear continuum model. If true community integration is the goal, we must admit that thus far it has not been realized. Instead, Carling has maintained that many residential treatment approaches "transinstitutionalize" consumers (Carling, 1995, p. 33), providing them with few opportunities to experience normalized community life. Likewise, in a system that currently professes to be consumer driven, both residential continua and long-term congregate care settings do not provide homes where most people want to live. Thus, the majority of residential service approaches that have been developed since deinstitutionalization began fall short on two key PsyR goals: community integration and improved quality of life.

Supported Housing: A New Approach to Residential Services

In addition to the fact that consumers prefer to live independently or with loved ones, studies have also found that people want support in order to successfully maintain their living situations (Tanzman, 1993; Yeich et al., 1994). According to the literature the most frequently mentioned supports include (a) availability of staff by phone 24 hours a day, 7 days a week for assistance in coping with crises; (b) financial resources; (c) assistance in budgeting money; and (d) house furnishings and supplies (Tanzman, 1993; Yeich et al., 1994). If a service system is truly responsive to consumer choice and committed to meaningful community integration, it should be helping people to attain independent housing and providing them with the supports to maintain that housing.

This approach to the provision of residential services was outlined by Paul Carling and Priscilla Ridgway in a set of principles of community residential rehabilitation (Carling & Ridgeway, 1991):

1. "The rehabilitation approach avoids the notion of 'placement' in favor of choice" (p. 72).
2. Rehabilitation-oriented residential services are "service systems that seek to expand consumer control, minimize rules, external (e.g., staff) structuring, while maximizing active consumer responsibility for day to day problem solving and promoting mutual support, self-help, and client operated services" (p. 73).
3. Many consumers choose to live with family members or to live alone with considerable support from family members. Family members thus need to be involved in the rehabilitation process and should be "given the support, information and resources they need" (p. 73).
4. Normalization, a guiding principle of PsyR, means normal environment, in this case the living environment, which is perhaps the most important environment in all of our lives. Normalization also means the recovery, creation, and maintenance of valued social roles (Wolfensberger, 1983), such as neighbor, tenant, and roommate, as opposed to group home resident or supervised apartment resident.
5. People with disabilities may need assistance in developing activity of daily living skills. Skill development occurs most productively when it is specific to the environment in which the person plans to live on a long-term basis. Thus skills developed in a transitional group home may be of little use to someone who plans to live independently.
6. Supports, both formal and informal, must be available and responsive to changing needs. Informal or natural supports include family members, neighbors, friends, peers, and other people in the community. "Natural support systems are most easily fostered in normal housing" (p. 73). Formal support services should also be accessible and well coordinated and should include crisis intervention and case management.
7. All needed supports should be flexible, individualized, and available for as long as an individual needs them. "Many programs, while acknowledging the need for longer term support, in fact invest most of their staff resources into 'transitional'

living programs, and significantly decrease support at precisely the time when the individual's needs may be the greatest (i.e., at the time of a move)" (p. 74).

8. Advocacy is greatly needed to combat stigma, community resistance, and the lack of decent and affordable housing options for people with psychiatric disabilities.

These principles provide the basis for what has become the residential service model of choice in the field of PsyR, **supported housing**.

"Supported housing embraces a vision of people with severe mental disorders succeeding in the community living situation of their choice through access to flexible, individualized services and supports" (Parrish, 1990, p. 10). Supported housing as an approach to residential service provision is a relatively new development. In 1987 a policy statement issued by the National Association of State Mental Health Program Directors (NASMHPD) recommended that states begin to move toward a more normalized model of residential services, which by the early 1990s was widely referred to as "supported housing" (Carling, 1990; Knisley & Fleming, 1993). Some state and local service systems have made significant progress in this area, whereas others are just beginning. In regard to the PsyR literature on supported housing, there is strong agreement on the key elements that define the approach (Ogilvie, 1997). Three essential elements are consistently mentioned: consumer choice, normal, integrated living sites, and provision of supports that are flexible and ongoing (Carling, 1990).

Implementing the Supported Housing Approach

PsyR residential services are in the midst of a paradigm shift from the linear continuum approach to a supported housing approach (Ridgway & Zipple, 1990). This shift involves a number of changes, not only in what type of services are provided but also in staff attitudes and in how financial resources are structured.

Key changes in service provision strategies include a shift in staff responsibilities, which requires a different set of skills and attitudes. In the linear continuum model, staff were expected to provide treatment and supervision in an effort to move residents to the next level of housing. Staff who work in supported housing programs provide individualized, as-needed supports, teach skills to consumers in their homes, and assist people in acquiring resources. They need to be both flexible and creative in determining the most effective way to help each consumer get what she or he needs to live successfully in the community. Consider the following vignette:

> Lisa used to live in a group home where staff supervised her in a number of ways. They watched her take her medication twice a day. They were always present when it was her turn to cook dinner. Staff reminded her (repeatedly if she procrastinated) to clean her room thoroughly every Saturday morning. Group home staff also provided psychiatric and mental health treatment. A psychiatric nurse met with her regularly to assess her current symptoms and monitor medications. Her case manager, a clinical social worker, met with her once a week to discuss any problems she was having.
>
> Now Lisa has her own efficiency apartment and receives services from a supported housing program. Initially, she asked staff for a great deal of help in getting settled and

learning new routines. For example, her laundry was building up because she wasn't sure how to get it to the laundromat and what to do once she got there. A staff member came over and showed her how to get her laundry done. Then the staff member helped her to write down a step-by-step procedure so Lisa could do it on her own. Staff also showed her how to fill a weekly medication dispenser and assisted her in establishing a routine for remembering to take her medication. She has now been in her apartment for 3 months and is doing well; staff members come over only when she asks them to. However, she likes knowing that she can reach someone 24 hours a day, if needed. Lisa sees a psychiatrist once a month and goes to a weekly support group at a local mental health center. She likes the fact that these treatment services are kept separate from her private home life.

Another important part of the paradigm shift is allowing consumers to take much more control over the services they receive. Supported housing promotes the notion of people making choices, not only in terms of where they live but also in terms of what supports are provided and how and when they are provided. Consider a typical day at a facility-based program that requires all residents to be up and out of the house by 9:00 A.M., involved in a PsyR program or otherwise productively engaged, and home by 4:00 P.M. to help cook dinner and then attend a community meeting. Contrast that picture with a supported housing program in which service recipients are not required to be accountable to support staff about how they spend their day and where a consumer's preference for having staff visit after 10:00 A.M. is respected. Such a program may support some people who only see staff occasionally, when they call to request assistance, whereas others, who ask for it, are provided with a more intensive level of services. Notice that for a supported housing program to be successful, staff must truly internalize the PsyR value of self-determination. For many practitioners, this involves a shift from thinking that staff always know what is best for the people they serve to building real partnerships with consumers (Pyke & Lowe, 1996).

PsyR practitioners involved in the provision of supported housing need to be much more active in both accessing and developing a range of community resources. For example, developing good relationships with potential or current landlords and affordable housing developers may increase consumer access to normal community housing. Finding out what support and social opportunities are available at a local church or synagogue may provide consumers with information about potentially useful natural support systems. Although group home staff may spend some time engaged in these types of activities, they must spend most of their time providing supports within their facilities. Supported housing interventions, on the other hand, provide more opportunities for people to live, work, and socialize with a range of people in their communities.

A number of supported housing programs have employed consumers (sometimes called consumer providers) in a variety of staff positions, including involvement in the provision of direct services and supports (Besio & Mahler, 1993; Butler, 1993). Using consumers as staff has a number of benefits. For example, consumers have a strong ability to empathize with the day-to-day concerns of other consumers, they are tolerant of unusual behaviors, and they are less likely to maintain a professional distance in the helping relationship. Each of these benefits can contribute to more comfortable relationships between consumer-providers and the people they serve, ultimately resulting in superior outcomes. Consumer-providers have also been found to be highly skilled in obtaining necessary resources and advocacy (Besio

& Mahler, 1993). Because of their own experiences, consumer-providers may be better attuned to what consumers need to accomplish independent living goals. They may also champion attitudes and behaviors that are respectful of consumers' right to privacy and need to be in control of their own home environment. More information about the use of psychiatric rehabilitation consumers as service providers can be found in chapter 10.

Among the greatest challenges to the implementation of supported housing are (a) accessing housing that matches consumer preferences, (b) helping people to acquire rental or mortgage assistance, and (c) financing individualized support services. Shifting service provision paradigms not only involve changes in what is provided but also changes in how services are financed. Adopting a supported housing approach may initially seem very expensive because the provision of off-site, individualized services can be less efficient than the provision of standardized, facility-based services. However, when estimating the cost of a service, long-term outcomes must be considered. Consumers who initially require numerous staff hours to get the level of support they need may need very little in the way of staff resources once they have adjusted to their new home and neighborhood and begin to make use of natural supports.

Accessing and financing enough decent and affordable housing for a local pool of consumers may present the biggest challenge to widespread implementation of supported housing services. As discussed earlier in the chapter, this is a problem throughout the United States for people who have low incomes. Entitlements such as SSI are not enough to cover average rental costs in most areas. Historically, mental health system resources used for residential treatment have reached only a small percentage of people. So the issue is not just reallocation of financial resources, it is facing the reality that we need to help consumers locate and access additional monies to rent or buy homes.

Although this is certainly a large barrier to the provision of supported housing, it is not insurmountable. Some states, such as Ohio, have had real success in reallocating capital funding—previously used to build and maintain hospitals, CMHCs, and residential treatment facilities—for use in developing integrated housing for consumers. Ohio also successfully used other strategies to increase funding for housing, such as attracting federal grant monies and increasing access to federal rent subsidies (Knisley & Fleming, 1993).

All efforts of this type require a tremendous amount of time, energy, and commitment by state department of mental health officials and consumer and family advocates (Knisley & Fleming, 1993). Other states and local communities, including Rhode Island, western Massachusetts, and Madison, Wisconsin, have also successfully increased consumer access to integrated housing. They have done so through use of creative financing strategies, such as housing cooperatives, assistance for first-time buyers, rental subsidies, and creative partnerships with state and local housing developers (Carling, 1995).

Outcomes of the Supported Housing Approach

As mentioned earlier, only in the past 10 years has supported housing has become an articulated model of residential service. Evaluations of this new approach have already been carried out and some of the initial studies are encouraging. An evaluation of supported housing demonstration projects in five states (Ohio, Oregon, Rhode Island, Washington, and Wisconsin) found that clients reported a high level of satisfaction with their lives (Livingston,

Gordon, King, & Srebnik, 1991). Although many of the people receiving services had a history of housing instability, most demonstrated a significant increase in stability once they became involved with the projects. Two critical factors were found to predict housing stability: symptoms and how much input a client had in choosing where he or she lived. The results of this study also suggest that along with providing consumers with opportunities to live in decent homes of their own choosing, communities need to focus on expanded social networks and employment opportunities.

Curtis, McCabe, Fleming, and Carling (1993) interviewed consumers, family members, agency staff, and administrators from seven supported housing demonstration projects in Texas. The most frequently mentioned client outcomes were decreases in hospital use and increases in community tenure, access to housing, motivation, hope and empowerment, normal role functioning, and overall quality of life. Clients also expressed a high level of satisfaction with the services they received.

A subsequent study of the Texas demonstration projects confirmed these initial findings (Texas Department of Mental Health and Mental Retardation, 1994). Utilizing client data from the year prior to project involvement, and comparing this data to information gathered after 1 year in a supported housing program, this study found that there was an increase in housing stability, level of functioning, and quality of life, as well as a decrease in hospital usage.

Another study by Brown, Ridgway, Anthony, and Rogers (1991) looked solely at individuals in supported housing. A group at high risk for rehospitalization and homelessness was compared to a group of people who were less disabled and had requested supported housing services. Both groups significantly decreased their hospital use in the 6 months following entry into the program, although as might be suspected the former group utilized more support services. The authors concluded that the supported housing approach is a viable option, even for persons who are severely disabled.

A recent literature review on supported housing concluded that there are still too few outcome studies on supported housing to draw firm conclusions about the efficacy of the approach (Ogilvie, 1997). In an earlier article, Carling (1988) had also called for more research on housing and community integration of people with psychiatric disabilities. In addition he recommended specific guidelines for studying this approach, including the following:

1. "A fundamental shift from professionally-defined to consumer-defined research" (p. 13). Such an approach calls for substantial consumer input in the development of outcome measures (e.g., How do they define *success* or *progress*?).
2. More longitudinal studies that consider the changing housing needs that accompany normal stages of adult development.
3. Separation of the evaluation of treatment goals and housing needs.
4. A greater emphasis on exploring which characteristics of communities promote successful integration, rather than just focusing on characteristics of consumers or program services.

These recommendations are consistent with the PsyR value of self-determination (through increased empowerment opportunities) and the principle of normalization.

BOX 9.1
Howie the Harp

Howie the Harp was a tireless advocate for the rights of people who have severe mental illness. His work spanned many areas of PsyR, including supported housing, self-help, and employment (particularly around the issue of reasonable accommodations). Howie was also remarkably effective in his work with individuals who were homeless and psychiatrically disabled. According to a former colleague, he had a unique ability to reach out and connect to people who came from the streets, to give them a voice, and to find ways to get them the things that they most wanted and needed (N. Thomas, personal communication, 1998).

Howie's motivation to help others was deeply rooted in his own experiences. In the words of his friend and colleague, Sally Zinman:

Having experienced the horrors of being in a mental hospital and being homeless as a boy, he spent the rest of his life advocating for people with mental disabilities (his self-definition), homeless and poor people. I don't know if many of us can trace so distinctly our life's pursuits to our childhood experiences. He never wavered in his direction, never took a detour. (Zinman, 1995, p. 1)

Howie became interested in patients' rights advocacy at the age of 16. At the time he had recently escaped from a psychiatric facility in New York City, following a 3-year involuntary hospitalization. He moved to Oregon, where he was exposed to an advocacy organization called the Insane Liberation Front. At 18 he moved back to New York to start a local chapter of the advocacy group: The Mental Patients Liberation Project. This led to the opening of a crisis center, which assisted people who were trying to get out of psychiatric institutions.

While working with the Mental Patients Liberation Project, Howie became aware of the thousands of ex-patients enduring atrocious conditions at local single room occupancy hotels (SROs). He organized Project Release, a tenant group dedicated to improving living conditions and advocating for residents' rights. Project Release was soon expanded to include a consumer run drop-in center and a self-help group. The group also obtained several apartments where people could live temporarily while searching for decent housing. All of these accomplishments occurred in the early 1970s, at a time when the ex-patient movement and consumer-run services were still very new ideas (chapter 10 traces the history of these efforts). Howie the Harp was one of the pioneers of PsyR.

When lack of funding opportunities in New York City became a major obstacle, Howie moved to California. There he became involved with supported housing services, working at the California Center for independent Living (CIL). This was the first of the independent living centers for people with disabilities. He actually began his association with the CIL when he was homeless and was helped to acquire and maintain housing. In addition to his psychiatric disability, Howie had a physical disability, and was thus uniquely qualified to understand the parallels in the service needs of both populations. One of his insights was that rather then treatment facilities, people with psychiatric disabilities needed access to individualized supports that would enable them to live independently. He was thus inspired to develop the Mental Disabilities

Independent Living Program, which was a precursor to the Oakland Independence Support Center (OISC) and also led to other projects. The OISC, which is still flourishing, provides a variety of services to people with psychiatric disabilities who are homeless or at risk for becoming homeless. Services include a drop-in center, which provides a safe alternative to the streets; support services; and independent living services, which utilize unique strategies to bring together homeless individuals and landlords who have vacancies (Howie the Harp, 1990). In 1993 Howie left a well-established OISC to return to his home town of New York City and work at a supported housing agency (Howie the Harp, 1993).

Howie had a way of describing himself and his viewpoint, which was direct, easy to grasp, and often had a touch of humor:

I am a former mental patient with a psychiatric disability. That does not describe who I am, but it

identifies a profound aspect of my life. I am also a musician, a lover of nature, and a frustrated comedian. At one time I was considered to be "chronically mentally ill," and in need of "treatment" for the rest of my life, most likely never able to live independently, and certainly never able to hold down a full-time job. That was a load of crap. I consider myself to be psychiatrically disabled, but I define disability as the disability rights movement has redefined the term. I have a condition that is neither positive or negative—not an illness to be "cured," but a condition that can be accommodated in order to enable me to live the way I choose. (Howie the Harp, 1991, p. 1)

Howie the Harp passed away in 1995 at the age of 42. Though his life was short, his accomplishments were many. His efforts to improve the lives of people with psychiatric disabilities will be greatly missed.

The Independent Living Movement

One of the influences on the previously mentioned paradigm shift from a linear continuum model of residential programming to a supported housing approach was the effort of people with physical disabilities to move away from institutionalized care to find innovative ways to live independently. Deegan (1992) described the **independent living (IL) movement** as comprised of three interrelated activities. The first is a grassroots advocacy movement in which people with physical disabilities have banded together and demanded civil rights and opportunities to live, work, and socialize in their communities.

The second piece of IL is a philosophy developed and lived by individuals who have physical disabilities. Some key principles of the IL philosophy are as follows:

1. Recognizing that it is not something internal, like a spinal cord injury, that prevents people with disabilities from living independently, although certainly these internal factors can make the day-to-day experience of living challenging. Rather it is external barriers, such as stairs, curbs, and stigmatizing attitudes, that prevent people from getting places that they want to go.

2. People with disabilities have a right to self-determination. They also have a right to make mistakes and choices that others may identify as risky. Deegan (1992) described a young man with a spinal cord injury and his adjustment to independent living. In the early days the young man repeatedly tried to do things in his apartment that caused him to fall from a wheelchair and lie on the floor for hours until someone arrives to help. Many professionals would cite these incidents as proof that he could not live by himself. Eventually, however,

the man learned his own limits and found the accommodations and supports to live more comfortably. Think about the many mistakes made, and risks taken, by people without disabilities as they first move away from the parental home. They may be criticized by their loved ones, but rarely are they threatened with professional interventions aimed at reducing their control over their lives.

3. "Integral to the philosophy of IL is the notion that people with disabilities can become experts in their own self-care. To live independently means to demedicalize our lives by learning self-care techniques that minimize the medical presence in our daily lives" (Deegan, 1992, p. 16).

The third piece of IL is the existence of independent living centers, which provide service delivery, coordinate advocacy efforts, and bring people with disabilities together to tackle mutual concerns. IL centers are primarily run by people with physical disabilities. Deegan (1992) described her efforts to develop an independent living center designed to meet the needs of people with psychiatric disabilities. She emphasized the importance of establishing both a grassroots movement and philosophy that are "similar in spirit to what people with physical disabilities discovered for themselves" (p. 17). She has been cautious, however, about determining what IL service centers should provide. She has not recommended trying to duplicate what other disability groups have done, nor has she favored a peer-run version of what is offered by the mental health system. Instead, she has envisioned a new service approach that "will grow out of our emerging sense of what it is we need to regain control over our lives" (p. 17).

More recently, Farkas and Chamberlain (1998) began research on applying IL strategies to develop supports for people with psychiatric disabilities. Specifically, they are teaching consumers to hire, train, and manage personal assistants, in much the same way that people with physical disabilities have utilized personal care assistants. Personal assistance services (PAS) are tailored to meet the unique support needs of a consumer. Examples of services that could be provided include daily reminders about when to wake up and when to take medications, assistance with paying bills and maintaining a budget, and driving a consumer to work. Basically PAS could involve anything that a consumer has difficulty doing because of his or her illness and wants help with. Services are provided by nonprofessionals who are hired by and work for the consumer rather than for the mental health system. Farkas and Chamberlin have developed a curriculum for consumers that helps them to analyze what they need from PAS, hire and train a personal assistant, and manage the employer-employee relationship.

Consistent with the supported housing model, utilization of personal assistance services is a strategy that enables consumers to live independently. When evaluating whether a person with a psychiatric disability is capable of living in a nonsupervised setting, it is important to remember that independent living does not necessarily mean going without supports or services. In the words of the late Howie the Harp, a consumer and an advocate:

> Independence involves freedom to choose, to choose whom to be independent with, for what purpose, and to what extent. Independence is one of this country's founding principles, and it should not be surprising that living independently is a goal of many disabled Americans. Inherent in their definition of independent living is the availability of support services. (Howie the Harp, 1993, p. 413)

Is Supported Housing for Everyone or Should Facility-Based Residential Care Continue for People with the Most Severe Disabilities?

Despite the paradigm shift outlined earlier and evidence that consumers prefer to live as most people do, in houses or apartments with friends and family (Tanzman, 1993; Yeich et al., 1994), we approach the new millennium with many people still residing in segregated facilities. Furthermore, in some parts of the United States, funding for community-based mental health services is still being channeled into the development of new facility-based residential programs, both transitional residential programs and long-term care facilities. If supported housing is an effective and philosophically sound model, why are many mental health administrators and providers passing it up in favor of what some call outdated models of service? Does the supported housing approach have the capacity to support all people with psychiatric disabilities who need assistance maintaining their home life? Or should it be conceptualized as one option among a wider range of community-based residential programs?

Supported Housing Is One Component of a Continuum of Housing Programs for People Who Have Psychiatric Disabilities

Supported housing is an important component of a community support system. For many years a major gap in the transitional housing model was lack of ongoing supports once people "graduated" from group homes or semisupervised apartments into the community. The ongoing, as-needed supports provided by the supported housing model do a great deal to help people who are ready to live independently to maintain their community tenure. However, some people with severe mental illness are either not ready to live independently or prefer congregate living arrangements (Tanzman, 1993). Some examples follow:

1. Some people who have spent many years in an institution are accustomed to being extremely dependent on hospital staff and may be reluctant to leave an institutionalized setting. For these individuals, a small (fewer than eight people) group home staffed by people who are familiar with the needs of people who have severe psychiatric disabilities can ease the stress of moving from an institution to the community. Some residents of such a facility may be ready to move on to independent living after a transition period. Others may desire long-term residency in a supervised setting.

2. People with more than one disability can benefit from round-the-clock supports and services that can be more accessible in congregate settings than in independent housing, for example, people who have a severe mental illness and a substance abuse disorder. A residential program that provides external controls and services specifically geared toward their needs can be a key to maintaining sobriety. A supported housing program would be hard-pressed to provide the same level of support, which may be essential during the early phases of recovery.

3. People whose disability is severe enough to require extensive personal care services may benefit from the accessibility of supports and services available in small, homelike congregate-care settings. These may be people who have chronic psychotic symptoms that interfere markedly with their ability to care for themselves or people with multiple disabilities including severe physical impairment (e.g., nonambulatory). Although the independent living movement (Deegan, 1992) and the experiences of supported living agencies that assist people with developmental disabilities (O'Brien & O'Brien, 1994) showed that people with severe disabilities who need a high level of daily personal assistance can live independently, the current service structure can make it extremely difficult to do so. Hiring a round-the-clock personal care assistant or a home health aide for a single individual can be very costly. Many insurance plans do not cover such services. Skilled and reliable care may be hard to find. Group homes with 24-hour staff coverage are often better equipped to solve these problems and provide services more easily affordable to residents with limited resources.

Supported Housing Is for Everyone

Supported housing is a flexible, individualized model that can be adapted to the needs of everyone.

It can be used by persons with varying levels of disability, but it is important to keep in mind that "the more severely disabled the client, the more critical the need for an individualized approach" (Carling & Ridgeway, 1991, p. 71). Supported housing is really about finding solutions to everyday problems. Some of these problems are just tougher to solve than others.

We can learn a lesson from the field of developmental disabilities, which has moved from an era of institutionalization, through a stage of deinstitutionalization in which people were served in structures (i.e., group homes, sheltered workshops) that were physically integrated into the community but fostered social segregation, and finally to an emerging stage of community membership (Bradley, 1994). This approach stresses that community membership is everyones right, not just a privilege reserved for people who are capable of a particular level of functioning. Keep in mind that some people with developmental disabilities have profound cognitive deficits or severe physical limitations. Nonetheless, local service systems have had real success in shifting from a residential treatment model to "supportive living," which is conceptually and practically similar to the supported housing approach (Carmody, 1994; O'Brien & O'Brien, 1994).

In Illinois, a project dubbed SPICE (Supported Placements in Integrated Community Environments) was created to help a group of people with severe cognitive or mobility impairments move from a nursing home into regular community housing (Carmody, 1994). The participants in the SPICE project were specifically selected because of the fact that they had severe and multiple disabilities, as the project sought to demonstrate that community integration could become a reality for the people considered to be the most disabled. From the very beginning of the project, the participants were encouraged to offer input and became involved. Some of them chose to live with families, others chose to live alone, still others opted for a roommate who was another project participant (such a decision had to be mutual). Participants helped interview and hire personal care assistants and other support staff. They were also assisted in accessing existing community resources (churches, community colleges, etc.). Outcome study results showed a significant gain in community living skills and participants reported a tremendous increase in satisfaction with their living arrangements. The project demonstrated "that anyone with disabilities can live in the community and that the community has the capacity to meet the needs of anyone, including people for whom nursing facilities had been thought the only 'appropriate' residential option" (Carmody, 1994, p. 479).

The history of service provision for people with psychiatric disabilities is clearly quite similar to that of people with developmental disabilities. However, the mental health system has not yet made as strong a commitment to the goal of community membership for all persons with psychiatric disabilities. The many obstacles include housing shortages, the high financial cost of providing in-home assistance (particularly to people who may need round-the-clock services), community opposition due to stigma, and the resistance of service providers who are reluctant to make major changes in how they think and operate. None of these obstacles is insurmountable, yet they often become excuses for maintaining the status quo. Supported housing is for everyone because all of us deserve the right to live in a place that is truly a home.

Summary

From the mid-19th century to the 1960s most people with severe mental illness spent a good part of their lives residing in psychiatric institutions. Once deinstitutionalization began, a key question was, where should consumers live? Some consumers returned to their families, who were often ill-prepared for their service and support needs. Other consumers were placed in boarding homes, nursing homes, and SROs where their quality of life was often little better and sometimes worse then what they left in the hospitals. A relatively small percentage of consumers were given residential treatment. Most of these housing options resulted in *transinstitutionalization* (Carling, 1995, p. 33), meaning that true community integration was not realized.

By the 1980s the preferred model of residential treatment was the linear continuum, which moved consumers through a series of placements that became progressively less supervised and restrictive. The goal of this approach was graduation to independent living, typically without any ongoing support. Eventually it became clear that this model was not meeting the needs of most consumers. The field of PsyR is now in the process of embracing a more normalized and individualized way to assist consumers in finding and maintaining homes. It is called supported housing. This approach seeks to support consumers in the home environments of their choice. Supported housing emphasizes integrated, long-term housing options. The philosophy of the supported housing approach is similar to the values and principles articulated by the independent living movement begun by people who have physical disabilities.

PsyR practitioners who work in supported housing programs do not provide treatment, as consumers can get that from psychiatrists and other mental health professionals. Nor do they provide supervision, which the vast majority of people with psychiatric disabilities do not want or need. Instead, they assist consumers in developing skills and obtaining the resources and supports that they want and need in their particular living situation. Supported housing is philosophically and practically similar to supported education and supported employment (see chapter 7 for more on these approaches). Despite barriers such as stigma, community opposition and lack of access to financial resources, these initiatives represent real hope to consumers who want to live, learn, work, and socialize in the same ways as nondisabled members of their communities.

Class Exercise
Designing an Ideal Residential Services Program

Imagine that you are a newly formed board of directors for a new residential services program. Your target population is adults who have a long history of a severe mental illness and are currently at high risk for psychiatric hospitalization or homelessness. Thus, you can assume that the people you will be providing services for have had a great deal of difficulty residing in the community because they are psychiatrically unstable, have severe functional deficits, have other issues such as problems with substance abuse, or most likely some combination of these. Your task is to determine what type of residential services you want to provide. Consider the following:

1. Do you want to establish group homes, develop a supervised or semisupervised apartment complex, help clients acquire regular homes in the community, or some combination of these?
2. If you choose to utilized facility-based housing, will it be transitional (i.e., residents must move on after a specified time period) or long term?

3. What types of services will the staff provide? How often will they be present in clients' living environments (e.g., 24-hour coverage? As-needed visits?).

References

Besio, S. W., & Mahler, J. (1993). Benefits and challenges of using consumer staff in supported housing services. *Hospital and Community Psychiatry, 44*(5), 490–491.

Bradley, V. J. (1994). Evolution of a new service paradigm. In V. J. Bradley, J. W. Ashbaugh, & B. C. Blaney (Eds.), *Creating individual supports for people with developmental disabilities*. Baltimore: Paul H. Brookes Publishing.

Brown, M. A., Ridgway, P., Anthony, W. A., & Rogers, E. S. (1991). Comparison of outcomes for clients seeking and assigned to supported housing services. *Hospital and Community Psychiatry, 42*(11), 1150–1153.

Butler, W. (1993). The consumer supported housing model in New Jersey (the cornerstone to a new paradigm). *Innovations & Research, 2*(3), 73–75.

Caan, R. A., Blankertz, L., Messinger, K. W., & Gardner, J. R. (1988). Psychosocial rehabilitation: Toward a definition. *Psychosocial Rehabilitation Journal, 11*(4), 61–77.

Campbell, M. E. (1981). The three-quarterway house: A step beyond halfway house toward independent living. *Hospital and Community Psychiatry, 32*(7), 500–501.

Carling, P. J. (1988). A review of the research on housing and community integration for people with psychiatric disabilities. *National Rehabilitation Information Center Quarterly, 1*(3), 1–18.

Carling, P. J. (1990). Supported housing: An evaluation agenda. *Psychosocial Rehabilitation Journal, 13*(4), 95–104.

Carling, P. J. (1993). Housing and supports for persons with mental illness: Emerging approaches to research and practice. *Hospital and Community Psychiatry, 44*(5), 439–449.

Carling, P. J. (1995). *Return to community: Building support systems for people with psychiatric disabilities*. New York: The Guilford Press.

Carling, P. J. (1994). Supports and rehabilitation for housing and community living. In The Publication Committee of IAPSRS (Eds.), *An introduction to psychiatric rehabilitation*. Columbia, MD: International Association of Psychosocial Rehabilitation Services.

Carling, P. J., & Ridgway, P. (1991). A psychiatric rehabilitation approach to housing. In M. D. Farkas & W. A. Anthony (Eds.), *Psychiatric rehabilitation programs: Putting theory into practice*. Baltimore: The Johns Hopkins University Press.

Carmody, K. (1994). Creating individual supports for people moving out of nursing facilities: Supported placements in integrated community environments (SPICE). In V. G. Bradley, J. W. Ashbaugh, & B. C. Blaney (Eds.), *Creating individual supports for people with developmental disabilities*. Baltimore: Paul H. Brookes Publishing.

Clermont, P. (1996). An interview with Howie the Harp. *Options, 1*(1) & 2(2).

Collaborative Support Programs of New Jersey. (1991). *Consumer housing preference survey*. Freehold, NJ: Author.

Collaborative Support Programs of New Jersey. (1996). *Boarding home resident survey for Monmouth and Ocean counties*. Freehold, NJ: Author.

Cook, J. R. (1997). Neighbors' perceptions of group homes. *Community Mental Health Journal, 33*(4), 287–299.

Curtis, L. C., McCabe, S. S., Fleming, M., & Carling, P. J. (1993). *Implementing the supported housing approach: An impact evaluation of the Texas supported housing demonstration initiative*. Burlington, VT: Trinity College, The Center for Community Change through Housing and Support.

Deegan, P. E. (1992). The independent living movement and people with psychiatric disabilities: Taking back control over our own lives. *Psychosocial Rehabilitation Journal, 15*(3), 3–19.

Fairweather, G. W., Saunders, D. H., Maynard, H., & Cressler, D. L. (1969). *Community life for the mentally ill.* Chicago: Aldine.

Farkas, M., & Chamberlin, J. (1998, May). *Developing supports, not just skill, through personal assistance services.* Paper presented at the VI World Congress, World Association for Psychosocial Rehabilitation, Hamburg, Germany.

Goldman, H. H., Gattozzi, A. A., & Taube, C. A. (1981). Defining and counting the chronically mentally ill. *Hospital and Community Psychiatry, 32*(1), 22–27.

Howie the Harp. (1990). Independent living with support services: The goal and future for mental health consumers. *Psychosocial Rehabilitation Journal, 13*(4), 85–89.

Howie the Harp. (1991). *A crazy folks guide to reasonable accommodation and "psychiatric disability."* Burlington, VT: Trinity College, The Center for Community Change through Housing and Support.

Howie the Harp. (1993). Taking a new approach to independent living. *Hospital and Community Psychiatry, 44*(5), 413.

Knisley, M. B., & Fleming, M. (1993). Implementing supported housing in state and local mental health systems. *Hospital & Community Psychiatry, 44*(5), 456–461.

Lamb, H. R. (1982). *Treating the long-term mentally ill.* San Francisco: Jossey-Bass.

Lehman, A. F., Ward, N. C., & Linn, L. S. (1982). Chronic mental patients: The quality of life issue. *American Journal of Psychiatry, 139*(10), 1271–1276.

Linn, M. W., Klett, C. J., & Caffey, E. M. (1980). Foster home characteristics and psychiatric patient outcome. *Archives of General Psychiatry, 37*(2), 129–132.

Livingston, J. A., Gordon, L. R., King, D. A., & Srebnik, D. S. (1991). *Implementing the supported housing approach: A national evaluation of NIMH supported housing demonstration projects.* Burlington, VT: Trinity College, The Center for Community Change through Housing and Support.

O'Brien, J., & O'Brien, C. L. (1994). More than just a new address: Images of organization for supported living agencies. In V. J. Bradley, J. W. Ashbaugh, & B. C. Blaney (Eds.), *Creating individual supports for people with developmental disabilities.* Baltimore: Paul H. Brookes Publishing.

Ogilvie, R. J. (1997). The state of supported housing for mental health consumers: A literature review. *Psychiatric Rehabilitation Journal, 21*(2), 122–131.

Onaga, E. E. (1994). The Fairweather lodge as a psychosocial program in the 1990's. In The Publication Committee of IAPSRS (Eds.), *An introduction to psychiatric rehabilitation.* Columbia, MD: International Association of Psychosocial Rehabilitation Services.

Parrish, J. (1990). Supported housing: A critical component of effective community support. *Psychosocial Rehabilitation Journal, 13*(4), 9–10.

Pyke, J., & Lowe, J. (1996) Supporting people, not structures: Changes in the provision of supportive housing. *Psychiatric Rehabilitation Journal, 19*(3), 5–12.

Ridgway, P., & Zipple, A. M. (1990). The paradigm shift in residential services: From the linear continuum to supported housing approaches. *Psychosocial Rehabilitation Journal, 13*(4), 11–31.

Tanzman, B. (1993). An overview of surveys of mental health consumers' preferences for housing and support services. *Hospital and Community Psychiatry, 44*(5), 450–455.

Texas Department of Mental Health and Mental Retardation, Research and Special Projects (1994, January). *TXMHMR supported housing program evaluation: year one findings.* Austin, TX: Author.

Torrey, E. F. (1995). *Surviving schizophrenia.* New York: HarperCollins.

Wolfensberger, W. (1983). Social role valorization: A proposed new term for the principle of normalization. *Mental Retardation, 21*(6), 235–239.

Yeich, S., Mowbray, C. T., Bybee, D., & Cohen, E. (1994). The case for a "supported housing" approach: A study of consumer housing and support preferences. *Psychosocial Rehabilitation Journal, 18*(2), 75–86.

Zinman, S. (1995, Spring/Summer). The legacy of Howie the Harp lives on. *National Empowerment Center Newsletter,* 1–9.

Zippay, A. (1997). Trends in siting strategies. *Community Mental Health Journal, 33*(4), 301–310.

Chapter 10

Consumers as Advocates and Providers of Supports and Services

*This chapter outlines the important contributions that consumers make to their own reha-
bilitation and the rehabilitation of others. Like the field of alcoholism and drug addiction
treatment, there is a long tradition of self-help among persons who have a severe mental
illness. Today, consumers are moving into professional psychiatric rehabilitation (PsyR)
service provider positions in larger and larger numbers. They are also involved in operating consumer agencies, participating on boards of directors and conducting sophisticated
research. Consumer involvement in all aspects of the rehabilitation process is a fundamental
principle of psychiatric rehabilitation that is being increasingly achieved.*

This chapter will answer the following questions:

1. How have self-help groups impacted PsyR?
2. What services are consumers capable of providing?
3. What are some of the issues around having consumers also provide services?
4. Should a consumer-provider disclose his/her condition to other professionals?
5. What are some of the benefits and concerns around consumers providing services?

Introduction

Consumers of psychiatric rehabilitation (PsyR) services have a long tradition of participating in self-help and mutual support initiatives. Despite the stigma associated with severe mental illness, PsyR consumers, like their counterparts in alcohol and drug rehabilitation, are moving into service provision roles in larger and larger numbers. The problems they face as they take on these new challenges are both complex and exciting. As many who have studied this phenomenon have pointed out, these developments represent real empowerment for consumers and an affirmation of the principles of psychiatric rehabilitation.

History of Self-Help and the Ex-patient Movement

Self-help has been a part of psychiatric rehabilitation since the field's beginning. The group of ex-psychiatric patients described in chapter 6, who dubbed themselves WANA (We Are Not Alone) in the 1940s and then went on to establish Fountain House, began as a self-help group. Other consumer support and self-help groups around the country helped establish services for persons with severe mental illness. Today the self-help movement plays an important part in the treatment, support, and public advocacy for persons who have a severe and persistent mental illness.

Recognition of the important role played by self-help has led to increased respect for these initiatives on the part of PsyR professionals. The idea that persons with the same problems can help each other is widespread and generally accepted today. One group of researchers has offered a general definition of self-help:

> Self-help is an attempt by people with a mutual problem to take control over the circumstances of their lives. Founded on the principle that people who share a disability have something to offer each other that professionals cannot provide, self-help efforts take many forms. (Segal, Silverman, & Temkin, 1993, p. 705)

Even before WANA, there were efforts by ex-psychiatric patients to provide mutual aid and support via self-help groups. Dr. Abraham Low, a psychiatrist, developed a treatment method in the 1930s that was similar to what we now call cognitive behavioral therapy. He worked with people who suffered from a wide range of mental and emotional disorders, teaching them to control their symptoms and take responsibility for their lives. His methods are outlined in a widely published book, *Mental Health through Will Training.* In 1952, 2 years before his death, he founded Recovery Inc., the second oldest self-help organization in the United States, which concentrated on the self-help aspect of his treatment. Alcoholics Anonymous, founded in 1935 (Robertson, 1988), is the oldest self-help organization in the United States. Over the years, Recovery Inc. has grown into an international organization totally run by its members. In meetings, members share examples of everyday life situations where they have applied Recovery Inc. principles. They share their stories in four steps. In the first step, the members summarize situations that trigger emotional distress. In the second step, members specify symptoms that they experienced. The third step involves relabeling symptoms using Recovery Inc. terminology. This part of the process helps members to cognitively reframe symptoms that they used to experience as devastating into manageable aspects of their day to day functioning. The last step requires members to speculate on how they would have handled the situation before they learned self-help techniques (Ackerman, 1997). Despite the fact that many mental health professionals either do not know about the organization or misinterpret its techniques, Recovery Inc. continues to be an important resource for people who are recovering from a variety of mental illnesses (Lee, 1995).

The civil rights movement of the 1960s helped give rise to the concepts of consumerism and empowerment. Although this movement may have begun as an effort to combat racism and sexism, it soon spread to other disadvantaged populations such as those confined indefinitely to psychiatric institutions. It was during the height of the civil rights movement that deinstitutionalization was bolstered by the reform of antiquated commitment laws throughout the United States. Many of those being released after long and sometimes abusive hospital stays found that the services being offered in outpatient settings were not meeting their needs. Overmedication, the stigmatizing attitudes of mental health professionals, diagnoses that became negative labels, and limited treatment options often combined to undermined their efforts to adjust to the community and lead a "normal" life.

Increasing numbers of ex-patients began to search for alternatives, and by the early 1970s the ex-patient movement, also referred to as the survivor movement (Rogers, 1996), had begun. Early on some of the names of local grassroots organizations were the Mental Patients Liberation Front, the Alliance for the Liberation of Mental Patients, and the Network Against Psychiatric Assault (Chamberlin, 1984). These names give us a clear sense of members attitudes toward the mental health system and their need to regain control over their lives. Although the **ex-patient movement** started primarily with advocacy efforts to deal with the devastation and disempowerment described, it soon expanded its focus and began offering support, mutual aid, information, and education (Rogers, 1996).

In contrast to groups opposed to the mental health system, some self-help groups developed in conjunction with existing services. A typical example might be a group of consumers attending a day program who express interest in forming a mutual self-help group. PsyR professionals who are aware of the benefits of such an initiative would provide consultation, space, and perhaps a supportive connection with an existing consumer-run group. Today there are numerous self-help groups around the country that operate in conjunction with regular mental health services, often sharing space, resources, and mutual referrals.

However, some people involved in the ex-patient movement maintain that separation from the mental health system is essential. Judi Chamberlin, a well-known activist for more than 25 years, stated "many of us in the ex-patients movement believe that it is only outside the mental health system that self-help and mutual support can flourish" (Chamberlin, 1984, p. 56). In her book *On Our Own*, Chamberlin described both her personal experiences as a psychiatric inpatient and her involvement in some of these early self-help initiatives. She described how "consciousness-raising" groups, which were not unlike those inspired by the women's movement, helped people labeled as mentally ill recognize the negative effects that the mental health system had on their self-image. Such groups helped ex-patients rebuild their self-esteem and inspired action such as the 1974 publication of a handbook,

Your Rights as a Mental Patient in Massachusetts. Other groups led to the development of drop-in centers, communal residences, and projects focused on publicizing the deplorable conditions of mental institutions (Chamberlin, 1988, p. 90). As we will see later in this chapter, consumer-run service initiatives have gained both momentum and credibility in recent years and have become essential elements in the recovery of people throughout the United States.

Self-Help Groups/Initiatives Today

Self-help and mutual support groups have become an accepted part of mental health services around the country. Numerous organizations throughout the United States provide information, referrals, and easy access to existing groups that offer support to people with a variety of psychiatric and medical disorders as well as other problems and issues (The New Jersey Self-Help Clearinghouse, 1997). The National Mental Health Consumers' Self-Help Clearinghouse is a noteworthy organization that provides a number of important services, including referrals to local self-help groups; information about other consumer-run services, such as drop-in centers and alternative programs; up-to-date information about the political activities of the self-help movement; training events, such as national and regional conferences; and access to consultation and technical assistance materials (Rogers, 1996). Information about self-help organizations can also be accessed through Web sites and Internet chat rooms.

Today self-help is an integral part of community support systems throughout the country. In fact, peer support has been listed as one of the ten essential ingredients of an ideal community support system (Stroul, 1989). Community support systems are covered in chapter 8. For some, self-help groups and other peer support services are an important adjunct to the professional psychiatric and rehabilitation services that they receive. For others, peer support initiatives represent a true alternative to the mental health system. We will take a closer look at consumers' experiences with both of these options, as well as examine professional attitudes about self-help.

Consumer Provider Collaboration

PsyR professionals are motivated to refer their clients to self-help and peer support services, as well as to collaborate with clients in developing such services, for two important reasons (a) they recognize that supports outside the mental health system are essential to the recovery process and (b) they see these services as cost-effective ways to provide clients with additional supports, particularly during an era of dwindling mental health dollars (Kaufman, Freund, & Wilson,1989). According to Joseph A. Rogers, executive director of the National Mental Health Consumers' Self-Help Clearinghouse:

> "Consumer run services are perfectly positioned to fill the service gap resulting from
> state and local cost-control measures such as managed care if consumers are educated

and supported in their efforts to expand existing consumer-run projects, launch new ones, and test new models." (Rogers, 1996, p.22)

Sometimes, however, the attitudes of mental health professionals interfere with both the utilization and further development of self-help efforts. Some of the concerns that professionals have about self-help efforts may stem from the following:

- A lack of information about key self-help initiatives (Lee, 1995)
- Underestimation of the abilities of consumers as service providers—for example, dismissing them as second-class workers (Mowbray et al., 1996; Solomon & Draine, 1996)
- Negative reactions to efforts associated with the ex-patient movement, such as concern that rebellion and noncompliance with treatment will be promoted (Kaufman et al., 1989; Mowbray et al., 1988).

Despite these potential barriers, consumers and providers can work together effectively when developing self-help initiatives. One model for consumer-provider collaboraton focuses on the changing roles of staff and consumers that are coming about as the PsyR field matures. As empowerment and self-help become more accepted, consumers increasingly take on more responsibility for supporting both themselves and their peers. In response to the same issues, the staff increasingly moves away from the role of helper and adopts a more professional consultative approach (Kaufman, et al., 1989). The model that represents these changes is a five-stage process:

1. In the investment/nuturance stage, the staff promotes increased social interaction between members of a psychiatric rehabilitation program, while members become more invested in the well-being of their peers.
2. In the initiative/delegation stage, consumers assume greater responsibility in planning program activities. Some program members begin to emerge as leaders. Staff members support these changes by delegating some of their responsibilities and teaching/modeling leadership skills.
3. During the rebellion/dialogue stage, members openly express dissatisfaction with both their role as patient or client and the control exerted by the mental health system, while staff recognize the validity of their concerns and promote open discussions about stigma and consumer rights. During this stage, work begins in the development of a self-help initiative. Staff members work toward reducing administrative resistance to the initiative and provide consumers with access to information about self-help organizations.
4. In the accomadation/collaboration stage, consumers deal with role shift issues and may begin to adopt new labels such as ex-patient. It is also typical in this stage for members to begin to meet informally outside of the program. Staff members can serve as important resources during this period of increased consumer autonomy.
5. In the self-help/consultation stage, consumers establish a formal self-help initiative. Staff members provide an as-needed consultant role (Kaufman et al., 1989, p.10).

The Case of David

Whether it is encouraged by professionals or generated entirely by consumers, self-help can be an important adjunct to rehabilitation. As you read about David, consider the role self-help plays in his rehabilitation process.

David is a 32-year-old man who has been coping with a severe mental illness since he was 19 years old. Over the past 13 years, he has been in a variety of inpatient and outpatient mental health services. David is currently attending a partial care program where, because of his interest in computers, he spends most of his time working in the prevocational clerical unit. His goal is to either get a job using computers or enroll in a computer training program. However, his caseworkers have told him that he is not ready for training or work yet. They feel he needs to be more compliant with his medication regimen and improve both his punctuality and concentration in the work area. David has tried to explain that he occasionally neglects to take his medication because he doesn't like to feel lethargic all the time. This lethargy is also the reason he frequently gets to the program late. He thinks his concentration problems have more to do with the boredom he experiences while working on tedious clerical tasks than with his symptoms.

Lately David is feeling more and more discouraged and frustrated. He feels that the treatment he is receiving at the program isn't getting him anywhere, but he doesn't know where else to turn. David is aware of the mental health/rehab services offered in his county and has been involved with many of them. In fact, he likes his current program better than the others he has been to, mostly because he likes some of the staff members and because he has made some close friendships with other members. One of these friends is Jean, who has been attending the program for several years herself. Jean tells David that while she finds the structure and support offered by the partial care program helpful in coping with her illness, she sometimes wishes she had more control over the focus of the group activities. They joke about starting their own program called CONTROL (Consumer-Owned Network to Recover Our Lives).

David and Jean continue to talk about the idea of starting their CONTROL. Eventually they present some of their ideas to Jill, a young, energetic caseworker who has empathized with their frustration in the past. Jill gives them some references and articles to read about the self-help movement. David and Jean get more excited about their idea and invite some other program members out for coffee to discuss the development of a self-help venture. Meanwhile, Jill speaks to both her supervisor and an agency administrator about supporting a member-run self-help group. Initially the idea is met with resistance. Concerns are raised about the direction the group might take and the implications around treatment and medication compliance. To address these concerns, Jill suggests that she function as the liaison between the mental health center and the new self-help group. This idea is acceptable and they agree to free Jill up one hour a week to act as a self-help consultant.

Jill uses the time to meet with David, Jean, and a few other interested members to discuss issues such as location, leadership, group dynamics, and dealing with potential crises. A month later they acquire space in a local community center one evening a week, and soon CONTROL, a mutual aid self-help group, becomes a reality.

> **The Case of David Continued**
>
> David and Jean continue to receive services at the partial care program, although David has cut back his involvement to 1 or 2 days a week. His contribution to the development and running of the self-help group has given him new confidence. His role in organizing and advertising the group's activities has convinced him that he can focus on and complete tasks that interest him. The enthusiastic encouragement and support he has received from other group members has helped him decide to start taking computer classes 2 mornings a week.

Self-Help and MICA

Participating with self-help groups may be even more important for people dealing with both a mental illness and a substance abuse problem. Historically, these individuals were the first to be referred to self-help groups in the form of Alcoholics Anonymous (AA). Sadly, these referrals were more often caused by an inability or unwillingness to deal with the substance abuse problem than an appreciation of the benefits of self-help. Still, professionals were aware that attendance at these substance abuse related self-help groups did help their clients. For many professionals, this knowledge led to an appreciation of the contributions self-help could make for their clients.

Mentally ill substance abuser (MICA) clients are still the consumers most likely to be referred to self-help groups. As mentioned earlier in the text, people with a MICA diagnosis often require specialized programs and supports. Caseworkers often encourage these clients to utilize self-help groups to supplement the professional supports and services that they receive. Alcoholics Anonymous and Narcotics Anonymous (NA) are the most commonly utilized mutual aid groups for persons recovering from alcoholism and other substance abuse disorders.

Many persons encountered stiff resistance from these groups when they disclosed they had a mental illness. Apparently, the stigma associated with severe mental illness exits even within groups such as AA and NA. In addition, AA and NA groups often discourage the use of psychotropic medications because they are viewed as obstacles to recovery from addiction. Partly in response to this resistance, many consumers have been receiving help in mutual aid groups known as **double trouble**. Double trouble groups are specifically geared to meet the needs of individuals who have a MICA diagnoses. Even so, they are very similar to AA and NA groups. Like AA and NA groups, double trouble groups utilize a 12-step process of recovery (Alcoholics Anonymous World Services, 1981). They are also frequently run by persons who have substance abuse problems themselves. In contrast, double trouble groups have two important differences from AA and NA groups: (a) acceptance of the importance of psychiatric medications and (b) a high tolerance of psychiatric symptomatology.

In at least one urban area, efforts to develop a much needed network of double trouble groups resulted in some variations of the traditional self-help model. Although the network strives to continue to support and develop consumer-run double trouble groups, they have also helped develop groups in which staff members were either present in the meeting or available nearby. This variation was utilized in certain inpatient settings and at community-based agencies where groups met on-site but regulations or insurance requirements necessitated staff involvement. Another variation of the double trouble support group has been used in situations where acute symptoms interfered with group leadership. In this version, staff members, who have received training and information by an experienced double trouble group member, provide interim leadership (Caldwell & White, 1991).

Although clients of MICA services and self-help groups specifically tailored to meet their needs are a seemingly good fit, researchers have found that in some settings the majority of clients who were strongly encouraged to utilize self-help groups did not do so on a regular basis. It may be that the stage of recovery a consumer is in is an important consideration in choosing to accept support from a self-help group. In particular, consumers with a MICA diagnosis may be able to make better use of self-help in the later stages of their recovery (Noordsy, Schwab, Fox, & Drake, 1996).

Self-Help as an Alternative to Professional Services

The ex-patient's movement described earlier has continued to make progress in its quest to provide people who are coping with mental illnesses and emotional problems with support and service options that are separate from the professionally driven mental health system. Whereas self-help group opportunities have flourished for many years, alternative programs, such as drop-in centers and residential facilities, were very difficult to start up and maintain without reliable funding sources. Obtaining funding became a controversial issue for many ex-patient groups. Some objected, in principle, to establishing relationships with traditional funding sources. Another concern was the creation of salaried staff positions in consumer-run organizations in which previously members had all shared the same volunteer status. These reservations were often irrelevant because potential funding sources, such as "mental health departments, were highly skeptical of the ability of ex-patients to run their own projects" (Chamberlin, 1990, p. 326).

By the early 1980s, however, people involved in the ex-patient movement began to establish greater credibility as presenters at national conferences, as articulate participants in legislative hearings, and as members of key boards and committees throughout the United States. Gradually, funding opportunities such as community support program grants from the National Institute of Mental Health and monies from state mental health and vocational rehabilitation departments became available. With increased funding and partnerships with other oppressed groups, such as the independent living movement for people with physical disabilities, the movement was able to help provide a wide array of services and supports (Chamberlin, Rogers, & Ellison, 1996).

In addition to playing a stronger role in service provision, the consumer movement continues to advocate for the rights of consumers by focusing on issues such as involuntary treatment, use of restraints and seclusion in psychiatric hospitals, and housing and employment discrimination. In 1996 the National Empowerment Center (NEC) of Lawrence, Massachusetts, listed 40 statewide consumer/survivor organizations located throughout the United States. The NEC is a nonprofit organization that was founded, and is primarily run by consumer/survivors. Its mission is to carry a message of recovery and empowerment, hope and healing to people with psychiatric disabilities, their friends and family members, professionals, and the general public. The NEC provides an array of information about the consumer/survivor movement, and about recovery and empowerment in the form of publications, training materials, and a speaker's bureau.

A study by Chamberlin et al. (1996) reviewed 64 self-help programs that were both administratively controlled and run by consumers. They found that a wide array of services were provided, including social/recreational activities, individual and system level advocacy, assistance with housing and employment, transportation, and assistance with activities of daily living. This study also found that the majority of people who utilized the self-help programs were very involved, spending an average of 15.3 hours a week at the program location (Chamberlin et al., 1996). These programs also received positive ratings on a variety of program satisfaction measures. Most of the self-help service recipients surveyed also utilized some type of professional mental health service.

BOX 10.1

A Consumer-Operated Agency Collaborative Support Programs of New Jersey

Collaborative Support Programs of New Jersey (CSPNJ), one of the agencies surveyed in the previously mentioned study, provides a good example of the kinds of services consumer-controlled and consumer-run programs can offer. CSPNJ is funded in part by the New Jersey Division of Mental Health Services. At the same time, all administrative positions at CSPNJ are held by consumers. The vast majority of the staff of CSPNJ identify themselves as mental health consumers as well.

The development and provision of supported housing is one of CSPNJ's key missions. Staff members assist consumers in obtaining homes and apartments and provide supports on an as needed basis. The agency also helps with the physical maintenance of the home. Monarch Housing, an affiliate of CSPNJ, provides other agencies around the state with assistance in obtaining decent and affordable housing for consumers. They provide a wide array of consultation services ranging from helping agencies obtain funding to consultation on how to deal with NIMBY (Not in My Backyard) issues. Chapter 7 covers the NIMBY issue in more depth.

Another key CSPNJ activity is the development and support of consumer-run drop-in centers. The agency has assisted in the development of 23 drop-in centers throughout the state. It provides self-help groups with assistance in obtaining funding and a site for the drop-in center, trains consumers in the provision of support services, and supplies ongoing consultation as needed.

CSPNJ is involved in other initiatives as well: the agency has a strong presence on mental health related boards and committees throughout the state, it maintains an advisory position with the state Division of Mental Health Services, it provides training and education to mental health providers, and it plays an active role in systems level advocacy.

BOX 10.2

Patricia Deegan

Patricia Deegan has a Ph.D. in clinical psychology. She has an impressive resume, having worked as a practicing psychologist, and a community mental health program director and having established a program for people with psychiatric disabilities within a cross disability, independent living center (see chapter 9 for more on the independent living movement). She

Patricia Deegan

is also a cofounder of the National Empowerment Center. Dr. Deegan has published numerous journal articles and is a much sought after consultant and lecturer. She has inspired thousands of mental health professionals, students, consumers, and family members in her speaking engagements throughout the United States, Canada, Europe, Israel, New Zealand, and Australia. In short, she is a leader in the field of psychiatric rehabilitation. Dr. Deegan also continues to cope with her own recovery from severe mental illness.

She was first diagnosed with schizophrenia as a teenager and was hospitalized on several occasions. In her writing, she describes her experiences as dehumanizing and the initial stages of her recovery as fraught with long periods of hopelessness and despair. Deegan's experiences, and the stories of other people with disabilities, led her to the realization that recovery is often impeded by mental health professionals whose low expectations and well meaning but coercive interventions prevent people from achieving true independence.

Deegan initially chose to work in a traditional mental health program, and she tried to change the system from within. She decided, at that time, not to disclose her illness to her colleagues. Eventually she became frustrated with both her attempts to help consumers within a system that frequently disempowered and stigmatized consumers and with efforts to keep her struggle with her illness under wraps. She began to speak at conferences about her experiences as a provider—and a consumer.

Eventually she left traditional practice and became active in the consumer/survivor movement, becoming a founding member of Massachusetts People/Patients Organized for Wellness, Empowerment and Rights (M-POWER). Dr. Deegan also began working with the Northeast Independent Living Program, "an advocacy and organizing program run by people with disabilities for people with disabilities" (Stevens, 1991, p. 20). At the same time she began writing articles and conducting speaking engagements to promote consumer's rights and her vision of recovery. In her own words:

> My real hope for re-humanizing the human services rests with people with disabilities as we begin learning that we can organize, that we have power in our numbers, and that we can overcome oppression through expression. The days of silence are over. As professionals and as fellow human beings, we have a great deal to learn from the people we seek to serve. It is important to listen to people with disabilities. (Deegan, 1990, p. 310)

Dr. Deegan currently works as the director of training at the National Empowerment Center and continues to speak, write, and provide consultation. A recent accomplishment was the publication of *Coping with Voices: Self Help Strategies for People Who Hear Voices That Are Distressing.* Although Deegan does not take an antimedication stance, she does object to mental health professionals who push consumers to become "medication compliant." Deegan's preference is to encourage people to use medications as "one tool among many tools that a person may choose to use in their recovery process" (Deegan, 1996, p. 1). Her recent publication provides other options for consumers who are coping with auditory hallucinations.

Consumers as PsyR Professionals

Consumers do not just act as service providers in alternative programs. In increasing numbers, consumers are being hired to provide a wide range of psychiatric rehabilitation and mental health services in the traditional mental health delivery system. Mowbray et al. (1996) examined this trend in which consumers work as regular service providers. Their work identified four principle reasons why this trend is going forward:

1. "[It is] consistent with a rehabilitation philosophy, [that] productive and important work is made available and accessible to consumers."
2. "Inclusion of consumers as mental health workers can increase the sensitivity of programs and services about recipients."
3. "[Consumers] can serve as effective role models for clients."
4. "The inclusion of consumers is an expression of affirmative action and consistent with contemporary civil and disability rights policies." (Mowbray et al., 1996, p. 48)

BOX 10.3
Prosumers (excerpt from Manos, 1993)

Acronyms, jargon, and buzzwords continue to clutter the world of discourse about mental health and illness. Knowing the meaning of this private vocabulary is a kind of ticket to the inner realm or backstage, separating the informed from the ignorant, or the insiders from the outsiders. *Prosumer* is the newest term to surface, born from a marriage of the words *professional* and *consumer*, so technically it is a neologism. A prosumer is a former pure consumer who has decided to look beyond self and toward the larger work to be done in the field. Interestingly, blending consumer and professional in the proper sequential order, with consumer first, would result in "confessional" and that just wouldn't communicate what this new being is all about. Prosumers are former mental patients, graduates of various forms of living hell, transformed into consumers and now activated toward a wide variety of work roles to help others who are still in the first stages of defining their selves and their beings.

Prosumers are a varied lot. Some go the whole distance and earn a professional degree in one of the mental health disciplines. Others work entirely as unpaid volunteers. Still others become paraprofessionals. And then there is the interesting group that started out as professionals, became patients, trod the long hard road to recovery, and now think of themselves as prosumers.

Prosumers seem to be particularly successful with patients and consumers who are still struggling actively with their illness and who have not been able to develop good interpersonal relationships with their professional caregivers. In these cases, people who have been there can develop the trust and show the way to new ideas and new ways of relating. The first step is very often simply to accept the illness. This is not so simple of course, but it is certainly rudimentary. We prosumers are more believable when we state that we've been there and know that there is a way out. We're seasoned travelers, we're excellent guides. We know the ropes and we know the paths, and we say simply, "Come, follow me."

There is, a great deal of variation in level of professionalism attached to the consumer-provider role. We will explore these various roles and review research findings regarding the strengths, potential limitations, and efficacy of consumer-providers who have also been called *prosumers* in the literature (Manos, 1993; see Box 10.3 for more about this term).

We will also examine the effect of being a consumer-provider on one's recovery, including the positive impact and the challenges that must be faced.

Efficacy of Consumer-Providers

Almost from its inception, the field of substance abuse counseling has recognized the benefits of utilizing recovering alcoholics and addicts as regular service providers (Moxley & Mowbray, 1997). An obvious benefit of this strategy is the ability of recovering alcoholics and addicts to truly empathize with the persons for whom they are providing services. Consumer-providers may also have an advantage over nonconsumer providers in the length of time it takes to establish trusting relationships with service recipients.

The field of mental health has been much slower to recognize these benefits, perhaps because there is greater stigma attached to having a mental illness than to a substance abuse disorder. The higher level of professionalism among mental health providers in terms of academic preparation, training, and educational degrees, compared to providers of substance abuse counseling, is another possible explanation. It is interesting to note that in some substance abuse treatment settings, counselors who are in recovery have a higher status then those who have not struggled with addiction. By contrast, in the mental health field, consumer-providers are frequently given job titles that indicate their consumer status and are viewed as second-class providers.

In addition to the advantages of consumer-providers mentioned earlier, the literature cites a number of unique strengths that people with psychiatric disabilities bring to the role of service provider. Life experiences, which may include survival on "the streets" and familiarity with successful resource acquisition strategies, provide many consumer-providers with an advantage not shared by some professionals, particularly those who are young and inexperienced (Paulson, 1991). One study found that peer specialists on an intensive case management team "developed a distinctive advocacy role, representing the client's perspective in discussions with case managers about clients' problems and needs" (Felton, Stastny, Shern, Blanch, Donahue, Knight, & Brown, 1995, p. 1039). These strengths may make consumer-providers especially effective in programs like Assertive Community Treatment, which emphasize mobile outreach and providing services directly to consumers in the community (Lyons et al., 1996).

Consumer-providers are frequently perceived by the people they serve as being more credible on medication compliance issues, particularly when they share their own experiences with medication. Along the same lines, consumer-providers can be particularly helpful in aiding consumers in recognizing the prodromal signs that precede acute episodes of mental illness (Paulson, 1991). Consumer-providers also supply consumers with important information about their rights and alternative treatment approaches, which allow consumers to choose from a wider array of options than nonconsumer providers may offer (Mowbray & Moxley, 1997a).

As Mowbray et al. and others have pointed out, a key strength of consumer-providers, and perhaps the best reason for promoting consumer involvement in PsyR service provision, is their ability to act as role models for other consumers. Their mere presence conveys the important message that people with severe mental illnesses can succeed in valued social roles. They convey competence and the ability to regain control over their lives to other consumers who may have lost hope of ever moving beyond the role of mental patient (Mowbray, 1997; Mowbray et al., 1996; Nikkel, Smith, & Edwards, 1992). In short, consumer-providers can be inspiring role models for other consumers. Consumer-providers also deliver a concrete message to other consumers about the reality and possibility of empowerment.

> Through the symbol and the reality of consumers who provide services, empowerment is actualized. Power is given away to those with a disability label, power to take control over their own outcomes and over systems operations. (Mowbray, 1997, p. 47)

Although other providers may be equally effective in assisting and supporting service recipients as they move toward recovery, consumer-providers have a unique capacity to inspire as well.

The impact of utilizing consumer-providers on client outcomes has not yet been widely studied, but initial research has found that consumer-providers compare favorably to non-consumer providers (Lyons et al., 1996; Solomon & Draine, 1995). One study found that intensive case management teams that incorporated peer specialists provided more effective case management and helped clients achieve a better quality of life when compared to teams which did not utilize consumer-providers (Felton et al., 1995). Recommendations for future study of consumer-providers includes utilization of a participatory action research approach so that consumer-providers have a voice in evaluating their contribution to the PsyR field (Leff, Campbell, Gagne, & Woocher, 1997).

Challenges for Consumer-Providers

In their efforts to assist consumers, it is important for consumer-providers to recognize and utilize their unique strengths. At the same time, they need to be aware of some potential limitations inherent in the their dual role as a consumer-provider. One of these limitations is the tendency by some consumer-providers to generalize their own experiences to the life situations of clients they are working with (Nikkel et al., 1992). They may "fail to fully appreciate the diversity of experiences of persons with major mental illnesses and the individuality of a person's response" (Paulson, 1991, p. 75). Some consumer-providers may make the mistake of thinking that their experience of a particular symptom of mental illness is typical, whereas it is much more likely that each person's experience is unique.

Another potential drawback involves the maintenance of confidentiality. Consumer-providers, particularly those who practice in or near an agency where they have received services, may struggle with boundaries due to prior relationships they have had with service recipients (Mowbray, 1997). This can also be a problem if staff who provided or still provide them with service are operating in adjacent services.

Because mental illnesses are stress related, many consumer-providers, and their employers, have concerns about coping with the high-stress associated with PsyR service provision. Will they be prone to burnout sooner than other providers? Will they need to take a lengthy sick leave if they become acutely ill? If they cannot handle the job stress and become unemployed, will they become reeligible for disability benefits? Such concerns plague many consumer-providers and can even have a negative effect on job performance.

Although many consumers establish comfortable relationships more easily with consumer-providers than nonconsumer providers, some are wary of receiving help from a person who may be struggling with their own mental illness. These concerns can stem from stigmatizing attitudes (consumers can be both victims and perpetuators of stigma!) or mistrust of peers once they move into a provider role (Mowbray, 1997). Such reactions can frustrate consumer-providers in their efforts to provide help and cause them to question their own capabilities.

Relationships with Nonconsumer Providers

For many consumer-providers, the most formidable challenge is establishing positive relationships with the nonconsumer staff (Mowbray, 1997; Macauley, 1993). This might come as a surprise for many people entering the field. After all, if PsyR staff members internalize PsyR values, goals, and principles, they should be pleased to work side by side with colleagues who are recovering from a mental illness. Unfortunately this is not always the case. Consumer-providers frequently report feeling discriminated against and stigmatized by coworkers. According to Daniel Fisher, a psychiatrist who is also an activist and self-described "person in recovery from a psychiatric disability":

> The mental health profession is one of the most discriminating and stigmatizing towards consumers/survivors. Consumer/survivors who work as providers are labeled and objectified in the same fashion as consumers. Their behavior and principles are filtered through their psychiatric disability. (Fisher, 1994b, p. 68)

A common complaint is being eyed suspiciously when expressing anger or simply having a bad day. Nonconsumer colleagues often jump to the conclusion that a consumer-provider is experiencing symptoms. In such situations, consumer-providers often report being treated in a way that is clearly different than the way other staff members are treated when they are having bad moods. For example, when a consumer-provider expresses too much emotion, the relationship may suddenly shift from collegial to therapeutic.

Stigmatizing attitudes may be expressed to consumer-providers in a variety of other ways. Nonconsumer staff may exclude consumer-providers from social events or act in other ways that distance consumer-providers. Nonconsumer staff may question the professionalism of consumer-providers, for example, by expressing resentment when reasonable accommodations are made for staff members who have psychiatric disabilities (Mowbray, 1997). Consumer-providers have also experienced harassment from colleagues in ways that are mean spirited and hurtful (Roberts, Rotteveel, & Manos, 1995). Stigma may not be the only reason that consumer-providers are sometimes treated poorly. Staff may fear being displaced by consumer-providers and thus exhibit resentful behaviors (Mowbray, 1997).

Happily, negative treatment of consumer-providers is not always the case. Many consumer-providers report very positive, supportive working relationships with nonconsumer colleagues. In fact many consumers cite a key reason for choosing a career in PsyR is working in an environment that is more supportive and accomadating than other work settings.

Disclosure

Should a consumer working in a PsyR professional role disclose to other staff or supervisors that he or she is also a recipient of mental health services? Although some consumer-providers are hired, in part, because of their experiences as mental health consumers, others are hired based solely on past work/educational experiences. This latter group may struggle with the issue of whether or not to disclose their experiences as a consumer. Dr. Deegan recounts such a struggle when she had to decide whether or not to disclose her own consumer status. Past experiences with stigmatizing attitudes of mental health professionals leave some consumer-providers determined to avoid self-disclosure at all costs. However, many consumer-providers report that this is a difficult stance to maintain. What if one were to come in contact with a consumer who is familiar with his or her status as service recipient? Another issue, raised by Patricia Deegan and others, is that one may diminish his or her efficacy by not disclosing relevant personal experiences to consumers (Deegan & Smoyak, 1996). Disclosing one's status as a mental health consumer also provides an important opportunity to act as a positive role model for both consumers and staff (Roberts et al., 1995). For more on the issue of disclosure, see chapter 7.

The choice is not only whether or not to disclose. Consumer-providers must consider a number of related concerns: who to disclose to, what to disclose, why is it important to disclose, when is an appropriate time to disclose, and how to convey what one chooses to share. Another important consideration is that it is necessary to disclose a disability to at least one staff worker in order to access the supports and protection via the Americans with Disabilities Act (Fisher, 1994a). Each consumer-provider must weigh her or his unique circumstances when grappling with the complicated issue of disclosure. However, in all cases it is essential that the choices are left to the consumer-provider; disclosure should never be required (Roberts et al., 1995).

CONTROVERSIAL ISSUE

Does Hiring Identified Consumer-Providers Promote Empowerment or Create a Subculture of Second-Class Workers?

The difficulties some consumer-providers face in their quest to become accepted by nonconsumer staff may be directly related to their assigned role in a particular program. There is much debate about whether the hiring of consumers on designated consumer lines to function as identified consumer-providers (in what some perceive as second-class positions) is a positive trend in the field of PsyR.

On one hand, this practice affords people who may have limited college education and vocational experience an opportunity to be employed in a profession that may provide them with many benefits. In addition, being hired in a way that allows one to be up front with the disability makes it easier to negotiate for reasonable accommodations such as a flexible work schedule and time off during periods of relapse. Some consumers state that there is less stress inherent in a job where one does not have to worry about an employer finding out about his or her psychiatric history. Many consumer-providers also appreciate the opportunity to work in a field that typically provides a supportive environment in which cooperation and strong interpersonal relationships between staff are encouraged. Consider the following situation:

———————————————

Before being diagnosed with bipolar disorder, Scott worked in a sales environment where competition often soured relationships and back-stabbing was commonplace. He lost his job after experiencing several acute episodes that required hospitalization. When he felt ready to return to work, Scott was hesitant to go back to the stressful world of profit-oriented business. Instead, he obtained a part-time job at a residential program affiliated with a clubhouse program he had attended. He found that he liked to spend his work time engaged in positive interactions with consumers and staff. Eventually he returned to school to get a counseling degree and got a full-time job as a residential case manager. He credits his work experience as an identified consumer-provider as being an important part of his recovery.

———————————————

Service recipients can also benefit when designated consumer-providers are incorporated into treatment or rehabilitation teams. Some of these benefits are cited in the section titled "Efficacy of Consumer Providers." Some models of programs for assertive community treatment (PACT) require that each team hire at least one peer advocate or consumer-provider. This worker functions on the team as an identified consumer. This strategy is commonly employed when the target population for the PACT are consumers in the community who have been resistant to establishing relationships with mental health professionals. Peer advocates can be important in helping to establish the initial contact, in the development of a positive working relationship, and for maintaining a positive relationship with consumers over time.

The other side of the argument maintains that job titles such as peer advocate, consumer-provider, and consumer case manager segregate these workers

from the rest of the staff. The mental health system has been criticized, and even accused of discriminatory employment practices, for requiring that people have a psychiatric history to obtain certain jobs (Stanek, 1993).

> *The concept of 'consumer professional' or 'client practitioner' may appear empowering and especially appealing when people with psychiatric labels are presented with previously denied opportunities for employment. However, the terms set up roles and determine relationships that ultimately create a second-class professional status. (Stanek, 1993, p. 10)*

Those working in designated consumer-provider roles may be paid less then other staff members, if they are paid at all. In some programs, consumers work as volunteer providers (Lieberman et al., 1991). Segregation may take the form of having certain restrictions inherent in consumer-provider positions, such as lack of access to case records or exclusion from certain staff meetings. Opportunities to move into higher level positions may also be limited to those on a designated consumer-provider track. Some agencies employ consumers in order to conform to current trends but then are not sure how to utilize the individuals that they hire. Such tokenism does little to change attitudes and tends to isolate those assuming roles that are not well defined (Griffin-Francell, 1997). Consider the following situation:

———————————————

Tony was initially excited when hired as a part-time consumer case manager for a mobile outreach team. But as he tried to settle into his job he became skeptical. He shared this during a consumer-provider support group: "They don't seem to know what I should be doing. I volunteer to go out to visit clients, but they always seem to have an excuse why someone else on the team should go instead. The other day when I asked how I could contribute, they suggested I should take some clients bowling. I feel I can make more of a contribution, but they don't seem to want to give me a chance."

———————————————

Needed Supports and Educational Training

Considering the many advantages of employing consumer-providers and the fact that the transition from consumer to provider can be difficult, the provision of supports both inside and outside of the work environment and the education and training needs of consumer-providers need to be considered. Strong and appropriate supervision is essential for consumer-providers who are dealing with both the standard issues around professional growth and development and the unique challenges outlined earlier in this chapter. Supervisors who are working with consumer-providers may need both specialized training and room in their schedules to provide additional supervision time when needed (Griffin-Francell, 1997; Mowbray & Moxley, 1997b). Group supervision in which several consumer-providers have the opportunity to address issues unique to their role may be helpful. Consumer-provider support groups outside the agency allow people to openly air feelings and concerns that they may not want to share in the workplace. These groups may also allow consumer-providers who have not chosen to disclose to obtain support (Fishbein, Manos, & Rotteveel, 1995).

It is likely that consumer-providers who move into normalized professional roles, rather than second-class roles, have a number of advantages. They are less likely to be segregated from other staff and do not have to struggle with role definition issues. They may also encounter less stigma, particularly if their colleagues perceive that they have appropriate qualifications. To move into these roles and become employed as legitimate professionals rather than being confined to consumer-designated job titles, consumers must have access to appropriate training, as well as opportunities to obtain academic degrees and required credentials. Attending college-level classes or training sessions required for credentialing may not be a viable option for all consumers who choose to provide services and supports to their peers, but these options do provide a distinct advantage, particularly for those seeking an upwardly mobile career path.

Any discussion of educational opportunities for consumer-providers must first recognize that there are many people with psychiatric disabilities already practicing in PsyR and related mental health fields who have professional degrees and credentials. Some have chosen to disclose their experiences as a consumer and utilize them in providing services. Others have remained quiet. Some of these practitioners became ill after receiving their degrees. Others, such as Patricia Deegan, were careful not to disclose their consumer status to college professors and administrators because of expected discrimination (Deegan & Smoyak, 1996). Historically, professional degree programs have shown biases against admitting consumers to their programs (Paulson, 1991). In some universities this trend is changing. Efforts to recruit consumers and integrate them into academic programs with students who are not identified consumers are well known by the authors, who teach in such programs, and are described elsewhere in the literature (Gill, Pratt, & Barrett, 1997; Paulson, 1991).

It is important to distinguish between integrated degree granting and training programs and those that are designed solely to prepare consumer-providers (Housel & Hickey, 1993; Sherman & Porter, 1991). Whereas the latter programs give consumers an opportunity to gain knowledge and skills that are essential for practice, they typically prepare consumers for second-class roles. They also ensure that consumer-providers emerge with a credential that is different than their nonconsumer colleagues. Such differences tend to promote segregation and discriminatory practices.

Appropriate supports and education for consumer-providers are essential, but the field also needs to address systemic and work culture changes that will reduce segregation and stigma and provide consumer-providers with well-defined and meaningful roles. Change is never easy, and many mental health professionals have spent years of education and practice creating clear boundaries between what they perceive as the capable helper and the dysfunctional helpee. Even those who have internalized the PsyR principle of reduced professional boundaries may have difficulty accepting a consumer as a full-fledged team member. Programs need to educate and prepare staff before they make a commitment to incorporating consumer-providers (Macauley, 1993). In situations in which consumer-providers are already on board, formal discussions and sensitivity training should be considered to ensure that the culture has adapted in a positive way. The following is an example of a PsyR program that still needs help in this area.

> Sara works in a clubhouse program as a rehabilitation counselor. She possesses educational and experiential qualifications similar to her colleagues, but she chose to disclose her status as a consumer when applying for the job. Surface reactions to her have been positive and she has not experienced any direct discrimination. However, the other staff members are sometimes uncomfortable around her, particularly when clubhouse members are not present. The staff culture is such that program members are sometimes joked about or imitated during informal staff-only interactions. Sara has noticed people looking at her uncomfortably when this occurs. Sometimes when she enters a room in which staff members were talking and laughing, she is met with sudden silence.

Other Influential Roles for Consumers

In addition to working in a variety of provider roles, consumers make other important contributions to the field of psychiatric rehabilitation. More and more, consumers are asked to participate in governing roles such as membership on agency boards of directors or administrative positions in state mental health departments. Consumers also participate actively in PsyR professional organizations such as International Association of Psychosocial Rehabilitation Services (IAPSRS) and its state chapters. Increasingly, consumers are also contributing in meaningful ways to program evaluation and the design of research studies. These roles allow consumers to have an impact on practice and policy issues, both on the individual agency level and on the state and national level. However this can only occur if consumers are allowed to hold real power. As with their provider roles, it is important that consumers in these influential positions are fully utilized in terms of their perspective and expertise and are not simply functioning as tokens to satisfy agency requirements or to help an organization appear progressive.

Activists in the ex-patient/consumer movement have had a meaningful impact on local, state, and national policy issues that relate to the concerns of people identified as mental health consumers. Typically, they achieve their goals by working outside of the mental health system. But to change a system that many consumers are dissatisfied with, the consumer perspective needs to be heard inside of the mental health system as well.

South Carolina is one of a number of states that has recently developed a director of consumer affairs position. This position is held by a consumer-provider who reports directly to the state mental health director. Part of this individual's responsibility is to administrate an initiative to hire 17 consumer affairs coordinators, one for each of the 17 community mental health centers located throughout the state. The positions are earmarked for self-identified consumers and are funded through the state's mental health plan. The main thrust of this innovative plan is to make consumer satisfaction with mental health services the system's number one goal (Bevilacqua, Gettys, & Cousins, 1997).

Consumer involvement on local mental health and PsyR agency boards is essential to the planning and implementation of consumer-centered services. A board of directors that has a substantial percentage of consumers filling meaningful roles is an excellent example of empowerment. It is important to realize that nonprofit agency administrators must answer to their boards of directors. The board has the power to hire and fire administrators, develop and refine the agency's mission and goals, and create policies that govern day-to-day service provision. Consumers serving on these boards also have a chance to combat stigma by serving as role models in their communities. For example, residential programs often have to deal with resistant community members when opening new group homes or apartments. Board representatives who are also self-identified consumers can help ease fears and misconceptions by speaking to neighbors and community representatives.

PsyR professional organizations are another place where consumer involvement is essential. Consumer participation on the boards and subcommittees of these organizations provides an excellent opportunity for collaboration between consumers and professionals that can positively influence both local and national service systems. Consumer involvement at local and national professional conferences, as both presenters and attendees, is another way that consumers can share their perspectives with PsyR and mental health professionals. Ten years ago many of these conferences were opportunities for professionals to talk with each other about their work with consumers. Now many of these conferences provide opportunities for professionals, consumer-providers, clients, and family members to share concerns and strategies for improving services.

Finally, research and program evaluation are areas where consumers are making important contributions. Increased collaboration between professionals and consumers in evaluating individual program outcomes and in rigorous studies are increasingly evidenced in the PsyR research literature. In addition, with the encouragement of the National Institute on Disability and Rehabilitation Research, participatory action research, a strategy which involves the persons under study fully participating in the research, is becoming an increasingly popular strategy (Rogers & Palmer-Erbs, 1994). Activist Daniel Fisher has recommended "basing total quality improvement of mental health services on outcome measures designed by survivors and consumers" (Fisher, 1994a, p. 915). He cited a group of consumers who are skilled in research methods and have formed the Consumer/Survivor Research and Policy Work Group as an important example of this goal. The group has worked with President Clinton's administration on national health care reform.

Summary

Peer support is an important component of community support systems, whether it is provided as an alternative to traditional mental health and psychiatric rehabilitation services (such as programs that are both controlled and run by consumer-survivor organizations) or as an adjunct to professional services (as in self-help groups that depend on professional consultation). Peer support can also be given by professionally trained providers who have also experienced mental illness. Consumer input into how services are provided is essential to the development of a truly consumer-centered mental health system. Such input helps to ensure consumer satisfaction and contributes to the protection of consumers rights and dignity. Psychiatric rehabilitation providers must learn to work in conjunction with the various types of consumer providers, activists, and policy makers. This means respecting the choices of consumers who utilize self-help groups or alternative programs and recognizing all of the valuable roles that consumer-providers can play within the system.

Class Exercise
Establishing a Self-Help Group

Imagine that you are a group of people who have a psychiatric disability and want to start a self-help group.

1. How would you begin the process?
2. What resources would you need to achieve your goal?
3. Would the group be open to anyone with a psychiatric disability, open only to people who had certain issues (e.g. diagnosis) in common, or closed to anyone outside your circle?
4. How would you deal with the issue of leadership? Some options are voting on a single leader or co-leaders, shared leadership among all group members, or rotating leadership.
5. Now that you have discussed your hypothetical self-help group in some detail, how would you define the mission and goals of your group?

References

Ackerman, L. P. (1997). A Recovery, Inc. group leaders story. In C. T. Mowbray, D. P. Moxley, C. A. Jasper, & L. L. Howell (Eds.), *Consumers as Providers.* Columbia, MD: International Association of Psychosocial Rehabilitation Services.

Alcohol Anonymous World Services. (1981). *Twelve steps and twelve traditions.* New York: Author.

Bevilacqua, J. J., Gettys, D., & Cousins, V. (1997). Mental health systems development: Benefits created by consumer engagement. In C. T. Mowbray, D. P. Moxley, C. A. Jasper, & L.L. Howell (Eds.), *Consumers as Providers*. Columbia, MD: International Association of Psychosocial Rehabilitation Services.

Caldwell, S., & White, K. K. (1991). Co-creating a self-help recovery movement [Special issue]. *Psychosocial Rehabilitation Journal, 15*(2), 91–95.

Chamberlin, J. (1984). Speaking for ourselves: An overview of the ex-psychiatric inmates' movement. *Psychosocial Rehabilitation Journal, 8*(2), 56–64.

Chamberlin, J. (1988). On our own (2nd ed.). London: Mind Publications.

Chamberlin, J. (1990). The ex-patients' movement: Where we've been and where we're going. [Special issue]. *Journal of Mind & Behavior, Special Issue, 11*, 323–336.

Chamberlin, J., Rogers, E. S., & Ellison, M. L. (1996). Self-help programs: A description of their characteristics and their members. *Psychiatric Rehabilitation Journal, 19*(3), 33–42.

Deegan, P. E. (1990). Spirit breaking: When the helping professions hurt. *The Humanistic Psychologist, 18*(3), 301–313.

Deegan, P. E. (1992). The independent living movement and people with psychiatric disorders: Taking back control over our own lives. *Psychosocial Rehabilitation Journal, 15*(3), 3–19.

Deegan, P. E. (1995). *Coping with voices: self-help strategies for people who hear voices that are distressing.* Lawrence, MA: National Empowerment Center.

Deegan, P. E. (1996, December). Using medication as part of the recovery process. Presentation at the *New Jersey Psychiatric Rehabilitation Association Annual Conference.* Eatontown, NJ.

Deegan, P. E., & Smoyak, S. A. (1996). Blending two realities into a unique perspective. *Journal of Psychosocial Nursing, 34*(9), 39–46.

Dincin, J. (1975). Psychiatric rehabilitation. *Schizophrenia Bulletin, 13*, 131–147.

Felton, C. J., Stastny, P., Shern, D. L., Blanch, A., Donahue, S. A., Knight, E., & Brown, C. (1995). Consumers as peer specialists on intensive case management teams: Impact on client outcomes. *Psychiatric Services, 46*(10), 1037–1044.

Fishbein, S. M., Manos, E., & Rotteveel, J. (1995). Helping the helpers: A unique colleague support system for mental health professionals-consumers. *Journal of Psychosocial Nursing, 33*(11), 41–43.

Fisher, D. B. (1994a). Health care reform based on an empowerment model of recovery by people with psychiatric disabilities. *Hospital and Community Psychiatry, 45*(9), 913–915.

Fisher, D. B. (1994b). A new vision of healing as constructed by people with psychiatric disabilities working as mental health providers. *Psychosocial Rehabilitation Journal, 17*(3), 67–81.

Gill, K. J., Pratt, C. W., & Barrett, N. (1997). Preparing psychiatric rehabilitation specialists through undergraduate education. *Community Mental Health Journal, 33*(4), 323–329.

Griffin-Francell, C. (1997). Consumers as providers of psychiatric rehabilitation: Reflections of a family member. In C. T. Mowbray, D. P. Moxley, C. A. Jasper, & L. L. Howell (Eds.), Consumers as providers. Columbia, MD: International Association of Psychosocial Rehabilitation Services.

Housel, D. P., & Hickey, J. S. (1993). Supported education in a community college for students with psychiatric disabilities: The Houston Community College model. *Psychosocial Rehabilitation Journal, 17*(1), 41–50.

Kaufman, C. L., Freund, P. D., & Wilson, J. (1989). Self-help in the mental health system: A model for consumer-provider collaboration. *Psychosocial Rehabilitation Journal, 13*(1), 5–21.

Lee, D. T. (1995). Professional underutilization of recovery Inc. *Psychiatric Rehabilitation Journal, 19*(1), 63–70.

Leff, H. S., Campbell, J., Gagne, C., & Woocher, L. S. (1997). Evaluating peer providers. In, C. T. Mowbray, D. P. Moxley, C. A. Jasper, & L. L. Howell (Eds.), *Consumers as Providers.* Columbia, MD: International Association of Psychosocial Rehabilitation Services.

Legal Project/Mental Patient's Liberation Front (1974). *Your rights as a mental patient in massachusetts.* West Somerville, MA: Author.

Lieberman, A. A., Gowdy, E. A., & Knutson, L. C. (1991). The Mental Health Outreach Project: A case study in self-help. *Psychosocial Rehabilitation Journal, 14*(3), 100–103.

Low, A. A. (1967). *Mental Health Through Will Training.* (15th ed.). Boston: Christopher.

Lyons, J. S., Cook, J. A., Ruth, A. R., Karver, M., & Slagg, N. B. (1996). Service delivery using consumer staff in a mobile crisis assessment program. *Community Mental Health Journal, 32*(1), 33–40.

MaCauley, R. (1993). Professionals need training to accept ex-patients as colleagues. *Resources, 5*(1), 18.

Manos, E. (1993). Prosumers. *Psychosocial Rehabilitation Journal, 16*(4), 117–120.

Mowbray, C., Wellwood, R., & Chamberlain, P. (1988). Project stay: A consumer run support service. *Psychosocial Rehabilitation Journal, 12*(1), 33–42.

Mowbray, C. T. (1997). Benefits and issues created by consumer role innovation in psychiatric rehabilitation. In, C. T. Mowbray, D. P. Moxley, C. A. Jasper, & L. L. Howell (Eds.), *Consumers as Providers.* Columbia, MD: International Association of Psychosocial Rehabilitation Services.

Mowbray, C. T., & Moxley, D. P. (1997a). Consumers as providers: Themes and success factors. In, C. T. Mowbray, D. P. Moxley, C. A. Jasper, & L. L. Howell (Eds.), *Consumers as Providers.* Columbia, MD: International Association of Psychosocial Rehabilitation Services.

Mowbray, C. T., & Moxley, D. P. (1997b). Futures for empowerment of consumer role innovation. In, C. T. Mowbray, D. P. Moxley, C. A. Jasper, & L. L. Howell (Eds.), *Consumers as Providers.* Columbia, MD: International Association of Psychosocial Rehabilitation Services.

Mowbray, C. T., Moxley, D. P., Thrasher, S., Bybee, D., McCrohan, N., Harris, S., & Clover, G. (1996). Consumers as community support providers: Issues created by role innovation. *Community Mental Health Journal, 32*(1), 47–67.

Moxley, D. P., & Mowbray, C. T. (1997). Consumers as providers: Forces and factors legitimizing role innovation in psychiatric rehabilitation. In, C. T. Mowbray, D. P. Moxley, C. A. Jasper, & L. L. Howell (Eds.), *Consumers as Providers.* Columbia, MD: International Association of Psychosocial Rehabilitation Services.

Murray, P. (1996). Recovery, Inc., as an adjunct to treatment in an era of managed care. *Psychiatric Services, 47*(12), 1378–1381.

New Jersey Self-Help Clearinghouse (1997). *The self-help group directory* (14th ed.). Denville, NJ: Northwest Covenant Medical Center.

Nikkel, R. E., Smith, G., & Edwards, D. (1992). A consumer operated case management project. *Hospital and Community Psychiatry, 43*(6), 577–579.

Noordsy, D. L., Schwab, B., Fox, L., & Drake, R. E. (1996). The role of self-help programs in the rehabilitation of persons with severe mental illness and substance use disorders. *Community Mental Health Journal, 32*(1), 71–81.

Paulson, R. I. (1991). Professional training for consumers and family members: One road to empowerment. *Psychosocial Rehabilitation Journal, 14*(3), 69–80.

Roberts, M., Rotteveel, J., & Manos, E. (1995, Spring) Mental health consumers as professionals: Disclosure in the workplace. *American Rehabilitation*, 20–23.

Robertson, N. (1988). *Getting better: Inside Alcoholics Anonymous.* New York: William Morrow.

Rogers, E. S., & Palmer-Erbs, V. (1994). Participatory action research: Implications for research and evaluation in psychiatric rehabilitation. *Psychosocial Rehabilitation Journal, 18*(2), 3–12.

Rogers, S. (1996). National clearinghouse serves mental health consumer movement. *Journal of Psychosocial Nursing, 34*(9), 22–25.

Segal, S. P., Silverman, C., & Temkin, T. (1993). Empowerment and self-help agency practice for people with mental disabilities. *Social Work, 38*(6), 705–712.

Sherman, P. S., & Porter, R. (1991). Mental health consumers as case management aides. *Hospital and Community Psychiatry, 42*(5), 494–498.

Solomon, P., & Draine, J. (1996). Perspectives concerning consumers as case managers. *Community Mental Health Journal, 32*(1), 41–46.

Solomon, P., & Draine, J. (1995). The efficacy of a consumer case management team: Two-year outcomes of a randomized trial. *Journal of Mental Health Administration, 22*(2), 135–146.

Stanek, L. J. (1993). Manipulative language, discriminatory practices. *Resources, 5*(1), 9–10.

Stevens, K. (1991, November). The mental health liberation movement. *Sojourner: The Women's Forum*, 20–21.

Stroul, B. A. (1989). Community support systems for persons with long-term mental illness: A conceptual framework. *Psychosocial Rehabilitation Journal, 12*(3), 9–26.

Chapter 11

The Role of the Family in Psychiatric Rehabilitation

*The role of the family in psychiatric rehabilitation(PsyR) and treatment has gone through
many changes. Previously viewed as a major cause of mental illness, today the family is seen*

as an important partner in the rehabilitation process. Family interventions are one of the few psychosocial strategies that have proven to be effective through research. This chapter describes the effect on the family of having a member with mental illness and the effect of the family on a person with mental illness. Finally, the chapter reviews the development of family advocacy movements like the National Alliance for the Mentally Ill (NAMI), which help to keep the needs of people with mental illness in the forefront of legislatures, administrators, and public policy forums.

This chapter will answer the following questions:

1. *What is the effect on the family of having a member with severe and persistent mental illness?*
2. *How does living with the family affect a person with major mental illness?*
3. *What kinds of family interventions have been shown to be effective for family members with mental illness?*
4. *How does the family fit into the concept of recovery?*
5. *What is the role of NAMI in supporting people with mental illness?*

Introduction

In many ways, the catastrophe of mental illness strikes not only the individual but also his or her entire family, placing an undue burden on them (Hatfield, 1987b). The role of the family in recovery from severe and persistent mental illness has become increasingly important as community integration has become a reality. Many of the first community-based psychiatric rehabilitation services were designed for single, deinstitutionalized adults, many of whom were completely estranged from their families. Today, when long-term hospitalization is the exception rather than the rule, families have once again become primary agents of care (Hatfield, 1987b). The opportunity for the individual to maintain a family life is greater than ever before. Today, people with mental illness are likely to stay involved with their family of origin, including parents and siblings. They are more likely to marry or stay in other long-term relationships and to have children.

At the same time, community-based care has also increased the burden that family members must bear, both subjectively and objectively. Shorter hospital stays often mean that many acutely ill individuals return home for continuing care in the community with their family.

In the past, families were incorrectly identified as etiological agents, literally causing serious mental illness. Mothers, in particular, have borne the brunt of these assertions. In fact, familial psychosocial factors, such as an environment high in criticism, hostility, and levels of emotional over involvement, may contribute to relapses in some cases (Anderson, Reiss, & Hogarty, 1986). This type of environment has been termed high in **expressed emotion** (EE). Nevertheless, most family households with members who have mental illness do not have high EE environments (Lefley, 1989). In addition, high EE environments can also be found outside family settings, such as other residential settings and some clinics (Hogarty, 1993).

Today, a paradigm shift is taking place. Families were formerly seen as dysfunctional, illness-causing systems. Now families are recognized as surprisingly resilient and resourceful with a potentially important role to play in treatment and rehabilitation. Despite the burden that a family member's illness often presents, some individuals have reported discovering strengthened familial bonds, stronger commitments, and a clearer identification of familial strengths and resources. Family members are finding they can make important contributions to the recovery process (Mannion, 1996).

Family interventions that capitalize on the strengths of families are among the most successful categories of psychosocial treatment and rehabilitation, actually reducing the frequency and length of psychotic relapse (Dixon & Lehman, 1995; Hogarty, 1993). These family interventions are typically designed around illness education, support, problem solving, and crisis intervention. Indeed, there is a body of data which show that the decompensation or hospital recidivism of persons with mental illness who reside with their families can be significantly reduced by this type of intervention in combination with psychotropic medication (Lehman & Steinwachs, 1998). This reduction is significantly greater than when medication alone is employed.

Family Work and Psychiatric Rehabilitation Principles

Like the rest of society, mental health professionals have traditionally let fear and blame dominate their interactions with families who have mental illness (Lundwall, 1996). All professionals, including psychiatric rehabilitation practitioners, need to be willing to create better options and resources for families and their members. One of the guiding principles of psychiatric rehabilitation is that the involvement and partnership of persons receiving services, as well as their family members, is essential to effective operation, evaluation, and governance of PsyR services (IAPSRS, 1996). Thus, family involvement in treatment, rehabilitation, and support are recognized as important elements in a person's rehabilitation (Cook & Hoffschmidt, 1993). In particular, the **psychoeducation** of families and consumers helps ensure that they have reasonable expectations regarding the disease, its treatment, and rehabilitation (Hatfield, 1990).

Because psychiatric rehabilitation is about community-based services, integrated settings, and natural supports, the involvement of family members (parents, spouses, children, and others) is essential for providing maximally normalized services. Clearly, many consumers may need treatment and a great deal of support for their entire lives. Thus, it is probably best if family members, if willing, can be engaged as partners in the long-term rehabilitation process (Cook & Hoffschmidt, 1993).

The Family as a "Caring Agent"

Today with very short hospital stays and deinstitutionalization a reality, in many cases families have reemerged as primary care providers. Since the early 1980s, more than half of all persons leaving state hospitals are sent to live with their family members. Among short stay patients, as many as four out of five individuals return to their families for care (Hatfield, 1987a).

Lefley (1989) noted that families must cope with both the positive and negative symptoms of severe mental illness (as discussed in chapter 2). But it is often the negative symptoms that have the most devastating effect on both the individual and the family. Impaired levels of functioning are related to loss of old skills and the failure to acquire new ones. This affects the person's productivity, self-concept, and potential for positive change. This, in turn, increases the family burden, both perpetuating and increasing the individual's dependence, socially and economically.

Independence/Dependence

Hatfield (1992) defined the central dilemma facing adults with serious and persistent mental illness and their families as being centered around the issue of independence/dependence. In our culture, the independence of young adults or even adolescents is seen as an important developmental goal. For many adults with severe and persistent mental illness, continued dependence on others is a virtual necessity. This requirement of continuing dependence often leads to great tension among family members. This is particularly true for parents who see fostering independence in their adult offspring as an important goal of parenting.

Pickett et al. (1997) found that adult children living with parents often creates a stressful situation regardless of the presence or absence of mental illness. Indeed, the variance in burden experienced by the parent was directly related to the degree of dependence of the adult on their parents, whether or not a psychiatric illness was present.

Burden and Stigma

Lefley (1989) discussed both the **family burden** and the **family stigma** associated with major mental illness. She noted that the emphasis on the family in terms of experience of mental illness has shifted from causing the disorders to being viewed as "potential precipitants of relapse" (Lefley, 1989, p. 556). Both the earlier and more recent views cast the family in a very negative light and contribute to the stigma experienced.

Lefley (1989) also reported that families fear, sometimes with good reason, that the behavior of a relative with mental illness diminishes their reputation as individuals and as a family, jeopardizing their relationships with friends and neighbors. Because of this stigma, family members wish to distance themselves from their ill relative, but often feel guilt if they do so.

Mental health professionals may be contributing to this stress by their own attitudes and behavior that reinforce the idea of "crazy-making families." Often, mental health professionals avoid family members or punish them in their efforts to seek information or support, particularly in times of distress. In a recent study, half of the parents and spouses of persons hospitalized for a mental disorder reported concealing the hospitalization to some degree

(Phelan, Bromet, & Link, 1998). Indeed, a significant portion of family members (16%) reported that they believed other people were avoiding them, suggesting a strong awareness of stigma by family members.

Marsh et al. (1996) collected many comments regarding familial burden. The burden the family bears has been described as suffering, very sad, draining, and lonely. Family members speak of the care of their loved one as being a full-time job. Some report the abandonment of their own jobs and careers. Often they feel as if they have not done enough. Some report permanent distraction. Others report anger toward their spouses or other family members. For example, parents of adults may be angry at the siblings of the person who is ill for their lack of support, involvement, and sometimes their unwillingness to acknowledge the existence of the sick family member to other people. Families coping with any chronic medical condition, mental illness, or otherwise attempt to adjust. Under conditions of constant strain regardless of the diagnostic category, family members see the illness as cycles or patterns of aggravation or exacerbation with contrasting periods of remission. Thus they experience many cycles of hope and disappointment.

Families experience a variety of stresses. These stresses can be very tangible, such as the economic burden of high health care costs, the loss of insurance, and so on. They can also be less tangible, but no less real, such as fear, anxiety, and fatigue. Thus, the stress on the family has been categorized into two broad areas: **objective burden** and **subjective burden**.

The Objective Burden

Objective burden deals with the actual, specifically identifiable problems associated with the person's mental illness. The objective burdens of families in which a member has a chronic developmental, mental, or physical disability have a degree of commonality. Objective burden includes financial hardships due to medical bills, the cost of the consumer's economic dependence, disruptions in household functioning, restriction of social activities, and altered relationships because of the demands of caregiving. There is often a significant time commitment to the mental health consumer's needs at the expense of other family activities. Individual members of the family, particularly the primary caregiver, may often need to change their roles in the family, often at the expense of the individual's own career.

The Subjective Burden

Subjective burden refers to the psychological distress borne by family members, which is engendered by the illness. Subjective burden is related to objective burden, but not always directly. A caregiver may carry the highest objective burden in the family, yet because she has accommodated herself to it, she may feel a relatively lower subjective burden than other family members. Other family members classified as second-tier relatives often bear a smaller objective burden but feel they have a greater burden because of the apparently abrupt disruptions in their routine, which they experience as a subjective burden.

Besides some of the chronic burdens families face, there are certain acute burdens that are no less troublesome. Families may have periodic crises involving interactions with emergency services and the police. In addition, in most states, involuntary commitment procedures pit family members against one another in an adversarial manner that is often poorly understood and causes resentment.

> Gina, a 28-year-old woman with four children had become very distressed. Her husband, Mike, had stopped seeing his psychiatrist. He had not bathed in months and had literally stopped speaking. He was not working and remained in the house. For weeks, she begged him to get help. When he became completely mute, she finally called crisis services and later filed the complaint to commit him. He was hospitalized, received medication, improved markedly and went back to work. But he was very resentful. Gina's father-in-law, Ralph, who was normally supportive and mild-mannered, said years later, "Do you realize she had Mike *committed!* I will never forgive her for that!" When other relatives pointed out it was the only option she had left to get Mike help, Ralph refused to listen.

Troublesome Actions that Contribute to Burden

In describing family life with a person with severe and persistent mental illness, Lefley (1987a, 1987b, 1989) noted a variety of behaviors of some mental health consumers that contribute to the burden borne by their family members. These include the following:

- Hostile, abusive, or assaultive behaviors (even if rare)
- Mood swings, other unpredictable behavior
- Socially offensive or embarrassing behavior
- Poor motivation, apparent malingering (often due to negative symptoms)
- Apparently self-destructive actions, such as poor handling of money, deteriorated personal hygiene, and neglect or damage of property

The burden that family members must bear occasionally includes abusive and assaultive behaviors in acute phases of the illness, especially in the earlier years. Although they are usually infrequent or even based on a single instance, these incidents within a family are very memorable and may be dwelled on for years to come. There are a variety of other troublesome behaviors that are particularly upsetting, including symptoms such as paranoid ideation about family members and negative symptoms that lead to poor self-care.

As if these problems were not enough, parents also worry about what will happen to their adult child "When I am gone." That is, they worry about who will provide care after their own deaths. Lefley (1987b) also described that many families experience a "dilemma of functional expectancy" (p. 114). This dilemma refers to the idea that having normal expectations for the role of a family member with mental illness sometimes leads to frustration because the person has difficulty meeting these expectations. For example, parents may attempt to promote the independence of their son or daughter—that is, they expect that as an adult he or she should be able to maintain an apartment. Yet when the person fails, the parents may think it is too much to expect. At the same time, if expectations are inordinately lowered, the individual may tend to live up to these low expectations, rarely reaching a level of functioning that would be considered normal.

Three Levels of Family Involvement

The burden experienced by family members varies based on their level of involvement with the member who is ill. Terkelson (1987b) proposed that there are three tiers of family involvement. In the immediate family, most often one individual, usually (but not always) a woman who is the mother, wife, sister, or daughter of the person with mental illness, assumes the role of principal caregiver. Much of her daily life becomes a series of illness-related occupations and preoccupations. She acknowledges the illness more than others and also suffers its impact more than others in this family. This individual, especially if she is the mother of the ill relative, may also feel responsible for the illness itself, an idea sometimes foisted on her by professionals. Terkelson (1987b) noted:

> She witnesses the impatient naivete of overworked, well-meaning professionals. She takes in their suggestions for modifying family life and suffers from the implications. (p. 131)

Often these implications are significant, asking a family to change its entire lifestyle, resulting in understandable resistance. Terkelson described this sort of caregiver as living a life that is a stream of nursing activities. Other activities include attempting to keep the illness from disrupting the rest of the family members' lives. Relief is found only when the consumer shows some progress. Time away from caring for the consumer is often filled with worrying or at least thinking about the person.

Second-tier relatives may live with or near the person with mental illness, but they are less intimately exposed to the ups and downs of the person's life. Thanks to the primary caregiver or first-tier relatives, as well as their own efforts, these second-tier relatives experience less frequent intrusion on their lives. However, occasionally they experience a more noticeable disruption when some troublesome aspect of the illness inserts itself into their lives. For example, although their daily routine is not burdened by the care of a relative with a disability, their lives may be more abruptly disrupted in the midst of an exacerbation of that person's symptoms. More than the primary caregiver or first-tier relatives, they may come to dread both the illness and the consumer, avoiding involvement whenever possible. In addition to avoiding involvement with the mental health consumer, they often avoid involvement with the primary caregiver. Thus, a husband may become estranged from a wife, siblings from each other, a child from a parent, and so on.

By contrast, there are also some second-tier relatives who, though they detach themselves from daily involvement with the consumer, involve themselves actively only during times of crises.

Third-tier relatives are not in the immediate household, but still share a common interest in the well-being of the consumer. At times, these individuals may play down or deny the presence of the illness and associated disability. Sometimes they regard the person with the illness as faking or lazy. Others may feel helpless in the face of the problem and wonder what they can do to help. They may also wonder if they have contributed to the adverse situation. Some may also have fantasies about rescuing the ill person. Occasionally, they may blame the primary caregiver or underinvolved second-tier relatives for the person's mental illness. As you can see by Terkelson's very insightful description of the situation, the objective and subjective burdens of each group vary markedly.

Case Study: A Confidentiality Issue

Maintaining the confidentiality of a person receiving services is considered a person's right as well as a good thing. But even with something as obvious as confidentiality, there can be problems. Consider this situation.

Kevin is a semiretired man in his early sixties. Almost every day, he drives his son, Brian who is about 30, to the local psychosocial rehabilitation day program. He drops him off at about 9 A.M. and picks him up about 3 P.M. One day, Kevin thinks he ought to talk things over with the staff at the center because Brian is sleeping poorly and often paces all night. He decides to call the center after he arrives at his part-time job. He asks for Brian's case manager, who gets on the phone. Brian's case manager makes the following response to Kevin's queries, ostensibly to protect confidentiality, "I cannot even say whether your son is served here or not." In fact, the case manager is upholding the agency's policy of not revealing information about the people they serve to anyone, unless the client expressly consents to the disclosure. Enraged at this "snippy" attitude and the rejection of his attempts to share information for his son's benefit, Kevin responds, "I know damn well he is there. I drive him there every day and pick him up, so don't give me that nonsense. Besides, you call my wife and me when it suits you; we have spoken before!"

Mental health professionals who are also members of families experiencing mental illness make up an interesting group of individuals in this regard. In many ways they are not different from other family members, except they may bear an additional stigma. Lefley (1987b) found mental health clinicians did not differ from lay family members in some important ways. Their assessment of the psychological burden or subjective burden of having a family member with mental illness was very similar to that of all family members. Like other family members, they assigned a high priority to education on symptoms and medications, techniques for managing difficult behavior, and involvement in support groups. Yet they were very uncomfortable discussing their family's experience with mental illness with their colleagues. The great majority had frequently heard colleagues make negative or otherwise disparaging remarks about family members of people with mental illness.

The Unique Burdens of Spouses

Spouses of persons with severe mental illness bear a unique burden. Mannion (1996) estimated that 35% to 40% of people hospitalized for psychiatric disabilities are discharged to live with their spouses. Mannion reported that the great majority of spouses surveyed reported a process of adaptation and recovery. Nevertheless, the burden of spouses includes the following:

- Marital dissatisfaction and disruption
- Financial problems
- Socialization difficulties

- Personal experience of emotional and mood symptoms
- Separations and divorce

Clearly, when one's spouse has a major mental illness, it puts a great deal of stress on the marriage. Despite this, it is often difficult for the well spouse to receive help keeping the marriage together. A reciprocal flow of information between spouses and professional caregivers would improve the quality of care and effectively reduce relapse, but unfortunately this is all too rare.

Siblings and Children

Siblings of people with mental illness also experience significant stresses (Kinsella, Anderson, & Anderson, 1996). Young family members, both siblings and children of people with the disorders, share a special vulnerability to the familial experience of mental illness (Marsh et al., 1993). For example, one grown child of a mother with mental illness reported:

> The mental illness shaped my life. . . . it revolved around her problems. (p. 15)

Adults who dealt with the mental illness of a relative during their own childhoods reported a variety of difficulties including subjective burden in the form of feelings of grief and loss, empathy for the suffering of other family members, stigma upon the individual and family, and objective burden in needing to deal with symptomatic behavior and illness-related crises. Specific problems include the following:

- Absence of a model of normal development
- Difficulty determining which experiences were "normal" and which were not
- Altered roles, such as *parentification* (a child having to care for the sick parent)
- Their own mental health problems
- Strain in relationships outside of the family, for example, at school
- Fear of developing mental illness themselves

In adulthood, these individuals attribute impaired self-esteem and self-concept and fear of rejection to their childhood experience (Marsh et al., 1993).

The Anguish of the Individual

Lefley (1987a, 1987b) suggested that the most devastating stressor for family members may be in learning to cope with the person's own anguish over an impoverished life, one's acute awareness of what he or she has missed out on or will miss out on. Not only does the individual with mental illness experience this extended grieving, so do the relatives who mourn the loss of the personality, skills, and strengths of the person due to the illness.

Family Dissatisfaction

Given the numerous burdens families must deal with, one would hope that the mental health system would be responsive to their concerns. Unfortunately, families are often unhappy with the way their relatives are served. They express general dissatisfaction with the service delivery system and often with mental health professionals themselves. They have frequently been subjected to irrelevant treatment models that do not meet their expressed needs. Traditional approaches often left them with inappropriate expectations about their family member. Expectations offered by professionals were often too low, too high, or absent altogether. For a number of reasons, professionals frequently withheld relevant information and did not help in managing difficult behaviors.

Consider the lot of the mother of a person with serious mental illness who was living at home after hospital discharge:

> She is suffering the pain of her child's illness, the stigmatization of having caused it, the burden of overseeing a treatment plan that may be unrealistic . . . at the same time, she is trying to balance conflicting advice. (Lefley, 1989, p. 557)

Seemingly logical instructions from professionals can be clearly contradictory. Family members, such as these mothers, can be accused of being overprotective at the same time they are being told to discourage their family member from taking unnecessary risks. She may be told that she has been neglectful or rejecting in the past, but that now she must encourage independence. If she does not take the advice of the professional she may be accused of sabotaging treatment (Lefley, 1989).

Too often professionals have been basically disapproving in the messages they give family members. Their overt or covert disapproval evokes defensive strategies on the part of the family members, thus fulfilling the bias of clinicians that the family is too defensive.

Given these communication problems, family members may become alienated and resentful. Other families may become overly submissive, inordinately deferring to the professionals. Some families, following instructions, have disengaged from or abandon their family member with mental illness.

Dual Diagnosis and the Family

The impact on the family unit of a member with a dual diagnosis of psychiatric disability and either a substance abuse disorder or a developmental disability can be complex. Depending on the severity and duration of the person's disabilities, the family may have expended considerable emotional and financial resources in coping with the situation. All areas of family functioning may be affected by the presence of a dual diagnosis in a family member, including the general atmosphere, the ways family members communicate with each other, relationships, roles, and responsibilities that family members assume or are assigned (Daley, Moss, & Campbell, 1993). Likewise, families affect the family member with a disability. In their attempts to "control the uncontrollable," families may become over involved (enmeshed) or completely shut off (disengaged) from their family member with a disability (Evans & Sullivan, 1990). In the case of a substance abuse disorder, sometimes well-intentioned behavior on the part of caring family members with a substance use disorder has the unintended effect of enabling the person to continue to abuse the substance. For example, money given to the individual for living expenses or rent may actually be spent on alcohol or drugs (Evans & Sullivan, 1990).

Nevertheless, families have often developed skills and strategies for coping with very difficult situations, and services to families should build on those strengths. Evans and her colleague (1990) talked about the need for families dealing with substance abuse and mental illness to enter a recovery process of their own. Education about chemical dependence and psychiatric disability, support groups such as Al-Anon, the 12-step program for families, and skill development in problem solving, negotiation, and communication are all services that are helpful to families in recovery (Evans & Sullivan, 1990).

The Burdens of Family Living for the Person with Mental Illness

Up to this point, this chapter has dealt with the burden of care associated with living with a relative with mental illness. But does family life present any unique stresses or burdens to the person with mental illness? As already stated, in the past it was inaccurately assumed that family living was not only stressful but also a possible cause of mental illness. Although today we understand that this is not the case, there is some evidence that a particular emotional environment of high expressed emotion (EE) may contribute to the relapses of some people with mental illness (Anderson et al., 1986).

British researchers observed an association between living arrangements and relapses among persons with schizophrenia (Anderson et al., 1986). Independent groups of investigators found that the emotional level within family groups with close ties presented a specific stress. Specifically, consumers whose families manifested high expressed emotion as demonstrated by criticism, hostility, and levels of emotional overinvolvement were at higher risk for relapse (sometimes 50% or more over a 9-month period), compared to consumers returning to low EE families (13% to 15% relapse rate). If a consumer had frequent contact (more than 35 hours per week) with a high EE relative, the increased relapse rate occurred even if they were compliant with their regimen of antipsychotics. A high EE environment apparently serves as a trigger for relapse. This negative high EE effect seems to be most relevant for unmarried men living in their parental homes (Harding & Zahniser, 1994).

A climate of high EE in one's family or other social unit apparently contributes to the onset of psychotic symptoms among people genetically at risk for schizophrenia (Anderson et al., 1986). However, it has also been found that most families with members who have schizophrenia do not have this high EE pattern, only those with high EE environments are more likely to relapse. Therefore, high EE does not appear to be either necessary or sufficient to cause schizophrenia (Harding & Zahniser, 1994).

The Dilemma of Functional Expectancy and Independence/Dependence Revisited

"The dilemma of functional expectancy" and the independence/dependence dilemma have been discussed in terms of their burden to family members. These two factors also present a potential burden to the person with mental illness. Living with one's family, especially one's family of origin, presents constant reminders of disabilities and unfulfilled plans and aspirations, which may not be helpful at all. For example, there may be the daily stress of being presented with the fact that one is not making a normal, expected contribution to family life. On the other hand, the lack of this expectation on the part of others may harm self-esteem. In addition, the lack of independence one has failed to achieve is also constantly "thrown in one's face" by having to depend on one's family for basic needs. These clearly are significant stresses that are more acutely felt in a family environment as opposed to solitary living.

Loneliness

One of the major complaints of persons with serious mental illness is their persistent loneliness. Are persons who live with family members less lonely than those who do not? Not necessarily (Brown, 1996). Both men and women with serious mental illness are significantly more lonely than the general population, as measured by the UCLA loneliness scale. In one study (Brown, 1996), consumers with mental illness were grouped according to different living situations: alone, with a roommate, with family, and group home. Those living with their families were no less lonely than those living in other situations. Indeed, there may be a special sort of loneliness experienced even when living among one's family.

Goals for Helping Families

Because families are the primary care agent, an enormous source of social support, and a strong contributing factor to recovery, the family-professional relationship should be one of collaboration, avoiding blaming and pathologizing family members. Given the objective and subjective burden of family members and the needs of their relative with mental illness, Anderson et al. (1986) specified the following goals in trying to help families:

- Establish a relationship with the family in which there is a genuine working alliance—that is, a partnership in order to help the consumer.
- Attempt to comprehend familial problems that may be contributing to both the stress level of the consumer and the family members.
- Gain an understanding of the family's resources and what successful and unsuccessful attempts to cope with the illness they have faced.
- Build rehabilitative and educational endeavors around the family's strengths.
- Develop appropriate expectations for the rehabilitation and treatment process through a contract that includes specific goals that are both mutual and attainable.

Family Interventions

Given the importance of the family in the rehabilitation process, a great deal of work has gone into studying how families can be assisted. Over the past 2 decades, sophisticated psychosocial interventions involving family members have been developed to assist in the rehabilitation of persons with serious and persistent mental illness (Dixon & Lehman, 1995). These methods have been studied empirically and rigorously evaluated, and they have been found to be effective (Lehman & Steinwachs, 1998). As it turns out, family interventions are one of the few PsyR strategies whose effectiveness has been confirmed by research. Some common assumptions are shared in all of these approaches:

- Schizophrenia and other major mental illness are regarded as medical, biological conditions.
- The family environment is not seen as an etiological factor.
- Social and emotional support is provided, often including support from other families.
- Routine psychotropic medication management is included as an essential component.

These approaches are emphatically in contrast to traditional family therapies based on etiological theories that assert that the family or its communication patterns are a major causative factor of the illness.

These rehabilitation-oriented interventions also tend to have common components, which only differ in emphasis or in the technique employed. These components include the following:

- *Psychoeducation:* Information about mental illness and its treatment, similar to the content of chapters 1, 2, and 3 of this book
- *Behavioral problem solving:* Structured problem solving about daily issues, crises, and so on, often beginning with brainstorming and moving to evaluation of specific alternatives (Hatfield, 1990)
- *Family support:* Empathy from other families and professionals regarding the plight of the family.
- *Crisis management:* Concrete information on de-escalation, coping with symptom exacerbation, and so on.

These interventions are delivered in a variety of formats, which may vary along a number of dimensions (Hatfield, 1990; McFarlane 1994). For example, sometimes interventions are aimed at a single family or at groups of families. Interventions are provided in different settings such as clinics, hospitals, homes, or church halls. The length of these interventions may range from a 1-day workshop to several years of monthly meetings. Also, the intervention may be designed to take place during different phases of the illness or to be carried out without regard for the phase of the illness. Some family interventions are conducted without the relative who has mental illness present, whereas others are only implemented with the relative present. In addition, these interventions can be conducted by professionals, family members, or a team consisting of both family members and professionals. Thus, in many family psychoeducational efforts, family members have leadership roles.

Similar to other psychiatric rehabilitation techniques, family psychoeducation involves connecting with family members by focusing on the here and now (Cnaan et al., 1990). Anderson et al. (1986) advised mental health practitioners to make themselves available to families immediately and not just at scheduled times. The initial focus must be on the present crisis that has brought them to seek assistance: a recent hospitalization, an impending hospital discharge, or a recent escalation in symptoms. In this collaborative approach, it is important not to treat the family as a patient but instead to treat it as a partner (Anderson et al., 1986). Some older family intervention models saw the family as "a system" that maintained pathology. Newer family interventions see families as having both strengths and weaknesses that, like many other psychosocial factors, have an impact on the course and adjustment of a person with serious mental illness. Working with families is a joint project in which the staff, individual family members, and the consumer all collaborate in the rehabilitation process.

Sometimes family members lack basic information regarding schizophrenia or other major mental illnesses. To address this deficit, Hogarty and his colleagues (Anderson et al., 1986) devised a single-day survival skills workshop. This approach has been adopted in various formats and often spread out over a series of sessions (Hatfield, 1990). This type of training provides family members with important knowledge about mental illness and its treatment, working on the premise that knowledge is power in itself. Typically, a survival skills workshop includes the following:

- Definitions of diagnoses such as schizophrenia
- History and prevalence of the disorder
- Personal and public experience
- The role of biology in the illness
- The role of antipsychotics, how they work, impact on outcome, therapeutic effects, and side effects
- Psychosocial treatments
- Course of the illness and impact of treatment on course
- Impact on family
- Familial responses
- Common problems families face
- Strategies for family coping, including revising expectations, avoiding overstimulation, selectively ignoring certain behavior, setting expectations, identifying signals of impending trouble, and effectively using professionals

Other groups (e.g., Hatfield, 1990) have expanded on this approach and spend a good deal of time teaching families to create supportive environments. In addition, there is explicit training around problem-solving skills and dealing with crises (Hatfield, 1990). Hatfield (1990) also recommended that besides addressing immediate family needs, realistic long-range planning should also take place to balance the needs of the family as well as the individual.

Summary of the Empirical Evidence

As mentioned earlier, family interventions, particularly psychoeducational and problem-solving approaches, are among the few effective methods of promoting better outcomes among people with severe and persistent mental illness (Lehman & Steinwachs, 1998). If family members can be engaged, certainly these interventions are among the most effective social techniques that can be employed to improve the course and outcome of illnesses such as schizophrenia (Hogarty, 1993). Family interventions that are primarily psychoeducational are particularly effective (Dixon & Lehman, 1995). Second, those that include the patient in the family intervention also appear to be superior. Multiple family groups working together are particularly effective, perhaps because of the mutual emotional support and practical advice they can share.

Many of these studies of family interventions began as part of an aftercare program following discharge from a psychiatric hospital. Some others began as a result of families simply providing support to other families in distress. Goldstein et al. (1978) found that even as few as six weekly sessions focusing on education, building acceptance, and planning for the future resulted in a significantly lower rate of relapses. Some family interventions were developed as explicit efforts to change high EE family environments, although, as discussed previously, most families who have persons with mental illness do not exhibit this high EE style. Nevertheless, Falloon and colleagues (Falloon et al., 1982; Falloon & Pedersen, 1985) studied this minority of families with a high EE environment. All the families included members diagnosed with schizophrenia who were predicted to be at high risk for relapse because they were living with high EE relatives. Falloon et al.'s treatment group included behavioral family therapy, problem solving, and communication skills designed to promote a low EE style. Training lasted for 3 months at the family's home with a 6-month follow-up period to provide familial support. This family intervention approach was compared to supportive individual psychotherapy and brief family counseling. Measured at 9 months and 2 years, the comprehensive family intervention produced significantly fewer relapses, increased patient functioning, reduced family burden, and lowered overall treatment costs.

Similarly, Leff et al. (1982, 1985) worked with the families of people with schizophrenia who were also classified as high EE. Psychoeducation of family members, a relatives' group, and individualized problem solving—oriented family therapy in the home were compared to minimal family contact and regular hospital follow-up. Measured at 9 months, it was found that the comprehensive family intervention reduced relapses.

As mentioned earlier, Hogarty et al. (1986, 1991) developed an approach that was very family centered and sought to empower families by promoting useful skills, knowledge, and attitudes. The family treatment focused on (a) building an alliance with the family, (b) providing concrete information and management suggestions, (c) building a support network at a 1-day survival skills workshop, and (d) providing workshop skills in individual family therapy with the patient included.

There is empirical support for the efficacy of Hogarty's approach. One of the most compelling findings from his studies, which employed random assignment, was that after 2 years only 25% to 29% of the individuals who received the family treatment relapsed, compared to relapse rates as high as 62% for individuals who received social skills training or day treatment alone.

Hogarty's approach was expanded by McFarlane to multiple family groups, which were later found to be superior. McFarlane (1994) and McFarlane and colleagues (1995) conducted studies of a psychoeducational family intervention delivered in a multiple family group format. Using content similar to that developed by Hogarty et al. (1991), but with single families, McFarlane and his colleagues began serving multiple families simultaneously.

The first study they conducted compared three groups: (a) the psychoeducation and multiple family group, (b) the psychoeducation and single family therapy group, and (c) multiple family groups without psychoeducation, known as the family dynamic group. Both psychoeducational conditions were similar in content. The psychoeducational interventions included initial family engagement and educational sessions followed by 2 years of biweekly sessions on illness management with clinicians using formal problem-solving techniques. This was followed by an additional 2 years of monthly sessions. Consumers did not attend initial family engagement and educational sessions but did attend the later monthly sessions. In the single family condition, clinicians met with one family at a time but covered the same areas over the same period of time at the same intensity of service as the multiple family group. In the multiple family group without psychoeducation (dynamic multiple group), no education was provided. The methods used by clinicians in this approach included opening intrafamilial communication, sharing emotional responses, and attempting to resolve familial conflicts. These groups met weekly for the first 2 years and twice monthly for the second 2 years.

After 1 year, the dynamic multiple family group condition was discontinued for ethical reasons, due to the inordinately high relapse rate. In the other treatments, after both 2 and 4 years, the relapse rates were significantly lower in the multiple family condition compared to the single family group. After 4 years, 78% of the single family condition patients had relapsed, compared to only 45% of the multiple family condition sample. McFarlane replicated this study using 172 families at six sites throughout New York State (McFarlane et al., 1995). The multiple family group condition again proved superior to the single family condition. There are a number of studies with related findings that support the efficacy of educational interventions with families and consumers (McFarlane, 1994).

The Effectiveness of Family Education and Support

In the report on the Schizophrenia Patient Outcomes Research Team (PORT), Lehman and Steinwachs (1998) summarized the research regarding family interventions and offered the following two recommendations about people with schizophrenia who have continuing contact with their families:

1. They should be offered a family psychosocial intervention that lasts at least 9 months.
2. This intervention should include education about mental illness, support for family members, formal behavioral problem solving, and crisis intervention skills.

These recommendations were based on the fact that these packages of interventions have been found to reduce typical 1-year relapse rates of 40% to 53% to as low as 2% to 23%. They are excellent examples of how a psychosocial intervention can help the course of a biological disorder.

Initially, it had been thought that these interventions should be limited to families classified as having high expressed emotion (criticism, hostility, and overinvolvement). Although there is substantial benefit to these families, these interventions have been found to be helpful regardless of the level of EE (Lehman & Steinwachs, 1998).

PORT (Lehman & Steinwachs, 1998) also added that family therapies based on the premise that family dysfunction is the etiology of a person's schizophrenic disorder should definitely not be used:

> The presumption that family interaction causes schizophrenia . . . has lead to serious disruption in clinician/family trust without evidence of therapeutic effectiveness. (Lehman & Steinwachs, 1998)

Other Family Psychoeducation Approaches

The family self-help movement has also been active in designing interventions including programming sponsored by the National Alliance for the Mentally Ill (NAMI), which is discussed later. In this framework, family education is targeted not only to help the patient but to help the family as well. These family education models reject the medical therapy concept that treatment is something done to the individual and that families must just comply. At the same time, they incorporate the reality that major mental illnesses are biological disorders. Like other rehabilitative approaches, these interventions concentrate on the competencies and strengths of family members.

Professional and Consumer Collaboration

Lundwall (1996) reported on an innovative approach that combines psychoeducation, support, and familial empowerment. The psychoeducational group is initially led by professionals and later is turned over to family members with the staff remaining in a case management or supportive role. Initially, the professional leads the rehabilitation process by providing psychoeducation, concrete guidelines, and coordination of service. Later, the leadership of the group is turned over to family members who have been empowered to lead their own groups. The professional continues in an advocacy, liaison, and service coordination role. The combination of education and support, followed by the assumption of leadership by family members increases the confidence of family members and, it is hoped, improves their ability to care for familial needs. In addition, the coordination of services helps meet the many needs of consumers and families. Families are supported in the experience of grief and loss of the ill family member. Also, the group empowers family members to help create positive changes in the service systems.

CONTROVERSIAL ISSUE
Supervision versus Self-Determination

In a new bill, a state legislator proposes that all state-licensed residences serving people with mental illness provide 24-hour supervision for their residents. This bill would even cover those programs that intentionally have minimal staff intervention because they are designed to promote independence. Not surprisingly, this bill receives a very mixed review from different groups. Some of the family advocate groups in the state praise the legislator for her vision, whereas other family advocates are uncomfortable with such a sweeping proposal. Some particularly vocal consumer advocates vigorously oppose the measure, whereas some other consumers prefer staff in the homes at all times. What psychosocial rehabilitation principles are at stake here? Why are some of the family members' advocates and consumer advocates on opposing sides here? Basically, they share the same concerns, the well-being of mental health consumers. One family advocate says he is for promoting quality of life and the 24-hour supervision will ensure good medication compliance and prompt crisis intervention. A consumer advocate says he is seeking a better quality of life by opposing the measure for his constituents, which he says will only hinder community integration, consumer choice, and self-determination. One wise observer comments, "I guess where you stand on this issue depends on where you sit." That is, some of the family advocates simply want their family member cared for, whereas some consumer advocates want to promote independence.

The Concept of Family Recovery

In our efforts to help consumers and their families, it might be useful to recognize that like the individual with mental illness, families may also go through a process of recovery. Spaniol and Zipple (1994) introduced this concept, seeing family recovery as an essential goal for helping people with mental illness and their families. Their conception of family recovery parallels the concept of recovery for individuals discussed throughout this text. Spaniol and Zipple identified four stages in a family's recovery from serious and persistent mental illness: (a) discovery/denial, (b) recognition/acceptance, (c) coping/competence, and (d) personal/political advocacy.

Stage 1: Discovery/Denial

Family members' initial response to severe and persistent mental illness may range from minimizing the importance of the condition ("Its not so serious") to active denial ("It's just a phase") or ("He or she is experimenting with drugs"). A lack of information and poor communication with professionals about what is happening can aggravate this situation. Sometimes, the best way to describe this stage is that it is characterized by a state of disbelief.

Stage 2: Recognition/Acceptance

As they become aware of the seriousness of the illness, family members may experience feelings of guilt, embarrassment, and self-blame. As they accept the reality of the illness, they experience a deep sense of loss. This sense of loss is often made more difficult by the cyclical nature of the illness, especially the periods of improvement that can cause a roller-coaster of repeated hope, followed by disappointment.

Stage 3: Coping/Competence

After acceptance, most families marshall their resources to try and cope with the illness. Coping strategies may be effective or ineffective, informed by so-called expert opinion, or devised on the family's own. As outlined earlier in this chapter, there are a variety of effective approaches to help families cope better and become competent in crisis intervention, problem solving, and understanding of mental illness.

Stage 4: Personal/Political Advocacy

Finally, many families reach the stage of personal/political advocacy. This stage is characterized by efforts to influence how the mental health system responds to the needs of the family member with mental illness and other individuals in the same predicament. These advocacy efforts often involve attempts to influence public policy through groups such as the National Alliance for the Mentally Ill (NAMI) and its local affiliates, which are discussed next.

The Story of NAMI

Family members are, and always have been, the caregivers for the majority of people with severe and persistent mental illness. Now, in many states and in other countries, they have assumed an organized advocacy role. The largest and most successful American group is the National Alliance for the Mentally Ill (NAMI). NAMI's major activities include families providing mutual support, sharing information, educating the public, and advocating for improved public policy and legislation.

Thanks in part to the efforts of NAMI, new and productive alliances between professionals and families are developing. These alliances are manifest with family representation on the advisory and governance boards of mental health services, as well as through family and consumer input in treatment, rehabilitation, and research. Family groups, in particular NAMI, have been very active in advocating, sponsoring, and raising funds for mental illness research.

History of NAMI

NAMI was founded in 1979, in Madison, Wisconsin, by people who wanted to help their relatives with mental illness and themselves. The first meeting included about 250 people who spent an emotional and memorable weekend together. While professionals were in attendance, family members who founded this organization were determined that it would be governed by and for families and consumers (National Alliance of the Mentally Ill, 1996, 1998).

Within 1 year, NAMI was incorporated, achieved nonprofit status, and elected a board of directors. Early efforts centered on making connections with small family support groups that had already been initiated throughout the United States. NAMI launched an annual conference and began publishing a newsletter. By 1982 NAMI opened its first national office in Washington, DC, and began the work of trying to influence legislation and policy with Congress, the administration, and other key lawmakers. NAMI describes itself as

> a grass roots, self-help, support, and advocacy organization of families and friends of people with serious mental illness, and those persons themselves. (National Alliance of the Mentally Ill, 1996, 1998)

NAMI has focused on the unfulfilled needs of persons with the most serious forms of mental illness including those served in PsyR programs. Many of the members of NAMI are parents who were blamed for their child's mental illness. As such, they have firsthand understanding of the social stigma their son or daughter has experienced.

NAMI families join together to advocate for both needed changes in public attitudes and public policy. They have been supportive of current research that has been demonstrating the biochemical basis of what they now call brain diseases. Unlike most other advocacy or professional organizations, NAMI's exclusive focus is on serious mental illness or brain disorders. It now has more than 140,000 members and approximately 1000 state, county, and local affiliates throughout the United States. NAMI's stated mission is to

> eradicate mental illness and to improve the quality of life for those who suffer from "no-fault" brain diseases such as schizophrenia, depression, manic-depression, schizoaffective disorder, panic disorder, and borderline personality disorder. (National Alliance of the Mentally Ill, 1996, 1998)

NAMI's current advocacy efforts are focused on achieving parity for mental disorders in all insurance plans. At both the federal and state levels, NAMI is working with legislators to introduce and pass laws that would end the discriminatory treatment of serious mental illness by insurance plans and companies. In short, NAMI wants mental illness to be treated like any other serious medical disorder.

Families Helping Each Other

One of NAMI's most recent education and support endeavors is called the NAMI Family to Family Education course. This family-to-family program is usually provided free of charge. In an intensive weekend training session, family members are trained as teachers and facilitators to provide both education and support to other families. The educational component consists of a 12-week course. Teams of two members cover the following areas regarding serious mental illness:

- Learning about feelings, learning about facts
- Introduction to schizophrenia (diagnosis, crucial periods, etc.)
- Introduction to depression
- Basics about the brain
- Problem-solving skills workshop
- Medication review
- What it is like to be mentally ill: empathy workshop
- Relative groups and self-care
- Communication skills
- Rehabilitation
- Advocacy: fighting stigma
- Certification and celebration

Familial Strengths and Resilience

As discussed in chapter 2, the available evidence suggests that schizophrenia and other major mental illnesses, like many other biologically caused disorders such as asthma or hypertension, have a large genetic component. Persons with this genetic component are often vulnerable to environmental stresses or triggers that promote specific biological events, such as changes in neurotransmitter functioning. Some aspects of family life may cause stress, which in turn may trigger relapse or the recurrence of symptoms. In any case, families are neither a necessary or sufficient cause of serious mental illness.

This discussion of the role of stress in the etiology of schizophrenia and other disorders is not to deny the fact that some people with serious and persistent mental illness have had traumatic or difficult childhood experiences involving their families (as have many people who do not have serious mental illnesses). Nor is it to deny that many individuals with serious mental illness live under adverse familial circumstances as adults.

Equally undeniable, however, is evidence of the resilience and strength of some families despite the objective and subjective burdens they face. Mannion (1996) reported:

> There have been few attempts to go beyond the concept of family burden and examine family resilience . . . a process of constructive change and growth in response to a serious psychiatric disorder in a loved one. (p. 4)

This positive outlook may strike some family members as looking at the world through rose-colored glasses, prompting individual family members to say, "What, are you kidding?"; yet others may note, "We are all surviving schizophrenia" (excerpted from Marsh et al., 1996). Nevertheless, Marsh et al. (1996) did identify many strengths among family members, which the authors termed as *resilience*.

In addition, families have been found capable of reducing relapse and promoting recovery among their relatives (Lehman & Steinwachs, 1998). There is little question that their burden is extreme. Equally extreme is the resourcefulness or strength of some family members in their efforts to live with mental illness. Perhaps more important, it has also been demonstrated that family members can do effective problem solving, intervene in crises, and promote recovery for their relative with mental illness (Lehman & Steinwachs, 1998).

Summary

The influence of family life on the lives of persons with mental illness can be both positive and negative. The effect of the person's illness on the family can be burdensome, although some families prove very resourceful. Family members bear a substantial degree of objective and subjective burden due to their relative's illness. At the same time, aspects of a family, with high expressed emotion for example, may present specific stresses to the relative who has a mental illness and produce negative outcomes.

The pathology or disorder in the lives of these families does not cause serious mental illness. Although such influences as hostile remarks, critical comments, and other high EE behavior have been found to be harmful to the course of serious mental illness, these same families have also been found to be capable of changing this style of interaction to promote coping, competence, and recovery.

Families go through their own process of recovery, adapting and incorporating severe and persistent mental illness into their self-image as a family. They can be a great source of support, not only to their own members but also other families. In the face of serious mental illness, many families are found to be ultimately resilient and quite capable. Many family members, after struggling with their own member's illness, become advocates for improved psychiatric rehabilitation policies and increased mental illness research. The PsyR practitioner must take the stance of partnership with family members. No other position can be considered responsible or ethical. If mental health consumers desire family involvement, and if family members can be successfully engaged, they are among the most important partners in the processes of rehabilitation and recovery. Most families can become knowledgeable about mental illness and its treatment. These families can effectively solve problems presented by their member's illness and disability. Most important, these families can be effective agents for promoting the attainment of their loved one's rehabilitation goals.

Class Exercise
Designing a Family Intervention and Support Program

Question 1

It is clear that family interventions that are primarily psychoeducational have been very effective, especially if started when the ill relative is in the acute phase of the illness. In this exercise, the task is to generate the variety of possible reasons that family psychoeducation can lead to a reduction in both the number and frequency of relapses. For example, how do knowledge and skills translate into a lower likelihood of relapse? Remember, this effect can take place in both high EE and low EE families. Also, consider the following questions about what these interventions actually accomplish for the family. Do they help families to (a) be better observers, (b) intervene sooner when relapse is coming, or (c) be better symptom management agents?

Based on the information in this chapter, generate a list of possible reasons why these psychoeducational family interventions have positive effects for people with mental illness. Provide the rationale for each reason on your list.

Question 2

Those family interventions that include people with mental illness directly in the training or group result in better outcomes. Is this fact consistent with PsyR principles? If so, which principles does it relate to and why?

Question 3

Mowbray and her colleagues (1995) found that high family contact was associated with poorer vocational outcomes, whereas less contact was associated with better outcomes.

Alternatively, McFarlane's group (1995) found that families can help to promote vocational outcomes. Are these two sets of findings inconsistent? If they are reconcilable, what do they imply about the role of families in the vocational rehabilitation of people with severe and persistent mental illness?

References

Anderson, C. M., Reiss, D. J., & Hogarty, G. E. (1986). *Schizophrenia and the family*. New York: Guilford Press.

Brown, C. (1996). A comparison of living situation and loneliness for people with mental illness. *Psychiatric Rehabilitation Journal, 20*(2), 59–63.

Cnaan, R. A., Blankertz, L., Messinger, K. W., & Gardner, J. R. (1990). Experts assessment of psychosocial rehabilitation principles. *Psychosocial Rehabilitation Journal, 13*(3), 59–73.

Cook, J. A., & Hoffschmidt, S. J. (1993). Comprehensive models of psychosocial rehabilitation. In R. W. Flexer & P. A. Solomon (Eds.), *Psychiatric rehabilitation in practice* (pp. 81–97). Boston: Andover Medical Publishers.

Daley, D. C., Moss, H. B., & Campbell, F. (1993). *Dual disorders: Counseling clients with chemical dependency & mental illness* (2nd ed.). Center City, MN: Hazelden Foundation.

Dixon, L. B., & Lehman, A. F. (1995). Family interventions for schizophrenia. *Schizophrenia Bulletin, 21*(4), 631–644.

Evans, K., & Sullivan, J. M. (1990). *Dual diagnosis: Counseling the mentally ill substance abuser*. New York: The Guilford Press.

Falloon, I. R., Boyd, J. L., McGill, C. W., Ranzani, J., Moss, H. B., & Gilderman, A. M. (1982). Family management in the prevention of exacerbation of schizophrenia. *New England Journal of Medicine, 306*, 1437–1440.

Falloon, I. R., & Pedersen, J. (1985). Family management in the prevention of morbidity of schizophrenia: The adjustment family unit. *British Journal of Psychiatry, 147*, 156–163.

Goldstein, M. J., Rodnick, E. H., Evans, J. R., May, P. R., & Steinberg, M. R. (1978). Drug and family therapy in the aftercare of adult schizophrenics. *Archives of General Psychiatry, 35*, 1169–1177.

Harding, C. M., & Zahniser, J. H. (1994). Empirical correction of seven myths about schizophrenia with implications for treatment. *Acta Psychiatrica Scandanavica, 90*, 140–146.

Hatfield, A. (1990). *Family education in mental illness*. New York: Guilford Press.

Hatfield, A. B. (1987a). Coping and adaptation: A conceptual framework for understanding families. In A. B. Hatfield & H. P. Lefley, *Families of the mentally ill: Coping and Adaptation* (pp. 60–84). New York: The Guilford Press.

Hatfield, A. B. (1987b). Families as caregivers: A historical perspective. In A. B. Hatfield & H. P. Lefley, *Families of the mentally ill: Coping and adaptation* (pp. 3–29). New York: The Guilford Press.

Hatfield, A. B. (1987c). Social support and family coping. In A. B. Hatfield & H. P. Lefley, *Families of the mentally ill: Coping and adaptation* (pp. 191–207). New York: The Guilford Press.

Hatfield, A. B. (1992). Leaving home: Separation issues in psychiatric illness. *Psychosocial rehabilitation journal, 15*(4), 37–47.

Hogarty, G. E. (1993). The prevention of relapse in chronic schizophrenic patients. *Journal of Clinical Psychiatry, 54*, 18–23.

Hogarty, G. E., Anderson C. M., Konrblith, S. J., Greenwald, D. P., Javana, C. D., & Moadonia, M. J. (1986). Personal indicators in the course of schizophrenia research group. Family psychoeducation, social skills training, and maintenance chemotherapy in the aftercare treatment of schizophrenia: I. One year effects of a controlled study on relapsed and expressed emotion. *Archives of General Psychiatry, 43*, 633–642.

Hogarty, G. E., Anderson C. M., Konrblith, S. J., Greenwald, D. P., Ulrich, R. F., & Carster, M. (1991). Family psychoeducation, social skills training, and maintenance chemotherapy in the aftercare treatment of schizophrenia: II. Two year effects of a controlled study on relapse and adjustment. *Archives of General Psychiatry, 48*, 340–347.

IAPSRS (1996). *Core principles of psychiatric rehabilitation.* Columbia, MD: Author.

Kinsella, C. B., Anderson, R. R., & Anderson, W. T. (1996). Coping skills, strengths, and needs as perceived by adult offspring and siblings of people with mental illness: A retrospective study. *Psychiatric Rehabilitation Journal, 20*(2), 24–32.

Leff, J. P., Berkowitz, R., Shavit, N., Strachan, A., Glass, I., & Vaughn, C. (1989). A trial of family therapy versus a relatives' group for schizophrenia: Two year follow-up. *British Journal of Psychiatry, 154,* 58–66.

Leff, J.P., Berkowitz, R., Shavit, N., Strachan, A., Glass, I., & Vaughn, C. (1990). A trial of family therapy versus a relatives' group for schizophrenia: Two year follow-up. *British Journal of Psychiatry, 157,* 571–577.

Leff, J. P., Kuipers, L., Berkowitz, R., Eberlein-Fries, R., & Sturgeon. (1982). A controlled trial of social intervention in schizophrenia families. *British Journal of Psychiatry, 146,* 594–600.

Leff, J. P., Kuipers, L., Berkowitz, R., & Sturgeon, D. (1985). A controlled trial of social intervention in schizophrenia families: Two year follow-up. *British Journal of Psychiatry, 146,* 594–600.

Lefley, H. P. (1987a). Behavioral manifestations of mental illness. In A. B. Hatfield & H. P. Lefley, *Families of the mentally ill: Coping and adaptation* (pp. 107–127). New York: The Guilford Press.

Lefley, H. P. (1987b). Culture and mental illness: The family role. In A. B. Hatfield & H. P. Lefley, *Families of the mentally ill: Coping and adaptation* (pp. 30–64). New York: The Guilford Press.

Lefley, H. P. (1989). Family burden and stigma in major mental illness. *American Psychologist, 44*(3), 556–560.

Lehman, A. F., & Steinwachs, D. M. (1998). At issue: Translating research into practice: The Schizophrenia patient outcomes research team (PORT) treatment recommendations. *Schizophrenia Bulletin, 24*(1), 1–10.

Lundwall, R. R. (1996). How psychoeducational support groups can provide multi-disciplinary services to families of people with mental illness. *Psychiatric Rehabilitation Journal, 20*(2), 64–72.

Mannion, E. (1996). Resilience and burden in spouses of people with mental illness. *Psychiatric Rehabilitation Journal, 20*(2), 13–23.

Marsh, D. T., Dickens, R. M., Koeske, R. D., Yackovich, N. S., Wilson, J. M., Leichliter, J. S., & McQuillis, V. (1993). Troubled journey: Siblings and children of people with mental illness. *Innovations and Research, 2*(2), 13–23.

Marsh, D. T., Lefley, H. P., Evans-Rhodes, D., Ansell, V. I., Doerzbacher, B. M., Labarbera, L., & Paluzzi, J. E. (1996). The family experience of mental illness: Evidence for resilience. *Psychiatric Rehabilitation Journal, 20*(2), 3–12.

McFarlane, W. R. (1994). Multiple family groups and psychoeducation in the treatment of schizophrenia. *New Directions in Mental Health Services, 62,* 13–22.

McFarlane, W. R., Lukens, E., Link, B., Dushay, R., Deakins, S. A., Newmark, M., Dunne, E. J., Horen, B., & Toran, J. (1995). Multiple family group and psychoeducation in the treatment of schizophrenia. *Archives of General Psychiatry, 52,* 679–687.

Mowbray, C. T., Bybee, D., Harris, S. N., & McCrohan, N. (1995). Predictors of work status and future work orientation in people with a psychiatric disability. *Psychiatric Rehabilitation Journal, 19*(2), 17–28.

National Alliance of the Mentally Ill. (1996, 1998). History of NAMI. Author: Washington, D.C. (Courtesy of NAMI-New Jersey).

Phelan, J. C., Bromet, E. J., & Link, B. G. (1998). Psychiatric illness and family stigma. *Schizophrenia Bulletin, 24*(1), 115–126.

Pickett, S. A., Cook, J. A., Cohler, J. B., & Solomon, M. L. (1997). Positive parent/adult-child relationships: Impact of severe mental illness and caregiving burden. *American Journal of Orthopsychiatry, 67*(2), 220–230.

Spaniol, L., & Zipple, A. M. (1994). The family recovery process. *The Journal of the California Alliance of the Mentally Ill, 5*(2), 57–59.

Terkelson, K. G. (1987a). The evolution of family responses to mental illness over time. In A. B. Hatfield & H. P. Lefley, *Families of the mentally Ill: Coping and adaptation.* New York: The Guilford Press, pp. 128–150.

Terkelson, K. G. (1987b). The meaning of mental illness to the family. In A. B. Hatfield & H. P. Lefley, *Families of the mentally ill: Coping and adaptation.* New York: The Guilford Press, pp. 151–166.

Glossary

acute phase—The period when the illness is most active and symptoms are most prevalent.

assertive community treatment (ACT)—A full support approach to the provision of case management, rehabilitative, and treatment services. ACT programs utilize assertive outreach and in vivo service provision techniques.

behaviorism—A psychological theory, popularized by B. F. Skinner, which focuses on the use of positive and negative reinforcement to modify behavior.

biological treatment—Also known as somatic treatment; the biological treatment of choice for severe mental illness is medication (e.g., antipsychotic medications, antidepressant medications, or mood stabilizers).

chronic—Meaning "over time," from the Greek chronikos, father of the gods, father of time; it is a term used to describe the long-term course of severe mental illness.

chronically mentally ill—Refers to persons with long-lasting mental illness who may suffer repeated relapses. Recently, the term *chronic*, which carries a negative connotation, has been replaced with *severe and persistent*.

client-centered therapy—A therapeutic approach introduced by Carl Rogers, which is based on a genuine, respectful, and empathic relationship between the client and practitioner.

clubhouse—A model of PsyR day programming, also known as the Fountain House model; clubhouses are places to congregate for social support, recreation, and to address community living needs and problems. Consumers who go to clubhouses are referred to as members and are involved in all aspects of their program's operation.

congregate care—Any community-based residential environment in which groups of people with psychiatric disabilities live together and receive services.

consumer-provider—A psychiatric rehabilitation service provider who has a history of severe mental illness; these individuals have also been called prosumers.

continuity of care—The provision of services both according to need and over time.

course—The natural history or sequence of events throughout the length the illness; for persons experiencing severe and persistent mental illness, the course can be life long marked by a risk of recurrence of severe symptoms.

decompensation—Failure to maintain a stable, relatively symptom-free status.

deinstitutionalization—The movement away from treating and housing people with mental illness in large mental hospitals, accomplished by discharging individuals to live in the community.

Delphi technique—A research strategy that gathers data by asking identified experts in a specific field or area. The name of this technique stems from the supposed wisdom of the Delphic Oracle in classical times.

delusions—False beliefs that an individual maintains, despite an absence of supporting evidence or despite evidence to the contrary.

depressive episode—Characterized by feelings of extreme sadness or emptiness lasting most of the day, every day, for a period of 2 weeks or longer.

diathesis-stress model—Also known as the stress/vulnerability/coping/competence model; an etiological theory that proposes that stress can trigger symptoms in individuals with a biological predisposition to severe mental illness; learning to cope effectively with stress is an important part of the rehabilitative process.

direct skills teaching—A skill development strategy developed at Boston University's Center for Psychiatric Rehabilitation; it is based on an educational model of "teaching as treatment."

disability—A functional loss due to the symptoms of mental illness (Lawn & Meyerson, from Liberman, 1993).

double trouble—Groups that offer 12-step programs to people who have both a mental illness and a substance abuse disorder.

earned income exclusion—Earnings that are excluded from the Social Security Administration's calculation of countable earned income.

empowerment—A term frequently used in conjunction with the PsyR value of self-determination, it is often addressed in PsyR programs via involvement strategies such as sharing knowledge, power, and economic resources with consumers; recently defined in the literature as being composed of three elements: self-esteem–self-efficacy combined with optimism and a sense of control over the future, possession of actual power, and righteous anger and community activism.

etiology—The cause or origin of a disorder.

eugenics—A science that deals with the improvement (as by control of human mating) of hereditary qualities of a race or breed.

ex-patient movement—An organized effort by people with a history of psychiatric illness to advocate for civil rights and humane treatment approaches; the movement has also provided access to a variety of self-help and alternative treatment opportunities.

expressed emotion—Familial psychosocial factors, such as an environment high in criticism, hostility, and levels of emotional overinvolvement that may contribute to relapse in some cases.

extended period of eligibility—A period of time following the trial work period during which the worker's eligibility for SSDI cash benefit depends on the person's earned income. Currently the EPE lasts 36 consecutive months.

Fairweather lodge—A residential service model developed by George Fairweather and characterized by groups of people with psychiatric disabilities living and working together on a long-term basis.

family foster care—A situation in which one or more consumers reside with, and are supported by, a family that is not their own.

functional assessment—An evaluation of a person's level of ability in specific life areas, such as one's vocational, self-care, or educational skills.

general income exclusion—Income that is excluded from the Social Security Administration's calculation of countable income.

gentrification—The buying and renovation of homes in deteriorating urban neighborhoods, which may improve property values but often displaces lower-income individuals.

global assessment—An overall assessment of a consumer that does not address ability to function in specific environments.

goals—Desired states or objectives to strive for and achieve.

hallucinations—Sensory perceptions in the absence of appropriate external stimulation, such as hearing voices.

independent living movement—The efforts of people with physical disabilities to advocate for civil rights, develop a shared philosophy, and provide peer support in order to recover and maintain control over their lives.

individual written rehabilitation plan (IWRP)—The plan written by the vocational rehabilitation counselor and consumer that describes the consumer's vocational goal and the services that will be accessed to reach that goal.

institutionalized—The negative behavioral effects of long-term stays in institutions such as state psychiatric hospitals, typically manifested by extreme dependency.

in vivo—Providing services to clients in the environments where they live, work, and socialize.

job development—The tasks involved in job acquisition. These may include developing relationships with the business community, investigating the hiring needs of a specific employer, communicating the program's available services to all customers, or, more specifically, assisting the consumer with job applications, resume writing, interview skills, and employer contacts.

linear continuum model—A residential service approach in which consumers move from a relatively restrictive congregate care setting to a series of progressively less restrictive living environments, and eventually to independent living.

longitudinal study—A research study that tracks subjects and relevant outcomes for lengthy periods of time (i.e., 10 or more years).

manic episode—Characterized by an elevated mood in which the person feels excessively "up" or "high", and occasionally feels excessively irritable, for a week or more.

medical model—An integral element of the medical system or profession; part of medicine.

milieu therapy—Milieu is a French term that literally means *environment*; milieu therapy is a technique based on the idea that every aspect (i.e., physical, social, and cultural) of a treatment setting or environment can be used to help achieve therapeutic or rehabilitation goals or results.

mixed episode—Meets the criteria for both depressive and manic episodes, cycling through each in turn.

natural supports—Supports provided by people or things naturally present in the setting, for example, paying to carpool with a coworker rather than being transported to work by a job coach.

negative symptoms—Symptoms that reflect a lessening or loss of functioning, essentially abilities or senses that are lost due to the disease (e.g., restricted emotional expression or reduced productivity of thought) *(DSM-IV)*.

neuroanatomy—The structure of the nerves or neurons composing the individual's brain and nervous system.

neurotransmitters—Chemicals that convey messages between neurons or cells in the brain and nervous system.

NIMBY—"Not in my backyard"; an acronym describing community opposition to living near a group home or other residential setting in which people with psychiatric disabilities reside.

normalization—The achievement or acquisition of valued social roles for consumers; normalization is a guiding principle of psychiatric rehabilitation.

normalized—A term used to describe an environment (such as a day program) that is consistent with the PsyR principle of normalization.

objective burden—Specifically, identifiable problems associated with a person's mental illness; the objective burdens of families may include financial hardships due to medical bills, the cost of the consumer's economic dependence, disruptions in household functioning, restriction of social activities, and so on.

outcomes—Specific results, the end of a specific course of treatment, or the end result of the course of an entire illness.

overall rehabilitation goal—A goal chosen and "owned" by a consumer, which usually involves a desire to achieve success and satisfaction in a specific living, learning, working, or social environment.

partial hospitalization program—Day programs that are essentially based on the medical model; treatment strategies include medication and medication monitoring; group, individual, and milieu therapies; and recreation and socialization. Some partial hospitals also incorporate PsyR intervention strategies.

positive symptoms—Symptoms that reflect an excess or distortion of normal functions, essentially symptoms that are added due to the disease (e.g., hallucinations and delusions) *(DSM-IV)*.

premorbid—The period of time before the psychiatric illness develops.

principles—Specific dictums designed to promulgate values and goals by providing guidelines for addressing specific situations or behaviors.

prodromal phase—Before the full syndrome; a period before the full onset of the illness characterized by deterioration in functioning and increasing positive and negative symptoms.

prognosis—The probable course or outcome of a disorder.

prosumers (or consumer providers)—A term used to describe identified consumers of mental health services who are also mental health professionals.

psychoanalytic—Psychological theories proposed by Sigmund Freud; psychoanalytic techniques emphasize the exploration of intrapsychic processes and their relationship to past events.

psychodynamic—A theory that psychopathology arises from conflicts from within the psyche or mind of the individual. These conflicts may be rooted in past events.

psychodynamic therapy—An insight-oriented approach that focuses on the interpretation of unconscious material and therapeutic transference; in the treatment of serious mental illnesses, this form of psychotherapy has been found to be generally ineffective.

psychoeducation—A PsyR intervention that involves connecting with family members by focusing on their current concerns, providing basic information regarding schizophrenia or other major mental illnesses, teaching crisis intervention techniques, and providing other resources that aid families in becoming effective partners in the treatment and rehabilitation process.

psychosis—Incorrect evaluation of reality.

psychosocial treatment—An approach that attempts to effect change through the manipulation of social or psychological factors.

quality of life—A person's subjective evaluation of the aspects of his or her life that the person deems important.

quantifiable—The ability to assign specific numbers to finite events in an objective fashion.

readiness assessment—A rehabilitation tool used to determine whether or not a consumer is ready to engage in the rehabilitation process.

reasonable accommodations—Modifications made to a job or work setting to enhance the ability of a qualified worker with a disability to perform the job. The Americans with Disabilities Act defines *reasonable* as an accommodation that is not excessively expensive compared to the resources of the business and does not fundamentally change the nature of the work being performed.

recidivism—Returning to the psychiatric hospital after discharge (e.g., relapse).

recovery—For a lifelong mental illness, recovery refers to a reformulation of one's self-image and an eventual adaptation to the disease; recovery is one of the goals of psychiatric rehabilitation.

rehabilitation—Any action intended to reduce the negative effects of the disease on the person's everyday life.

rehabilitation diagnosis—The initial phase of the rehabilitation process, in which the consumer chooses an overall rehabilitation goal, and then participates in the completion of a functional and resource assessment related to that goal.

rehabilitation intervention—A strategy used to assist in the completion of goals and objectives; rehabilitation interventions include skill development and resource acquisition and development.

rehabilitation plan—A tool used to designate consumers' goals and objectives, as well as their skill and resource acquisition needs and the strategies to be used to achieve them.

relapse—The recurrence of acute phases after periods of remission or lack of symptoms.

remission—Time period when an individual is essentially symptom free.

residential treatment facility—Congregate care settings, such as group homes, that are operated by mental health professionals.

residual phase—The period after the acute phase of the illness when symptoms become milder.

resource assessment—A rehabilitation tool used to determine which resources (i.e., persons or things) are needed to assist consumers in attaining their overall rehabilitation goals.

schizoaffective disorder—A psychiatric disorder characterized by both symptoms of schizophrenia and symptoms of a mood disorder.

self-determination—A PsyR value that is based on the belief that consumers have the right to participate in all decisions that affect their lives; closely related to the concept of empowerment.

self-help—Involvement in nonprofessional activities that provide support and information for oneself and others who share a similar illness or problem.

situational assessment—An evaluation of the presence or absence of the skills and resources needed for a consumer to function successfully in the environments (i.e., situations) of their choice; this is in contrast to doing a global assessment, unrelated to specific client goals.

skills training—A skill development strategy developed by R. P. Liberman and his colleagues at UCLA; it is based on social learning theory and behavioral techniques.

somatic—Of the body; biologically based.

staff burnout—A general loss of motivation, meaning, or interest in one's job, which may present itself as frustration or hopelessness.

subjective burden—The psychological distress, borne by family members, which is engendered by the severe mental illness of a relative.

substantial gainful activity (SGA)—An amount of earnings designated by SSA as an indication of a worker's ability to be self-supporting. Currently this amount is $500 per month.

supported employment (SE)—An individualized approach to help consumers achieve integrated employment. SE emphasizes training and support provided in settings of choice rather than a demonstration of skills prior to one's access to vocational services. Supported employment services provide support to the individual in selecting, obtaining, and maintaining employment.

supported housing—Integrated, community-based housing opportunities for people with psychiatric disabilities, which emphasize consumer choice and provision of flexible and ongoing supports.

transitional employment (TE)—A program of time-limited jobs in regular work settings for real pay. Agency staff acquire the job from an employer and subsequently provide training and support to consumers in that job. Consumers in TE jobs earn the going rate of pay from the employer and remain in the job for a specified period of time. The job is then filled by another consumer.

treatment—Any action designed to cure a disease or reduce its symptoms; treatment for serious mental illnesses can be broken into two broad categories: biological (somatic) and psychosocial.

trial work period—Nine nonconsecutive months in which SSDI recipients can earn income while maintaining their cash benefits, thus allowing the individual to try working with limited risk.

values—Deeply held beliefs that may inform specific behaviors, attitudes, and ideas.

Index